YOUR
ADOLESCENT

ALSO BY THE AMERICAN ACADEMY OF
CHILD AND ADOLESCENT PSYCHIATRY:

Your Child:
What Every Parent Needs to Know:
What's Normal, What's Not, and When to Seek Help

THE AMERICAN ACADEMY OF
CHILD AND ADOLESCENT PSYCHIATRY

YOUR
ADOLESCENT

*Emotional, Behavioral, and
Cognitive Development from
Early Adolescence through the Teen Years*

■ ■ ■

David B. Pruitt, M.D., Editor-in-Chief

HarperCollins*Publishers*

FIRST EDITION

Designed by Helene Wald Berinsky

Br 27.50/15.13   2/99

Library of Congress Cataloging-in-Publication Data

Your adolescent : what every parent needs to know : what's normal, what's not, and when to seek help / by American Academy of Child and Adolescent Psychiatry ; David B. Pruitt, editor-in-chief.
    p. cm.
  ISBN 0–06–270182–7 (hardcover)
   1. Adolescent psychology.   2. Adolescent pyschopathology.   3. Parent and child—Psychological aspects.   I. Pruitt, David B.   II. American Academy of Child and Adolescent Psychiatry.
BF724.Y68   1999
155.5—dc21   98-34587

99 00 01 02 03 ❖/RRD 10 9 8 7 6 5 4 3 2 1

Contents

Part I ▪ THE LIFE OF AN ADOLESCENT

Part II ▪ DAY-TO-DAY PROBLEM BEHAVIORS

Part III ■ SERIOUS PROBLEMS AND ABNORMALITIES

Part IV ■ SEEKING HELP

The Contributors

■ **EDITOR-IN-CHIEF**

David B. Pruitt, M.D.
Professor of Psychiatry
Director of the Division of Child and
    Adolescent Psychiatry
University of Tennessee, Memphis
Medical Director, TLC Family Care
    Healthplan
Memphis, Tennessee
President 1997–99, American Academy of
    Child and Adolescent Psychiatry

■ **ASSOCIATE EDITORS**

Claudia Berenson, M.D.
Associate Professor, Psychiatry and Pediatrics
University of New Mexico
Albuquerque, New Mexico

William Bernet, M.D.
Associate Professor of Psychiatry
Vanderbilt University School of Medicine
Medical Director
The Psychiatric Hospital at Vanderbilt
Nashville, Tennessee

Jerry Heston, M.D.
Associate Professor of Psychiatry
Division of Child and Adolescent Psychiatry
University of Tennessee, Memphis
Medical Director, Behavior Health Unit,
    Le Bonheur Children's Medical Center
Memphis, Tennessee

Paramjit T. Joshi, M.D.
Associate Professor
Director of Clinical Services
Division of Child and Adolescent Psychiatry
Johns Hopkins University School of
    Medicine
Baltimore, Maryland

Penelope Krener Knapp, M.D.
Professor, Psychiatry and Pediatrics
University of California, Davis
Davis, California

James C. MacIntyre II, M.D.
Associate Professor of Psychiatry
Albany Medical College
Albany, New York

■ **Deputy Editors**

Paul L. Adams, M.D.
Louisville, Kentucky

Virginia Q. Anthony
Washington, D.C.

■ **Contributing Editors**

Thomas Anders, M.D.
Davis, California

Alan Axelson, M.D.
Pittsburgh, Pennsylvania

Larry Brown, M.D.
Providence, Rhode Island

Catherine DeAngelis, M.D.
Baltimore, Maryland

David Fassler, M.D.
Burlington, Vermont

Henry Gault, M.D.
Northbrook, Illinois

Gerald Golden, M.D.
Philadelphia, Pennsylvania

David Herzog, M.D.
Boston, Massachusetts

Steven Jaffe, M.D.
Atlanta, Georgia

Allan Josephson, M.D.
Augusta, Georgia

Henrietta Leonard, M.D.
Providence, Rhode Island

Alexander Lucas, M.D.
Rochester, Minnesota

Bruce D. Miller, M.D.
Buffalo, New York

Frederick Palmer, M.D.
Memphis, Tennessee

Rachel Z. Ritvo, M.D.
Rockville, Maryland

John Schowalter, M.D.
New Haven, Connecticut

Robert Schreter, M.D.
Lutherville, Maryland

Larry Silver, M.D.
Washington, D.C.

Michael Silver, M.D.
Wynnewood, Pennsylvania

Deborah Simkin, M.D.
Fort Walton Beach, Florida

■ **Editorial Director**

Hugh G. Howard
Red Rock Publishing, Inc.
East Chatham, New York

■ **Contributors**

Dale Gelfand
Spencertown, New York

Elizabeth Lawrence
East Chatham, New York

Dawn Micklethwaite Peterson
Maplewood, New Jersey

Elizabeth Tinsley
Chatham, New York

Lyn Yonack
Great Barrington, Massachusetts

Acknowledgments

Your Adolescent is the result of a group effort by many of the more than 6,300 members of the American Academy of Child and Adolescent Psychiatry and a range of consultants concerned with the needs of children, adolescents, and their families. This book and its companion volume, *Your Child,* focus on the goal of parent education as the primary vehicle to bring about better health and health-care for children and adolescents.

The Academy has a long-held belief that parents are a precious resource that must be supported and strengthened for the well-being of children and adolescents. *Your Adolescent* and *Your Child,* which offer the collective wisdom of many child and adolescent psychiatrists who trained to serve children, adolescents, and their families, represent this philosophy.

The creation of these books was a team effort, much like the collaboration within a functional family or a high-quality child and adolescent mental health-care team. The process included support for the individuals in the group as well as careful coordination of the group. Both are essential for any team project to succeed.

We started with a small group of Academy members working with our wonderful panel of writers led by Hugh Howard. We progressively developed an organization, content, chapters, and finally these books, always broadening our circle of consultants and experts, always attempting to reach consensus about what works and what doesn't, what advice to give, and most important, when to say that we don't know.

This project has come to realization with a lot of help. Beyond those listed on previous pages are the following: J. Graham Brooks, M.D.; Lee Combrick Graham, M.D.; Geraldine Fox, M.D.; Kevin T. Kalikow, M.D.; Jack M. Reiter, M.D.; Alvin Rosenfeld, M.D.; Dorothy Levine, M.D.; Carrie Sylvester, M.D.; Martin Drell, M.D.; Elizabeth Wright, M.D.; Moisy Shopper, M.D.; Barbara Stilwell, M.D.; Shaun C. McDevitt, Ph.D.; Diane Shrier, M.D.; Andrew Russell, M.D.; James

Harris, M.D.; Joseph J. Jankowski, M.D.; Richard Angell, M.D.; John O'Brien, M.D.; Bennett L. Leventhal, M.D.; Owen W. Lewis, M.D.; John Reinhart, M.D.; Ms. Abby O'Neil; E. James Anthony, M.D.; Harold Kopelwicz, M.D.; Larry Stone, M.D.; Peter Jensen, M.D.; Marilyn Benoit, M.D.; Theodore Petty, M.D.; Clarice Kestenbaum, M.D.; Alvin Poussaint, M.D.; Gloria Powell, M.D.; Bruce Perry, M.D.

Many at my university, the University of Tennessee, Memphis, also supported this effort in the belief that this kind of commitment strengthens and serves the university mission. Among them are Chancellor William Rice, Dean Henry Herrod, and Department of Psychiatry Chairman Neil Edwards; the faculty, past and present, of the Division of Child and Adolescent Psychiatry, including Kris Douglas, Constance Durbin, Laurel Kiser, Marilyn Paavola, Jerry Heston, Ewa Ostoja, Jyothsna Kumar, Mark Sauser, Rita Porter, Robert Pugh, Suzanne Fischer, and Edgar McColgan; and the trainees of the Division both past and present, including recent fellows Anthony Jackson, Kendall Vitulli, Yolanda Gilbert, Yanco Gavrizi, Monica Salgueiro, and Nick Sansait.

I also want to give thanks to Karl Kovacs, Executive Director of TLC Family Care Healthplan, whose friendship and guidance in our collegial day-to-day work has allowed me a sense of mission in the rapidly changing healthcare marketplace, and to Eric Brown, President of Communication Associates who has helped me over the years to learn the value and effectiveness of clear thinking and talking.

I want to thank several other individuals at the Academy who have supported this work with their insight and assistance through the long writing and editing process: Virginia Q. Anthony, Executive Director of the American Academy of Child and Adolescent Psychiatry; Patricia Jutz, Director of Communications; Tamara Hodge-Wells; and Tonya Cook. They have provided immeasurable support.

A special thanks as well to Bettye Fleming, my long-time Administrative Assistant, who kept the whole project glued together through the many overnight mails, faxes, conference calls, due dates, and deadlines that she, as always, gently and effectively made happen.

Finally, a very special thanks to my wife and colleague, Laurel, who, with our two children, Peter and A.J., has helped me move through the wonderful stages of growth and development as a parent.

David B. Pruitt, M.D.

Foreword

Child and adolescent psychiatry begins with a profound respect for your adolescent, his or her endowments, and a deep regard for the task of parenting.

For more than two decades, I have attended seminars, case conferences, grand rounds, scientific meetings, and committee meetings. Both as a parent and in my professional capacity, I am invariably struck that this respect pervades virtually every presentation about individual youngsters by child and adolescent psychiatrists. Discussions, publications, and stories share this appreciation for the adolescent, and the individual's strengths and uniqueness. And so, you will find, does *Your Adolescent.*

The Academy was founded in 1953 by eighty-one child and adolescent psychiatrists who saw a need for a forum to focus on the clinical, educational, and research problems unique to children. The early meetings were informative. The struggles for separation from other medical and mental health groups, for new ties, and for a sense of identity were earnest and absorbing. Differences in values and focus from other professions led to the founding of the Academy as an academic association, but over more than four decades of growth, the agenda here at the Academy has developed to include vigorous advocacy for children and adolescents, an outstanding program of professional education, and an increasing focus on prevention and public health.

In the past fifteen years, the Academy has reached out to you as parents and members of extended families. We recognize that you are on the front line, whether your role is as a parent, grandparent, or caregiver. You deal daily with disorders of adolescence and other parenting issues and concerns. Since early identification is one of the most effective forms of prevention, we believe our outreach can help in preventing or limiting the pain, trauma, and failure experienced by children and adolescents—and perhaps reduce the anguish and heartache felt by parents of youngsters in distress.

Our attempts to inform the public are not aimed solely at the parents of the children and adolescents who need professional help. Often, in part because of today's very stressful home–work environment, parents need reassurance about the differences between personality and temperament, and education about what constitutes the normal phases of growing up. We can provide guidance about when you should be concerned about your adolescent and, ultimately, whether you should seek treatment.

Over a career, a child and adolescent psychiatrist learns a great deal from and about families, about specific resilience and breaking points, about vulnerabilities and elasticities, and about how teens with the same parents can be so alike and yet so different.

This book is an outgrowth of a vigorous parent education effort based on that learning. This volume addresses normal development, normal problems, as well as more serious disorders and concerns with adolescents. It is a way of sharing child and adolescent psychiatry's appreciation of the teenage years, developmental milestones, and adolescent achievement with you, the parents, grandparents, and caregivers, who are caring and concerned, anxious, or just inquisitive.

The Academy is very proud of *Your Adolescent* as a key part of our ongoing partnership with parents. We commend David B. Pruitt, M.D., Hugh Howard, the editorial board, and the many authors, readers, and critics who have contributed to this offering.

Virginia Q. Anthony, *Executive Director*

Introduction

A parent helps her fifteen-year-old son pack for a summer program at a college some 200 miles away. When she pushes aside a pile of underwear to squeeze in some clean socks, the mother notices that in the bottom of the suitcase, along with the shaving equipment he thinks he needs, her son has stowed a family picture and a small stuffed animal. She muses that even though he has a girlfriend, will soon have a driver's license, and can be as exasperating and opinionated as any adult she has ever met, within his grown-up–size body, underneath the deep voice and behind the often-defiant eyes, is a tender, tentative, uncertain child.

Every parent forgets, at moments, that there is a child still lurking within their adolescent. That forgetfulness is particularly likely when you are in the grips of the power struggles that all too often characterize the parent-child relationship during the teenage years. By the time your child has reached adolescence, chances are that you have succeeded in providing him (or her) with a firm sense of roots, a sense of belonging, of love and attachment. You may have afforded him ample opportunity to develop and test his wings, too, to gradually and increasingly experience himself as a separate, independent being.

Adolescence is the time when teenagers focus on the wings of independence—how far they can fly, how fast, what new adventures are offered them—rather than on the nests from where they came. To parents, that soaring may seem dangerous, and you may worry about when, how, and even whether your teen will return to you. Perhaps you fear losing forever the compliant child you once held in your arms, the adoring, trusting child you tucked in each night—and that thought may compel you to hold tighter to your teenager, to try to restrict his or her freedom.

As the two of you negotiate this juncture in your teen's life and in your relationship, maintaining your patience, flexibility, and the joy you have felt as a parent may seem like a tremendous challenge. In order for this stage to be fully enjoyable, rich, and auspicious, it helps if you can cultivate an appreciation of your teenager's complexity, your own complexity, and the complexity of the relationship.

The journey that began at childbirth, zoomed through infancy, toddled on through childhood, and now moves in fits and starts though adolescence into adulthood is traveled by both parent and child. The adventure is mutual, the direction shared, and the paths corresponding. Yet the experience is not identical.

Just like every other human relationship, the parent-child relationship embraces two distinct points of view. Teenagers, however articulate they may be in other areas, can be notoriously inarticulate when it comes to putting forth their own perspectives, needs, and purposes to their parents. During this time of dramatic and perplexing change, adolescents often have difficulty understanding their own inner states and behaviors. At the same time, parents frequently share the confusion and turmoil of adolescence. You may well misread or misunderstand your youngster's communications. Frequently you may find yourself at a complete loss in terms of what your teenager is communicating and how you are to respond.

In a way, this book functions to put forth your teenager's point of view in a manner that can guide you, the parent, in your day-to-day interactions with your teen within the context of his or her development and your own development as a parent.

We at the American Academy of Child and Adolescent Psychiatry developed *Your Adolescent* to provide the kind of information you need to supplement your instincts and your knowledge of your teenager. In these pages, you will find, in very broad strokes, your youngster's point of view— what she is likely experiencing at a given age or during a given event or life circumstance—within the context of your relationship. We will look at what to expect from your adolescent, in terms of emotional, cognitive, moral, physical, and behavioral development, at each point along the way. What, for example, does a typical twelve-year-old girl feel, think about, and wish for? What can you anticipate from your sixteen-year-old as he drives off alone for the first time? How will your eighteen-year-old handle the burgeoning responsibilities of going off to college or work every day after leaving high school? What will it mean to your teen when there's a death in the family or you and your spouse are divorcing? What does it mean that your fourteen-year-old has taken up smoking marijuana?

This information is not presented merely for its own sake. By describing in some detail the developmental milestones and concerns common to all parent-teen relationships, by discussing particular questions that may arise during the course of parenthood, and by examining more worrisome problems that may present themselves, we hope to provide broad guidance in your day-to-day interactions with your adolescent. Given what you know from the years of childhood of your youngster's singular temperament and developmental expectations, how do you best handle such issues as teenage peer pressures, a family move, aggressive behaviors, masturbation, money, and the like?

This book offers suggestions for handling practical matters: How do you monitor the television he watches or the movies she goes to see? What about grooming—when is grunge cool and when is it unacceptably grungy? What about discipline, rebellion, and dating? When do certain behaviors become problems requiring professional help? This book is intended to be used as a touchstone—a way of measuring when a certain behavior, though irritating and confusing, is perfectly normal and when it is a signal to consult a child and adolescent psychiatrist or other professional. It is a reference intended to offer reassurance, perspective, and guidance.

When all is said and done, successful parenting requires not just instinct, familiarity, and reflexes, but thoughtful reflection as well. Another purpose of this book is to provide the information, and perhaps a dollop of wisdom, to nurture your understanding in such a way that you can facilitate your adolescent's development. Indeed, it is our intention to help you and your teenager over the inevitable bumps of the teen years—even when your instincts are blunted by irritation at being pushed away and even insulted, by too much anxiety over seemingly risky behavior, by too many conflicting responsibilities, and strained patience, flexibility, and creativity.

Parenting is truly one of life's greatest pleasures, as well as one of its greatest challenges. It is the hope of all of us who contributed to this volume that you will find encouragement and help within its pages to guide your adolescent as he or she engages richly and meaningfully in the developmental processes.

How to Use This Book

Your Adolescent is organized to make it easy for you to browse through at your leisure, to satisfy your curiosity on a given subject, or to direct you quickly and methodically to areas of specific interest when you are pressed to know. The book is divided into four parts plus several appendices.

Part I. The Life of an Adolescent

Part I presents the milestones of a teenager's development, starting with early adolescence and working through to the departure of the adolescent from home to lead an independent life. This section presents an approximate chronology of what to expect from your adolescent in terms of physical, emotional, behavioral, cognitive, social, and moral maturation.

The concerns discussed in this section of the book—for example, *Where do I set limits on my daughter's desire to go out on dates? Is there anything I can do about my son's choice of friends? How do I adapt my thinking on discipline and punishment to the challenges of parenting a teenager?*—are typical of those you will routinely encounter as a parent. The issues and information presented here center on what almost every teenager experiences during the course of adolescence.

Chapter 1: Early and Middle Adolescence describes the developmental stage during which your child moves into puberty. Your teenager's peers become more important; members of the opposite sex acquire a new and surprising attractiveness. And you, as a parent, may find that you play an increasingly secondary role in this emerging adolescent world. This chapter includes discussions about such topics as acne, dating, menstruation, and autonomy.

Chapter 2: The High-School Years looks at the life of the adolescent as he or she continues to pull away from you and enters the ranks of young adulthood. It's a busy yet ambivalent time, as growing independence is tempered with worries and uncertainties about new freedoms and challenges. Subjects covered in this chapter include sexuality, money, the emerging sense of identity, and communication with your teenager.

Chapter 3: Leaving the Nest concerns the major transition that teens and parents alike face as the youngster leaves home to begin a largely independent life. This chapter considers, among other issues, how older adolescents must deal with separating from their parents and reworking the parent-child relationship; exploring, experimenting, and establishing rudimentary adult identities; engaging in mature, intimate relationships; and charting occupational paths.

Part II. Day-to-Day Problem Behaviors

Part II describes those everyday behaviors, feelings, and reactions that may be bewildering to you but are by no means aberrant. Rebellion, teenage fads, and even sexual experimentation are all perfectly normal parts of growing up, yet they may be distressing for you and your adolescent. Other behaviors, however natural for the teenager, may be quite problematic. You may wonder how to deal with your child's shoplifting, cheating, and drinking and driving, and whether there is a need for serious concern. In many cases, even such worrisome behavior does not signal serious trouble. Yet, it may

require your attention and necessitate that you respond in an immediate and measured way. This section places such concerns in the context of the teen's development.

In addition, this second part of the book addresses those issues faced from time to time, not by all children but by many, in their singular paths towards adulthood: divorce; death or serious illness in the family; moving; changing schools; extracurricular activities; chores and jobs; experimenting with alcohol and drugs; and other challenges. By addressing these issues in greater detail, we hope to offer reassurance and direction so that you can interpret and respond to your youngster's behavior in a helpful manner.

Chapter 4: Challenges at Home centers on some of the common issues and problems that face adolescents. Communication difficulties, sexual experimentation, and learning to manage responsibility and independence are common issues for parents and adolescents; less usual are problems such as runaway teens and date rape. These and other dilemmas will be discussed in this chapter.

Chapter 5: The Family Redefined grapples with the question: "What is a family?" Countless youngsters today are being raised by single parents, stepparents, grandparents, gay parents, and foster families. Other factors, including adoption, sibling rivalry, and poverty, have a direct impact on development in adolescence and the relationships teens have with those who care for them. They are addressed in this chapter.

Chapter 6: School-Related Concerns includes discussions on such subjects as motivation, homework, student-teacher conflicts, learning difficulties, school failure, and over- and underachievement.

Chapter 7: The Adolescent and the Community addresses the issues involved in living in the larger community of family, friends, neighbors, and strangers. It touches on such subjects as curfews, thrill-seeking behaviors, antisocial and delinquent behavior, violence in the media, gangs, guns and adolescents, children having children, and homosexuality.

Chapter 8: The Adolescent With Chronic Illness describes the special challenges that families contend with when an adolescent has a chronic illness such as diabetes, seizure disorders, and cancer or another life-threatening disease. It will also address concerns about growth, menstrual problems, and chronic pelvic inflammatory disease in girls.

Part III. Serious Problems and Abnormalities

In Part III, we move beyond day-to-day quandaries and concerns to those that in fact represent serious obstacles to a teenager's development and family life. This section reviews those emotional, behavioral, and developmental problems that usually require professional intervention. The information provided in these chapters will help you understand what is going on with your adolescent so that you can ask a child and adolescent psychiatrist or other mental health clinician the right questions and get the right kind of help for your teen and your family.

Today, we understand that when a youngster experiences serious problems, it is not only or not simply a product of faulty parenting. Rather it is a result of the elaborate interplay between the youngster's temperament, strengths, vulnerabilities, family, and environment. This chapter presents serious problems within their context and complexity without blame or judgment. This section is intended to help parents recognize and understand these serious illnesses and their inevitable repercussions.

Chapter 9: Emotional Disorders, for example, elucidates those disturbances, including depressive disorders, anxiety disorders, and posttraumatic stress disorder, in which an adolescent internalizes or feels profound and constant distress to the point that the normal involvements of her life—school, friends, family—are significantly disrupted.

Chapter 10: Disruptive Behavior Disorders focuses on those disturbed behaviors that indicate a considerable degree of internal upset or represent a symptom of a larger, underlying emotional problem. Such conditions include attention-deficit/hyperactivity disorder, conduct disorder, and opposition defiant disorder.

Chapter 11: Developmental Disorders deals with mental retardation, pervasive developmental disorder, learning disorders, language and speech disorders, and other related problems that can impede a youngster's development.

Chapter 12: Eating and Nutritional Disorders will consider disorders in which teenagers distort their bodies' nutritional needs. The serious and potentially life-threatening disorder anorexia nervosa is discussed, as well as bulimia nervosa and obesity.

Chapter 13: Psychotic Disorders examines schizophrenia, psychosis due to mood disorders, brief reactive psychosis, and toxic psychosis, in which a teen's thought processes are severely and consistently impaired.

Chapter 14: Substance Abuse Disorders will consider the use of alcohol and drugs by teenagers. While many teens experiment with alcohol or drugs, some go on to regular and dangerous abuse. In this chapter, the topics discussed include alcohol abuse, the four stages of substance abuse, and drug abuse.

Chapter 15: Sleep Disorders reviews the possible causes and repercussions of an adolescent's sleep difficulties. While sleep problems may signal only mild, passing problems, they may also represent more persistent, troublesome ones. In this chapter we explore some of the most common sleep problems that occur in adolescence, which include narcolepsy, circadian rhythm sleep disorder (delayed sleep phase), nightmares, and sleepwalking.

Part IV. Seeking Help

Part IV offers practical advice and useful information to guide parents when it seems that professional mental health intervention may be appropriate. This section presents the who, where, when, and why of getting help. We discuss in detail the many aspects of treatment (individual psychotherapy, medication, cognitive-behavioral techniques, family and group therapies, and psychiatric evaluation and diagnosis), as well as the professionals involved (child and adolescent psychiatrists, psychologists, social workers, counselors, and psychotherapists).

As you determine whether your adolescent—and your family—could benefit from professional treatment, *Chapter 16: When and Where to Seek Help* offers direction. This chapter will help parents understand just what is involved in seeking help, what mental health intervention can reasonably be expected to accomplish, and how to go about finding the right clinician for your teen and your family.

Chapter 17: What Are the Treatment Options? provides a detailed discussion of the fundamentals of choosing and using mental health services—specifically, the various types of therapies available and the issues and problems each typically addresses.

Appendices

The Appendices include a list of basic identifications and descriptions of commonly used psychiatric medications (*Appendix A: Psychiatric Medicines*); a list of medical and others tests commonly used by mental health clinicians in assessing or diagnosing adolescents (*Appendix B: Medical, Psychological, Educational, and Developmental Tests*); and a glossary of psychiatric and medical terminology that you may encounter in discussing your youngster's status with his child and adolescent psychiatrist or other clinician. We have also included a complete index to ensure easy access to specific topics throughout *Your Adolescent*.

A Note to the Reader

We used male pronouns (*he, him, his,* and *himself*) when referring to the early adolescent in the opening chapter of this book. We used female pronouns (*she, her, herself*) in the second chapter. Thereafter, pronoun forms alternate from one chapter to the next.

There are a handful of exceptions. These occur in response to conditions or disorders found predominantly in males or females. We chose to use this approach to make the book more readable and evenhanded and to acknowledge that our readers are the parents of both boys and girls.

The Editors

Part 1

THE LIFE OF
AN ADOLESCENT

■   ■   ■

In the three chapters that follow, the milestones of development are described, including those of early and middle adolescence, the high-school years, and the time of separation that follows. In addition to providing a chronology of what to expect from your adolescent, this part discusses many of the common physical, emotional, cognitive, social, and moral issues and the challenges of parenting that you will confront in raising a teenager.

1

Early and Middle Adolescence

■ ■ ■

Perhaps as you held your newborn you tried to envision him at later stages—as, say, a teenager. At that time that image must have been difficult to imagine.

Yet children grow up quickly and the boy who, only a short while ago, still slept with a special blanket is now lobbying for an earring. Adolescence is the time when childhood is left behind and your young teen begins to cross the long bridge that separates childhood and the adult world.

That transition is not an easy time for either the adolescent or his parents. During this time, your son or daughter's body is being bombarded by hormones, which results in a growth surge, as well as the reproductive maturation that makes the teen physically capable of becoming a parent. For some young adolescents, this hormonal onslaught is tantamount to being on an emotional roller coaster, a difficult ride for the teen as well as for the rest of the family.

Adolescence is also a time when most children begin to pull away from their families. Once a homebody, your son may suddenly announce that he'd like to go away to camp for the summer rather than go on the annual family trek to the beach. Peers become more important than ever. Although your son used to (and still may) pretend to gag every time he saw kissing on television, he's discovering that girls aren't so bad; in fact, they're quite nice—and getting close to one may have become an intriguing prospect.

In this chapter, we will focus on the issues that your child faces as he enters adolescence. Peer pressure, burgeoning sexuality, and the quest for autonomy are some of the topics that we will discuss. First, though, let's cover the developmental milestones that children go through as they enter the adolescent years.

Milestones

Adolescence is a stage of life when, with the exception of infancy, the body grows and changes more dramatically than at any other time. During these few years, your child will attain most of his adult height and become biologically capable of having his offspring. His reasoning capabilities will rise to a new level of complexity. As he prepares to make his own place in the world, he begins the process of discovering exactly what he wants that place to be. These are also years when it may seem as though you, his parent, have been pushed from the front to the backseat of his life. You may feel superfluous now that his friends, more than family, occupy his spare time.

These are exciting days of endless discoveries. But they are also filled with the pain of uncertainty, of not always knowing if one fits in. Watching your adolescent grapple with

these doubts may sometimes seem like a rerun of your own early teens; perhaps you can still sense the sting of humiliation over being the shortest or the tallest, the most or the least developed in the class. You want to protect him from insecure feelings; you want somehow to devise a way to ensure that he stays confident about his sense of worth. Yet you also realize that you no longer have that kind of power over his life.

In this section, we will discuss the developmental milestones of early adolescence from physical, psychological, moral, and social perspectives. Keep in mind that although it is natural for your relationship with your child to change as he begins to grow up, this does not mean that it diminishes in importance. Strong parental support and guidance have never been as important as they are during adolescence.

■ PHYSICAL CHANGES

The growth spurt is one of the first signs that a child is beginning puberty, the series of biological events that transform the immature body into one that is physically capable of reproduction.

As with any aspect of human development, there is no precise timetable. But there is a fixed *sequence* for the physical changes of adolescence. For example, the average boy begins his growth spurt at about age twelve. This doesn't mean, however, that as a parent you should be concerned if your thirteen-year-old is the shortest kid in his class. Chances are that everything is fine and that he is simply developing slower than his classmates. If at fifteen, however, he still hasn't begun a significant growth spurt, consult your adolescent's physician.

For girls, the average age at which the growth spurt begins is ten. The growth spurt, during which the child attains 98 percent of his adult height, usually lasts anywhere between two and three years but can be a lot shorter. During this time, a boy may grow as much as nine inches, while most girls add six or seven inches to their height.

Different parts of the body grow at different rates during this spurt. Perhaps you've wondered why your son's jeans are too short long before his shirt sleeves have crept far above his wrists? Typically, the adolescent leg grows faster than the body trunk. As a result, the legs stop their growth between six and nine months earlier than the rest of the body, while the shoulders and chest are the last parts to attain full growth. During the growth spurt, the bones of the face also change, with the features becoming sharper and less childlike.

As the body gets taller, its shape changes. The body of a girl becomes rounder. She develops breasts and a soft padding around what was once boy-like hips. Boys, on the other hand, lose their baby fat, becoming more muscular, with wider shoulders and thicker necks. Gone are the days when almost any girl in the class was a physical match for most any boy: Adolescent boys *are* physically stronger than their female counterparts because of their more muscular physical makeup. By contrast, adolescent girls can be reassured that women are more likely to live longer and enjoy better health and appear better able to tolerate stress than men.

However dramatic an adolescent's growth, it is only part of the story. Inside, the adolescent is changing, too. The reproductive organs, targeted by hormones, are enlarging and maturing in preparation for future reproduction. During puberty, girls generally first develop small breasts, then pubic and underarm hair grows, and finally menses begin. The first sign that a boy is entering puberty usually is an enlargement in the testes and growth of pubic hair. Next the penis begins to grow in size. About a year later, most boys have sperm in their semen.

■ PSYCHOLOGICAL DEVELOPMENT

Adolescence—the transition between childhood and entry into the adult world—is a relatively new concept and not a universal one. Prior to the nineteenth century, life was radically different for most teens. People tended to marry well before they were out of their teens and were quickly burdened with the responsibilities of parenthood. The reality for children in the past was a few years of schooling—enough to learn to read and write, if they were lucky—and then a job in a factory or the fields.

In our and other industrialized societies, adolescence is seen as an apprenticeship. Just as the craftsman trains for years before gaining full status in his field, the adolescent is learning to handle adult responsibilities. Many changes must occur during this time in order for an adolescent to be fully prepared to accept these responsibilities. In addition to the physical changes that will transform him from a child into a young adult capable of starting his own family, the perimeters of your adolescent's mind are expanding, allowing him to think in new ways. Moreover, he is struggling with the formidable but crucial task of forming an identity.

By the time your child is in seventh or eighth grade, you should be noticing subtle differences in the way he thinks. The Swiss developmental psychologist Jean Piaget contended that by age twelve a child develops a more logical structure to his thought processes and some capacity for abstract thought and reason. The adolescent should be able to think about possibilities, consider hypotheses, think ahead, consider the thought process, and think beyond conventional limits. Under Piaget's theory, an elementary-school child, for example, when asked to combine chemicals in various combinations to change the color of a liquid, would test only one chemical at a time. If someone suggested that he try two or more at once, he would become confused. A fourteen-year-old, on the other hand, might start out testing one but would quickly realize that he needed to combine chemicals to produce the desired result. Piaget called this ability to think systemically about all the logical possibilities within a problem *formal operations,* as opposed to the *concrete* operational thought that enables elementary-school students to complete each part of a task without relating one to the other. Brain maturation coupled with experience results in these new thinking capabilities.

Adolescents also have an increased ability to use abstract verbal concepts. In one study, children and adolescents were given a series of sentences. Each sentence contained the same nonsense word, and the youngsters were asked to figure out the meaning from the context. The tendency of the younger children was to evaluate each sentence as though it had no relationship to the next. Thus, they thought the nonsense word had one meaning in the first sentence and a different meaning in the next one. The adolescents, however, were more likely to deduce the meaning for the nonsense word and apply that same meaning in the entire series of sentences. Adolescents also fared much better in tests that require constructing comparisons.

The adolescent's increased cognitive sophistication goes beyond the ability to link the parts of a process or decode meanings. An increased ability to engage in abstract thought enables him to examine complex issues that previously were beyond his intellectual grasp, issues such as politics, religion, and morality. As the adolescent grows older, his thinking becomes even more abstract.

If you ask a ten-year-old, for example, what should be done to stop the crime wave, he will probably advocate severe punishment for all those who break the law as the best deterrent he can think of. An adolescent, however, is likely to consider the complexity of the problem. He is apt to introduce into the argument other elements such as leniency for first-time offenders, reform programs, and the revision of laws that no longer work. The older teen is beginning to consider issues within a larger framework.

Logical questions emerge as one's cognitive capacity expands to examine the whole picture: *Who am I? Where do I fit in?* During adolescence, the individual begins to consolidate an identity that is expressed in terms of his beliefs and goals for the future. When asked who he is the six-year-old will proudly describe himself as the best baseball player in the class or the fastest reader. But ask your fourteen-year-old the same question and you'll get a very different kind of answer. He may say, for instance, that he's a person who doesn't like to hurt others. He also is more likely than the younger child to list the multiple pieces that he considers to be part of the puzzle that is his identity. Thus, he isn't simply a good athlete, but he's also an understanding friend, loyal, considerate, well-mannered, and a good student in everything except math.

He is aware that his personality is multifaceted, and he senses that there are facets still to be unearthed. At home, for instance, he may be a constant cutup, a practical joker who keeps the family in stitches. Yet, his school persona is very different, perhaps that of a quiet boy who fades into the woodwork. Sometimes these contradictions are difficult for teens in early adolescence. Generally, as an adolescent grows older, he becomes more comfortable with the different parts of himself and learns to use different behavior in different contexts.

The adolescent is an explorer, discovering himself. This is a heady time, when the possibilities seem exhilarating. Yet, on some days, you may have to drag him out of bed and use threats to get him on the school bus. For all their bravado, young adolescents are rather delicate from a psychological viewpoint. The self-esteem that in elementary school seemed so solid may now be as flimsy as gossamer.

Studies have shown that self-esteem plummets during early adolescence.

If you have a daughter, you may especially notice the change. Self-esteem in girls is thought to be more fragile during these years because of the emphasis on physical attractiveness. With their rapidly changing bodies, many girls don't feel very good about the way they look. Fortunately, this decline in self-esteem is only temporary, and as they move through the early years of adolescence, most teens reclaim the self-esteem they lost along the way. (See also *Building Self-Esteem*, page 75.)

■ MORAL DEVELOPMENT

As an adolescent's reasoning abilities increase, he begins to focus more on the deeper questions of right and wrong. *What kind of person do I want to be? How should I react in certain situations? When is it important to stand firm and when is there room to be flexible?*

In his move through life, your child's moral standards evolve. When he was a kindergartner, for example, he followed the rules because he didn't want to get into trouble and he didn't consider the feelings of others or recognize that they might differ from his own. A year or two later, he had a growing awareness that sometimes his needs conflicted with his classmates', but right or wrong, those needs were fixed and universal.

By the end of elementary school, in determining the "right" course of action, your child is likely to take into account the expectations of his family, teachers, and peers. Much of his behavior is still geared toward avoiding punishment and gaining rewards, but he is beginning to see that many factors go into the moral choices that every individual must make. During the middle-school years, his moral development continues to evolve as he becomes more aware of the relationship between the individual and society. A teen at this stage of moral development is likely to conform to the views of society—he will probably accept the notion that laws are there for a purpose and that those who break them must pay a price. Some adolescents break the law. The typical teen tests limits and society's tolerance of behaviors. Yet the majority don't break laws and commit crimes.

As your teen gets older, his moral reasoning shifts to a new plane. Able to view moral conflicts in more abstract terms, he realizes that widespread societal views do not always reflect the moral high ground. He may decide that in certain areas his own behavior has to be above that of the law or societal norm. He can readily cite examples of justice and injustice. He is becoming more sensitive to the impact of his own actions on those around him. In essence, he is evolving the moral standards by which the rest of his life will be lived.

Unfortunately, not every teen (or every adult) has strong moral convictions. As a parent, however, you can help your teen develop moral standards by setting a good example yourself. If your adolescent sees you dealing with other people in a forthright and fair manner, the teen will have a model to follow. Teens are more likely to exhibit greater self-control and mature moral judgments when they are reared by parents who are consistent in their rules of behavior, who don't make arbitrary rules but explain the reasons behind the rules, and consider the feelings and opinions of all members of the family and community.

■ SOCIAL DEVELOPMENT

The world is a much bigger place for the adolescent. Suddenly, he expects freedoms that until now have not been an issue. Perhaps in the interest of safety you've driven him to school all these years; now he wants to walk with friends, even though the school's more than a mile or two from home. On the weekends, he used to be happy to play soccer or go on an outing with the family; now he wants to hang out at the mall with his friends.

There's no question that most adolescents pull away from their family to some degree. In elementary school, he used to love it when he saw you volunteering in the school library or helping with a class party. But these days you notice that when you are out together, he walks slightly behind you—as though you're strangers—especially if a group of teenagers happens to pass by.

The move away from family and toward peers is a normal part of adolescence. This does not mean you are not important to your child. A solid, loving relationship between parent and child remains as critical during this period of development as it was in his preschool years. He needs to know that you are still there for him.

Studies have shown that although adolescents between the ages of twelve and fifteen are spending more time with friends than they did as younger children, there are still times when they like to be with Mom and Dad. When it comes time to relax and hang out, though, they prefer to be with friends. Why? Simply because they enjoy being with people their own age. They feel that they are better understood by peers and that they can be themselves. This is important to their social development, in learning to make close relationships with others, to their identity formation, and to understanding who they are.

Even though your middle-school child may be exposed to a wider variety of children, most likely his best friends are from similar social and ethnic backgrounds, even more so than during elementary school. Moreover, his criteria in choosing friends have changed. In elementary school, most children will choose friends based on similar interests. But seventh graders, in addition to similar interests, also want friends to have similar attitudes and values. They also cite loyalty and closeness as important characteristics.

This shouldn't come as a surprise, especially with teenage girls, who spend a good part of their socialization time involved in private conversation with their friends. The long-winded telephone conversations, while aggravating for parents with only one phone line, serve the valuable purpose of helping the teen define who she is, a process termed *identity formation*.

Boys, on the other hand, are less likely to discuss their most private thoughts with a friend. Boys want friends whom they like and trust to do things with and who will stand up for them if they're in trouble. Girls want friends who understand their feelings.

These are also the years when an interest in the opposite sex develops. Not all children in the early middle-school years are interested in dating. Your child may belong to a group where sports are the main focus or perhaps he is academically gifted and socializes with kids who are more concerned with making the honor roll than with whom they're going to go out on Friday night. Yet many twelve- or thirteen-year-olds do have a growing interest in boy-girl relationships.

Typically, small groups of boys and girls begin to sit together on the bus and hang out at lunch and after school. School functions such as dances also are geared to bring the sexes together socially. Many adolescents are content with being part of a loosely organized group and wait until high school or after to date seriously. Others, however, begin pairing off in middle school.

Peer Pressure and Influence

The thought that an adolescent will be influenced unduly by peer pressure has crossed even the most relaxed parent's mind. From the time they are little, children are encouraged to do right and avoid wrong choices. *Just say no,* they are told about drugs, sex, and anything that we believe will lead them away from the path of right and good behavior.

During adolescence, signs of social conformity begin to appear—conformity, that is, to expectations and influences of peers, not yours. Your son begs to have his ear pierced like the rest of his friends. His sneakers have to be a certain brand and his hair cut just so.

Although these are often superficial fashion statements, parents wonder whether this is a harbinger of more drastic changes and choices in the future.

Peer approval and acceptance during these years *is* important. More and more, as children grow into adolescents, they come to rely on their friends for everything from companionship to understanding. This "youth culture" serves to separate the current generation from the previous one. Your son may dress in clothes that you think belong in the rag bag, listen to music that sounds like construction noise, and wear a ring through his nose. You may not understand any more than your parents did when your hair was longer. For your son, though, there's nothing to understand. He's trying to express himself, to make a statement about his identity, to demonstrate that his generation is different. He wants to be like his friends and for you to respect him as an autonomous person.

Many parents—especially those with clear memories of their own adolescence—don't lose any sleep over such signs of peer conformity. Of much greater concern is whether a teen is being led into self-destructive or antisocial behavior by his strong desire to be part of a group.

Studies have shown that young adolescents are more willing to follow their peers than are younger children. The more a middle-school child is pressured by peers, the greater the chance that he will go along or join in. This tendency, however, does decrease later in adolescence. Students in one study said that they were more likely to be influenced toward prosocial behaviors than into antisocial acts.

What about parental influence? Are the morals you have taught your child forgotten in the face of peer pressure? Although much has been written about the generation gap, current research shows that the differences between parents and adolescents are not as great as many people think. Most adolescents do, in fact, hold their parents in high regard. One study of 1,000 teens and their mothers found that 60 percent of the teens rated their relationship as extremely close, while only 11 percent said they were not close with their mother. An interesting finding was that both parents and peers had influence over the adolescent but in different areas. Adolescents tended to agree with their parents' ideas on marriage and religion yet often disagreed on issues related to drugs and sex. Another study found that while most adolescents adhered to the basic moral principles learned from parents, they conformed to peers when it came to clothing styles, hairstyle, and hours of sleep.

Your adolescent feels dual pressures to conform—both to peers and to the standards you have established at home. Understand this struggle to balance those pressures. Your teen needs rules that are considered and consistent, as well as some room to experiment safely. Yet your adolescent also needs to know you are a constant presence, providing support and enforcing the rules and limits.

Dating and Groups

In general, social life in middle school follows a familiar progression.

Initially, most children emerge from their elementary school with a few close friends. In middle school, which may well be much larger and may draw students from several elementary schools, the young adolescent comes into contact with many children he's never seen before. The tendency at first may be to cling to familiar faces. Gradually many begin to break through the barrier of comfortable familiarity and make overtures to kids they didn't know from the old school.

In early middle school, an adolescent's social life usually revolves around a few friends of the same sex. These friends may or may not form a *clique*, a small group of perhaps half a dozen peers who do things together. As adolescents progress through middle and high school, cliques become more common. The clique, in a sense, is like a family of peers, the difference between this and a real family being that the adolescent is free to leave the clique and join another if the first one no longer is satisfying. Cliques are thought to be so pervasive and attractive during this stage of life because they offer a transitional sense of security, a haven where the adolescent feels in social control. When cliques enlarge and turn aggressive, they may become gangs.

As your child progresses through middle school, his circle of friends is likely to broaden. He still may be a member of a clique, but his clique may join with other cliques to form a larger *crowd*, typically of about fifteen to thirty members. A crowd is generally identified by a common denominator of its members. Hence, you may hear him label members of a crowd as the *jocks,* the *druggies,* the *fast* or *cool kids*, the *brains* or the *nerds,* the *rednecks*, and so on.

By the time an adolescent is near the end of middle school, he has probably begun to spend time with members of the opposite sex. These interactions across sexual lines may begin when a clique of boys and one of girls—often the most popular students—get together to form a heterosexual crowd. Initially the crowd's socialization may be simply eating lunch together or hanging out in the school parking lot for a few minutes each day before or after school. School dances, extracurricular activities, and private parties also provide chances for boys and girls to mingle. Attractions develop and soon you see boys calling girls or girls calling boys. These first calls are usually nervous affairs, and are often made with a cheering section of one's friends near the telephone, offering encouragement and muffled giggles.

In many areas, group dating begins during these middle-school years. Several girls arrange to meet a group of boys at the movie theater or at the mall or library and may pair up there. Adolescents are more likely to start one-on-one dating in high school, especially after they or some of their peers have a driver's license.

As a parent, your first impulse may be to continue to exercise strict control over your adolescent's social interactions and choice of friends. As you become more of an outsider in his social life, however, that becomes increasingly difficult. Yet, remaining a presence *is* important. Parental limits, including curfews, age thresholds (*you may not date until you're sixteen*), and codes of behavior, are important for both parent and adolescent. Your opinions may rarely be solicited, but thoughtful, reasoned reactions to your teen's friends or activities are often registered and can affect decisions.

Baby-sitting and Other Work

When many children reach middle school, they are able to perform some work to earn spending money. Such work can introduce them to the responsibilities that come with formal jobs and employment.

Baby-sitting, caring for neighbors' pets, delivering newspapers, mowing lawns, and yard work are probably the most common job opportunities for young adolescents. At age sixteen, teens are legally able to be regularly employed, to work in stores, restaurants, and offices.

If your teen wants to work, encourage him. These informal jobs can give the teen self-confidence and pride. He is proud to have accomplished something on his own, and he knows his work was worth something to another adult. In addition, being able to buy things with his own money gives him a sense of independence.

For most middle-schoolers, work is a positive experience because they are only allowed to work in casual jobs that demand little time and do not interfere very much with their studies or school activities. Older teens, however, may overdo it by working too many hours in their quest for the latest fashions or to put extra food on the family table. Although these part-time jobs are useful,

long work hours can be associated with a drop in school performance. Studies have shown that teens who work more than twenty hours a week are more likely to drop out of school than those with less demanding work schedules.

Maintaining Lines of Communication

As your teen becomes more self-sufficient, there will be days when it seems that he no longer needs you. More than ever, however, there needs to be an open line of communication between him and you, his parent. He needs to know that you are there for him.

You may be eyeing this advice skeptically. How many times, you ask yourself, have you tried to get him to open up? Yet all he does is sit there, looking bored, making you feel as though you're intruding. Adolescents can be masters of noncommunication—he won't talk if he doesn't feel like it, and many days he simply doesn't feel like it. It's not necessary that you know everything that's going on inside your adolescent's head. What is important, however, is that if something is bothering him or he has matters that he wants to discuss, he feels comfortable coming to you.

Contrary to parental worry, the majority of adolescents love and respect their parents and want to have a close relationship. One of the ways you can help this happen is to maintain open communication with your teen. Communication patterns are best established much earlier, but they do evolve over time. Don't try to pull information out of your teen; when he does decide to open up, be a good listener. Don't interrupt. Try to be as nonjudgmental as possible. Among the biggest dangers to the parent-teen communication are harsh criticism and attempts by parents to solve their teen's problems prematurely or preemptively. (See also *Talking to Your Teenager,* page 38.)

Use criticism sparingly. Instead, rely on praise and trust to help build your teen's self-esteem. Remember, too, it is not your responsibility to solve all your adolescent's problems. When he brings his problems and concerns to you, listen, and offer your opinion if he asks. But ultimately, the problems are his, and he must take responsibility for resolving them. Certain more serious issues such as drug or alcohol use or illegal acts, however, do require parental intervention.

Discipline and Punishment

From a developmental standpoint, adolescence is the time when a person begins to experiment with freedom. No longer a dependent child unready to assume the responsibilities of adulthood, the adolescent is attempting to bridge two worlds. Sometimes he is successful and you, bursting with pride, marvel at his maturity and strong character. At other times he fails and you find yourself disappointed or in a shouting match.

As an adolescent, your child has a series of complex and difficult tasks to master. In a few short years, he will sever the intense dependency of childhood and develop a more mature and equal relationship with his parents. To do this, he requires emotional space and freedom to experiment. Rebellion, turmoil, confusion, alienation, and indifference are all common emotional states for adolescents. Not every adolescent declares war on his parents—most kids and their parents coexist in relative peace. But even kids who are not notoriously rebellious or in turmoil will have days when any attempt a parent makes at conversation is met with stony silence or an indifferent shrug.

Although parents may be tempted to try to crush adolescent rebellion, this strategy often makes the teen more defiant. As a parent, you have to define limits of behavior that are acceptable. Your teen must be taught that he is accountable for his actions and decisions.

Even if they won't admit it, teens need and want guidance and rules to help them learn the boundaries of acceptable behavior. With adolescents, you need a different approach to discipline and punishment. Your teen's more sophisticated thought processes and increased freedom demand different approaches than when he was younger. For example, the time-out may have been a successful method for disciplining unacceptable behavior in earlier years, but it isn't likely to be effective in dealing with a fourteen-year-old. For teens, the loss of a privilege is a more appropriate punishment.

The following guidelines may be helpful in disciplining your adolescent:

- **Make the Rules Clear.**
  Most experts recommend having fewer rules but insisting that rules be followed. You may, for example, not object to his

playing music in his room but insist that all is quiet by 10 P.M. Similarly, it is up to you to set rules regarding television and telephone privileges, curfew, and use of your possessions. Your teen should know the penalty or consequence for breaking a rule. For example, if he loses or destroys something, he should be expected to replace it. Or the consequence for a bad math grade might be more study time and loss of a favorite television program.

- **Be Willing to Negotiate.**
Adolescents realize that many rules are fairly arbitrary, so parents shouldn't be surprised when a teen questions a rule. Many families help lessen tension and conflicts by having occasional family meetings where issues can be discussed and, in some cases, negotiated. Perhaps your teen doesn't like his arbitrary bedtime. He wants to be allowed to stay up an extra hour, and he has a list of reasons to support his request. Whether his reasons persuade you to alter his bedtime is not really the point. More important is that you've discussed the issue with him in a reasoning, adult manner. In this way, he feels like his viewpoint received the respectful consideration it deserved.

- **Avoid Criticism.**
Many parents express concern about the way their teens look. They may not like their hair, clothes, music, or friends. But if parents voice all these criticisms, their relationships with their teens will suffer. Many negative parent-adolescent relation-

ships arise from too much criticism. So choose battles wisely. If his behavior is potentially harmful or infringes on your rights or the rights of others, then you should set firm limits. Otherwise it's preferable to allow your teen some freedom to experiment and rebel.

- **Teach Responsibility.**
No matter how hard you try to teach life's most important lessons, ultimately your teen learns through trial and error. He makes a mistake, pays a price, and learns the consequences of the error.

You can't be with your teen twenty-four hours a day, whispering what is right and what is wrong. His own conscience has usually taken that over by age fourteen. It is up to him to make decisions and then accept responsibility for his choices. If he decides to spend all his allowance on a new CD and then doesn't have enough money for a Friday night movie with his friends, he learns the consequences far better than if you were budgeting his money for him.

- **Keep Your Cool.**
Children learn by example. Thus, if you scream at your teen, he will think it's all right for him to use the same behavior with you. Adolescents can be disrespectful and rude to their parents. Teach your teen, through your own behavior, that it is acceptable to disagree and to feel angry but that screaming and rudeness will not be tolerated. If your teen says something mean to you, explain how that makes you feel.

Puberty: Its Biology and Psychology

If you are the parent of a child in middle school, you have probably seen firsthand the highly variable timetable of sexual development.

Some seventh-grade girls have the bodies of mature women, while others are just beginning to wear training bras. As for the average twelve-year-old boy, he probably is several inches shorter than many of the girls in his class. At a glance, most of the boys could be mistaken for the girls' younger brothers.

Puberty—a series of biological changes that enable an individual to be capable of reproduction—begins when a part of the brain signals the pituitary gland to increase its production of hormones. In addition to the hormones that promote growth, the pituitary gland also releases hormones that increase the production of two main sex hormones. In a girl, the ovaries release large amounts of estrogen and progesterone; in boys, the testes and adrenal gland (located adjacent to the kidneys) manufacture testosterone. These hormones trigger the physical changes that we associate with puberty.

Many factors determine when a person starts puberty. Heredity has a role. If you, for example, started puberty later than average, your son or daughter is more likely to follow that pattern than the child of a person who started maturing earlier. Heredity is not the only factor. Studies of girls have shown that environmental factors such as nutrition, stress, exercise, and socioeconomic background also influence the age at which a girl starts her menstrual period. American girls today, for example, start menstruating eighteen months earlier than did their great-grandmothers at the turn of the century.

Boys, too, enter puberty earlier than their great-grandfathers did. Most boys today have reached their full adult height by the time they turn eighteen; fifty years ago, the average male achieved his full height at the age of twenty-six. Although there are wide variations in the age and speed at which individuals go through puberty, the sequence of events is always consistent.

In girls, the first sign is usually the appearance of a small rise or breast bud around the nipple. As the breasts continue to grow, the girl develops sparse pubic and underarm hair. Her shape begins to change; in addition to growing taller, her hips become more rounded. The sebaceous glands in the skin often become overactive during puberty, which may result in acne on the faces or bodies of both boys and girls.

In addition to these visible signs, there are internal changes occurring as a girl's body prepares for menstruation. The ovaries are growing, and the cells destined to become ova are slowly beginning to develop. The uterus is also enlarging and the vaginal wall thickening. Prior to the onset of menstruation, many girls notice an increase in vaginal discharge. Menstruation occurs toward the end of puberty, on average about eighteen months after the peak of the growth spurt. In the early months of sexual maturity, menstrual periods tend to be erratic, and many girls have periods without the release of an egg (ovulation) for a year or more. The average age in the United States for the onset of menstruation is between twelve and thirteen.

As a boy's testes begin to produce testosterone, the first noticeable sign of puberty is a difference in the way the genitals look. The testes become larger, and the skin of the scrotum thickens and becomes redder in color. Light-colored sprigs of pubic hair appear around the base of the penis. The penis itself becomes larger and will grow for the next two years. After the penis begins to grow, most boys begin to ejaculate semen. Although even the infant penis is capable of erection, the ability to ejaculate comes with puberty. Initially, the semen is scant of sperm, but the sperm count will increase as the boy matures. In addition to these genital changes, a boy will develop hair under his arms and on his face. Chest hair doesn't appear until the late teens or even well into young adulthood. During puberty a boy's voice begins to change gradually as his larynx expands and the vocal cords lengthen. Before the high voice of the young boy evolves into the deep voice of a man, it goes through a period of cracks and squeaks that we have come to associate with adolescence.

The complete pubertal process for both boys and girls typically lasts between four and five years. Many girls and boys admit to being a little frightened over menstruation or ejaculation. Some have strong negative feelings about what is happening to their bodies; others are reticent, preferring not to talk about it.

What about the age at which an adolescent enters puberty? Does an early or late puberty have psychological or emotional effects on a boy or girl?

Unfortunately, there are not clear answers because of mixed findings from various studies. One study of boys found that when peers and adults were asked to rate the boys, they rated the early maturing boys as being more socially and psychologically mature. These boys tended to have a more positive attitude toward their bodies, presumably because their physical maturity enhanced their athletic capabilities. Another study, however, found that the early maturing boys were less curious intellectually, more serious, and more prone to anxiety than their late-developing counterparts.

Early maturation for a girl may also have risks. Girls who mature early may have lower self-esteem. Because their bodies are physically mature, these girls often are attractive to older boys. They are more likely to have a boyfriend at a relatively young age and have early sexual relations, which can lead to a pregnancy. A study has also shown that early maturing girls tend to be shorter and weigh more than our society's idealized vision of the slim, long-legged teen. Although girls who develop later may feel badly because they're not initially popular, as they grow older they tend to be more satisfied with the way they look than those who mature early. The timing of puberty, however, is biologically programmed.

While parents cannot alter the timing, they may be able to help their teen examine his feelings and be more comfortable with the changes that are occurring. Fundamental to this is educating the youngster about puberty. Help your adolescent understand that puberty is a natural process, that everyone experiences intense moods, and, over time, learns to adjust to the changes. (See also *Building Self-Esteem*, page 75.)

If you are the parent of an adolescent, you have probably noticed emotional changes in your child. Your son may be moodier than usual, preferring to hang out in his room rather than with the rest of the family. You sense that he is pulling away, trying to put both emotional and physical space between himself and the rest of the family. This is a natural consequence of puberty, and if you haven't noticed it in your child yet, you may in the future. After a girl starts menstruating, both parents may tend to tighten the tether in an attempt to increase control. Frequently, the girl balks at this and becomes argumentative. Interestingly, the conflicts that arise during puberty are more often between the mother and her son or daughter. Some researchers speculate that this tension may reflect the early closeness with the mother, making it more difficult to achieve emotional separation. Then, too, mothers are often placed in the role of enforcing the family rules.

If you are frequently arguing with your adolescent, know that more peaceful days probably lie ahead. Remember that it takes two to fight; resist the temptation to engage in pitched battles over small matters. Look for opportunities to talk things through peacefully. Timing is important, so don't insist if your youngster isn't receptive— peacemaking, too, can be seen as interference at the wrong moment. Make sure your

adolescent understands you're available and willing to talk when he's ready. As you and your child adjust to the changes both in his body and in your relationship, tensions should ease and you should find yourself back on solid ground.

Menstruation

The majority of girls will start menstruating sometime during these middle-school years.

Menstruation—the monthly flow of blood from the uterus—is a signal that a female is physically mature and capable of becoming pregnant. Although the onset of the menses is a physical event, it also has psychological ramifications.

It wasn't that long ago that menstruation was something not discussed in polite society. Mothers failed to prepare their daughters for the impending changes in their body, and more than one young woman awoke to the shock of her life, no doubt thinking she had contracted some dreaded disease or suffered some unknown injury. In certain societies, girls and women are still considered unclean when they are menstruating.

Fortunately, for the most part such thinking has changed. Thanks to information provided by parents and schools, few young adolescents today are unaware of the physical changes they can expect. This does not mean, however, that every adolescent feels comfortable with what is happening to her body. Girls are extremely self-conscious. Your daughter may look at herself in the mirror and feel fat in her body's newfound roundness. As her breasts grow larger, she may be teased by boys in her class or even by her siblings. Part of her may long for the days when she felt comfortable wrestling with the neighborhood boys, while the other part yearns to grow up, to know what it's like to be a woman.

Researchers have conducted studies that focus on girls' attitudes and beliefs about menstruation. In one study, 20 percent had positive feelings about their first period, 20 percent said they had negative feelings, and 40 percent said they were both pleased and scared about what was happening to their body. Similar studies have found that girls who have unpleasant physical symptoms during their period are more likely to have negative feelings about the experience, as are those who start menstruating early and girls who were not sufficiently prepared for the event. Moreover, girls tend to be secretive about what is happening to them. One-fourth of girls interviewed for a study said they had told only their mothers when they started their periods, although usually after six months or so most girls become more open and share their secret with friends.

Whether a girl feels comfortable about beginning menstruation is related to how well she has been prepared for the event. Those who report negative feelings are more likely to have been unprepared or to have received information about the process from a person who expressed negative feelings. When a mother refers to her period as the "curse" and constantly complains about how lousy she feels, her daughter will often have similar feelings when she starts menstruating.

You can help pave the way for your daughter by preparing her for the changes that will take place. Speak about menstruation in positive, rather than negative, terms. To prepare her and help her avoid embarrassment, show her what to do when she starts menstruating.

It's also particularly important during this stage of development that daughters aren't sent the message that they are inferior to their brothers: If a girl is made to feel less significant than the boys in her family, she may have a difficult time accepting herself as the androgynous body of her childhood evolves into that of a young woman. Consider carefully your attitudes toward your children. Be evenhanded and sensitive to the reality (or even the perception) of unfairness in the way you treat your youngsters. If you treat your daughter with added respect, that may help her understand that menstruation signals a new level of maturity and help foster her sense of responsibility.

Above all, keep the lines of communication open between you. A girl who has a loving relationship with her mother is more likely to feel good about growing up herself.

Body Image

As boys and girls enter adolescence, it is easy for them to find fault with their bodies. The boy who never minded being the shortest kid in the class now feels dwarfed. A girl whose body has raced ahead of most of her peers suddenly feels fat and bloated.

Teenagers, like many adults, are often disappointed with their bodies. A girl may feel that she is flat-chested or that her breasts are too large for her to wear the latest fashions. Boys may long for the well-defined muscles that they see on athletes. The glamorous male and female body images they see on television and in magazines—retouched and manipulated as they often are—tend to establish unrealistic and even unreal expectations.

Girls are vulnerable to developing poor body images. During puberty, many girls gain weight. In many cases, the weight is shed as the girl matures, but sometimes not before it has left its mark; we all know thin women who insist that they are obese. Fad diets that provide inadequate nutrition are common among adolescent girls. Boys in sports such as wrestling or gymnastics sometimes put exaggerated emphasis on body size and appearance and may also experiment with their diet. Such preoccupations with developing the "perfect body" can place a teenager, especially girls, at risk for the potentially fatal eating disorder anorexia nervosa or for bulimia, a disorder characterized by bingeing and purging. (See *Eating and Nutritional Disorders*, page 260.)

As part of the maturation process, most adolescents learn to feel comfortable in their "new" bodies. For example, the small-breasted girl learns to appreciate her attractive legs, and the short boy takes pride in his ample biceps. If your teen is worried about his late puberty and physical development, reassure him that in time he will catch up to his peers. The teen who is unhappy with the shape of his body and who wants to slim down or develop a more well-defined contour should be encouraged to start an exercise regimen.

If weight is a problem, discuss a sensible diet with your adolescent's doctor. Beware of teens wanting to use steroids or other drugs to build muscles. Such medications can pose serious health risks, especially in developing adolescents, as well as be against the rules in competitive sports.

Acne

During their adolescent years, three out of four teens have acne, which consists of pimples, blackheads, or whiteheads.

As an individual begins puberty, elevated hormonal activities cause the skin's sebaceous glands to produce an excessive amount of oil. The oil can then block the hair follicles. Add common bacteria to the blocked pore and you have a pimple. Girls often notice an aggravation of their acne prior to their menstrual period each month.

Acne is a relatively minor physical problem for many teens, but for others, the ramifications extend beyond the physical. Severe acne can affect an adolescent's self-esteem, self-confidence, and social life. Moreover, cystic acne—a severe form of the disease—can permanently scar the skin.

If your teen has acne, you may be able to treat it at home. A mild oil-free soap can be used to cleanse the skin and an over-the-counter lotion that contains benzoyl peroxide can be applied afterward to dry up the pimples. If this doesn't clear up the problem, don't assume that he simply has to endure this phase, however unpleasant. Great strides have been made in recent years in the treatment of acne, which requires consulting with a dermatologist, a physician who specializes in the treatment of skin disorders. Depending upon the severity of your child's acne, the doctor will choose from an assortment of treatments, which may include a combination of oral and topical antibiotics or possibly Retin A, a vitamin-A derivative that has proven effective in treating some types of acne. If cystic acne has left scars or pits on the skin's surface, a surgical procedure (*dermabrasion*) may be used to abrade the skin surface, exposing smoother skin.

Self-Consciousness

Adolescents are notoriously self-conscious. Your adolescent probably feels as though the world is watching his every move. It sees when he sneezes into his sleeve, notices when he picks up the wrong fork at a friend's house for dinner, and is eyeing that pimple that right now is percolating beneath the surface of his chin.

It's as though they imagine others sizing them up through a magnifying glass that enhances every little flaw. Suddenly, the child who in the past seemed comfortable in his own skin looks as though he'd like to jump out of it. Any little defect is exaggerated— the slight bump on his nose, the gap between his front teeth, his skinny legs—all are cause for alarm.

Self-consciousness is not confined to appearance. The way he sits, moves, and talks with people he doesn't know well also speaks of uncertainty and lack of confidence.

If you make the mistake of teasing him or telling a joke that he considers corny in front of a friend, he may refuse to speak to you for the rest of the day.

Parents should be patient at a teen's shyness or apparent unsociability. Try to understand his concerns and be sensitive and supportive. Parents can help bolster uncertain self-esteem through praise and positive feedback. (See also *Building Self-Esteem*, page 75.) When his friends visit, be polite and hospitable, but stay out of the way, as most young teens dislike it when their parents try to act young and cool around their friends. Most teens become less self-conscious as they adjust to the physical and emotional changes taking place.

Sexuality

One of the greatest concerns of many parents as their children grow older is their youngsters' emerging sexuality. It may be shocking to realize how rapidly the baby you once nursed is developing into a young man. A father who delighted in roughhousing with his little girl suddenly understands that this is no longer appropriate behavior now that his daughter is growing up.

Not only must a parent confront his or her own feelings about the changes taking place as a child enters adolescence but he also must consider the external factors and risks that cannot help but increase parental fear over this period of life. These include early sexual intercourse, teenage pregnancy, and, perhaps the most frightening risk of all, AIDS.

Parents must resist the impulse to avoid these issues and hope that with a little luck everything will turn out all right. As a parent, it is important for you to understand your teen's emerging sexual feelings and to communicate information about sexual activity and its emotional and physical consequences. In the same way, a preparatory conversation should be initiated with sons about nocturnal emissions ("wet dreams"). When unexpected, these normal occurrences can be both surprising and a source of concern to an adolescent boy.

In the early middle-school years, many adolescents are uncomfortable with their changing bodies and emerging sexual feelings. As a result, you may notice your teen going out of his way to deny these changes. He may, for instance, insist that girls are gross, even though you find a magazine with pictures of naked women under his bed. A girl who is developing breasts may wear loose-fitting shirts to cover up this early sign of puberty. Young adolescents gravitate toward friends of the same sex, and part of the interaction with peers may involve talk about sex and dirty jokes. Masturbation also offers a sexual outlet for many young adolescents. (See *Masturbation*, page 22.)

In the years that follow, most adolescents develop a greater awareness of their sexuality. Girls begin menstruating, and boys experience the changes of puberty. Girl-boy relationships begin to develop. Some teens actually begin dating before high school; even those who don't actually go out on dates often find opportunities to be alone with a member of the opposite sex. By the age of fifteen many teens are beginning to engage in some form of sexual experimentation, which may include kissing, petting, oral-genital contacts, mutual masturbation, and even intercourse.

Although it may be difficult to imagine your child growing up so fast, statistics show us that many teens are doing just that—and teenagers *do* get pregnant and some *do* get AIDS. A survey by the Kaiser Family Foundation found that by the ninth grade, 38 percent of teens were sexually active. Despite its availability and a national campaign to encourage the use of condoms to help prevent AIDS, many teens have sexual relations without using condoms or any other form of contraception; one study found the average time between the onset of intercourse and birth control to be one year. The Kaiser survey found that while more than half the teens said they had some information about sex and birth control, many said it did not include enough detail about how to use or where to obtain contraceptives. Given these findings, it shouldn't come as any surprise that one in five teenage girls between the ages of fifteen and nineteen will become pregnant.

Teens who have early sexual intercourse often report strong peer pressure as a reason behind their decision. Everyone else is doing it and they don't want to be left out, they say. Many say they are simply curious about sex and want to experience what everyone is talking about.

How do a boy and a girl feel after they've lost their virginity? One study found marked differences between how the sexes feel after their first experience of sexual intercourse. The study, which involved more than 1,000 American teens, found that boys were more likely to describe their first sexual partner in casual terms—as in *she's a friend,* for example, or *she's just a girl I know*—whereas 75 percent of the girls surveyed said their partner was their boyfriend. The majority of the boys said they were glad they'd had sex. Girls, however, were not so positive about the experience. Sixty-one percent said they had conflicted feelings, and 11 percent said they were sorry it happened.

As the parent of an adolescent, it is up to you to make sure your child has the information necessary to make intelligent choices. Most schools today provide some sex education, but you shouldn't assume that all the questions are answered in the classroom. The more important aspect of sexuality, intimacy, is rarely discussed in education classes. There is no substitute for parental involvement in this crucial part of your teen's life. (See *Talking About Sex With Your Teen,* page 33.)

Parents often say they don't want to discuss sexuality with their teens because they are afraid that any in-depth discussion will appear as a license to indulge in sexual behavior. Experts, however, agree that parents need to do more than tell a teen to say no to premature sex. Since statistics show that a large number of teens are sexually active, parents have a responsibility to prepare their adolescents, who may well be considering having intercourse. This preparation includes a discussion of the emotional aspects of physically intimate behavior, of the risks of AIDS and other sexually transmitted diseases, and about pregnancy prevention (contraception).

Discussing sexual matters with your teen does not condone early sexual intercourse. During your conversations, in addition to supplying information, you should also make your personal feelings and values known. You may say that you wish your adolescent would wait to have sexual intercourse and explain the reasons why. But recognize that if your teen decides to have sex, there's not much you can do other than provide information that will enable the adolescent to act responsibly and make appropriate choices. Don't wait to have the conversation only *after* the event.

Above all, make sure your teen knows that whatever happens, you are always available for guidance and counsel or just to listen.

Masturbation

Masturbation, the stimulation of one's own genitals for sexual pleasure, is a normal activity and one that even young children engage in. As children's bodies mature, they develop powerful sexual feelings. Masturbation can help release this sexual tension and lessen sexual impulses.

The majority of boys—approximately 82 percent, according to one study—have masturbated to orgasm by the time they are fifteen years old. Girls, on the other hand, are less likely to masturbate; the same study found that only 20 percent of fifteen-year-old girls had masturbated to orgasm.

Masturbation itself holds some interesting

insights into the difference between male and female sexual behavior. A boy who masturbates learns to associate his feelings of sexual desire with his penis. Conversely, a young female adolescent's erotic feelings are less easily defined unless she knows what her clitoris is and how it feels when stimulated. Unlike her male counterpart, she is not as likely to equate sexual feelings with one exclusive spot on her body.

Masturbation is usually associated with fantasies or daydreams, but these differ between the sexes. Boys are taught to be aggressive and competitive, and their sexual fantasies during masturbation reflect this training, with sexual aggression and dominance as popular themes. When a boy masturbates, his fantasy probably has very specific sexual behaviors, yet little emotional involvement.

A girl's upbringing, however, often involves an emphasis on relating to others. A girl in early adolescence who does masturbate is likely to fantasize sexual acts that she has already performed. She might, for instance, imagine kissing a boy she knows from school or her favorite movie actor. The context also is different. A young girl probably won't imagine a wild sexual romp but is more likely to imagine a softer and more romantic setting.

As a parent, you have little control over whether your young teen masturbates. Unlike some younger children who masturbate in public, most adolescents are very secretive about anything that relates to their bodies. Chances are, if your adolescent elects to masturbate, the chosen site is probably in the privacy of his own room or in the bathroom. Respect his privacy.

The Teenage Identity

During this time, your teen is struggling to define himself. *What kind of person is he? What does he want to do with his life? What is truly important? Who are his intimates?* Adolescence is a time of experimenting with new roles.

One day you come home to find him meditating in the lotus position, the next he's trying out for the football team. Two weeks later, he joins a rock band, yesterday's role cast aside as easily as a dirty pair of socks.

One of the ways your teen searches for his spot in the world is through friends. These are years when belonging to something is everything. Adolescence can be a lonely time. It is often difficult for the young teen to realize that his feelings are also shared by others, that he didn't invent this feeling of isolation or confusion. Then, one day while talking to another adolescent, things suddenly click into place: Someone else likes this song or feels the same way about that book. This can be one of the most comforting feelings he will ever know, this sense of mutual understanding.

As your teen moves through his adolescence, it will become more important than ever to be liked and accepted. To be popular, one of the "in" crowd, is a goal that many teens in middle and high school aspire to. What leads to social success during the teen years? In an early study on teens' opinions as to what made a student popular, boys and girls both said that a good personality was the most important characteristic. After that, boys listed a good reputation, athletic ability, looks, nice clothes, and good grades as being important for entrance into the best crowd. For girls, in addition to having a good personality, good looks, good clothes, and a good reputation were desirable traits.

Typically, every school has a leading crowd against which every other teen measures his social status. Sometimes in the quest for popularity an adolescent disowns part of himself. He may, for instance, let his grades slip because being too smart is not cool in the crowd he wants to join. Don't be surprised if your teen tries to cultivate a certain image that matches the classmates that he's trying to attract. If he has to make too many concessions to fit in, he may eventually realize this and look for friendships that offer a more comfortable fit. While you cannot set your adolescent's social agenda, maintaining open lines of communication with him may allow you to help him see himself from a larger perspective and to better understand the advantages of cultivating a wide range of friendships.

Aggressiveness

Aggression is fairly common in young children and takes many forms—hitting, kicking, yelling, biting, throwing. Part of the socialization process in a young child involves mastering more constructive ways to obtain what he wants and to accept delays in gratification. By early in grade school most children have learned—often the hard way—the rules of getting along with others. A child who baits, bullies, flies into rages, or picks fights is simply not well liked. If he does not learn to modify his behavior, he may be shunned by other youngsters and their parents, and often his desperate bids for attention make him only more unpopular and may lead to social isolation as he gets older.

Aggressive behavior typically subsides after the age of six or seven but may surface again during the junior-high years. In the adolescent, aggressive, antisocial behavior in school typically leads to academic and disciplinary problems, and possibly to school failure.

Aggressive behavior is generally learned at home but is often enhanced by the culture. Teens whose parents relied upon corporal punishment may be more likely to resolve conflicts with aggression, too. Many movies and television programs feature casual violence that may seem like normal behavior, particularly to children already predisposed to aggression. Physical aggressiveness is also praised and rewarded in many sports. Children who grow up with these messages from family, coaches, the media, and, in some cases, from the streets outside may have difficulty controlling their own aggressive or violent impulses.

The hormonal and physical changes during adolescence make some teens more volatile and more likely to challenge both adults and peers in a belligerent way, particularly if their self-confidence and self-esteem are low. As both boys and girls grow bigger and stronger—and especially as they develop athletic prowess—the temptation to prove themselves physically often proves impossible to resist. Also the cliques and gangs to which many teenagers belong, or want to belong, sometimes command an intense loyalty that can lead to aggressive confrontations between groups.

■ HOW TO RESPOND

It may be helpful to remember that boasting, bullying, and other aggressive behavior often have their roots in insecurity and low self-esteem. Does your adolescent feel loved and valued for who he is? Do you praise his achievements, no matter how small? Have you allowed him to make decisions for himself and to take responsibility for them? Have you emphasized and modeled self-control and constructive problem-solving? Does he have a solid sense of competence and self-worth?

Contrary to appearances, teenagers still care deeply about their parents' opinion of them. The self-image they've built over the years determines in large part their behavior outside the home.

In mild cases of aggression your teen may need no more than some extra attention and a little help with social skills, particularly in the area of making friends. When aggression crosses over into antisocial behavior, however, professional intervention may be necessary, and you will have to work closely with school counselors or psychologists, teachers, and possibly social-service agencies and juvenile court to prevent the problem from turning into a pattern of delinquency.

Activities

Although it may mean that you spend much time ferrying your adolescent from place to place, extracurricular activities should be encouraged during the teen years.

One of the ways your teen learns about himself and others is through exposure to a wide variety of life's offerings. He takes an art class and gains the confidence of knowing he has some talent; joins an athletic team and realizes that, while not a star athlete, he is a good team player; or tutors a disadvantaged student and learns to give of himself.

Not only do extracurricular activities help young people expand their circle of interests and friends, but it also keeps them occupied. A teen who is busy is less likely to be sitting around brooding or getting into trouble out of boredom. A word of caution, however. Some adolescents are so eager to try everything that they become overextended, which leads to stress and sometimes lower grades in school. As his parent, encourage your teen's involvement while at the same time making sure the activity schedule is not so packed that there's too little time for homework and simply relaxing.

A child in middle school generally has opportunities to explore various activities within the context of school itself. Many middle schools have a vast assortment of clubs and athletic teams that meet during or after school. Scouting or church youth groups are good ways for boys and girls to meet others with similar interests and participate in both indoor and outdoor activities. Or, if your adolescent has a specific interest in dance or playing a musical instrument, for example, you can help develop that talent with lessons.

Middle school is not too early to encourage volunteerism in your child. Throughout the country young volunteers are making a difference in their communities by giving of their time and energy. Encourage your teen to help out at your church or synagogue, or perhaps a local food bank is in need of help, or the children's ward at a nearby hospital has a volunteer program. Young people who are involved in community service typically view that experience with a real sense of having accomplished something important and an appreciation for what they have in life.

Developing Autonomy

The middle-school child is a study in contradiction. One day your teen acts very grown-up, the next very childish. One moment, your adolescent demands more freedom; the next, it's as though your teen is frightened by the freedom already granted.

As a result, parents often don't know how to treat the middle-schooler: as a child or as a young adult. Invariably, you will make mistakes, treating your teen like a child on a day when he's feeling very proud of newfound maturity.

During these years, parents need to develop fairly thick hides. They need to understand their children still love and need them, even though they decline your invitations for evenings out in favor of movies with friends.

Your adolescent is working to achieve a sense of autonomy or separateness from you.

Your teen will pull away, becoming less interested in family activities and more so in spending time with friends. Whereas your opinion about everything from clothes to homework once mattered, the adolescent is less willing to accept your advice. Your teen may get testy if you dare to open your mouth about anything that even hints of criticism. Conversely, you may find yourself the object of criticism.

A part of this move toward becoming more independent is an increased demand for privacy. Perhaps your adolescent is spending more time alone, forbidding you or a sibling to cross the threshold of the teen's private space. Your attempts at meaningful conversation are thwarted—your adolescent balks at even removing headphones to converse with you.

While these years can be trying for parents, they are a vital period for healthy development. You must continue to enforce the rules of your house, but beyond that, allow your child the space and freedom needed to grow up and find his own identity. Be available—but maintain some distance when your teen needs that. By late adolescence most teenagers have gained the maturity to realize that they can be their own persons without completely severing ties with the ones they love. When this happens, don't be surprised if your advice is suddenly in demand again from a more mature teen who realizes that parents do know something.

2
The High-School Years

■ ■ ■

If a single theme can characterize a time of life, for the teen in high school it would probably be the challenge of continuing to pull away from you and entering the ranks of young adulthood. To put it another way, it's your teenager's struggle to consolidate her individual identity. This is no easy task for either parent or teen.

When your child as a toddler insisted on climbing the stairs without holding your hand, you may have been nervous, afraid the child would get hurt. Nevertheless, you swal-lowed your fear and let the experiment commence. The look of pride on the child's face after accomplishing the desired goal on the tenth try was enough to tell you that your instincts to let go had been correct. These days you may be having an equally difficult time letting your teen go.

If your adolescent takes risks and makes the wrong decision, you fear the conse-quences will be much more severe than the bruised bottom that would have resulted from a fall down a few stairs. Casual sex, pregnancy, drugs, alcohol, and drunk driving may be dangers that flash through your mind every time your teenager is ten minutes late arriving home or gets invited to a party. You don't want to nag too much or be too controlling. You sense you should be saving your objections for the really important issues, and yet it's so hard to watch your teen go out into the world alone, without your protection. Intellectually, you understand your teenager will make mistakes and learn from them; yet you also hope she will not be seriously hurt in the process.

For a high-schooler, these years can be filled with ambivalence. The average teen relishes newfound freedom and rarely gives up an opportunity to show that you're not in control. Yet, at other times she will want you in the driver's seat, assuming responsibility for what happens, right or wrong, good or bad. Your teen may, for instance, mention a party where people are going to be using alcohol, hoping that you will not let her attend; it's easier to blame you when her friends wonder why she wasn't there. During high school, most teens experience pangs of uncertainty. As graduation approaches, your teen may worry about making new friends at college or express concerns about living away from home for the first time.

High school is also a busy time for most teens. For those academically inclined, there is the push to achieve, score high on tests, and be accepted by a good college. Extracurricular activities or a part-time job will also draw an older teen out of the home, making you feel as though your child has already left the nest. Then there is the new world of teenage social life—parties and football games with peers, and a new level of dating and intimacy.

In this chapter we will look at some of the important issues for teens during the high-school years. With more teens engaging in sexual relationships, sexuality and its ramifications raise many important concerns. Preparing your teen to function as an independent adult, establishing parameters of behavior for the older teen, and keeping the lines of communication open between parent and teen are some of the topics we will explore. First, however, we will examine the developmental changes that occur as your teen moves through the high-school years.

Milestones

By high school, it is easy to see some of your teen's adult physical qualities. The teen's body is closer to being that of an adult than of a child. While the high-school girl's body has softened and the boy's hardened, the bones of their faces have emerged from the soft cushioning of childhood to be more clearly defined.

Intellectually, your teen's powers have taken on a new sophistication. An increased ability to engage in abstract thought enables the teen to grasp issues that were previously beyond understanding. This ability emerges during the middle-school years and continues to deepen across the high-school years and young adulthood. As a result, the teen in high school is better able to dissect moral dilemmas with newfound insight. The teen who once saw the world in terms of right or wrong, black or white, now sees a wide field of gray with many gradations.

The move toward greater autonomy that you noticed in middle school is accelerated during this time as the adolescent continues to build on the foundation for future independence.

In this section, we will explore the physical, psychological, and moral milestones of high school. As you read this, remember that the tasks that you face as a parent and that your teen confronts as a soon-to-be young adult are challenging. The adolescent is defining a life apart from you, and you must assist her by providing her with the freedom to do it.

▪ PHYSICAL CHANGES

In middle school, your child had one foot in the land of the child while the other had just begun its stretch to step into adulthood. In high school, though, there's no doubt from a physical standpoint which land the late adolescent inhabits.

Thinking back to her early adolescence, you remember seeing her with a group of her friends and being amazed that they were all roughly the same age. In sixth grade, one towered over the boys, while another was already in possession of a woman's body; a third was as thin as a reed. If you are the parent of a boy, the disparity was similar. Although boys typically begin puberty two years later than the average girl, there is still a wide variation in development. One thirteen-year-old boy may be taller than most of the girls in his class, while his best friend may

look as though he belongs in elementary school.

High school in many ways is the great equalizer. By the time they are sixteen, the vast majority of girls are close to their adult height. They have larger breasts and more rounded hips than in earlier adolescence. Their menstrual cycles are regular and they are biologically capable of becoming pregnant.

Boys are on their way to becoming men. Most boys are well into their growth spurt by this age, but boys continue to grow until age twenty-one. During his two-to-three–year period of accelerated growth, a boy may add as much as nine inches to his height. Moreover, his body, like his female counterpart's, is changing. Unlike a girl, however, he is replacing more fat with muscle, which makes him stronger, and his shoulders and neck are becoming thicker. His penis is growing and his voice becoming deeper. Some facial hair may be evident, but this is a later development, and many boys in high school do not have enough to require regular shaving.

▪ PSYCHOLOGICAL DEVELOPMENT

During these years, your teen may become more assertive about individual rights. Your adolescent will probably be less interested in family activities and less willing to accept parental advice and controls.

The struggle for independence is often at its most ardent during these high-school years. You may find your rules are regarded as unfair; your teen may test your authority. Rebellion is not uncommon during these years, although only a relatively small minority of teens display antisocial behavior such as heavy drug use or delinquency. For most teens, rebellion involves more minor issues: outrageous clothes, heavy makeup, a certain kind of music, or political views contrasting to your own.

The cognitive changes that you noticed in your teen in middle school continues during these years. The capacity for logical thought and the ability to use abstract verbal concepts are increased as the teen grows older. An increased ability to engage in abstract thought enables the older teen to examine issues that once were beyond her grasp. If, for instance, you ask a twelve-year-old how to stop the wave of crime, the early adolescent is likely to advocate severe punishment for lawbreakers. A high-school student, on the other hand, is better able to examine the complexity of the problem, looking at the various elements and how they fit together. These cognitive changes are also related to exposure to more varied and complex experiences and dilemmas.

Like the younger adolescent, the older one is still attempting to forge an identity. *What do I want to do with my life? What kind of person am I? What do I feel strongly about?* These are all questions that everyone asks during these formative years and that must be eventually resolved if the person is to be psychologically healthy. The high-school student is more likely to be put to the test than a younger counterpart. Increased freedom may put the adolescent into situations where the teen's ideas are tested. She, for instance, may think of herself as a person who would never take

drugs. Then she attends a party where almost everyone is drinking or using drugs. Her dilemma: Does she risk having her friends thinking she's weird or decide to give up the ideals she has set for herself?

Research has shown that during middle school teens often feel unsure about their self-esteem. In high school, however, most teens experience a steady increase in their sense of self-worth that continues to grow well into their twenties. Girls may more often express feelings of loneliness than boys do and may also be more sensitive to the opinions of others.

In establishing a healthy identity, the teen must strike a balance between being with others and being comfortable when alone. As a result, parents often see shifts in their teenagers' need for social time and private time. It's part of the exploration characteristic of the high-school years.

■ MORAL DEVELOPMENT

She's spending a lot of time in her room these days, and you assume she's either in one of her moods, listening to music, or talking on the phone. But don't be surprised if she's simply thinking.

Step back to the days of your own youth and you may recall a time when an injustice left you brooding. You questioned a world that could tolerate such injustice; you dreamed of change, and perhaps even acted on your desire to make your opinion heard.

The high-school years are a time when the issue of right and wrong may preoccupy a teen's thoughts. Increased reasoning abilities allow the older adolescent to examine the complexity of moral issues. Better than younger adolescents, high-schoolers realize that even though society takes a certain stand, it is not necessarily the right one. Your teen may, for example, understand all the reasons behind capital punishment—yet, while our society accepts it as a punishment for the worst crimes, the teen may decide killing another human being cannot be condoned, whether licensed by the state or not. In parallel with such thinking about moral or political issues, teens may also explore the complexity of their own feelings.

During this time, expect your teen to search for inconsistencies in your behavior. You've always told her it's wrong to lie, but then she hears you on the phone begging off a dinner invitation with the excuse of an appointment that she knows you don't have. She has known for quite a while that you're not perfect; now she's quick to point that out.

Some teens become very focused on finding a person or system that replaces the parents as role models. This may be one of the reasons that young people have in recent generations been attracted to politics or religious ideologies outside the mainstream. They are searching for things that enhance their independence from their parents and allow them to be responsible for their own behavior; at the same time, a strong sense of idealism may propel them to seek out an alternative system in hopes of improving the world. The need to belong to a group may also substitute for family ties.

Not all teens, of course, are idealistic. Many, in fact, are increasingly cynical to the idea that one person can affect change.

Sexuality

For many of us, the subject of sex is a difficult topic to discuss. When it comes to talking to our children about one of life's most intimate aspects, many parents understandably have difficulty discussing it openly. Some parents permanently table the discussion, hoping the teen will get answers to the questions from friends or at school. But sexual feelings are a relatively new experience for the adolescent. Teens need help understanding and dealing with these feelings.

The reluctance of parents to discuss sexuality is nothing new. Parents have always found the subject difficult to broach, and in the past, many simply let it slide, perhaps rationalizing that there was plenty of time to get to the specifics. Today's parents don't have that luxury.

More teens are having sex at a younger age than previous generations, in many cases with multiple partners. According to recent statistics, over half of teens between the ages of fifteen and nineteen have had sexual intercourse. The age-old consequence of teenage sex, unplanned pregnancy, continues to be a risk. Other risks include sexually transmitted diseases (STDs), such as chlamydia, gonorrhea, trichomonas, genital herpes, and human papilloma virus. Any of the STDs can render a teen infertile, and some have also been associated with long-term development of certain types of cancer. The incidence of AIDS, the most dangerous STD, is rapidly increasing among the heterosexual adolescent population. Despite recent advances that appear to prolong and improve the quality of life in some patients, AIDS is still an incurable and ultimately fatal disease.

Parents should not assume that their teen will be one of those who decides to wait to have sexual intercourse. Thus, it becomes critical for you to provide necessary information before your teen becomes sexually active. Some parents may be reluctant to provide information about contraceptives, in the belief that by talking about birth control they are, in fact, giving their teen license to have sex. In fact, the reverse may be true. As a parent, you are in the best position both to provide factual information and to discuss your own moral principles and feelings regarding sex, including arousal and the pleasurable aspects of sex. Although most schools provide basic sexual education, they typically avoid discussion of morality and intimacy. It is up to you to help your adolescent make moral choices. For example, you can explain that you think waiting to have sex would be wise and list the reasons why. But you can't enforce virginity. This is why it is so important to have discussed with both teenage boys and girls how to prevent pregnancy and disease if they decide to have sex.

Ideally, sex education is not an event but a process, which begins when the child is young and asks you where babies come from. With a young child you give enough information to satisfy the immediate question. As the child gets older, the questions become more complicated, although some children may stop asking questions because they sense that the subject is taboo or pick up their parents' ignorance of or discomfort with the topic.

Some form of sex education is taught in most schools, so a basic understanding of the mechanics of the male and female reproductive systems should have been reached by the time your teen is in high school. The teen knows how men get women pregnant and has probably sat through a discussion of contraceptives. She may also know that some contraceptives can decrease the risk of sexually transmitted diseases. Your teenager may understand all this intellectually; but she may not have related it to her own experience or may not have been paying close attention or failed to ask questions because she was afraid or embarrassed.

Parents often wonder how to initiate an open discussion of sex with a teen. Pick a quiet time when no one is rushing out the door. If you're nervous, that's all right, but make it clear that you're nervous because you want to explain everything correctly, not because you think sex is wrong. You might start out talking about where sexual urges come from and how the body responds. You might also talk about the powerful sexual feelings that can accompany falling in love or having a crush on someone. Talk about the forms of sexual behavior—kissing, petting, and intercourse. Explain that intercourse is not the only way to reach orgasm. Other important topics include masturbation; contraceptive methods; prevention of sexually transmitted diseases; and how to avoid situations where date rape or other forms of sexual abuse can occur.

Help your teen understand that movies and television do not paint a realistic picture of sex. Remind her that having sex

TALKING ABOUT SEX WITH YOUR TEEN

As daunting a task as it may seem, this is one of the more important jobs of parenthood. Teenagers need not only the biological basics they get in health and hygiene classes at school—they need parental guidance, too. Thoughtful but frank talk about sexuality before sexual experimentation begins may also open lines of future communication about your teen's sexual concerns and behavior. If you're afraid of this subject and keep avoiding it, your youngster may develop the same attitude and may avoid discussion and sharing with you. Be honest and sensitive as you employ some of the following strategies for discussing sex with your teen:

Be proactive rather than reactive.
Teens often say they'd like to discuss sex with their parents but can't seem to get the words out. Don't wait for your teen to come to you. Initiate the discussions yourself. Teens whose parents discuss sex openly with them are more likely to wait to have sexual intercourse than their uninformed counterparts. The issues of pregnancy and contraception are equally important for boys and girls to understand.

Give her permission to say no.
If you issue an edict that under no circumstances is the teen to have intercourse, don't be surprised if she rebels by doing just that. On the other hand, she's more likely to feel good about saying no if you help her understand why that is a wise option. For example, you might want to acquaint her with some common ploys, such as *If you love me, you'll sleep with me,* and so on. Let her know that a truly loving relationship between two people doesn't involve coercion.

Avoid trying to scare her into abstinence.
If your teen is feeling rebellious, scare tactics may push her over the edge or scare her so badly that later it will prove a burden to enjoying an adult sexual relationship.

Help her understand that sex is more than intercourse.
Sex is an act that also involves the feelings of both partners. Let her know that there are ways to express her sexuality without having intercourse before she is

ready. She should be aware that it is not all or nothing. She can enjoy a physical relationship without having intercourse.

Respect her privacy.
The minute your teen walks in the door from a date, don't demand to know what happened that evening. Let her know that you trust her. Stress, however, that if she is being sexually active or considering it, you expect her to behave responsibly.

Try to avoid overreacting.
If your teen comes to you with a question about AIDS, for example, don't automatically assume the adolescent has been exposed to the virus. Simply answer the question without accusations or jumping to conclusions. Later ask if there was a particular reason for the question. Use this topic as a way to keep channels open. Don't insist there must be some secretive reason for the curiosity.

If, despite your efforts, you just can't discuss sex with your teen, have someone stand in for you—your spouse, perhaps a relative or a trusted friend, your teen's doctor, or a favorite teacher. If your teen has been active in church, then a trusted member of the clergy may also be helpful.

does not make her more grown-up and will not make her more like some admired TV star. Many girls, in fact, express regret after losing their virginity and admit that their first sexual experience was not pleasant or was even disappointing. Don't try to cover too much at one time. Convey the message that you're always there for her and available to answer questions or simply to talk about feelings.

Discipline and Punishment

Despite her increasing independence and even though she would never admit it, your older teen still needs you to propose clearly defined rules of behavior.

This doesn't mean that your teen will smilingly acquiesce to rules that are seen as arbitrary. Some parents may be able to get away with that when a child is young, but in adolescence more sophisticated thought processes, exposure to differing styles of child rearing, and the struggle for autonomy enable the teenager to question the validity of the rules parents impose. Parents' control over a teen diminishes as she moves through high school. As more time is spent away from you, it is impossible to know what she is doing every minute of every day.

Thus, rather than simply laying down the

law, it is usually more productive if the parent and teen sit down together and talk about acceptable behavior in the household or in the community. During the discussion, stress the importance of trust in a relationship. Since she has her own conscience to govern her behavior, it is up to the adolescent to behave in a responsible manner. Keep in mind that most teens respect their parents, and it is this respect along with their conscience that keeps them from breaking more rules than they do. The idea that you want to reinforce is that your teen should do the right thing because she knows it is right, not out of fear of parental disapproval or threatened punishment.

In general, most experts advise that by the time a teen reaches high school, the fewer rules, the better. This doesn't mean that anarchy should reign in your home but that a move to award mutual respect must occur. Instead of establishing a rule for every possible infraction, it is more effective to have rules only for the most important elements of your teen's life. For the typical high-school student, this would mean establishing rules regarding dating, curfew, homework, telephone, and driving privileges. Parents should also discuss the principles behind a set of rules. If your daughter frequently comes home, however, with a different hair color or a newly pierced hole in her body and that bothers you, then you should talk with her.

When you want to establish limits for your teen, expect to negotiate. Rarely will teens stand by mutely and permit their parents to dictate rules to them. More likely there will be some balking and some arguing. You will be more successful if you allow the adolescent input and the opportunity to negotiate. With a grown daughter, you can no longer expect an authoritarian approach to be successful.

Listen carefully to reasoning on why the curfew should be extended. This doesn't mean you have to accept uncertainty or abandon rules altogether. After all, you do have more experience, and if you are confident that your judgment is correct, your manner should convey that message. This confidence is actually reassuring to the teen. So even if her argument fails to sway you, by listening and treating the teen in a more adult-like fashion, you demonstrate your respect. As a result, your teen feels she has been recognized as more mature and is likely to behave more responsibly, even if she continues to disagree with the limit.

The tone you take during these discussions may well determine the outcome. If you assume the voice of authority and issue edicts, your teen may refuse to listen or ignore your limits or rules. In essence, the rebellious side of your teen may feel that you are presenting a challenge that needs to be taken up. Similarly, actually forbidding something may make it seem more attractive to the teen.

On the other hand, if your teen is involved in self-destructive behavior or is a threat to others, negotiation will not be productive. In some cases, strict parental discipline isn't effective. Most of these situations require careful assessment by a qualified clinician to determine an appropriate course of action.

No matter how good your relationship is with your teen, most adolescents test limits. Parents should expect adolescents to make more choices and decisions as they progress through high school. Like all of us, your teen will learn through trial and error and by being accountable for choices and decisions.

What should you do when a rule is disregarded? There is no point in having a rule if it can be broken without consequence. Society doesn't work that way and neither should you. Therefore, you must make it clear that you expect rules to be followed. Your consequences should relate directly to the actual behavior. Thus, if your teen breaks a curfew, she may have to spend the next Saturday night at home as a consequence. Or if your teen can't follow rules for using the telephone, you might revoke phone privileges for a day or two.

Avoid being too harsh with consequences. Parents are sometimes tempted to use an I'll-show-her-who's-boss approach by grounding a teen for a month because she was an hour late coming home from a date. Not only is it impractical for you to carry through with such a long-term punishment, but it will also create resentment and tension in your relationship. Spending a night or two at home is usually ample time for her to get the message that she needs to take her curfew seriously.

Peer Culture

These days she spends more time with her friends than with her family. You'd think

that it would be enough that she sees them all day in school. But then she comes home, holes up in her room, and chats on the phone until you pull the plug on her conversation. She seems to long for peer relations that are informal and less regulated than at school.

You'd heard it would be like this, that a time would come when your teen would prefer the company of friends to spending time with you. And, looking back, it didn't happen overnight; this trend was beginning in middle school. Now, as a high-schooler, your adolescent's friends and their approval occupy a primary place. Their opinions seem more important than yours and appear to have more credibility to your teen.

Studies have shown that teens spend more time with their friends as they progress through adolescence. The reason they most often give is that their friends understand them better and allow them to be themselves. Girls especially crave intimate self-disclosing relationships with other girls, which accounts for the oft-reported telephone problems in households with teens. Although it is easy to be annoyed when your teenager monopolizes the phone, keep in mind that it is through these intimate conversations with friends that she begins to define herself and discover facets of her identity.

Girls' relationships with their close friends change with their development. Middle-school girls may display some jealousy even toward their closest friends, but high-school girls are more tolerant of their friends and their differences. This may reflect the fact that they are surer of themselves and are less fearful of being abandoned or betrayed by their friends. It also may be a sign that they have progressed to a more mature stage of friendship. Rather than simply viewing it as a means of developing mutual intimacy and support, they recognize a friend's need to establish close relationships with other people as well.

Unlike girls, boys' friendships tend to be less close. But boys in high school may still spend lengths of time on the phone, usually with a preferred girl. Boys are more likely to gravitate toward an alliance with a group. Instead of revealing innermost secrets as a girl is likely to do with a best friend, a boy tends to gain approval by his actions. When asked about the qualities that are important in a friend, a boy will tend to focus on attributes such as being cooperative and able to work toward a common interest, whereas a girl in her late teens will say a friend is someone to turn to for support, a confidante.

Much has been made of the power of the peer group to influence behavior. Parents often worry that their teen will be influenced negatively by a peer group. While peers do exert influence, the vast majority of teens seek out friends with similar views about drug use, drinking, delinquency, dating, academic achievement, and so on. Thus the "good" kid who falls in with a bad crowd is the exception, not the rule. Moreover, research shows that middle-school students are more likely to conform to the will of their peers than high-school students. The pressure to have sex, smoke, and drink alcohol, however, increases in late adolescence. Yet, in surveys teens report that they are more likely to be influenced by peer pressure that is positive rather than negative.

Despite these reassurances, the outside trappings of peer conformity—the clothes, pierced body parts, dyed heads, and so on—can be annoying for any parent. Many parents wish they could see their daughter in a dress or their son in a tie occasionally. Unless she wants to do something that you absolutely can't live with (a pierced eyebrow, green stripes in the hair) it's probably best just to swallow your criticism and ignore the way she looks. There will undoubtedly be more important issues to negotiate with her. It may help to remember your own youth and how counterculture dress or other such statements seemed so important at the time. As she matures and develops more confidence in herself and her judgments, she will be less interested in conformity with peers.

What should you do if you don't like or approve of your teenager's friends? Unless you believe an individual or a peer group poses an actual danger, the best strategy is to be low-key. You cannot pick your teen's friends; to try to do so is to interfere in a way that is almost guaranteed to create resentment. On the other hand, if you can keep lines of communication open, you may be able to encourage a diversity of friendships without specifically criticizing or condemning certain individuals. In the end, you want to help your youngster develop a broader perspective of her peers so that as she matures she will see all of her friends more clearly and be better able to develop healthy, positive relationships.

Talking to Your Teenager

There are days when it seems you'd have more luck initiating a meaningful conversation with the family cocker spaniel than with your high-school sophomore.

"How was school today?" you inquire over dinner.

She shrugs. "All right."

You nod, trying to encourage her to go on. "Well, what did you do?"

"Not much."

"How's French going?"

She pauses between bites. "It's boring."

You frown, thinking that last year she loved French. "What exactly is the problem? The teacher? Is the work too hard?"

"I just hate it, that's all. Can I have some more pasta?"

One of the major complaints voiced by the parents of teenagers is that they might as well be speaking in different languages for all the communication that is taking place. They complain that no matter how hard they try to talk to their teen, they just can't seem to penetrate the wall that has grown between them. It may help to know that you're not alone. Not only do many other parents have the same communication problems, but teens also are quick to say that they can't seem to get through to their parents. They just don't understand what I'm saying, is a common criticism of parents by teens.

Communication should be simple—we've been doing it since we were infants when all we had to do to summon Mom or Dad was let loose with a plaintive wail. Why then do many teens and their parents go through a period where they can't seem to express what they mean? A big part of the problem has to do with both the parent and the teen being suspicious of the other's motives. For instance, a parent may be convinced that the teen is up to something and will adopt a prosecutorial approach. *Why were you late? What were you doing? The least you could have done was called.* The teen, on the other hand, resents the third degree. The adolescent feels these questions are an invasion of privacy and decides not to answer them. This only serves to make the parent more angry and suspicious, which, in turn, makes the teen more reluctant to reveal anything. Maturity in your daughter means she shares a more equal existence with you, her parent.

Another major problem is the style in which parents and teens communicate. Perhaps you remember that years ago you told your young child what to do and the instructions were routinely followed. The attitude was, I'm the parent and you're the child, so I know what's best. While that may have worked on a six-year-old, the approach isn't effective or helpful at sixteen.

Teens have a radar for condescension. When they feel this from parents or teachers, they dismiss the message no matter how important it is. Beginning a conversation by accusing the teen of something will appear condescending. Yelling, giving lectures that don't permit input from the teen, and refusing to listen to the teen's point of view will stop communication.

A less blatant but equally divisive style occurs when parents insist on communication only when it's convenient to them. It doesn't matter that their teen stayed up half the night studying for an exam and is now so tired that picking up a spoon at breakfast is a challenge—the parents insist now is the time for a talk, regardless of her feelings. On the other hand, when this teen really does feel the need to talk, she may believe that, chances are, busy parents won't be available.

This isn't to say that parents are the only ones whose communication style can be a problem. Teens themselves block effective communication. They act bored, come up with quips or silly behavior, deliberately distort what the parent is trying to say, or simply close their ears to what is being said.

Parents who put down a teen, who issue orders like a drill sergeant, who use sarcasm, or who make rejecting remarks will be unlikely to communicate successfully with their teen. On the other hand, parents frequently feel offended when their teen asserts, *You don't understand*; or when the teen uses the argument "everyone's doing it" as an excuse for unacceptable behavior; or when their teen sees a problem only from the standpoint of how it affects her.

One step toward better communication is sending a clear message to your teen. While this seems obvious, many parents send mixed messages. This may occur when a parent doesn't say what he or she means. Perhaps your teen asks you whether birth control pills are safe. You want to say that they are safer than getting pregnant, but you don't want to give her the impression that having sex at her age is acceptable to you. So you simply tell her that she's too young to be worried about contraception. In doing so, you have failed to answer the question (and treated her like a child).

Another way we send ambiguous messages is when one part of the message contradicts the other. You may, for instance, tell your daughter that as long as she does her best, you'll be happy. Yet, when she brings home a B in calculus, you express disappointment. Your teen may also be confused by vague instructions. You might have told your teen that you wanted her to baby-sit her younger sibling on Saturday night, only to have been annoyed when she didn't return home until after seven o'clock that evening. You had dinner reservations at seven, but she didn't know that. She thought she was home in plenty of time for you to have your evening out.

To help make your messages clearer, consider the following:

- Use "I" messages to explain your feelings. Rather than yell at her for leaving the kitchen a mess after a snack, explain that you get upset when you come home to a mess and that you'd appreciate it if she could help out by cleaning up after herself.

- Before tackling a difficult subject, organize your thoughts.

- Be sure she knows your priorities. One day you tell her to clean up the kitchen, the next you have a discussion about the importance of taking good care of her younger brother after school. Make sure she knows that you consider one job more important than the other.

- Don't make her guess what you want. Be specific about her responsibilities.
- Be concise.
- Ask for feedback. This will let you know whether she has misunderstood.
- Be attentive to her moods. If she's on her way to rehearse the school play, now is not the time to initiate a conversation. Wait until she isn't distracted.

In order to communicate effectively, you must be able to listen to what the other person is saying. While this sounds easy, most people aren't particularly adept at listening. Good listening is an active rather than passive process, one in which the listener not only hears the words being spoken but is sensitive to other nuances such as emotions and nonverbal cues.

To enhance your listening abilities, first limit your distractions. Prior to the conversation, turn off the television or radio. Try to have your conversations when neither you nor your teen is late for an appointment or thinking about rushing off somewhere. If you are rushed, your teen will sense your impatience and may refuse to talk. When your teen is opening up, ask questions to make sure that you understand, but keep in mind that if you interrupt too often, your teen may become defensive and close off communication. If you feel that you are beginning to interrogate your teen, back off.

Patience is a necessary component of teen-parent communication. Teens are sometimes nervous about initiating certain discussions, so they will begin the discussion with seemingly meaningless chatter about this or that. If they feel their parents are tuning out, they will terminate the conversation. If you are patiently listening, however, the conversation is more likely to move on to the subject that the teen really wants to discuss.

The following tips may improve communication with your teen:

- Never talk down to teens. With each passing day, they're becoming your intellectual equals, with an ever greater knowledge of the world, its people, and its problems. Don't treat them as if they're still children.
- Don't be afraid to admit that you're wrong. Teens know that parents aren't perfect and make mistakes.
- Repeated criticism rarely leads to constructive changes and does create a wall between the two of you.
- Don't initiate a conversation when you're angry. Cool off first and then talk about it.
- Don't pretend to have all the right answers. By now your teen has learned that there is often more than one solution to a problem.
- An argument between the two of you should not be viewed as a win-lose situation. Instead, your goals should be to understand why you're arguing and to turn the conflict into a productive discussion.
- Talk often—about current events, politics, even the weather. It's easier to talk about personal things if channels are

already open. Communication isn't only necessary for personal issues.

- Try to remember what it was like to be a teenager or try to see the world as your teen does.

- Be honest with your teen, but try to avoid hurt feelings.

- Avoid ultimatums and commands unless absolutely necessary.

- If you listen to what your teen says, she is more likely to listen to you.

The Group vs. Coupling Off

At the end of the middle-school years, your teen may have had friends of both sexes. Boys and girls roamed the mall together, congregated in one corner at school dances, and met at the movies.

Upon entering high school, though, the crowd has changed. Boys and girls who as middle-school students may have done little more about an attraction to a classmate than talk on the phone or hang out after school are now seen holding hands in the halls or kissing when the teacher's back is turned. After school hours, they're busy plotting and planning ways to be together. Instead of getting together with the group for pizza on a Friday night, they prefer to be alone or with one or two other couples.

While younger adolescents often get an early taste of a romantic relationship—a crush on an older boy, flirting at the school dance—most teens don't begin to date or form couples until they get into high school.

This pattern appears to be a progression of the skills teens learned in early adolescence. Very young teens, for instance, tend to run in same-sex groups. A young adolescent, especially if she is a girl, is apt to be particularly close with one or two special friends, to whom she will, in a sense, bare her soul. She discloses her true self and her best friend does the same, the result of which is the birth of intimacy. As she becomes older and attracted to boys, the skills that she has learned in developing and maintaining friendship are further honed but this time expressed in romantic relationships.

Often, the first teens to begin pairing off are the more popular students, typically in the so-called in crowd. These social leaders tend to influence the rest of the group's transition to dating relationships and later to going steady and even having sex. A teen who does not date at all in high school may be rejected by her peers. Teenagers who are or think they may be gay or lesbian may also find themselves struggling with being different from what their peers regard as the social norm. (See *Homosexuality,* page 163.)

What do teens get from dating that they couldn't from simply being part of a mixed-sex crowd? Dating serves a number of functions, some of which can be gained with any friendship. Entertainment, socialization, the enhancement of one's prestige, and the desire for romance are some needs that dating satisfies. Teens who date learn about intimacy and emotions, how to cope with an infatuation, how to express themselves to another person, and, oftentimes, how to deal with the pain of rejection.

Many high-school students are able to maintain a somewhat blasé attitude toward dating. They enjoy it when the right person is involved, but they also maintain close ties with friends of the same sex. Some teens, however, become so caught up with trying to find someone special or, once they do, with being part of a couple, that they neglect their other relationships. No matter how intense, many high-school romances don't withstand the test of time, and when they do end, many teens have a difficult time reestablishing their old friendships. A study that followed graduating teens into college found that nearly one-half broke up with their high-school steady during the first few months of college; most of the others reported some dissatisfaction with the relationship that carried over from high school.

As a parent, what should your role be in your teen's social life? First of all, don't push it or worry about your teen's lack of a social life. Many teens date little or not at all until college. If your teenager has a range of friends but shows no interest in dating, don't be alarmed. The teen might simply be shy and need to develop confidence before dating. Or other activities may be more important and allow little time to invest in dating. Once your teen expresses the desire to date, however, it is up to you to set the ground rules.

You may, for instance, give your fifteen-year-old permission to go to the movies with a classmate but instantly reject her request to go on a weekend ski trip with a college man she met at a rock concert. You will also need to establish a curfew and other rules such as calling home if she is delayed.

Many parents who don't object to casual dating become upset or worried when their teen begins to date someone exclusively. On the positive side, if she does decide to go steady, you will get to know the boy much better than you would otherwise, and the chance of her having indiscriminate sex is greatly decreased. Yet you may also fear that a close attachment to this one person will result in an earlier sexual relationship. You may also believe these years should be a time for getting to know lots of people and you fear she is limiting her opportunities.

Unless you've seen evidence that her steady is abusive, either physically or emotionally, it is best to resist the urge to try to control or oppose the relationship. Parents who adamantly object or forbid teens to see their steady friends are inviting rebellion. Suddenly, the issue becomes us-against-the-world, and parental objections will drive the teens closer together. If left alone, the majority of these high-school romances will come to a natural end.

Identity

One of the most important things your teen must accomplish during these years is to form an identity.

Psychologist Erik Erikson theorized that a person must work through four developmental issues on the way to forming an identity during adolescence: in short, they are trust, autonomy, initiative, and industry.

According to Erikson, establishing trust is

the process by which a teen seeks and finds friends who are trustworthy and admirable. Initially the friends are of the same sex, but in later adolescence the focus shifts to partners of the opposite sex. The teen also begins to search for political causes and leaders worthy of support. By establishing autonomy, the teen attempts to chart an independent course instead of simply going along with parental wishes. As the teen takes the initiative, the teen sets her own goals. To Erikson, the term industry characterizes the older teen's realization, as she progresses through adolescence, that she alone must take responsibility for setting her goals and for the quality of the work that she does toward achieving those goals.

Other theorists have characterized elements of the emerging adolescent personality in other ways. Daniel Offer, M.D., in the Offer Self-Image Questionnaire for Adolescents, devised a personality test to help assess the adjustment of self-image during adolescence. Offer found normal adolescents to be happy with themselves and their physical development. In social terms, they were found to be work-oriented and to see themselves as making friends easily. Sexually, they desired opposite sex friendships, in general liked the changes in their bodies, and were not afraid of their sexuality. From the perspective of family, surprisingly few adolescents reported major conflicts with their parents. In the same way, they saw themselves as having no major problems in their lives and were confident in their ability to cope with the challenges they faced.

The views of Offer and Erikson support the complexity of the identity issue. The challenges of the process are considerable for the teen, but how, as a parent, can you create an environment supportive of your teen's forming a healthy identity and self-image?

One interesting study that addressed that question involved asking parents and their teen to plan a two-week vacation together in twenty minutes. Researchers then interviewed the adolescents about their future goals, hypothesizing that their identity exploration would be related to whether the adolescent had developed an independent point of view.

In evaluating the data in this study, the researchers found that the way the teens related to their parents was associated with exploring their identity. For boys, greater identity exploration was associated with their fathers' willingness to allow their sons to disagree, their fathers' willingness to compromise and to change their own suggestions to take into account the desires of their sons. Girls who had the highest degree of identity exploration came from families where they openly communicated and the girls felt comfortable in disagreeing with their parents and were assertive in making suggestions.

This study concluded that identity formation is more likely to prosper in a family environment that offers support and security while at the same time encouraging the teen to form independent opinions. Helping your teen solidify her identity and crystallize her self-image cannot be translated into a few simple rules. But providing your teen with a stable family structure that gives support and guidance and offers open communication even in disagreement can allow your youngster the flexibility and acceptance to flourish as she develops her own sense of who she is and will be.

Work/Jobs

The vast majority of teenagers have some source of income other than an allowance. In many cases, especially with young teens, the work is sporadic, perhaps baby-sitting on Saturday night for neighbors or mowing lawns. But by the time they reach high school, more and more teens want a regular part-time job with a steady income, even though the legal jobs available to them nearly always pay only minimum wage for work in fast-food restaurants, grocery stores, hospitals, and laundries.

Recent statistics note that more high-school students than ever are working. Surveys indicate that as many as 60 percent of sophomores have regular jobs, while 75 percent of juniors and seniors work. Very likely you as a parent are going to be faced with a teen asking for permission to work.

The issue of teenage employment is double-edged. On one hand, you admire the fact that she is ambitious enough to want to earn her own money and accept the responsibility that goes with having a job. Yet you worry about the impact on the rest of her life. Will her grades suffer? Will she still have time for her friends and the extracurricular activities she loves? And what about you? As it is, you don't see much of her.

What will happen to your relationship when she adds a job to her agenda?

There is no doubt that employment, when carefully monitored, does have its benefits. A job can increase a teen's self-confidence and help develop a sense of responsibility. Although the majority of teens work in jobs that require minimal expertise and do little to prepare them for future careers, they do learn simple work skills, such as being on time, following directions, and taking orders from a boss. They also gain the pride that comes from earning one's own money, which, in most cases, is minimum wage or just above (girls tend to earn less than boys). With some parental guidance, the working teen also can develop a greater appreciation for the value of money, drawing up a budget and learning to stick to it, a valuable skill no matter what her age.

The negative side to having a job is that the teen is spending time earning money that could be spent doing other things, such as developing interests and talents, socializing with friends, and spending time with the family. Moreover, employed students spend less time on homework, are absent or tardy from school more frequently, and have fewer friends. Students who occasionally work long hours also may become increasingly stressed and discouraged as they fall behind in school. They also are more likely to smoke and use drugs and alcohol.

Despite the risks, it may be difficult for a parent to forbid the teen from working.

There are many opportunities for middle-class teens who have access to malls and other retail centers where jobs are abundant; inner-city teens typically have a more difficult time becoming employed and, when they do, are forced to work longer hours. The deciding factor in whether a job becomes an asset or a liability seems to be in the number of hours worked. In one study, researchers found that sophomores and juniors who worked twenty or more hours per week had a drop in grades and were more likely to quit school than those who worked fewer hours. Interestingly, seniors who worked the same number of hours were not similarly affected, leading to speculation that since the older students can choose more elective classes, working seniors are less likely to enroll in tough academic courses that require a heavy time investment.

A nationwide study conducted at the University of Colorado found that a part-time job is a positive factor when a student works no more than 13.5 hours per week. The students who worked this amount of time or less had higher grades than those who didn't work at all.

These findings suggest that a working teen needn't sacrifice academic performance. Employers, however, are rarely concerned about a worker's school performance, and a teen may be hard-pressed to decline when asked to work extra hours. So it is up to parents to set employment conditions. Insist upon a ceiling of 13.5 hours per week during the school year. Moreover, recognize that a job done on the weekends is less disruptive than one that requires late nights during the week. You may also want to consider an agreement with your teen that if academic performance drops, the work will stop or the hours will be decreased.

Driving

Probably the biggest status symbol among the high-school crowd is a driver's license. This one little piece of paper cannot only be a social asset (especially if your teen's the first in her crowd to get one) but also makes the adolescent feel more independent than ever before. No longer do Mom or Dad have to do the delivering; the teen can get there on her own.

The sixteenth birthday—the age at which in most states a person can earn a driver's license—is a long-awaited event in most households. The teen counts the hours until the magical day of the driving test and the opportunity to demonstrate driving competence. Parents, on the other hand, may view the day with less enthusiasm. They fear for the teen's safety on the road and the increase in auto insurance.

Unless you're a city dweller and don't need a car to get around, you might as well face the fact that your teen is going to want to get a driver's license. Even if you've never balked about endless chauffeuring, your teen will probably want to drive. Some peer pressure may be involved. To be the only teen in the crowd who doesn't drive may be regarded as a major humiliation.

In most cases, the best way to teach a teen to drive is through a driver's education class, which is usually sponsored by the school. In many states, a benefit of passing such a course is a reduction in insurance premiums. In addition to on-the-road training with a driving instructor, your teen will probably need extra practice with you before becoming competent enough to pass the driving test required for a license. You may also choose to put limits on your new driver.

Teaching a child to drive can set the pulse racing in even the most relaxed parent. Remember, if you show how nervous you are, you'll make your teen more nervous. So start off in a relatively nonthreatening place, such as an empty parking lot. Wait until your teen has had some instruction in driver's education and then see for yourself how well the youngster does.

Not all parents have the temperament to teach driving. Some people just can't handle the pressure of teaching a novice to drive. If you find yourself yelling, making sarcastic remarks, or otherwise being difficult or upsetting to your teen, ask your spouse, or perhaps a friend or relative, to take over.

Even though your teen has a driver's license, it is up to you to establish rules for safe and responsible driving and use of the car such as setting specific guidelines. For instance, one rule should be that everyone in the car, including the driver, always wears a seat belt. Other rules need to address when your teen can drive; the allowable range; who puts gas in the car; and what infractions would result in a suspension of driving privileges.

Before your teen takes the car out alone or gets into a car driven by a friend, you should discuss safety issues in detail. Even if you're confident the rookie driver won't drink alcohol when doing the driving, your teen may be faced with a situation where others drivers are drinking or using drugs. Make it clear that this is an unacceptable risk. Tell your teen that rather than get into a car with an unreliable driver (or if your teen decides to drink alcohol), she should call home, no matter what time it is, so that you can pick her up or arrange for a taxi.

Increasing Independence and Responsibility

It hardly seems possible that your adolescent will soon be leaving home, but when you have a teen in high school, the day is not far off when she will be going out into the world, whether it be to college or into the workforce. There are days when both you and your teen will wonder whether you're ready for this change.

These years can be difficult for both the parents and their older teenager. The parents, accustomed to nurturing their child, must now focus on letting go with confidence so that their teen can assume independence and greater responsibility. Your feeling of helplessness may be similar to the one you felt when you watched the child learn to walk. She tried to get up on her feet, faltered, fell, tried, and failed again. You wanted to help—but you knew that she had to do it on her own. You could only be a witness; you couldn't do it for her. The older teen is also conflicted as she reaches out to the world one day, only to withdraw the next, part of her hoping that you'll take over.

As difficult as this transition can be, becoming autonomous is absolutely necessary if your teen is to forge ahead successfully into adulthood. Studies have shown that those who have the easiest time achieving independence come from warm, supportive families who operate under clearly defined rules and who enjoy open communication between the parents and their children. Conversely, teens who grow up in restrictive homes where parents constantly criticize them have more difficulty becoming independent. If your teen is shy or timid by temperament, more patience and encouragement may be needed in this transition.

How can you go about creating an environment that encourages your older teen's growing independence? The first step is to make it clear that she is responsible for beginning to manage her own life. She wants to use the family car? Fine, you say, as long as she fills the gas tank. Let her manage her own money and help her work out a budget. Your teen may relish her increasing independence, which is wonderful as long as she also understands that the price is greater responsibility.

Moving through high school means increased autonomy both physically and emotionally. You may find your values being questioned or even shunned. You may suddenly find yourself on opposite sides in religious or political discussions. In short, your teen is thinking independently, rather than simply parroting your views. Discussing politics, morality, and other values with your teen during this phase of life can be exhilarating for adults and teens alike. Teens who have their own ideas are more likely to evolve into adults who are tolerant of others' beliefs.

Perhaps you get the feeling that you've fallen a notch or two in your teen's estimation. For the first time, you are seen as a real person—and not simply a mother or father. Encourage this new insight. It is healthy for a soon-to-be adult to know that you are not perfect and that, yes, even an intelligent person such as yourself makes mistakes. This will take some of the pressure off the requirement to be perfect. It is all right to fail sometimes, and this realization may enable your teenager to take the risks necessary to achieve desired goals.

Finally, let your teen know that it is all right to be afraid. Leaving home for many of us is one of the hardest things we'll ever do, but most of us not only survive but also thrive in our adult independence.

Money Issues

By high school—if not before—your teen should begin learning what things cost.

In many households, an adolescent asks for something and automatically gets it. Even in families where the teen is expected to pay for some things, many teenagers have no concept of what it costs to maintain their standard of living. They look at their house or apartment and don't automatically connect the fact that it takes two parents working to pay the mortgage or rent. They see a refrigerator filled with food and fail to equate that with a hefty chunk of a parent's paycheck.

While it's not necessary to perform a budget analysis for your teen's benefit, now is a good time to start talking about family expenses. You may be surprised at how shocked your teen is when you explain how much it costs simply to heat your house during the winter or buy holiday gifts. Such explanations prepare the teen for the day—not so far off—when a teen's independence will also mean assuming the responsibility to meet expenses. Many young people are amazed when they discover how difficult it is to stretch their paycheck to cover the expenses of their first apartment. Many find it upsetting to learn that economic changes make it more difficult for today's teenagers to attain the affluence that their parents know.

Even young children should be given a weekly allowance to help teach them about money. In some households, the money is tied to the successful completion of some chores; in others, the child gets the allowance regardless of behavior. Ideally, a large allowance should be earned so that the teen learns the value of work—the message being that if you work, you are paid; if you don't,

you're not. Earning an allowance can provide an excellent transition to earning money from a part-time job, which is a common occurrence in high school.

Finally, parents can help their teen develop good financial habits. Instead of letting your teen, for instance, spend everything on whatever appeals, insist upon a savings account in which an agreed upon portion of monthly earnings are deposited. Even if you can afford it, you shouldn't automatically buy the teen everything she desires. Saving for the mountain bike will lead to a greater appreciation than if you automatically buy it for her. One last point: Don't give access to your credit cards. That can give teens the false impression that you can buy things without having the money to pay for them. Letting them use your credit cards can create serious financial problems later when college begins and expenses soar.

3

Leaving the Nest

■ ■ ■

During the last few years of adolescence, parents and teens are likely to be caught up in the practical matters of leaving home: finishing up high school; deciding whether to get jobs or go on to college after high school; considering different schools and their programs; choosing between colleges in the area and those away from home; completing college applications; arranging for housing, financial aid, and on-campus jobs. With all this external activity, an important process going on under the surface may be largely ignored: Adolescents are approaching the end of high school and continuing to experience change and growth within themselves.

Unless a family has experienced a death or divorce, this is the first transition since the birth of the youngest child that actually transforms the family's composition. When your teenager is ready to leave home, the family must confront its shrinking size, acknowledge and recover from a sense of loss, and begin to make accommodations to the changes.

While children prepare to leave to make lives of their own, parents must prepare to let go. This happens most successfully when parents are able to make subtle shifts in their own personal and inner lives. Sometimes as they shift away from parenting as a central preoccupation, they discover new interests or increase their involvement in existing work and leisure activities. Often parents deepen their relationships with friends, siblings, and other family members. Most important, as children leave home, a mother and a father must return to their roles as wife and husband and find a different sort of companionship in each other. As their primary parenting functions decrease, more than a few husbands and wives find themselves regarding each other more directly than they have for years. In the best of all circumstances, they renew and perhaps improve their personal and intimate life together.

For the youngster, the transitional process that characterizes the latter part of the teenage years is perhaps the most dramatic of the life cycle. It begins in growth, the hormonal storm and stress of adolescence. Somewhere around their eighteenth birthdays, most teenagers complete high school and begin to plan what to do as a young adult. This could mean travel, work, college, or a combination.

Along the way, older adolescents have to deal with the tasks inherent in this developmental phase: separating from their parents and reworking the parent-child relationship; exploring, experimenting, and establishing a rudimentary adult identity; engaging in mature, intimate relationships; and charting an occupational path.

Thus, the developmental work of late adolescence involves both the teenager and his family. For some, the bulk of the work is done during the late teenage years. In many cases, though, these tasks are not successfully completed until a young person is well into his twenties or even thirties.

In this chapter, we will look at the tasks of late adolescence. We will describe the milestones that the late teen passes on his way to adulthood, as well as some of the more critical decisions to be faced concerning school, work, and relationships. Finally, we will look at the ways in which the parent-child relationship must change to permit a young person to leave home, both actually and emotionally.

Throughout the chapter, as throughout the process, it is important to remember that even as a child turns away from parents and the parental connection to embark on his own life, the parent-child relationship, in its many, complicated configurations, remains the bedrock upon which his adult life will be based. Even as he turns away, he carries his parents with him at the core of his being.

Milestones

By the time a teenager reaches the end of adolescence, the youngster has assumed the look of an adult. All visible traces of childhood have vanished. In intellectual terms, the teen has the capacity to think abstractly and solve ever more complex problems. More ideas and information can be grasped, more of their complexities appreciated. In terms of emotional growth, an eighteen-, nineteen- or twenty-year-old continues to grapple with the basic issues of identity (self) and relationships (other).

During adolescence, physical, emotional,

and intellectual development progress at different rates, confusing parents and teachers alike. At thirteen or at sixteen, a youngster may look remarkably mature, yet the teen's emotional or cognitive level may seem strikingly immature. There will be other times, however, when the same youngster says something so sophisticated in its wisdom and clarity that it causes others to do a double take.

In most instances, the pieces come together at the end of adolescence to create a physically, emotionally, and intellectually mature young adult, one who is ready to leave home and to solo in managing and navigating out in the world. Yet there isn't one point when this consolidation occurs; the pattern is neither possible to predict nor easy to discern. In recent generations, puberty, which clearly marks the beginning of adolescence, starts earlier than in former generations. In general, the expectation is that adolescence will evolve into young adulthood somewhere around the age of nineteen or twenty. Yet the end of this phase is not clearly marked.

The process of adolescence concludes and adulthood arrives usually long after the teenage years have ended. As our world becomes increasingly complicated and its demands more exacting, most young people achieve actual independence when they are well into their twenties. Economic integrity and independence may come many years later.

▪ PHYSICAL DEVELOPMENT

The physical process that began with the onset of puberty becomes fully established at the end of the teen years. Basic physical and physiological changes have taken place. A boy's voice has found its deeper tenor. His penis, testicles, and pubic hair are mature. Facial hair has appeared. At eighteen or even earlier, a girl's breasts, pubic hair, and body shape have assumed their mature appearance, and her menstrual rhythm has regulated itself. Usually, late adolescents have also developed emotional and intellectual understandings of their maturing physical selves—body image, gender role definition, sexual identity, gender preference, sexual orientation, and even adult sexual patterns may be well established, all within the boundaries of socioeconomic class.

▪ COGNITIVE DEVELOPMENT

Much of the more conflicted, awkward feelings that color the way a young adolescent processes information abate toward the end of the teenage years. Earlier, self-consciousness and swings between feelings of grandiosity and invincibility on the one hand, and powerlessness and disorientation on the other, shaped much of the teen's thinking. Now, as the teenage years give way to the college years and beyond, thinking becomes more reasonable and moderate.

Most youngsters readily handle abstract ideas and concepts by the end of adolescence. They can make judgments based on more comprehensive and complex thinking. Plus, they can think about thinking—the late teen may frame an argument for discussion or debate and, simultaneously, make an internal judgment about the strengths and weaknesses of his arguments.

More than ever before, an older teenager

notices and understands how past actions shape and have an impact on the present. He can anticipate consequences of present actions.

Because their thinking is more flexible and fluid, older teens may have the cognitive tools to begin to struggle with many of the larger decisions that they will be called on to make. Though they may still turn to their parents and other adults for counsel, teenagers as they gain maturity use an increasingly sophisticated and realistic appraisal of the real possibilities and their own abilities and interests when they make decisions.

They wish and should be encouraged to make their own decisions: whether to work or to go on to further their education, which school to attend, which job to take, whom to date, when to marry, when to begin to have sexual relationships and with whom. They can also consider various career directions, religious questions, and political involvements. In addition, many young people cultivate a philosophical interest in such subjects as love, morality, politics, religion, and philosophy. They may even begin to wrestle with such major questions as the purposes of life.

■ EMOTIONAL AND SOCIAL DEVELOPMENT

Older teenagers are working to leave the world where they lived as children and enter a world where they will be considered adults. Like other transitions, this shift from childhood to adulthood brings reflection, self-evaluation, and possible upheaval. In order to make this passage successfully, they must reassess their current values and goals and explore their options for internal growth and growth out in the world.

During adolescence, youngsters build upon their earlier ways of being in relationships and of getting along with others. This means that they have to find a different balance between their dependence on their parents and their growing independence from them. Late adolescence involves making a shift toward equality in the parent-child relationship. Gradually, responsibility for a youngster's decisions and personal well-being must move almost completely from the parent to the child. Power struggles that occur and dependency issues inherent in the process should resolve by the end of adolescence. This resolution happens most smoothly in families where intergenerational communications are open and easy.

By the end of adolescence, your youngster will react more consistently as an adult. There will probably be a lessening in the intensity and volatility of feelings and in the need for frequent and immediate gratification. The teen's judgment will become realistic and less grandiose; the youngster will show more concern for others. The young person emerging from the teenage years will be able to make and keep commitments and make choices based on actual skills and abilities.

Even when most of the challenges of puberty have passed and the most dramatic feelings have dissolved, an older adolescent may experience considerable anxiety about the risks and uncertainty of the future, grief over the loss of past ways of being, and vague uneasiness about the changes to be faced.

For the adolescent on the threshold of adulthood, past relationships and institutions—parents, school, teachers, religious organizations—may no longer provide the coherence and stability they once did. An adult is expected to be self-motivated and self-directed; accomplishing things requires skillful navigation of the adult world. While this will ultimately lead to greater freedom and more options, the separation may lead a young person to feel temporarily burdened and distressed.

Many teenagers experience the imminent responsibilities of adult choice and independence as an encumbrance. The range of new choices and expectations can be daunting. It is not uncommon for teenagers in late adolescence to feel particularly alienated, vulnerable, and uncertain about their ability to thrive in the adult world. You can offer support and help your teen develop confidence and build up self-esteem. (See *Building Self-Esteem,* page 75.) To some degree, however, this difficult passage is his to make alone.

Until individuals develop internal measures for their accomplishments, they tend to evaluate worth, success, and maturity relative to those of friends, classmates, and coworkers. They compare themselves to a rigid internalized vision of what society expects of them. Often, this self-evaluation can be painful, as they feel particularly invested in being socially effective and appropriate. They may not feel that they measure up.

Yet as a young person ventures away from childhood and enters adulthood, the teen's sense of independence gradually becomes more secure. Unmoored from parents, the late adolescent begins to experience the world unassisted by parents. An emerging sense of competence allows one's operation as an independent agent; the teen takes stock of his own successes and failures to live up to his own expectations. The result is a stronger sense of personal identity.

As their identities strengthen, young people feel more comfortable breaking away from an indiscriminate acceptance of their peer group's value system. Their thinking about their parents and their family roles has evolved over time. Relying more on inner strength, they do not need peer support to take issue with their parents. A young person may take parental advice or not. That same teen, a short while before, might have felt the need to react strongly against what were perceived as attempts to control him. Now, more secure in his own autonomy, he can see parental advice and peer values as elements to include in the decision-making process.

In short, late adolescence is a stage rich in potential and energy and fraught with external pressures and anxiety. It is the time when your child must separate sufficiently from you and truly become a unique individual. More and more, the teen will make independent life decisions; settle into a preliminary adult identity; engage in intimate relationships; make occupational commitments; and decide on a system of morals and values.

■ MORAL DEVELOPMENT

As teenagers consider ways of being and thinking in the world, most evolve a reasonably clear sense of right and wrong. In childhood, their behavior was driven by the fear of punishment and the need to rebel and test limits. Now, their behavior is guided by a true sense of caring about how their actions affect others.

Teenagers in late adolescence become more responsive to a standard of behavior based on broad ethical principles. In many instances, they choose to do what is right and fair, and turn away from what is wrong and unjust. Because they can view real moral issues in abstract terms, they are likely to be sensitive to everyday examples of honesty and mendacity, responsibility and irresponsibility, cooperation and selfishness, and reciprocity and egocentrism.

Whereas a young teen might feel delighted to get away with something, an older teen is more likely to feel guilty at having violated personal principles. With maturity, a person's sense of self may include a moral code to be followed relatively independently of the endorsement or disapproval of others.

Not everyone reaches this level of development by the end of adolescence; not all adolescents reach the same understandings at identical ages. For that matter, some adults never embrace strong moral convictions, but most do.

The development of a moral framework arises out of a complex interplay of factors. Teens who engage more fully in social interactions have greater opportunities to observe social cause and effect, which then can help them form a mature moral judgment and a sense of fairness. Also, intellectual maturity can promote an appreciation of the various roles, perceptions, and feelings of others. And, of course, teenagers whose parents have consistently provided a sense of love, respect, and discipline tend to conduct their own lives in a responsible, measured, and caring way.

A moral framework is no more than a basis for decision making that will help the teen react to situations consistently and with fairness and reasonableness. In developing moral standards, the teen must consider how to distinguish between right and wrong; the adolescent must consider how to balance the wishes of the self against the wishes of the other, and how to act in ways that accomplish the greatest good for the greatest number. Ultimately, moral standards will guide a young person as he strives to contribute in meaningful ways to the larger society of which he is becoming a part.

Identity Consolidation

In the 1960s, the term *identity crisis* was used loosely to describe the volatile nature of the teenage years. Yet, rather than describing a troubling quality, the term actually refers to a teenager's developmental struggle with the question: *Who am I?*

During this time of self-scrutiny, the teen needs to look inward, to consider personal history, and gain perspective on past, present, and future. Exploration will give way to reorganization into a cohesive sense of self that satisfies both internal needs and external demands. The resulting sense of self will encompass an autonomous relationship with parents, a realistic view of the teen's capacities, practical plans and goals for the future, and a firm sexual identity. At some point or other, it may also include an increasingly clear set of moral standards and spiritual life.

During this process of *identity consolidation*, teenagers actively experiment with a variety of identities and identifications. They try on miscellaneous styles, associate with and date different kinds of people, investigate various interests, and consider an array of goals and paths. Only after a period of exploration and experimentation can they evolve an enduring sense of self and a system of behavior, values, and goals to serve them in adulthood. They usually ape their parents in outward behavior after all.

During the course of identity exploration, the way a teenager thinks about the world, selects people to associate with, and chooses activities and occupations to engage in may undergo a series of noticeable changes. This is all in the service of learning and making internal adjustments.

Many of a youngster's beliefs and patterns have been adopted from his parents. These, too, now must be examined and reconsidered. Without such investigation, it is doubtful that a young person will find such adult roles as worker, adult, sibling, husband, or wife satisfying.

As a teenager relinquishes the emotional investment in the roles of childhood, there may be an accompanying sense of acute discomfort, confusion, and loss. The teen is no longer a child. The old manner of relating to parents, siblings, friends, and mentors no longer works. Old interests, activities, and involvements may seem immature and irrele-

vant. The teen will likely experience considerable anxiety until a comfortable new sense of self evolves.

Today's society, with its complexities, conflicting demands, and its array of options, makes the process of identity consolidation more onerous than in the past. Young people face innumerable choices in terms of where they will live, whom they will love, and what they will do for work. As people live longer, it is probable that the choices they make early in life will need to be reconsidered, adjusted, modified, and, in many instances, changed altogether later on.

Many parents look on with grave concern as their teenager seems to flit from relationship to relationship, from interest to interest, from ambition to ambition. *How many times, you may wonder, is he going to change his major?* However disconcerting this may be to you as parents, your teenager is doing just what he ought: exploring various possibilities before committing to a rudimentary adult identity.

When parental relationships are excessively conflicted and critical, the exploration may be largely reactive. The teens may adopt values, goals, and styles that stand in stark contrast to their parents' and reject those that might please their parents. By not considering and accepting those parental qualities that would in fact serve them well, they narrow their exploration and compromise their identity.

Then there are others for whom identity becomes diffused. This is seen often in people who, well beyond adolescence, cannot make commitments. Even in their thirties, they hop from job to job, from career to career, from partner to partner, from town to town. They may move from one religious affiliation to another. In extreme instances, an individual might go back and forth in terms of his sexual orientation. Sometimes, the inability to commit to any identity arises from parental ties that are too distant or negligent.

When a young person's identity begins to consolidate, the teen experiences an increased capacity for mutually satisfying relationships. Somewhere between late adolescence and early adulthood, most people become more secure in their sexual identity and emotionally ready to engage in sexual intercourse with someone they care about.

As a rule, fulfilling love relationships are the primary positive way people connect with the outside world. When they know who they are, they can give more fully of themselves without feeling depleted or compromised. They can take responsibility for themselves and others.

Once they feel stabilized and settled, young people tend to experience less emotional conflict and increased energy and have more consistent motivation. They are better able to tolerate whatever conflicts and frustrations inevitably arise and have a growing awareness of their abilities to influence the world around them. It becomes easier to invest in educational pursuits, career explorations, and new interests and activities, and to be confident of the potential for personal growth. They can comfortably go about learning the ways of the world and will feel anchored enough to take risks.

Intimacy

The capacity and willingness to commit to intimate relationships stand as hallmarks of adulthood. Built on mutuality, such relationships entail compromise and sacrifice. The ability to tolerate and enjoy intimacy is reflected not only in adult sexual relationships but also in rich friendships. At the heart of adult friendships is mutuality, openness, generosity, concern, and amiability.

True mutuality becomes possible as a young person separates from his parents. When an adolescent can experience himself as a separate individual, greater energy can be invested in love interests outside the family without burdening the relationship with inappropriate reactions and judgments from the past. Young adults who have unresolved conflicted feelings about their parents tend to approach relationships from a confused, insecure, and mistrustful vantage point.

The capacity for intimate ties arises from a strong sense of personal identity. Only after resolving some of the basic issues around identity can a person evaluate new relationships according to self-knowledge and a clear awareness of his own system of values and goals. Then he can make compromises without fearing that he will compromise his own sense of self. There often are, however, gender differences. For a girl, for example, *being close* may mean a willingness on the part of the girl to subordinate her identity to the evolving relationship with a boy. With a male, there is a tendency when young to want to feel masterful and be concerned about power and status.

By their very nature, intimate relationships require that each person defer his or her own needs and wishes out of consideration for the other and for the good of the partnership. In many ways, the notion of adult commitment and compromise runs counter to the emphasis in today's society on self-fulfillment. Yet, in fact, commitment to adult relationships reflects maturity and a strong identity. Such relationships arise out of devotion and, in the long run, lead to vitality, strength, and cohesiveness.

Wellness and Health

Late adolescence is the time when the values and caring that you have communicated through your parenting pay off. You can no longer tell your child how to eat, what to wear, how to behave, and what to avoid each day. While there are ways in which you can still offer guidance and advice, mostly, by this age, teenagers are ready to assume almost complete responsibility for their own care.

Because older teenagers can grasp the full implications of specific actions and circumstances, they are truly able to assume full responsibility for their own care. They can appreciate the cause and effect relationship between destructive behaviors and low achievement, between good habits and good health.

At this age, most can understand the nature of personal responsibility and anticipate the consequences of behavior. They have begun to comprehend that what they do, the activities they engage in, and the people they associate with can have repercussions in other areas of their lives and in their future.

By now, the need for frequent and immediate gratification, which characterizes early adolescence, begins to fade. Thus, as the teen approaches and enters his twenties, he is more likely to abstain from such risky behaviors as drinking, drug use, irresponsible sexual behavior, and reckless driving.

Most older adolescents have had encounters with the dark side of life: people who are willing to take advantage of their trust and loyalty; actions and activities that are pleasurable in the moment but destructive in the long run. Reaching maturity means knowing what is out in the world—good and bad—and making informed choices.

Having said all that, certain concerns bear reconsideration.

Exercise. Little by little, the notion that teenagers are invincible begins to dissolve. As they get older, teenagers begin to appreciate that they must live, not just for the moment, but live in ways that lay a solid groundwork for the rest of their lives. Many youngsters have always enjoyed an active lifestyle. They don't have to be convinced that exercise is an important aspect of a healthy life. While even at this age there may be some inactive kids who cannot believe that they will be anything other than young and healthy, most can take to heart the advice that exercise now can mean greater health later.

Eating. By the time youngsters reach late adolescence, their growth has leveled off.

Chances are that their appetite has moderated as well. Although many at this age still prefer soft drinks, salty snacks, and high-fat foods over well-balanced meals, they can begin to recognize how good nutrition translates into good health. This is especially true if parents have encouraged well-balanced, nutritious eating all along.

Smoking. Today, even with the dangers of smoking so well publicized, many teenagers smoke. Some do it for the sensation that nicotine provides of increasing alertness yet also relaxing the smoker. Others begin because family members and friends smoke. To many, it seems like the grown-up thing to do.

Though it is best not to begin smoking in the first place, once a teenager starts, stopping requires motivation. Some quit when they become part of peer groups that disapprove of smoking. Others become deterred by the high price of cigarettes. Still others stop when they realize that smoking leaves them short-of-breath or smelling like smoke.

After making every effort to keep your child from harm, discovering that your teen has started smoking can be extremely distressing. Unfortunately, you cannot simply establish by decree that the smoking will stop. You can, however, prohibit smoking in the house. And perhaps you can help your teenager find personal motivation to stop. Nagging almost certainly won't work, but as adulthood approaches, your teen may be more responsive to occasional warnings about the health dangers of tobacco. Be truthful about your concerns and the consequences of smoking.

Research shows that children are more likely to smoke if their parents smoke. If that's the case in your household, you can most effectively dissuade your child by quitting yourself.

Drug and Alcohol Use. By the time youngsters reach late adolescence, most have been introduced to drug and alcohol use. By the age of eighteen, most drink on occasion, and many have experimented with illegal drugs. Young people from all backgrounds use illegal drugs and abuse alcohol, but when parents use drugs or alcohol, teenagers are more likely to follow their example.

Like adults, teenagers often use drugs and alcohol to manage unhappiness, depression, and routine pressures. When this is the case, abuse can become habitual in adulthood. Teenagers who abuse drugs or alcohol have trouble dealing with the challenges of moving from childhood to adulthood. They may have difficulty finishing high school, staying in college, acting reliably in a job, or be more prone to accidents. Their personal relationships, with peers and family, are likely to suffer.

Parents are best equipped to help their teens if they do not abuse drugs or alcohol themselves. There may be a genetic component: Is there a history in your family of alcohol or drug abuse by adolescents? If so, educate your youngster about the risks of substance abuse and about how that may foretell a family's tendency to depression and mood problems. Strive to maintain and strengthen communication with your child as an added protection and warning system. In general, substance abuse is most effectively curtailed by addressing those factors that lead teenagers to seek escape from stress through drugs and alcohol.

Most important, parents who have consistently provided a supportive home base, treated their children with respect and sensitivity, bolstered their children's sense of self, listened without judging, and offered a sense of their own values and standards have likely engendered within their adolescent enough inner strength to deal with life's stresses. When youngsters have true inner strength, they seldom have to look to alcohol and drugs to manage their problems.

If you suspect alcohol or drug use, however, it is important that you face it directly and honestly with your teen. If reducing the pressures does not reduce the usage, or if it seems that your teenager is addicted, you should discuss the need for professional treatment with your teen, and seek it out. (See also *The Four Stages of Substance Abuse*, page 285.)

Breast Self-Examination. Beginning with the onset of puberty, your daughter should perform a monthly examination of her breasts. Even though breast cancer is rare in teenage girls, these routine exams encourage girls to be more familiar with their bodies. In addition, early attention prepares girls for adulthood when breast cancer is more common, and regular self-examination is so important.

Breast self-examinations are best conducted right after a menstrual period. The easiest time is when she showers. Before stepping into the shower, she should look at her breasts in the mirror for irregularities in shape or nipple discharge.

In the shower, she simply soaps up each breast. Imagining that each is a circle divided into four quarters and raising her right arm behind her head, she feels each segment of the right breast with her left hand. Next, moving her fingers to the center, she feels around the nipple. The process is then reversed, as she uses her right hand to examine her left breast.

Most normal teenage breasts have fibrous texture and spots. It is not uncommon for lumps to come and go throughout a girl's menstrual cycle. Therefore, if your daughter detects something other than soft tissue, she should not feel alarmed. It is important, however, that girls become familiar with the feel of their own breasts so that if any lumps or such irregularities as knots, depressions, or unusual textures suddenly appear she can recognize them. A doctor should examine such irregularities, especially if they persist.

Sexuality. By late adolescence, most youngsters are secure in their sexual identity. Around this time, many feel emotionally ready to engage in heterosexual intercourse with someone they care deeply about. It is unlikely, though, that they are ready to become parents. In most cases, an early and unwanted pregnancy will limit the choices that these young adults will have on the threshold of adulthood. It may interfere with their ability to finish their education or to pursue certain career paths.

If your teenager has decided to engage in sex, it is imperative that proper precautions be taken to prevent pregnancy and guard against sexually transmitted diseases. Objections about the awkwardness of using condoms during lovemaking must be overridden: A teenager old enough to take part in sexual behavior is old enough to take responsibility for it. If one partner is reluctant to talk about or use condoms, the intimacy and compassion of the relationship may need to be reconsidered.

If you have not had a serious talk with your teenager yet about the risks involved in sexual activities, now is the time to do so. Though we may hope that our teenagers will wait until marriage before engaging in sexual activities, chances are, they will not. If they are not already sexually active, they may be soon. It is always risky on your part to make any assumptions about your youngster's sexual behavior and understandings. Make sure your teen is armed with complete and correct knowledge. (See also *Sexual Experimentation* and *Intimacy,* pages 90 and 56).

Late Adolescent Separation

In late adolescence, youngsters face the task of separating from their parents in such a way that allows them to experience themselves as unique individuals. This does not necessarily entail reacting negatively and rebelliously in relation to their parents and what they represent. Rather the process means that teenagers progressively change their connection to their parents. Only by doing so can young people enter into more adult love relationships.

Often as they give up some of the more childlike ties to their parents, teenagers feel mournful. It is not unusual for teenagers in the last part of adolescence to experience a sense of loss, vague feelings of emptiness and depression, as well as an intense hunger for love. This may produce some uncertainty and insecurity in dating, sexual relationships, and their commitment to more adultlike relationships.

To an outside observer, or to a concerned parent, dating and relationships at this stage may appear excessively volatile and intense, perhaps even disturbed. While some adolescents have actual emotional disorders that manifest in their social and love relationships, most are working through the vestiges of separation from their parents and taking stock of themselves, an often painful and confusing but very normal process. (See *Identity Consolidation,* page 54.)

As young people accumulate experience, most of them naturally achieve greater constancy in their relationships. Their peer, romantic, and sexual relationships build upon their experience with parents; a teen's relationships are first formed by observing his parents' relationships before moving on to experience other forms of relationships. These intermediary and often intense adolescent love relationships serve as important catalysts to change and maturity.

THE SEPARATING PARENT

As a parent, you may find the unconventional quality of your youngster's choices during this period troubling. Nevertheless, because reaching young adulthood means assuming new roles and shedding old ones, it is essential that a young person re-evaluate, adjust, and relinquish antiquated beliefs, values, and behavioral patterns—and do so independently.

Still, you must be aware (without being nosy), attentive (without being intrusive), supportive (without being domineering), informative (without lecturing), and open-minded (without being valueless).

When parental relationships are excessively close and over-involved, teenagers can settle prematurely on a rigid identity without sufficient exploration. This usually happens because they cannot distinguish their own values and commitments from those of their parents. Teens who have in this way limited their exploration are likely to commit to values, goals, and behavioral styles that are imitations of their parents'.

To help your child mature, allow your adolescent to develop an independent identity, one that isn't simply a wholesale, uncritical adoption of yours. It is much more difficult to wait for the moment when your teen wants to talk about what is on his mind than it was to ask your fourth-grader what he did in school. Yet wait you must, allowing your adolescent to seek, and find, his own solutions and understandings.

Going to College

For many seventeen- and eighteen-year-olds, going to college is the first big step towards true independence. Not every student leaves home and moves to campus, but for those who do, college is often the first time a young person will live away from home for more than a few weeks.

Although the college experience offers many opportunities for independence, students are usually able to keep a toehold at home, at least for a while. They usually return at vacation times to their old room.

Throughout the college years, most youngsters rely on their parents for financial support, at least in part. As a result, college not only prepares a young person for his roles and place in the adult world; it also provides a gradual transition away—a weaning of sorts—from the world of their childhood.

Today, the competition for places in prestigious schools is fairly intense. Yet there are so many truly excellent colleges, with so many worthwhile and interesting programs, that painstaking research should turn up a suitable match for most students.

Look for a college that offers a match for the teen's particular abilities, interests, and personality. This requires research about the college and an honest assessment of the student's interests, goals, strengths, and weaknesses.

In general, choosing a college is easier for those students who have clear interests and career goals. At the age of seventeen and eighteen, though, most find that their goals are less well-defined. Therefore, many teenagers prefer to keep their occupational options open and use the first couple of years in college to explore different areas of interest before committing themselves to a definite course of study.

The size of the school may be a consideration for some students. Large universities offer a vast array of academic, social, and extracurricular opportunities, as well as anonymity and diversity. Yet, for some students, being part of a large school may feel daunting and intimidating. Some teens find a small college offers a sense of belonging, which may be welcome if they are coping with living away from home for the first time.

At eighteen, many kids are not sure whether they are ready for college. Others are not sure whether college is the right course for them at all. Such teens may be particularly well-suited for a couple of evening classes or a semester at a nearby community college.

Some youngsters are not ready at the age of eighteen to leave the sense of familiarity and security that they get from living at home. Some feel that they have enough to contend with as they meet increased responsibility and greater academic demands in college without having to deal with independent living. Still others want to live away from home while enjoying the reassurance of knowing their families are nearby. For these students, a college in the area may be the best choice.

Most families today must consider the cost of a college education. Many decisions are based in part on the availability of scholarships and financial aid. As our economy changes, competition for these awards becomes greater: Many students apply for several financial packages.

Choosing a college is a major decision and important step toward independence. Most teenagers want and need to make this decision even if you, the parents, will be paying the bills. Certainly it is reasonable for you to have a voice in the process. You can help by taking your teen on tours of selected colleges. You can also help in the application process, which can be anxiety-provoking and demanding. You can share your thoughts and opinions on the pros and cons of each college as well as your feelings about which one appears to be the best match. But remember that your judgments are pieces of information added to the mix. They may well be useful in making the selection, but neither you nor your teen should regard your preferences as the one and only path to follow.

It is not uncommon for a teenager to make a decision only to find that the choice falls short of his expectations and hopes. Frequently, students need to switch schools after a semester or two. If it appears that your youngster's concerns are substantial, support the decision to transfer. Making decisions is an important aspect of adulthood. But equally important is being able to admit that a decision was wrong and to take steps to correct the mistake. In most cases, teenagers who switch schools do better in the new school.

Before your teenager departs for college and as he eases into its rituals and routines and makes new friends, be sure that he understands the risks of substance abuse. Often in the past, colleges and universities have taken a very casual approach to disciplining students for drinking on campus, but more recently, deaths associated with binge drinking have raised the consciousness of parents and college administrators alike. The use of drugs is against the law, as well as dangerous. You can't be there to forbid drinking and drug abuse, but you can be sure your teenager has an informed perspective on alcohol consumption and drug use. One of the greatest dangers is ignorance of the risks, both to the body and from the law, posed by casual and careless substance abuse. (See also *Experimenting With Alcohol and Drugs* and *The Four Stages of Substance Abuse,* pages 94 and 285.)

Work

Whether a person enters the job market directly after high school, during college, or later, work plays a crucial role in entering young adulthood. For many young people, work provides the first occasion to measure their performance against adult norms and expectations. Work influences a person's values, intellectual development, self-concept, and relation to society. In addition, it offers opportunities for socialization and responsibility that are key to a successful transition from childhood to adulthood.

Work offers an important situation in which to experiment with different aspects of identity. Through work, a teenager can assume various real-life roles. As an employee, the youngster will likely be encouraged and expected to manage independent responsibilities, to take the initiative, and to act responsibly and reliably. This helps develop greater independence and a sense of autonomy.

Through work, a young person usually comes into contact with a more diverse group of people than at school. In the workplace, there are more opportunities to interact with adults, as peers and supervisors, and to identify with new role models. In addition, the quality of relationships at work will likely be different from those in the family and at school. As a rule, work relationships spring from common, task-related goals.

Work offers young people the chance to establish an occupational identity, which naturally bolsters their autonomy and sense of self. Also, earning their own money helps them feel more independent of their parents. There are usually attendant gains in responsibility, financial independence, and a chance to establish a foothold in the adult world outside of the parental home. The self-supporting worker can lay legitimate claim to adulthood and expect the world to accord greater levels of respect and responsibility. Such gains in social recognition reinforce the sense of self. If the work involves membership in a particular profession—as a teacher or a carpenter, for example—further identity definition can be attained.

As young people enter the workforce, they are called upon to reevaluate and abandon unrealistic fantasies and dreams. In place of those, they must formulate realistic ideas of their own capabilities and opportunities. Forced to become pragmatic, they must assess their skills, the job market, and the match between the two. Often, teens have to compromise on their earlier, more idealistic ambitions. Entering the job market makes young people acknowledge that their choices are no longer limitless.

Given the nature of most jobs, the young person must learn to be less self-centered and more aware of individual differences. Youthful dreams for changing society through ideology may need to be reassessed. Work often transforms a teen from an idealistic reformer to an achiever.

As with any situation that changes the nature of relationships, expectations, roles, and orientation, working can cause a young person considerable confusion concerning his identity and self-image, at least initially. As young people enter the workforce, it is not unusual for them to find that their basic ability to feel safe and anchored to the environment is temporarily lost.

With the shift in identity to incorporate the role of worker, teenagers may become particularly vulnerable to social mandates. A young person who in early adolescence was wildly rebellious may become rigidly conventional and intolerant of deviance in late adolescence and early adulthood. Young people tend to feel a sense of loss as they separate from parents and their values and behaviors. As they shed old roles and assume new ones, societal and cultural forces—especially those communicated at work—may exert an unusually strong influence on their choices and goals.

During this transition to adulthood, some young people try to fill the temporary emotional vacuum by assuming wholeheartedly conventional values and behaviors. When this happens, they may place great significance on achievement and its markers, such as status, money, and material acquisition. At this time, individuals may become less critical of the status quo and less invested in independence.

Ideally, by the end of this transitional period, young adults strike a balance between self and work—retaining and finding expression for their own values, self-identity, and integrity in the culture of the workplace.

Leaving Home: How Difficult Does It Have to Be?

Crossing the bridge from childhood to adulthood is no easy task. Teens in the latter part of adolescence often oscillate between self-sufficiency and dependency. Like infants taking their first steps, teenagers take tentative steps into adulthood, holding on to their parents for support and reassurance.

Most teenagers feel ambivalent about the process. As they grasp at the security and the familiarity of the past, adolescents are likely to resent their need to do so. Yet a teen's leaving home is, in a way, the moment that all other moments of parenting have led up to. Each lesson you helped your child learn—to feed himself, to control his bladder and his bowels, to tie his shoes, to control his rage, to tolerate frustration, to share, to make decisions—prepared him for independence so that he could make his way in the world. Yet, with each step, parents feel ambivalent as well. Now, as it comes time to celebrate your child's leaving, you also mourn the loss of the family as you've known it.

Although the notion of completely renouncing ties may be compatible with Western culture's goals of "the strong individual," reflection shows this may not be ideal. Instead, it appears that development and growth are enhanced when the process of separation is fluid and continuous, involving adjustments and modifications rather than renunciation. Maintaining the relationship with parents and grandparents seems to foster development. Family interactions that are enjoyable, fulfilling, and generally free from intergenerational conflicts about separation allow best for both continuity and change.

As the parent-child relationship is transformed, there has to be continued engagement. Yet, the terms of the relationship must be renegotiated to accommodate each member's changing needs. In this way, the need for closeness and connection and the need for autonomy and independence are accommodated. A close relationship between parents and an adult child based on mutual respect, friendship, and love, rather than on duty, does not evolve on its own. It takes energy, attention, and work—by child and parents alike.

On the teen's part, a balance must be struck between viewing himself as separate and maintaining a satisfactory, primarily positive relationship with his parents. Gradually, he must accept responsibility for his decisions and for changing the way he relates.

Rather than putting the onus for change and autonomy on his parents, a young person must let go of those aspects of the relationship that are no longer adaptive. For example, sooner or later, a young person must recognize that rebelliousness or excessive compliancy no longer serves a purpose in the relationship with parents. As immature behaviors are abandoned, the parental relationship can move toward increased levels of mutual respect and a growing awareness and appreciation of each other's unique and separate identity.

The fact that the relationship increasingly embodies balance and equality means that more and more, a young person's parents can be appreciated for who they are, limitations, blemishes, and all. Once the teen achieves a significant and separate sense of self, it is easier to return home to parents, confident of the ability to make independent choices and take responsibility. Defensive anger and rebelliousness can be replaced by reciprocity and empathy. A successfully renegotiated parent-child relationship blends an appreciation and tolerance of each member's individuality with a strong sense of connection.

All parents make mistakes while raising their children. Yet, many parents and children alike blame these errors for the problems youngsters have as they become adult. It is important that, as they mature, young people take responsibility for themselves. At a certain point, it is up to them to correct the effects of parental mistakes. When adults blame their parents for the difficulties in life, it becomes an excuse for avoiding adult responsibility. Part of growing up is saying, *I know my parents did their best. Now that I'm going to be an adult, I can change if I wish.*

Once they are sufficiently confident in their autonomous self, older teenagers may be able to ask their parents for advice. Knowing that they can disagree and take only what seems in keeping with their own evolving standards, they can allow themselves to value their parents and what they have to offer. The more independent and confident a youngster is, the easier it is to listen to others without feeling threatened by other peoples' values.

Parents help with this process in ways that have been evolving throughout the years. Beginning with the birth of their first child, most parents work to establish a delicate and ever-shifting balance between providing love, support, and understanding for their children on the one hand and setting standards and limits on the other. Now, the process accelerates. Now, more than ever, you must trust that your child will be guided by the internalized self-control and self-respect developed through the consistent discipline and love you have provided during the earlier years.

Parents, however, also have internal work to do. Now is the time to contemplate and deal with empty bedrooms in the house. Soon, when your children return home, whether it's from college or from work, it will be for only a brief visit.

As children vacate the house, one by one, husbands and wives must face each other directly, not just for an hour or two, but for most of the time and, perhaps, for the first time in a couple of decades.

Parents must let go. When children leave home to make lives of their own, parents must deal with an inevitable sense of loss as their family transforms itself. This is an essential task of this transitional stage, for unless a family has experienced a divorce or death, this is the first time in its history that a transition means not only a shift but also an actual coming apart.

Families let go in ways consistent with their own particular styles. Some families release members abruptly. Others wean departing members slowly.

For mothers, this period can be particularly stressful, especially if their primary focus has been on home and family. As their role and sense of self abruptly change, mothers can feel acute loss of self-esteem, disorientation, and depression.

It is not uncommon in the early years, when there are small children around, for husbands and wives to replace romance and adult socialization with family activities. As children leave, it is time for romance and socializing to regain its prominence in the marriage. Children leave, and husbands and wives are faced with the necessity of finding companionship with each other.

For many, there is great joy in this recoupling process, in knowing privacy without having to retreat to their bedroom. Other wives and husbands, though, find themselves miles apart, bored with each other, angry, disappointed, and indifferent. Often, the children have been their major shared interest. When the last child leaves home, parents sometimes face choices for their futures.

Without children to act as the conversational focus or the go-between, however, many couples are able to revitalize their marriages, relishing their time together and the opportunity to reacquaint themselves with each other. When the marriage is vital enough to generate closeness between partners, parents are able to make the transition successfully and to face the *empty nest period* with pleasure and enthusiasm.

Part 2

DAY-TO-DAY PROBLEM BEHAVIORS

■   ■   ■

In the following five chapters, you will find discussions of issues faced from time to time, not by all adolescents, but by many, in their singular paths towards adulthood. Some are everyday behaviors, feelings, and reactions that are perfectly normal but are distressing for you and your teenager; others are more problematic. Guidance will be offered here for dealing with a range of such day-to-day problem behaviors as your child's rebellion, stealing, aggressiveness, or sexual behaviors; dealing with a death in the family, moving, or changing schools; and other life transitions. As always, the goal of these chapters is to offer reassurance and direction so that you can interpret and respond to your adolescent's behavior in a helpful manner.

4

Challenges at Home

■ ■ ■

Some teens appear to sail through their adolescent years as effortlessly as a seaworthy boat in calm waters. But for the majority of teens, the passage is more likely to be comparable to crossing a mountain range with its towering peaks that overlook deep valleys. One day your teen is bubbling over with enthusiasm, walking on top of the world; the next it takes every ounce of effort to crack a smile.

Much has been made of the war between adolescents and their parents. Although an important task of these years is separation between parent and teen, this can be—and typically is—accomplished without turning the home into a battleground. Despite the stereotype of the rebellious youth who sneers in the face of authority, most teens and their parents maintain close ties during these years, and the most recent research shows that the majority of adolescents respect their parents.

This isn't to imply that there won't be problems. There may be some days when you wish you could start over again. She may spend hours locked in her room, reject some of your rules, refuse to talk about what's bothering her, and hang out with friends who you think are a bad influence. Then there are the more serious issues that may arise. Many unhappy teens run away from home; others begin experimenting with drugs or alcohol.

In this chapter, we will address some of the common problems that face adolescents. Some aren't necessarily even problems. A part-time job, for example, doesn't become a problem and can even be an asset unless the teen begins working so many hours that work interferes with academics. On the other hand, sexual experimentation, date rape, and severe loneliness or the feeling that one is isolated from the group are more serious problems that often have long-term consequences for the adolescent. These and other daily dilemmas will be discussed in this chapter.

Responsibility and Independence

From the moment of her birth, your child begins a journey toward independence. In the early years, the steps taken away from you, though small, were nonetheless significant: the first time she let a stranger hold her without screaming, the day she let go of your hand and ran off to join her class of kindergartners, the first night she slept over at a friend's house.

Now that she is a teenager, though, these steps toward establishing herself as a person separate from her family are getting bigger and more frequent. These days the issue isn't just staying overnight at a friend's house but spending the summer in France with a school group or dating a boy you think is too old for

her. There are days when you find yourself trying to pull her back to you, while she pushes with all her strength to widen the distance. Other days you convince yourself to give her the space she needs and she rejects your offer, preferring instead to stay close, in essence, to forget if only for a brief time that she is growing up.

The process whereby an adolescent becomes increasingly independent is not easy for the teen, her parents, or their household. On one hand, the teen can't wait for the privileges of adulthood but may shy away from the responsibilities. At the same time that she is attempting to break away from her parents, part of her yearns for the comfort and safety of Mom's or Dad's arms.

Shepherding a child into adulthood can be daunting. Parents may find it difficult to look at their fifteen-year-old and acknowledge what they see: a teen on the verge of learning to drive, date, and, in a couple of years, go off to college or into the workforce or to marry. Instead, you may wish to see a child in elementary school, riding bikes with friends or playing for the softball team. *My parents treat me like I'm still a baby,* is a common lament among teens. Yet an adolescent can't possibly understand that it doesn't matter how old or successful she is, she will always be her parents' "baby." And there is nothing wrong with that, as long as the need for the individual to separate from the family is achieved.

In our society—unlike some others—an individual does not go directly from childhood to being an adult but passes through adolescence, a transition between the two worlds. It is one of the tasks of this crucial time to prepare the young person to take on the responsibilities of full-fledged adulthood and become independent of the family.

The first steps toward this independence generally occur in early adolescence or, in some cases, even preadolescence. Perhaps your child convinces you that she should be allowed to baby-sit and control her own money. Or maybe she begins meeting her friends for lunch and a matinee, something you wouldn't have permitted when she was younger. Summer camp, a plane or train trip to visit a friend or relative alone, or joining a volunteer organization on her own are all ways in which a teen begins to declare her independence. Of course, the price is that she be willing to accept greater amounts of responsibility. The teen who baby-sits must assume responsibility for arriving on time to care for younger children, to feed, entertain, and put them to bed, whereas the teen allowed to go away to summer camp must shoulder the responsibility of taking care of herself in an environment different from home.

As your teen gets older, her behavior will become increasingly more autonomous. Moreover, a more difficult form of independence begins to blossom. Gradually, you will notice a move toward more emotional strength. Your teen may begin questioning and even criticizing your values, the way you lead your life. Her beliefs, which usually begin to differ from your own, will begin to take shape, and she may be quite vocal about disagreeing with your points of view. She will begin to see you not simply as her parent but as a person with many sides—weaknesses and strengths included.

Some teens develop close relationships with other adults during this period. Parents who watch their teen grow close to another parent, a friend, or teacher may feel threatened, thinking that somehow this interloper has replaced one or both parents in the teen's eyes. Don't worry. You're not being replaced. Your child doesn't view the adult friend as a surrogate parent. On the contrary, the appeal of the relationship is that it is not governed by parent-child rules. The adult is simply a friend who accepts the teen for who she is without being critical.

As a parent, one of your jobs is to nurture your child. You take care of material needs and give her the love and emotional support she needs to thrive. Part of life's most important job, often the most difficult part, is sensing when it is time to begin letting go. Then it is up to the parent to begin preparing the adolescent to take on the responsibilities that the parent once shouldered.

Studies have shown that teens who come from warm, supportive families with clearly defined rules and open communication between parents and children have an easier time accepting increasing levels of responsibility than do those whose parents are too quick to criticize or who create a hostile home environment. Adolescents who grow up in restrictive, hostile homes have more difficulty becoming independent than do other adolescents. One study found that teens whose families used a democratic/authoritative approach to governing the household were more likely to feel independent than those who lived with either openly permissive or restrictive parents.

If you were teaching your teen to drive, you would probably not begin by taking her out into rush-hour traffic. More likely, you would take her to a deserted parking lot and, after talking though the steps involved, let her get behind the wheel. Only after you saw for yourself that she was capable of driving in a straight line and had mastered stopping quickly would you allow her to venture out onto a sparsely traveled road. Teaching independence and responsibility is also accomplished in small steps that gradually cover more ground as the teen becomes more mature and capable.

The following are some suggestions to help you encourage your teen's burgeoning independence:

- **Gradually give her responsibility for managing her life.**

  For the young teen this may mean insisting that she take responsibility for keeping her room clean or doing her own laundry, while a teen driver might be required to return the family car with a full tank of gas to retain driving privileges. Teens need to realize that the price of increasing independence is responsibility, so make sure that one does not come without the other.

  Over time, let her manage her own money. Your teenager will eventually have to support herself, so now is a good time for her to learn how to budget. Whether her source of income is from an allowance you give her every week or from a part-time job, it is important that she have her own money to spend and save, and support charities of her choice.

- **Encourage her to think for herself.**

  Involve her in open discussions of morals, politics, religion, whatever comes up. Don't be surprised if she questions your values, and don't criticize her for having different beliefs. Teens who hear their own internal voices rather than simply echoing the thoughts of their parents are in a better position to become adults who are tolerant of others' beliefs.

- **Let your teen see you as a real person and not simply as her parent.**

  A young teen may think you've never done anything wrong in your life, while an older one might be convinced you have never done anything right. Now is the time to shatter both illusions. The child who is becoming an adult needs to understand that her parents are people who have both strengths and weaknesses. No, parents aren't perfect, but successful adulthood does not require perfection. This simple message can help release some of the pressure to perform that the adolescent may feel. Teens who know that intelligent people make mistakes and even fail sometimes are more likely to try new things and, in doing so, discover something about themselves.

- **Let her know that it's all right to be scared.**

  Separating from the people who love her

BUILDING SELF-ESTEEM

In a child, emotional security is the foundation upon which are built a youngster's sense of self, her self-esteem, and her ability to establish and maintain social relationships in the world outside of the family. Yet the solid self-esteem of childhood often appears to be more fragile during early adolescence. In a daughter you may notice that sudden changes in her body have left her worrying about whether she's attractive. In a son, there may be awkwardness about his changing voice or acne problems. These changes lead many teens to feel unsure and less confident as they navigate the adolescent years.

As the parent of a teen, your task increasingly is to offer support and act as a resource. Consider these suggestions as you consider your role:

- **Offer reassurance.**
  Everyone experiences the complex and powerful changes of adolescence—be sure your child understands that. Sharing or confiding similar experiences from your own past may be helpful.

- **Use criticism sparingly.**
  Praise and positive feedback build self-esteem better than reproaches and harsh assessments. Make sure criticism is constructive (not destructive to self-esteem).

- **Offer praise.**
  Congratulate her on her victories, no matter how small, and acknowledge her attempts, even if unsuccessful.

- **Encourage your teen's interests.**
  Sports, hobbies, community service, music, art, clubs, and jobs can help promote a sense of competence and self-worth. Additional benefits may be the camaraderie and friendships with other teens who share the same interests.

- **Be patient.**
  Parents should be patient with a teen's shyness or apparent loss of self-worth: Try to understand her feelings and to be supportive.

■ **Encourage independence.**
No longer is your job to solve your child's problems. Give the youngster the room and the responsibility to address her own challenges and problems. If your teenager asks for your counsel, grant it gladly but remember you're advising not instructing. Within reasonable limits, she should increasingly be making her own decisions and assuming responsibility for the consequences and outcomes.

■ **Keep lines of communication open.**
Conversations with your teen about her concerns can establish new lines of communication. These can both buttress the youngster's self-esteem and foster a positive parent-adolescent relationship.

■ **Encourage your teenager's friendships.**
Close adolescent friendships have been shown to bolster self-esteem, social skills, and a sense of connectedness and belonging.

■ **Love her for herself.**
On good days and bad, make sure she feels loved and valued. A youngster without a sense of belonging to and being loved by her family is lacking an important stabilizing element in life.

most may be one of the most difficult things she has ever done. Studies have shown that the transition as a teen leaves for college or goes off to join the work-force is an extremely difficult one for both adolescent and parents. A study by the Yale Psychiatric Institute found that many incoming college freshman become extremely angry toward their parents, apparently as a way of making the emotional transition. The students who were the most afraid of leaving home were the most hostile, although when interviewed months later after they had made the adjustment, they were more attached than ever to their parents.

Rebellion

It was once believed that rebellion was simply part of being a teenager and that parents might as well get used to several turbulent years.

If you are the parent of a teen, however, you'll be happy to know that recent research is more optimistic. Several large studies of adolescents and their parents indicate that three-fourths of families have warm, loving relationships during the teen years. Most teens surveyed admit to admiring their parents, feel loved and appreciated, and are likely to turn to them for advice.

Thus, it appears that only about 5 to 10 percent of families with teens experience a significant deterioration in the parent-teen relationship during these years. These teens are more likely to rebel with delinquent behavior or to be emotionally or behaviorally disturbed.

This isn't to say that you should expect absolute tranquillity during adolescence. Even the nicest, most cooperative kid in the world has days when there's an almost visible chip on her shoulder. Arguments with you, yelling at her siblings, and slamming of doors may ensue. Expect some mood swings as well as arguments; they are completely normal and healthy.

Keeping your teen talking will help keep your relationship on an even track. Discuss issues, but refuse to get into a shouting match. Instead, table the discussion while everyone regains their composure, but schedule a time to talk again.

Communication Difficulties

She used to tell you everything. Now that she's a teenager, though, you find that sometimes you may as well be talking to a brick wall for all the answers you're getting.

Not all teens, of course, stop talking to their parents. Some routinely confide in one or both parents. Research has shown that these teens tend to be ones who conform rather than rebel. They also, according to one study, appear better adjusted socially and at school than are those who keep their thoughts to themselves, although some researchers speculate that these teens may be more dependent upon their parents during the transition than their more reticent counterparts.

In many homes, however, teens who once never seemed to stop talking seem as though they have lost their voice. As a parent of a suddenly mute teen, you wonder if you should be concerned.

Again, teenagers value their privacy, so it isn't uncommon for an adolescent to want to spend a lot of time alone. Teens also are notorious for being moody and withdrawn. These behaviors all fall within the normal realm of adolescence. They can, in fact, be healthy. Like everyone, a teen needs time alone to sort things out; in essence, to make sense of the world. Behind the closed doors of the teen's room, creativity can bloom, plans for the future can be formulated, and wounds allowed to heal.

Remember that communication is a two-way activity. Teens that don't seem to want to communicate may have parents who cut them off, who won't tolerate dissenting views, and who ridicule their teens or jump to conclusions. Communication is more than a matter of simply asking and answering questions. Communication is about giving and receiving; it's about talking *and* listening.

If your teen has gone silent, look for other signs before you convince yourself that something is seriously wrong. Is she suddenly without friends, refusing to talk on the phone, picking at her food, or crying often?

(See *Depressive Disorders,* page 209.) Are there signs of drug abuse? (See *Experimenting With Alcohol and Drugs*, page 94.) If there are other behavioral changes, then her silence may be a symptom of a problem that requires your intervention.

A teen in pain or who is angry is often unequipped to deal with these feelings directly, so she retreats behind a wall to avoid having to cope with her feelings. In some cases, adolescents engaged in destructive behavior—drug or alcohol abuse, gangs, school problems, and so on—believe that if they hide from you, you won't find out what they're doing. For other teens, silence and withdrawal are symptoms of depression or other emotional problems.

If you suspect your teen's desire to be alone is due to an underlying problem, you can't afford to sit and wait until she decides to confide in you. There is no magic formula for getting a teen to tell you what's bothering her. You, more than anyone, know your child and are in a position to observe the behavioral changes. Let your intuition guide you. If you suspect a problem, there probably is one. If, despite your efforts, she refuses to open up or continues to deny that something is wrong, it may be time to seek help.

Grooming

She spends hours in the bathroom primping. Yet when she emerges, hair wild, face pale, it looks to you as though she just climbed out of bed and you're tempted to order her at least to comb her hair before she goes out.

Grooming is often a source of conflict between parent and adolescent. In the very young teen, it may be a lack of grooming that is causing the problem. Accustomed to caring for a child's body, the teen may continue her habit of showering every other day. But what's adequate for the ten-year-old simply won't do once the hormones and odors of adolescence arrive. These days you notice that her hair, once silky and lustrous, is stringy and speckled with flakes of dandruff, her skin has an oily, unwashed look, and when she walks into a room, you notice an odor.

Like anything else, talking care of one's person is learned. A parent shouldn't assume that a teen on the brink of adolescence automatically knows what to do about underarm perspiration or skin blemishes. It's up to you to help. Buy some antiperspirant. Explain that a daily bath or shower is necessary. Demonstrate proper skin care to help keep it clean and clear. This should all be done in an informational tone. Remember, adolescents can be extremely self-conscious about the way they look and the changes in their bodies. An insult or critical remark about a teen's appearance can inflict just as much pain as a slap across the face.

Beyond teaching your teen the mechanics of cleanliness and then encouraging that they be followed, try to be tolerant of personal styles. Perhaps the prescribed uniform is a pair of baggy jeans and an oversize flannel shirt. *Wouldn't it be nice,* you think, *to see her wear some of those nice clothes hanging in the closet?* If you're tempted to burn the jeans, try to remember back to your own adolescence and the strange outfits that you put together in an effort either to conform with what your peers were wearing or, if you were a bit of a rebel, make your own statement. If your teen dresses in jeans for a family event that you feel requires more formal attire, explain that you think a formal restaurant or wherever it is you're going requires a different outfit. Otherwise, let the teen pick the outfits, within reason.

Naturally, there are times when a parent needs to intervene, especially if a fashion statement has long-term repercussions. You may, for example, think it reasonable to add a second earring—but balk when you hear of a plan to pierce a nostril or a nipple. Dying one's hair green, getting a tattoo, or wearing sexually suggestive clothes may all go against your grain. If you strongly disagree with something, say so. Explain why you feel that a tattoo, for example, would be a mistake. These discussions are difficult as both sides have very strong opinions.

As teens get older and more interested in the opposite sex, they often develop a preoccupation with the way they look. Some parents at these times rarely get to see the inside of their own bathrooms. The teenager can spend hours in front of the bathroom mirror experimenting with new looks. Beyond patience and possibly instituting a time limit on bathroom use, there's not a lot a parent can do about this. Most teens eventually become more comfortable with their looks and decide that life wasn't meant to be lived in front of a mirror; there are more exciting things to do.

Loneliness and Isolation

When you were young, did anyone ever tell you that your high-school years were supposed to be the best time of your life? Even if nobody actually said those words, chances are that magazines, television, and the movies you saw echoed that sentiment. The teens in the movies had flawless skin, wore bikinis with no sign of self-consciousness, and always knew the right words to say. Life was portrayed as one big party. But maybe you were one of the many kids who wasn't invited.

Contemporary media have attempted to show the gamut of adolescence, from teen mothers caring for infants to young debutantes selecting a dress for the ball and on to high-school seniors agonizing over whether they'll be accepted to a good college. Mainstream society still has an idealized view of youth as happy and carefree—but statistics tell us that life is anything but carefree for today's teens.

At least 32 percent of fifteen-year-old girls are sexually active. The United States has the highest rate of teenage pregnancy of any Western industrialized nation. Drug abuse is widespread in our high schools and even in middle schools. And an estimated 500,000 teens each year in this country survive suicide attempts.

For many teens, these years are defined not by football games and endless parties but by loneliness and isolation. Adolescence is a time when most adolescents need to share their feelings with others who will understand. Hence, the strong desire to find teens with whom one can relate. This is not always easy to do. Many teens, however hard they try, are so self-conscious and shy that they have a difficult time in social situations, even in those that call upon them to mix with members of the same sex. They're so worried that they will say or do something wrong that they say nothing at all. In social situations, these teens are easy to ignore, and most soon get the message not to try. They feel undesirable, and it becomes easier to retreat behind the closed door of one's room rather than risk rejection.

What characteristics make a teen someone others want to know? Research on what makes a teen a desirable companion places spontaneity and a willingness to try new things high on the list. Other attributes that correlate with being well-liked include interest in others, liveliness, cheerfulness, and gaiety, characteristics that the shy teen may not exhibit.

A common protection against loneliness is to belong to a circle of friends. There are many teens, however, who don't fit in with a crowd or group. Adolescents who are suddenly thrust into a new school as a result of a move often have a difficult time making new friends. A new girl in school may be simply ignored, or—if she looks promising—she may be courted by several groups and then later dropped when it becomes clear that she is different. Sometimes, especially if she has moved often, she may be the reluctant one who avoids establishing new friendships in order to avoid the pain of severing the ties when she moves.

Americans tend to be joiners. As a first-grader, your daughter joined the Brownies; in middle school, the soccer team; in high school, the glee club. She was part of something, a group, singing friendship songs, working toward the common goal. Yet, these outward signs of connection are not enough for most people. Many teens discover they feel the most isolated and alone when they are in the middle of a crowd, even their own group of friends. What is missing is often the special connection that comes with having a close friend, someone who likes you for yourself.

If social acceptance during adolescence can be likened to a spring shower that revives a drooping plant, then rejection is a long, hot summer. It isn't necessary for a teen to be especially popular to be happy, but studies have shown that adolescents who have friends have a better self-image and a better relationship with parents and teachers than those who have no close relationships with peers. Teens who are repeatedly rejected in their attempts to initiate friendships often give up trying. Some may become self-rejecting, feeling undeserving of success. The self-rejecting teen feels inferior. She is apt to consider the opinions of others more valid than her own. In an attempt to impress her peers or at least get their attention, the self-rejecting teen may do things that go against her grain. Sadly, these actions often serve only to reinforce others' negative opinion of the teen. That, in turn, makes her dislike herself even more.

As the parent of a teenager, you've grown used to seeing your daughter arrive home from school, utter not a word, and bolt into her bedroom, to be lured away only by the call of an empty stomach. But lately you've noticed a sadness that wasn't there before, and you wonder if you should be concerned.

Although in this book we've talked about the importance of privacy during these years, don't confuse isolation and loneliness with your teen's need for privacy. Yes, healthy and happy adolescents do spend time in their rooms. They sometimes are moody, they often argue with their parents, and getting them to open up may require the skills of an investigative reporter. But they are not habitually sad. If your daughter spends hours in her room programming her computer or practicing her cello, that is probably by choice. If, on the other hand, she does little but lie on her bed and stare at the ceiling, she may be feeling sad due to loneliness.

Although you can't take your teenager by the hand and find her a best friend, there are things you can do to be supportive. Remind her that there are other kids in school or in your neighborhood that share her interests and attitudes. Without nagging, encourage her to participate in activities that are not threatening. Offer to drive her and a friend to the movies. Don't try to hang out with them—let them know when you'll pick them up.

If you suspect your teen is unhappy, reach out to her. It is important that she know you are there for her. Offer advice, but don't pretend there are easy answers; there aren't. In some cases, the source of the problem may be apparent. A girl who has severe acne, for example, may feel extremely self-conscious and retreat into isolation. A few trips to the dermatologist may help bolster her self-esteem and get her ready to face the world again. Or, if you suspect your teen simply has a skill deficit—perhaps she doesn't know how to go about making up with her best friend after a fight—you can suggest a role-playing session where you act out the various scenarios. This can both give you insight into what's going on in her life and help her arrive at an acceptable solution to her problem.

Sometimes, despite a parent's good intentions, nothing seems to make a difference. The teen's sadness and sense of isolation isn't transient. If your adolescent seems profoundly unhappy for a prolonged period, she may have depression, a condition that, if left untreated, may last for months. Signs of depression include a loss of interest in nearly all activities, changes in appetite and weight, trouble sleeping or excessive daytime sleeping, fatigue, feelings of worthlessness or inappropriate guilt, difficulty concentrating, and recurring thoughts of death or suicide. (See *Depressive Disorders,* page 209, and *Teenage Suicide,* page 213.)

It is critical that parents take chronic sadness seriously. Don't assume that this is just a phase that will pass. Seek help for your adolescent and family. (See *When and Where to Seek Help,* page 302.)

PEER INFLUENCES

The average American teenager spends 22 hours a week, not counting classroom time, with friends. For many, more time is spent with friends than with family. So it shouldn't come as a surprise that peers have a great deal of influence on behavior.

We've all heard of "peer pressure," a fear high on many parents' list of concerns. We imagine our teens buckling under the pressure to have sex, skip school, take drugs, get drunk and drive, and so on. But peer influence is not always negative. In fact, it is more often a positive factor. Studies have shown that teens tend to choose friends with similar feelings about drug use, drinking, dating, and delinquency.

Envision a party where marijuana is being passed around. It's not as though someone is actively pressuring her to use the drug. But everyone is doing it. She says she'd feel weird if she didn't join in. Peer pressure is rarely as overt as someone shoving a beer at a friend and ordering her to drink. Rather, it is generally a subtle influence.

Researchers studying peer group influences and have found: (1) early adolescents are more susceptible to peer influence than either younger children or older teens; (2) girls may be slightly more susceptible than boys; (3) teens who are not confident about their social skills are more likely to succumb to peer pressure; and (4) even those most susceptible are less likely to follow friends involved in antisocial behavior than they are when the behavior is neutral or positive.

Do teens feel under pressure to conform? In one study where researchers asked teens to describe the pressures from peers, older teens were more likely to be pressured to use drugs or have sex than their younger counterparts. Peer pressure to behave in a positive manner, however, was still substantially higher. Interestingly, the greatest pressure teens reported from friends was to finish high school.

The evening news features the most negative peer influence—skinheads, rival inner-city gangs, teen murderers, and so forth. Could the so-called good kid that you send to school end up in such a crowd? That is not very likely. For the most part, serious juvenile delinquency appears in a very small number of adolescent groups. Although disturbing and certainly visible, the small percentage of teens involved in these extreme antisocial acts tend to be abnormally aggressive kids who are shunned by the rest and seek out others with similar behavior. Membership in the group provides emotional support, while at the same time the antisocial norms of the group give its members license to engage in more negative behavior.

TELEVISION

Television is ubiquitous in American homes, lives, and conversation. At the same time, TV is also a source of complaint from parents who feel they cannot control what and how much their children watch, and who further suspect that it has as bad an effect on homework as it does on language and attitudes.

As with other technologies, television has the potential for both good and bad, for both wise use and abuse. You may enjoy fine historical dramas or thoughtful news analysis but abhor the violence in police shows or be offended by the values displayed in some sitcoms. Although TV can be a source of creatively presented information ("educational" TV), you may feel that information is better gathered from books or firsthand experience. Many educators tend to agree.

You may decide there's no place for television at all in your home. Some families where there is no TV do report that kids read more, spend more time playing outside, use their free time more creatively, and are more likely to participate in dinnertime conversation. In other families, TV by its absence becomes a volatile issue. Friends talk about shows your children haven't seen and they feel left out; sometimes even teachers expect them to be familiar with certain aspects of popular culture. Television can play an important role in peer socialization, and many youngsters break the embargo anyway by watching TV at friends' houses.

A middle ground that seems to work for many families is to keep the TV but to establish viewing rules. Consider limiting hours: only Friday and Saturday nights, for instance, or an hour a night on school nights and two on weekends. Agree that homework be completed before the TV is turned on. Requiring that the kids plan beforehand what they're going to watch (with your approval) cuts down on channel surfing, on flipping on the TV as an antidote to boredom, or on leaving it on as background noise. Make sure your kids have choices available to them for activities other than TV, including time with you. And remember: You must abide by the same rules.

Making sure everyone watches only the programs they really want to see makes television a more positive experience; talking about shows in the same way you might discuss books helps transform it into a less passive activity. You can also educate your kids about advertising and how it works, which helps them become more discriminating consumers.

As your teen moves into the high-school years, monitoring the programs your adolescent watches becomes more and more difficult. Your teen will use the principles and judgments you've helped establish in the preceding years. Almost inevitably, television exposes teens to violence and drug and alcohol use. Your teen may be naturally curious about the sexuality apparent on MTV. The adolescent's self-image and ideas about relationships are informed in part by what they watch, even though what she sees on television may offer a grossly distorted view of how people should regard themselves and relate to one another.

As a parent, you can help provide a broader perspective from which to understand what your adolescent sees on television. Television is one influence in a teen's world—and part of your job is to frame discussions about sexuality, violence, substance abuse, and other issues in a way that allows you, teachers, and others to contribute to the debates. Television—whether it's pure entertainment or intended to be educational—can contribute to a wider understanding of the world when put into a broader perspective. In fact, with a little discipline and flexibility, you just might actually be able to turn television-watching into a learning experience.

Extracurricular Activities

Most adolescents today don't simply go to school. Rather, they go to school and then play soccer and then attend meetings of the French Club and then have a piano lesson and then work in a food bank. . . and on and on and on.

There is no doubt that extracurricular activities can be a positive factor in a young person's life. Talents not always discovered in the classroom may emerge. Friends are made. And, sometimes, lifelong interests solidified. Occasionally, teens become overextended in their desire to sample from a vast menu of choices. When this happens, school perfor-mance may suffer or a teen feels stressed or pressured.

What drives teens to take on so many activities? The usual assumption is that they find the activities fun and they want to try new things, but sometimes fun isn't part of the equation. Research has shown that teens become involved in extracurricular activities for a variety of reasons—because their friends are doing it, to increase their popularity, to have their picture appear more often in the school yearbook, because it looks good on a college application, to meet members of the opposite sex, and so on. Some of these reasons may be good ones but some not.

Parents may find it difficult to say no

when a child expresses an interest in drama or photography, for instance. These are the years for exploration, and part of exploring is venturing into new realms. So a big part of you wants to encourage your teen to embrace new challenges and opportunities. Yet, you know how easy it is to become too busy.

As an aware parent, you are in a good position to monitor your teen's choices. If, for instance, the decision is between a part in the school musical, an activity that will require daily rehearsals for several months, or being involved in student government, a one-hour weekly commitment, you may want to try to steer her toward the latter by pointing out how little free time she already has.

Discuss the pros and cons of each activity with your teen. What is the time commitment? Is your adolescent really interested in the club or project, or is the focus actually social, the opportunity to do something with a particular friend or group? Is there a connection between the activity and a continuing interest or long-term goal of the adolescent's? Stress to your teen that nobody can do everything, and help her make good choices for the right reasons.

If you see that your teen is so busy that no time remains for study, you should further limit extracurricular activities before academic performance is affected.

Chores and Jobs

Running a household is a lot of work, and teens as well as younger children should be expected to share in that work.

This isn't to suggest that you turn your children into domestic laborers. But having a reasonable number of chores benefits the teen by teaching responsibility. She learns that as a member of your household she is expected to contribute. In most families, dinner does not magically appear out of nowhere; it is planned and prepared by someone. Yet the adolescent who isn't expected to as little as set the table or rinse a plate after a meal goes away with the feeling that no contribution is necessary because someone else will do the work. This may not have as much influence on a very young child, but an adolescent on the threshold of leaving home will have a rude awakening upon discovering how great is the teen's ignorance of everyday tasks.

Chores are a source of conflict in many families. In families with more than one child, there is bickering because each child feels as if the tasks allotted to them are greater than those assigned to a sibling. Parents, too, get angry when they discover that their teen didn't mow the grass or do the laundry on schedule.

To help alleviate conflicts over chores in your house, make sure that tasks are allocated fairly. If your fourteen-year-old is expected to mow the grass, your twelve-year-old also should have an age-appropriate chore, such as washing the car. Where possible, rotate chores. There are some chores that nobody likes, while others, such as walking the dog on a nice day, may actually be pleasant. Make sure that everyone has a chance to do the full range of chores appropriate to their age and capabilities.

Be specific about each household member's responsibilities. You may want to post a chore chart or checklist with detailed instructions.

Show your children how you want the chores done. If, for example, you merely tell your adolescent to dust the furniture in the living room, don't be surprised if it fails your white-glove test. Explain that your idea of a thorough dusting is more than a flick of the feather duster, and make sure you demonstrate how you want it done.

Be flexible. You know yourself that there are some days you don't mind cooking dinner but the thought of facing laundry is enough to ruin your day. In assigning chores, you may want to give a liberal time frame. Instead of insisting, for example, that laundry be done on Monday, you might want to say that laundry has to be done by Wednesday. This takes into account the days when your teen has conflicting activities, an unusual amount of homework, or simply doesn't feel like folding clothes. Not only does this make for a happier, less pressured teen, but it also teaches a lesson on budgeting time.

Balance the level of responsibilities with the privileges or freedom granted. Reward jobs done well, but also develop consequences for chores left undone. Most teens will comply with reasonable chores if they know that they will be given more privileges. And the thought of not going out with friends on the weekend is a strong motivator for completion of chores during the week.

A natural progression from household chores is to a job outside the home, a coveted prize in many communities. Typically, the first taste a young adolescent has of gainful employment is in informal neighborhood jobs—mowing lawns, baby-sitting, walking pets. Fourteen- and fifteen-year-olds often are hired in more formal work settings such as in libraries, fast-food restaurants, and camps, although child labor laws prohibit these teens from working more than three hours a day and after 7 P.M. on school days. Teens who are sixteen and older have a greater range of employment opportunities and no time restrictions under federal law, although some states have established restrictions on the hours teens can work.

There is much to be said for part-time work for teens. A job helps teach the teen about responsibility and offers firsthand experience in managing money. There is also a sense of pride and self-confidence that comes with earning one's own money and doing a job well. When money is in short supply, a job may enable a teen to buy the extras that can make the adolescent feel good or even to help pay for basic necessities. Research shows that teens in the workplace acquire practical skills that ease their transition into adulthood.

The downside of teen employment is that instead of being a complement to school, it often becomes a primary force in a teenager's quest for a car or other goods. Many teens work twenty or more hours a week, often late into the night, making it difficult to get adequate sleep needed to perform well in school. Grades can suffer, extracurricular activities become a thing of the past, and in many cases, the teen simply drops out of school.

Despite the risks, studies show that as many as 60 percent of high-school sophomores and 75 percent of all juniors and seniors work at some point during the school year.

Should your teen be one of them?

If your teen has been pressuring you about a job, here are some things to consider before you nod your head:

- A nationwide study conducted at the University of Colorado showed that students who work more than 13.5 hours per week have lower grades than those who are unemployed or who work fewer hours. Interestingly, those who work under that 13.5-hour-per-week threshold have better grades than teens who don't work at all.
- When a teen works is as important as the total number of hours. A teen required to close a fast-food restaurant at midnight is one who may sacrifice the energy she needs to get through the school day.
- Increased absenteeism, neglected homework, and, ultimately, lower grades are all consequences of too many work hours.

Should you decide to let your teen try a job, help the adolescent to choose wisely. A job that involves a few hours of work after school or on the weekends is preferable to one with night hours. Remember, too, the 13.5-hour threshold. If an employer wants more time, say no and stick to your guns.

Use the job to help teach your teen the importance of saving. Insist that a portion of the money be put in the bank. Finally, make sure your teen understands that you will be monitoring grades and school performance. If you have any inkling that the job is adversely affecting her schoolwork, insist on shorter hours or that the job be eliminated from the schedule.

Changing Eating and Sleeping Patterns

If your teen's eating and sleeping habits have changed, you're not alone. Many parents of teens notice a real change during these years. Most of the changes are the result of growing bodies and the increased demands of hectic lifestyles. But as a parent you should also be alert for signs of problems. These are the years when dangerous eating disorders may appear, especially in teenage girls.

■ EATING

These can be difficult years for the nutrition-conscious parent. On one hand, you're aware that your teen needs a nutritious diet to enable the body to grow and one that is low in fat to minimize the risk of diseases that may surface during adulthood. On the other hand, your teen may rarely be home for a meal, what with working a part-time job, activities, and a busy social life. Thus, even if you've tried to teach nutrition and introduce healthy foods, fast food may be the nutrition of choice much of the time.

These high-calorie meals often lead to weight gain. That can be complicated during these years when teens go on strict diets that don't come close to meeting their nutritional needs and deplete them of valuable energy. While a large number of teens are concerned about weight and diet, a small percentage (0.5 percent) develop anorexia nervosa, a sometimes fatal eating disorder in which the teen sees herself as fat and starves herself. Between 5 and 18 percent of teen girls develop bulimia, an eating disorder characterized by bingeing and purging. (See *Eating and Nutritional Disorders,* page 260.)

Although conflicting schedules may make it difficult to monitor your teen's eating habits, try to have dinner together at least several times a week, a practice that has social and other benefits beyond nutrition alone. You can also exert some control by packing a lunch to take to school rather than having her opt for the selections in the school cafeteria. While it's unlikely you'll be able to convince her to avoid French fries with an explanation of the long-term dangers of atherosclerosis, you might try appealing to her more immediate sense of self. Let her know that these foods may taste great, but they add lots of calories, little nutrition, and won't do for her hair, skin, and shape what fruits, vegetables, and grains will. Beware of remarks that may make your daughter especially self-conscious about her body image—careless, though well-intentioned comments about baby fat, weight gain, or body type have been known to be a factor in precipitating anorexia.

If your teen insists on dieting, encourage her to develop a sensible weight-loss plan. Be observant for the signs and symptoms of anorexia nervosa, which include continued reduction of food intake, strenuous exercise, secrecy about food, skipping meals by saying she isn't hungry, and cessation of menstruation.

■ SLEEPING

Many parents with a teen are familiar with this weekend scenario: The rest of the family is up early and ready to begin the day, while the teen emerges from bed groggy and disheveled, barely in time for lunch. Does your teen really need thirteen hours of sleep, you wonder? In fact, extended periods of sleep are quite normal during the teen years.

Most teens need at least eight hours of sleep every night to feel their best. It is during this "down" time that they refuel and that most of the hormones their body needs for growth and development are secreted. Do most teens get eight hours? Many are so busy with jobs, school, activities, and their social life that sleep takes a backseat, and they end up getting six hours or even less. Then you have the teen who, in an effort to catch up, seems to sink into a coma on the weekends.

The fact is that many teens are simply too busy. Not only do they have too much going on, but they're not adept at organizing their time. Therefore, you may have a teen who spends two hours on the phone after dinner and only later begins to tackle three hours of homework. As a parent, you can help your teen get needed rest by encouraging a reasonable bedtime. Part of growing up is learning to manage time, and one of your parenting tasks is to help your adolescent master such skills.

Illness in Adolescence

The average teenager misses five days of school per year as a result of illness or injury. Except for very young children, whose immature immune systems make them susceptible to a host of viruses, adolescents have the highest incidence of illness among all age groups.

Teens become ill for a number of reasons, the most common being:

- ACUTE ILLNESSES.
  Colds, the flu, menstrual cramps (see *Menstrual Problems*, page 182), mononucleosis, and other temporary ailments occur frequently during adolescence. Appropriate care should be taken in treating each of these, but increasingly, the adolescent can assume responsibility for self-care just as she is becoming more independent in other areas. Illness can be used to educate teens about how to care for themselves when ill, how to maintain responsibilities when ill (after all, parents usually don't miss work for headaches, menstrual cramps, or other minor illnesses). It's also time for parents to remain in the waiting room as teens begin to establish and learn to manage independent relationships with their doctors.

- ACCIDENTS.
  Nonfatal injuries from accidents are responsible for the largest number of hospitalizations for adolescents between the ages of twelve and seventeen. Most accidents involve a motor or recreational vehicle, and the majority of accidents involve alcohol. In fact, one-third of eighth graders and 44 percent of high-school sophomores polled in one study admitted to having been in a car with a drinking or drug-using driver the previous month. Skateboard and bicycle mishaps also frequently send adolescents to the hospital.

- CHRONIC ILLNESS.
  Six percent or two million adolescents between the ages of ten and eighteen suffer from a chronic disease, the most common being mental illnesses, asthma, and diseases of the musculoskeletal system. (See *The Adolescent With Chronic Illness,* page 166.)

- SEXUAL ACTIVITY.
  The main health problems associated with teenage sexual behavior are sexually transmitted diseases and pregnancy. One-fourth of all sexually active adolescents are infected with a sexually transmitted disease before they graduate from high school, while about one million teens become pregnant each year, with 480,000 of that number actually giving birth.

- MENTAL ILLNESSES.
  Mental disorders also occur during adolescence. Among those that may require

intervention by a mental health professional are depression (see *Depressive Disorders*, page 209), anxiety disorders (*Anxiety and Avoidant Disorders,* page 196), sexual abuse (see *Physical or Sexual Abuse,* page 117), and alcohol or drug abuse problems (*Substance Abuse Disorders,* page 279).

Sexual Experimentation

Most of us—with a little effort—can accept the fact that our children's bodies will mature. A more bitter pill to swallow, though, is what they may be doing with those bodies.

Whether we like it or not, teens today are experimenting with sex in unprecedented numbers. Aside from the emotional fallout of having sex too early, teens who engage in sexual intercourse expose themselves to the risk of sexually transmitted diseases in addition to an unwanted pregnancy. Consider the following statistics:

- Fifty percent of girls and 60 percent of boys between the ages of fifteen and nineteen have had sexual intercourse.

- The number of girls under the age of fifteen who have their first experience with intercourse is on the rise. In 1982, 19 percent of girls had had intercourse by the time they were fifteen, but five years later that number had climbed to 27 percent.

- Fifty percent of teens report using no birth control the first time they have intercourse; only one-third of all sexually active adolescents routinely use some method of contraception.

- Sixty percent of sexually active girls between the ages of fifteen and nineteen have had two or more partners.

- One million American teens become pregnant each year.

- Many teens who opt for premature intercourse are unhappy about the experience. In one study of 1,000 American adolescents, 11 percent of girls said they were sorry after intercourse, while 61 percent had ambivalent feelings. Conversely, only 1 percent of the boys interviewed regretted the experience, and 34 percent admitted to having mixed feelings.

For most teens, sexual awakening is a gradual process that starts slow and builds to a crescendo. Long before they reach their teens, many children masturbate, a practice that usually continues throughout the teens and indeed throughout life. As a teen masturbates, she may engage in erotic fantasy to excite herself. These fantasies become more explicit as the teen ages. So an eleven-year-old might fantasize about kissing a boy at school, while a seventeen-year-old's fantasy might involve having intercourse with a rock star.

These fantasies are important to your teen's sexual development. Not only are they pleasurable, but they can also act as a safe substitute for a real sexual encounter. Moreover, autoerotic behavior helps teens learn about themselves sexually. Through trial and error they learn what works sexually for them and what doesn't. In a sense, masturbation and fantasy can be a safe dress rehearsal for more mature sexual behavior.

Not all teens have a positive experience with masturbation, sexual fantasy, or with their own sexuality. Some feel guilt or shame at what they are doing. Others may be so caught up in their sexual fantasies that they resist the impulse to move on to a dating situation. Or they may be so afraid of entering the social arena with its sexual risks that they deliberately make themselves socially undesirable, wear clothes that hide their bodies, grow lax about grooming, or simply avoid social encounters. Others are anxious about their bodies: A girl may be embarrassed that her breasts are small; a boy may feel that he isn't muscular enough. Teens with strong religious convictions may feel uncomfortable even thinking about sex.

Experimentation in homosexual relationships also is quite common during the teens. Just because a teen has a homosexual interest or encounter does not necessarily mean she is gay. Because many teens openly disapprove of homosexuality, it is difficult to get reliable statistics regarding homosexual encounters. One study, however, found that 5 percent of boys and girls between the ages of thirteen and fifteen reported having had at least one sexual experience with a member of the same sex. More than half of these teens said the incident occurred when they were eleven or twelve. Girls usually indicated that their partner was the same age, while boys said that in most cases he was either younger or close to the same age. Twelve percent of these boys, however, disclosed that their sexual partner was an adult male. (See also *Homosexuality*, page 163.)

The culmination of any sexual awakening for heterosexuals is intercourse, a finish line that is being increasingly crossed by teenagers. An obvious question, and one that cannot fully be explained, is, why?

There are many factors that experts say contribute to earlier sexual experimentation. In general, our society presents sex as an exciting, very adult thing that people who like each other do. You would have to lock your teen up to avoid exposing the adolescent to the pervasive presence of sex in movies, television, books, and even billboards. The sex is all too often *not* between two mature married people who happen to love each other but involves the coupling of two gorgeous and young bodies with little shared history.

No doubt society's acceptance toward earlier sex also is a factor, although societal sexual mores have been loosening since World War I, when the number of nonvirgin brides doubled. Premarital sex does not elicit the guilt it once did. Society does, however, still tend to take a dim view of female promiscuity.

At the same time your teen is being exposed to society's none-too-subtle sexual message, she is experiencing strong sexual feelings. A boy she likes in school accidentally brushes up against her and she tingles all over. She may dream about the boy. This could be the one. They'll marry and have children and live happily ever after. The boy's fantasy is quite different, even assuming he likes the girl. He's thinking how good she looked in that clingy sweater. What would it be like to kiss her or do more? Gender differences during adolescence cannot be ignored. Girls are raised to please people and to value commitment and emotional intimacy. Unlike boys who tend to focus on sex itself and the physical pleasure from it, most girls view sex within the context of a romance. Thus, teen boys are more likely to have sex when the opportunity presents itself, while girls are more concerned with establishing meaningful relationships, sexual and otherwise.

Peers also have a role in swaying a teen toward or away from early sexual intercourse. In a 1986 Harris poll, 1,000 teens were asked why they had not waited to have sexual intercourse until they were older. The top reasons given by girls were peer pressure (34 percent), pressure from boys (17 percent), curiosity (14 percent), and "everyone is doing it" (14 percent). Boys cited as their reasons: peer pressure (26 percent), curiosity (16 percent), "everyone is doing it" (10 percent), and sexual gratification (10 percent). Teens tend to gravitate toward a best friend who shares the same sexual values and behavior. Thus, a girl who has not had sex is more likely to be friends with a girl who is also a virgin. If one of them then becomes sexually active, the other may feel that she has to choose between ending her friendship or following her friend's example and becoming sexually active herself. There is immense pressure

during these years to conform, and studies have shown that peer pressure to drink, smoke, and have sexual intercourse increases as the teen ages.

Finally, parents have a role in influencing their teen's sexual behavior. Teens who live in families who value strong academic performance are less likely to have early sexual experience. The composition of the family also has an impact. Girls from single-parent families are more likely to have early sexual intercourse than those who live with both parents. Whether this is a function of the absence of a second parent, a lack of supervision, or being witness to a sexually active dating parent is not known.

Some teens use sex as a weapon against their parents. A girl who sexually acts out may be using her behavior as a way to rebel against her family. The daughters of mothers who are unaffectionate, yet strict about rules, are more likely to have sex early as a way of expressing their defiance and autonomy.

While most parents probably would prefer that their teens waited until they were older to become sexually intimate with another person, the reality is that most adolescents will discover sex during the teen years. As a parent, it is important for you to understand that your teen's sexuality is not in and of itself a problem. The physical and emotional evolution of a child into an adult becomes a problem only when the wrong choices lead to dire consequences. Having consensual sex in her mid-teens will not ruin your teen's life; contracting AIDS from that sexual act will. Regardless of their sexual circumstances, we owe it to our children to make sure that they are equipped with the knowledge that will allow them to live with the choices they make.

Date Rape

When most people think of rape, they see a stranger who follows his victim along a darkened street or breaks a window to get into her apartment. In fact, more than half of rapes reported to the police are committed by acquaintances of the victim, in many instances during a date. Since many women don't report acquaintance rape, this type of rape is probably even more prevalent than statistics tell us.

Although boys certainly are vulnerable to sexual abuse in other forms, the victim in a date rape is almost always a girl.

Teens are much more vulnerable to rape by a date or acquaintance than by a stranger. While a young person may avoid exposing herself to unsafe situations where she could be attacked by a stranger, teens often underestimate the potential danger in social situations. These are years when the pressure is on to have an active social life. They go to parties with lots of people, many of whom they don't know well. Alcohol and drugs may be easily available, and people under the influence of alcohol and drugs may put themselves into situations that they normally wouldn't. A college freshman who has had too much to drink, for instance, may agree to go to a stranger's room at a party; the same teen, when sober, might feel uneasy about the same situation and refuse the invitation.

In recent years, the issue of date rape on college campuses has surfaced. In a survey at one Midwestern college, more than 20 percent of the women questioned said they were victims of rape or attempted rape. In most cases, the women knew their attacker. Typically, the date rape scenario on a college campus goes something like this: A young woman goes to a party and meets a man. She dances with him, they drink, and later she agrees either to go to his room so they can talk or to allow him to walk or drive her home. They hold hands, and they may kiss, but when things start heating up, the girl says *Stop!* The rapist, of course, just keeps on going, overpowering his partner, perhaps threatening her, and inflicting physical pain.

Oftentimes the victim is so confused about what has happened that she decides not to report the rape. *After all,* she rationalizes, *I was drinking, I did agree to go to his room, and I enjoyed kissing him. Maybe I led him on? Maybe it really was my fault? Maybe no one will believe me?*

Recently the problem has become so often reported that more cases are being successfully prosecuted than in the past. Rape specialists say the fault lies in our cultural assumption that the natural masculine role during sex is to go aggressively after one's sexual goal, while the natural feminine inclination is to either resist or submit. Implicit in the way date rape was once viewed was that a woman who really didn't want sex couldn't be made to have intercourse by her date, the idea being that she must have done some-thing to make him feel his advances were welcomed.

As her parent, teach your teen some basic safety strategies to help keep her safe. While these may protect her from strangers, they won't help her when someone she knows becomes sexually violent. Much of the pre-vention of date or acquaintance rape involves being alert and sensitive to others—and in the realization that her body belongs to her and is not available to anyone who wants to touch it. Here are a few messages that you can communicate:

- No one has the right to touch her without her permission. Ideally, you begin com-municating this message in early child-hood when you assure her that it's all right if she doesn't want to kiss a relative or family friend good-bye.

- Teach her how easily signals can be misin-terpreted. Many teens don't understand that what she regards as innocent and playful sexual behavior can be read as provocative and seductive by others. Explain that in her sexual encounters she must set boundaries. She must make her partner aware of what she wants to do and what she will not do.

- Let her know that she has the right to stop any sexual activity at any time. She does not have to go through with inter-course simply because her partner is excited and expects it.

- She always has the right to say no. Some-times girls believe that because they've had intercourse with someone before, they are not entitled to decline. Make sure she understands that she must be in control.

- If you are the parent of a boy, teach him to respect women. Along with the self-control that both sexes must learn, a male has to know that the word *stop* means just that. If he forces himself on someone, he needs to understand that he is breaking the law and that punishment may involve prison.

- Since most date rapes involve alcohol, it is prudent to avoid excessive drinking in social situations.

- Tell her that if she is in a situation where a date refuses to stop, she can try scream-ing, getting away, or fighting, but in many cases there's nothing she can do to stop the rape. Stress that it is not her fault; she is a victim. Afterward, however, encour-age her to notify the police and prosecute her attacker.

Experimenting With Alcohol and Drugs

Consider the following statistics:

- According to a 1991 report by the Sur-geon General's office, 20.7 million junior and senior high school students said they drink alcohol; 8 million admitted to drinking every week, while 5.4 million said they occasionally binge-drink (five or more drinks in a row). For 500,000 high-schoolers, getting drunk is a weekly event.

- Drug use among teens started dropping in the late 1980s, probably as a result of a national awareness campaign. It remains, however, a pervasive problem. While the number of students who had tried the powerful drug cocaine or its derivative, crack, fell from 15 percent in 1987 to 6 percent in 1993, 35 percent of high-school seniors polled in 1993 had tried marijuana. Although this is way down from the 60 percent who admitted using the drug in a 1979 survey, 3 percent more students had tried marijuana in 1993 than in 1992. It appears that the number of young adolescents experimenting with drugs is on the rise.

- Thousands of young lives are lost due to drugs or alcohol. Eight thousand adolescents die each year in alcohol-related car accidents, while 45,000 are injured, many of them seriously.

Your teen may not seem to you to be the type to get involved in drugs or alcohol. You may be right—but keep in mind that drug and alcohol abuse occurs in every neighborhood in every town.

Do your adolescent's friends experiment with drugs or alcohol? Studies have shown that teens choose friends with similar beliefs and attitudes. Thus, if her friends use drugs or alcohol, the chances are that she does, too.

From the time they are young, children today are taught the dangers of drugs and alcohol. Drug and alcohol abuse awareness is a part of the curricula in most schools. Many parents reinforce that message at home. Yet teens (and many adults) continue to experiment despite the risks.

Teens say that there are many reasons why they use drugs. Peer pressure is a common one. Your teen may be at a party when someone begins passing around a marijuana joint. The first impulse may be to decline, but then everyone is taking a puff and what teen doesn't want to be part of the gang? Many teens desperately need the emotional support of friends, the sense that they belong and are accepted by a group of peers. In some circles to pass on a marijuana joint is tantamount to rejecting the group. Moreover, the use of drugs is often part of a social ritual. Everyone sits around smoking marijuana and talking, reinforcing the sense of camaraderie and shared experience.

Other reasons that teens give for taking drugs or drinking include simply for the fun of it, to escape reality, to improve creativity, because they like themselves better when they're high, as a way to prove that they are grown-up, and because substance abuse is condoned in their family.

What should you do if you suspect your child is using drugs or alcohol? Although it may be difficult, try to avoid losing your cool. You'll get farther if you try not to be accusatory as you question your teen to identify the drug or drugs being consumed, the frequency of use, and the source. If you determine that experimentation has been limited to a few times but the teen feels little need to continue, avoid emphasizing guilt.

Instead, reinforce the decision to abandon the behavior.

On the other hand, you may learn that getting high has become a common and much-desired pleasure for the teen. Then it is up to you to decide the limits of your tolerance. Some advise parents to make it clear that they will not tolerate their teen using drugs or alcohol no matter how infrequently. Some experts suggest a contract that stipulates that the teen agrees not to drink or do drugs.

Preventing your teen from using drugs and alcohol is easier than curing addiction. Here are some ways to help keep your teen from becoming a substance abuser.

- Be a good role model. Parents who come home intoxicated are giving their teens license to do the same.
- Teach your children about drugs.
- Help your adolescent recognize the power of peer pressure, and teach her that strong people follow their own values.
- Set clear limits for behavior and establish consequence if rules are broken. A major infraction of the agreed-upon rules should require appropriate consequences. For instance, if your teen takes the car without your permission, taking away the teen's driving privileges for two weeks sends a message and helps teach that the rules aren't meant to be broken.
- Help keep your teen busy. Sports are great tension releasers and also promote healthy camaraderie. Community service, music, art, clubs, all can provide challenges that, when met, bolster self-esteem. Moreover, they keep the teen from getting bored and encourage friendships with other teens with similar interests.

(See also *Substance Abuse Disorders,* page 279.)

Running Away

When most people think about teenage runaways, they tend to envision a disturbed teen with serious emotional problems. The fact is that most runaways don't fit into that category. The majority who leave voluntarily are seeking a solution to a problem. Rather than stay home and try to work things out, many simply bolt when the situation seems hopeless.

What would cause a teen to leave home for the uncertainty and risks posed by life on the streets? At least one-third of runaway teens don't make that choice: They are thrown out by their parents or guardians. The reason may be as seemingly insignificant as breaking a household rule or a major infraction such as a pregnancy. A sizable number of teens who leave home are literally running for their lives. These are adolescents who live in homes where they are being sexually or physically abused. For them, life on the streets, for all its danger, may be safer than staying home.

Dysfunctional families, school-related problems, and harsh demands or restrictions imposed by parents are all reasons that alone or in combination can cause a teen to run

RUNAWAY PREVENTION

Here are some runaway prevention tips from the North America Missing Children's Association:

- **Pay attention.**

  When your teen talks, listen. Don't think you can simply nod your head in the right places and continue watching television. Your teen will know the difference.
- **Hear her out and follow up.**
- **Be respectful.**

  Acknowledge and support your adolescent's need to grow up.
- **Understand.**

  Try to see things as she does and to sympathize with the struggle she's going through. Remember what your own adolescence was like.
- **Don't lecture.**

  Answer her questions with clear information, but avoid lecturing.
- **Discuss feelings.**

  Set the tone by telling her your own feelings. Encourage her to talk about hers. Show her through your behavior that intense feelings can be managed. Help her deal with hers.
- **Create responsibility.**

  Don't order, but instead give her choices, and help her to understand that there are consequences to the choices she makes.
- **Praise.**

  Describe both her positive and negative behavior and how it affects others. Be specific, and praise her good behavior at least as often, if not more so, than the behavior that you find objectionable.
- **Stop hassling.**

  No one likes to be grilled for information. Asking her too many questions will make her shut down. Give her the opportunity to volunteer without probing too much.

> ■ **Don't always give the answers.**
> You will not always be available to solve your teen's problems, so let her get used to doing her own problem-solving. She must learn to take responsibility for her own life.
>
> ■ **Use teamwork.**
> Work with your teen to define the problems in your household and to explore mutually satisfying solutions.
>
> ■ **Love.**
> Don't assume that she knows you love her. Tell her often. Make sure she understands that your love is secure no matter what happens.

from home, according to the National Network of Runaway and Youth Services. But by far the most common reason is poor communication between the teen and her parents.

An estimated 50 percent of teens who run away complain that they are unable to communicate with their parents. A common approach used in many of these households is one where the parents set rigid rules that they expect the teen to follow without question. The teenager sees these rules and restrictions as unfair, yet the lack of communication doesn't allow for open discussion. Oftentimes mixed messages are being sent. The teen may try to interpret what her parents need from her, but invariably, because of the lack of communication, she will fail. Many of these teens eventually give up trying and run.

Typically, a teen decides to run away after a problem has simmered for months or longer. Initially, a teen who is having family problems may make an attempt to rectify the situation. She may, for example, change her behavior if she perceives that that is the cause of the problem. If she thinks her parents are highly stressed, she may take on more duties around the house in an attempt to improve family life. When it appears that her efforts are fruitless, she then decides to get out rather than make further attempts to solve the problem. Whenever a child disappears from her home, however, let the police know. Take it seriously. Do not say, *You are free to get out if you don't do as I say.* That invites runaway behavior.

There are two types of runaways: those who run with the intention of leaving forever and casual runaways—teens who, in response to a family fight or what they regard as overly strict rules, take off for a few days, knowing they will return when the air clears. A casual runaway can come from even a close-knit family with good communication between parents and child. Ninety percent of these teens return home within a few days.

There are usually warning signs before a teen leaves home. Unfortunately, parents often miss them. Yet no family—not even loving, nurturing ones—are immune to the problems that can precipitate a teen's need to run away.

Thinking About the Future

When she was little she wanted to be a ballerina when she grew up. Soon, though, the allure of wearing a pink tutu wore thin and she decided to dedicate herself to the care of animals. Now, many years later, having weighed and later rejected the merits of a handful of careers, she is nearing graduation and scared to death. What does she want to do with her life? She hasn't a clue.

Although it may be tempting to blame such uncertainty on poor career counseling, your teen does not lack for company. There will always be a few individuals who know with absolute conviction from early childhood that they want to build bridges, heal people, or write poetry. But for the majority of teens, the answers require a more thorough search. Even a teen who aims to be a history teacher, for example, may enter college, take an anthropology course only because it's required, and be so thoroughly captivated that history is quickly superseded by anthropology.

As a parent, you can help your teen by not letting your own expectations get in the way of the adolescent's search for a career identity. Don't assume that a student with a gift for math should choose a career in mathematics. Perhaps the teen's passion is really for counseling troubled children rather than computing logarithms. Just because a teen's grades have never been better than average, don't assume that a goal of being a pharmacist is

beyond reach. High schools are full of underachievers who later buckle down, narrow their sights on a goal, and succeed.

To help yourself develop a realistic idea of your teen's capabilities and as an exercise to make the youngster think about the future, encourage the adolescent to list personal strengths and weaknesses. You may also want to check school records. Sometimes teacher comments are more revealing than a grade point average. Talking to school personnel also is a way to really find out more about your teen's capabilities. Teachers and counselors have relationships with hundreds of other teens and may be able to give you valuable insights. School guidance counselors have access to interest and skills inventories that might suggest possible careers.

Finally, whether she's going to college or entering the workforce, remember career choices are reversible. Countless confused college freshmen have entered with the idea of finding out about themselves in the process of becoming educated people. Sometimes it takes several false starts, but most do connect with something they like and careers are born. Likewise, an entry-level job in the workforce may, after some experience, lead to a better job or to additional training or education that would ensure a better job.

While your teen is grappling with the frightening prospect of deciding what to do, don't be surprised if it causes anxiety in your household. These are traumatic times for both parent and teen. Watching a child go away to college or move into an apartment may mean some sleepless nights for you, worrying whether you've adequately prepared your child to make countless choices responsibly and independently. For the teen, the idea of leaving home also is riddled with anxiety. On one hand, the adolescent wants to fly solo; on the other, the idea of being totally responsible for oneself can be frightening.

About the only thing you can do is reassure your teen that you will always be there if you're needed. If the new job is located in your area, you may want to extend an invitation to live at home. Some teens assume that once they are out of high school, they're expected to move out. Asking the teen to stay may ease everyone's anxiety. At the same time, new rules and expectations will need to be developed. These may involve paying rent, fewer rules, and other adjustments so that the youngster doesn't feel like life after graduation is just a continuation of high school.

5

The Family Redefined

■ ■ ■

Family means different things to different people. All of us have our own associations with the word, colored by childhood experience, but most of us would agree that, in one way or another, our families shaped who we are.

Our family helps teach us how to be human. From our earliest bond with mother and father as newborns through the day we leave home, the family is the workshop in which we learn how to communicate our needs and to form reciprocal attachments.

Through language, spoken and unspoken, we learn to understand others—to establish rapport, empathy, and compassion; to listen for multiple meanings; to develop a sense of irony and humor. We also learn both to express and to control powerful emotions. These skills, so essential to getting along with other people and building meaningful relationships, come into full play during adolescence, as the teenager begins the work of separating from parents and establishing an independent identity and place in the world.

Like many parents, you might find yourself wondering just how important your family is to your adolescent, who has become considerably less interested in spending time with you than with peers. When at home, your teenager may be closeted away in his room. He's suddenly more critical of you, less likely to accept what you say at face value and more likely to question your rules. One moment the teen loudly proclaims the right to independent decisions; the next you may be presented with a minor problem that the youngster seems incapable of handling independently. This vacillation between dependence and independence recurs, between bold steps into the outside world and retreat to the safety and security of home. Your authority and control diminish as the teen gets older, and the boundaries you established during childhood must now be internalized so that the youngster can ultimately control and assume responsibility for his own behavior.

This process is a gradual one, however. Adolescents do not have the maturity of judgment or experience to run their own lives until they approach the end of their teens, or even later. As a youngster becomes increasingly mobile and independent, you may sometimes feel superfluous. Keep in mind that many teens go through a stage of rejecting their parents' lifestyles and beliefs, because being different from their parents is the first, most obvious way to establish who they are not, if not necessarily who they are. But they still need your love and approval. If you can avoid overreacting and tolerate what you can—but also set limits on what you cannot, such as swearing or smoking in the house—you should all cope somewhat more easily.

Other shifts may be necessary as well. Cultivate your adolescent's intellectual growth and independence. Encourage dialogue and communication. Be open to discussing ideas, some of which may be quite radical to you. Ask questions, try respecting views expressed that are unlike your own, and resist jumping in with your own facts and conclusions. Encourage your adolescent to take on more responsibility around the house, including some of the things you would normally do yourself, such as grocery shopping and cooking. Support new friendships, and open your home to teenage friends, even those whose haircuts and torn jeans make you nervous. (See *Diversity of Friends,* page 150.) Help broaden your teen's horizons, perhaps by suggesting community involvement or by taking advantage of a foreign exchange program. Such strategies may help counteract the self-absorption you've noticed in your adolescent. Above all, let your teen make decisions for himself as long as he is prepared to accept the consequences.

The challenge with parenting an adolescent is to be able to let go. This is difficult for many parents, who may genuinely want to protect their child. But if the goal is to send him into the world as a responsible, self-sufficient adult, hanging on only delays and often jeopardizes what should be a positive, joyful event. The family that has nurtured and unconditionally loved the child must support the youngster's growth toward individuality and full selfhood, confident that the teen is mature enough to meet life's challenges.

Family Rituals

The routines and rituals that mark a family's day, week, and year serve not only to organize family life but also to reinforce the emotional bonds that tie members together. They range from the mechanical weekday morning routine, when children prepare for school and Mom and Dad get ready for work, to the more complex and meaningful rituals of religious worship.

In many families, taking leave and coming together are marked by small rituals—the good-bye kiss, the welcome-home hug, the chat over an afternoon snack about the teenager's day. While some adolescents make a great show of shunning such displays of affection, they would feel neglected and unloved without them.

The evening meal, however simple, is an important ritual, because often it is the only time of day when the family can sit down together to share not only a meal but their abiding interest and concern for each other. A relaxed and convivial dinner is an important daily affirmation of parents' love . Over the years it also teaches your child the manners and social graces that will be critical to acceptance by other people outside the family. With your teen's busy schedule, you'll be lucky to collect everyone for dinner every night, but aim for several nights a week. Sunday breakfast or brunch is a great opportunity for a special, more elaborate meal that many children—even adolescents—look forward to. Sunday dinner can be a special event, too, especially if extended family or friends are invited.

Don't invite television to be a guest at the table no matter how loudly your children protest. Engage your teen in dinnertime conversation instead. Find topics that interest him, and keep it a dialogue, not a lecture. Many parents complain that their teenagers can barely carry on a coherent conversation; it may be that they simply do not get enough practice.

Involve your teen in before- and after-dinner chores. Helping with preparation and clean-up emphasizes the importance of family mealtime and everyone's role in it. Many teens enjoy cooking and should be encouraged to develop their own specialties, be they spaghetti or duck à l'orange, and to cook for the family once or twice a week. Youngsters who come to the table at the last minute, wolf down their food, and jump up to go back to their rooms or call their friends seldom have much interest in exchanging information and ideas with the rest of the family.

After-dinner activities can include games, playing musical instruments, singing, or projects. Even if television is the activity of choice, that, too, can be a family ritual: The family learns each other's favorite shows; the members negotiate what each gets to watch; they laugh together, and, in general, share the time rather than going off in solitary fashion to watch their own televisions.

The family vacation is another kind of ritual. It is eagerly anticipated by young children, but as they get older they often become reluctant to go along. Time with peers seems to be more important now than time with family. It's difficult to know how to handle this situation; is leaving your sixteen-year-old at home preferable to dragging him around for two weeks, pouting and complaining? You may have to compromise if you want to keep the annual vacation a true family event—let him bring a friend along, or perhaps go to New York City rather than the coast of Maine.

Religious beliefs and rituals are central to the lives of many families. Church attendance, other spiritual practices, and the celebration of religious holidays and festivals all enhance the moral guidance you yourself provide every day. They also strengthen a youngster's sense of belonging to a historical tradition as well as to a living community of fellow worshipers.

In some families, adolescents reject their parents' religion, which can lead to bitter and fruitless battles of wills. Keep in mind that in the process of separating from you and finding an independent identity, your adolescent will question the beliefs and practices that you take for granted. The teen may explore other religions or follow an agnostic path for a while. It is probably wise to respect your teen's need to search for a spiritual home, barring dangerous involvement in a cult. As often happens, the youngster may later return to the religion encountered during childhood, his faith strengthened by his peregrinations. In any case, the values and principles taught during childhood will be valuable later, regardless of the belief system ultimately adopted.

Separation and Divorce

Divorce has become a common feature of American life. The rate of divorce in the U.S.—now at about 50 percent of all marriages—is one of the highest in the world. While it may be true that the stigma of divorce has been erased, the breakup of the family is not a normal event for the children involved. It is one thing to know other kids who've experienced divorce and quite another to have it hit one's own home. Children want their parents to stay together. Divorce means loss and abandonment, pain, and grief.

In a few cases divorce is the only tolerable alternative to a home environment that is abusive, violent, and harmful to the child. In other cases, where the parents' relationship is strained but not violent, where daily discourse is marked by argument, distrust, and tension, professional counseling may serve to teach both spouses how to communicate, express needs and feelings, and resolve conflicts. Especially if there are children involved, parents should make every effort to save their marriage. Working through a crisis ultimately strengthens the marital bond, renews commitment to the family, and serves as a valuable lesson for adolescents in interpersonal relationships. The children, too, learn that conflicts can be resolved.

If, with or without professional help or other attempts to shore up a failing marriage, a couple decides to separate, they must keep in mind that their children need them more than ever. When both parents strive to keep disruption to a minimum and their own dealings amicable and respectful, the children stand a much better chance of coming through emotionally intact. But if divorcing parents are unable to rise above their own anger and bitterness and see to their children's needs, the long-term consequences can be wrenching. For divorce usually brings with it a host of upheavals: the loss of the everyday relationship with one parent, generally the father; a sharp decline in family income, which may require moving to a new neighborhood and a new school; and a pervasive sense of unease and insecurity.

Many people assume that young children are more traumatized than adolescents by divorce, but according to the research this is not always the case. Some teens are so self-absorbed they do not realize anything is amiss until the separation is announced. But many more are surprisingly perceptive and miss very little. Either way, divorce is a blow to their world, and they respond in a number of ways. Most feel deep sadness and loss. They may be angry at one or both parents, and often align with one against the other. Their schoolwork suffers, and behavior problems are common. In junior high, when the opinion of their peers is so important, they may feel ashamed and isolated, even if some of their friends have gone through the same experience. Their self-esteem may plummet. Adolescent boys seem to suffer particularly keenly from the absence of fathers, their primary role models in the transition to adulthood. As teenagers and adults, children of divorce often have trouble with their own relationships and may continue to experience problems of self-esteem into adulthood.

■ HOW TO RESPOND

If you and your spouse have decided to separate—and there is absolutely no chance of reconciliation—don't wait until the last minute to tell your children. You're turning their world upside down as it is; why compound it by, for instance, announcing to them when they come home from school one day that their father has moved out and isn't coming back. Instead, give them time to absorb the news, to ask questions, and to express their feelings while they have both parents at home.

Even if your marriage has come to a painful, sudden, or unexpected end, you and your spouse should talk to the children together if at all possible. A parent who must face his or her teen alone bears the brunt of their disbelief, anger, and despair. If both parents can tackle this painful task together, the children may be less likely to take sides. It may also be easier for them to understand and accept that a parent is leaving the marriage, not the children. If your spouse has simply walked away, appeal to him or her to join you in talking with the children. Both of you must do your best to keep bitterness and recriminations out of the discussions with the children: This is about them, not you.

Agree on an explanation beforehand. Keep it simple, straightforward, and honest. You might say, for instance, that your fighting has been making everyone unhappy, that you've tried to work things out but haven't succeeded, and that separation seems to be the only alternative to a tense and unhappy household. Assure them that the decision is between the two of you and has nothing to do with anything they've done.

Acknowledge that the divorce will be painful and sad for everyone, but affirm that you both love the children and will both always be their parents. Be specific about the logistics of the new arrangement—where Mom and Dad will be living now, where the kids will be living, how often they will get to see the other parent, what else will change, and, most importantly, what will not. In other words, present the bad news honestly and then leaven it with the assurance that although Mom and Dad are splitting up, neither one will ever leave the kids or stop loving them.

No matter how positively you've presented the news, your teen will likely need to talk about it repeatedly in the weeks and months to come. You will have your own emotions to deal with, as well as the logistics of the change, but be available to your kids, particularly if they seem angry, withdrawn, or depressed. Encourage them to express their feelings, however hurtful these are to you, and respect their rights to those feelings. But gently correct any misconceptions they might harbor about you or your spouse, especially those that have to do with abandonment and losing the other parent's love.

Perhaps the single most important thing each spouse can do to ease the devastation of divorce is to encourage an ongoing relationship between the child and the other parent. Try to complete the legal procedures as quickly as possible—a prolonged custody battle is painful and demoralizing for a child—and do it amicably. Agree to work together through the coming years as two parents who are both concerned about the well-being of your youngster. If you can, schedule regular conversations, either in person or by telephone, to keep each other apprised of problems, important events, and

milestones. Remember that you may no longer be husband and wife, but you will always be your children's parents.

Whether you choose joint custody or sole custody with visitation for the other parent, once that issue is settled, honor it fully. Don't turn visitation into a bargaining chip. Don't fight in front of your child, or through him. Resist the temptation to pry information out of your teen about your ex-spouse's new life. Don't complain to your youngsters about late alimony or child-support payments. Don't test their loyalty. Your teen is probably confused and ambivalent as it is, and you should support a strong, loving relationship with the other parent. Keep in mind that the driving principle must *always* be the question *What does OUR child need?*

If you're the noncustodial parent, stick to your visitation schedule while allowing your teen some latitude for his social life. Those visits should be a priority in your new life. You should not plan something grand or special for every visit; your teen will probably appreciate just hanging out, talking, fixing meals together, activities that feel natural and normal. For both of you it may feel like getting to know each other all over again.

Resist the urge to turn your adolescent into a confidant. Your concerns and anxieties belong to you, the grown-up, not to him. It is not his place to give you advice or neglect his own needs to take care of yours.

As much as you can, try to keep family life normal, predictable, and routine. That includes maintaining the same household rules and expectations that applied before the divorce. Sometimes parents feel so guilty or are so entangled in their own problems that they let rules slide, but adolescents need the security of structure and boundaries as much as before. Don't let chaos set in. (See also *Family Rituals*, page 103.)

Finally, it's important to recognize that taking care of yourself and your children after divorce is a very tough job. The emotional and economic toll on both parents can be enormous. If you feel overwhelmed or close to burnout, ask for help—from extended family, close friends, clergy, a support group, or a clinician. Often, kids and parents both benefit from support groups aimed specifically at addressing the effects of divorce; many civic and religious organizations offer such workshops at low or no cost. Seeking help is not a sign of weakness or failure; if anything, it signals strength and dedication to your family. With parental commitment and goodwill, children of divorce can come through the experience resilient, independent, and even more empathetic—and prepared to meet the challenges of their lives.

Single-Parent Families

The economic and social changes that have affected the U.S. over the past few decades have transformed the American family. What was once considered the norm—two parents, father employed, mother at home, stable financial picture—is now rather the exception. Half of all marriages end in divorce. Roughly half of all children spend several years in a single-parent household because of divorce, the death of a spouse, mothers who

have never married, and unmarried individuals who adopt children.

According to the statistics, a single-parent family is at greater risk for such negative outcomes as a decline in income, poverty, social isolation, child abuse, and behavioral problems. While the stresses on such families are great, these problems are not inevitable. If the parent can successfully juggle the multiple tasks of caring for her children and taking care of herself—single mothers far outnumber single fathers—her family stands an excellent chance not only of surviving but of thriving.

Even with child support, most single parents are hard pressed to meet their financial obligations. The drop in family income may require moving to a less expensive home or neighborhood, transferring the children from private to public school, giving up vacations, cutting back on consumer purchases, and often much more.

The great majority of single mothers work. Absence from the home carries both benefits and disadvantages. If you are a working mother, you likely feel a sense of competence and accomplishment, because you're paying the bills and keeping your children fed and clothed. This is no small achievement. You might also take satisfaction in the fact that, according to several studies, daughters of working women tend to be stronger and more independent and have a more positive view of women in the workplace.

In contrast, you may feel guilty about not being home with your children. If any of them are preteens, child care may be an issue. But that's only one of the problems facing you as a single parent. After a full day at work you return home to what may feel like your second shift—buying groceries, cooking dinner, cleaning up, doing laundry, and, most importantly, giving time to your children. It's a rare parent indeed who can consistently manage a schedule like this, and if time and financial constraints keep you from pursuing personal interests or friendships, you run the risk of burning out. You suffer from an overload of chores and responsibilities.

If you have gone through a divorce or your spouse has died, your children are experiencing their own grief. Behavioral problems may surface, such as increased aggressiveness or emotional withdrawal. Your children's needs only compound your own struggle to come to terms with your situation. You may respond with guilt and resentment or even rage that they are making it all so much more difficult for you. You may also bitterly resent what your ex-spouse has done to you, making parenting discussions very difficult.

■ How to Respond

In order to adequately meet the demands of the family, it is crucial that you attend to your own needs, too. Don't be afraid to ask for and accept help with housework and care of your youngsters. Enlist the aid of grandparents, aunts and uncles, neighbors, good friends, and baby-sitters. Give yourself time off to do some of the things that give you pleasure. Give your adolescents more responsibility for some of the housework—feeding and walking pets, washing dishes, doing laundry, mopping or vacuuming, cooking simple dinners a few times a week. Teens benefit

from regular chores in any household; in a single-parent one, chores give them a sense of control and mastery in a situation that might otherwise feel ambiguous.

Teens are rarely eager to take on austerity measures and may resent you, the remaining parent, for making them necessary. Explain the realities in a matter-of-fact manner, without giving in to the temptation to blame your ex-partner or paint a more frightening picture than is accurate. Be patient and sympathetic when they protest, but be firm. A teen who wants extra money for clothes and CDs should be encouraged to take on part-time work, if only baby-sitting, and begin to learn about saving, budgeting, and long-term planning. As much as possible try to keep his routine the same as before, however, keeping social and extracurricular activities intact. Assure the child of your continual love and caring.

Keeping to routines established before single-parenthood will also help with difficult behavior that arises afterward. Be understanding. Your children need time to adjust to a painful transition. Do not, in your guilt, allow behavior that would have been unacceptable before. Boys, who in their adolescent years need a strong male role model as they begin to separate from their mothers, may challenge a mother's authority. If you are in this position, you will need to reestablish again and again who the boss is and what the rules are—lovingly, compassionately, and firmly—and ask your ex-spouse to support you. You might also call on adult male relatives to spend time with your son. Family therapy may be in order if your chil-

The Family Redefined ■ 109

dren are having a particularly difficult time adjusting.

Under the best of circumstances, being a good parent is one of the toughest and most rewarding challenges in life. Doing it alone, especially with adolescents, is even harder, but single parents everywhere are proving it can be done even with limited help.

Stepfamilies

With the current high rate of divorce and remarriage in the U.S., the number of children living in stepfamilies, now about 10 percent, is growing. For the adults, remarriage is something that they have looked forward to; mothers in particular can now share the emotional and financial responsibility for the family, and because both partners' emotional needs are being better met, they can be more available for their children.

Children may experience remarriage differently. Even after years of living without the other biological parent, many hold on to the hope that their parents will reconcile. The arrival of a stepparent dashes that hope. In addition, over the years of single parenthood children grow very close to their mother or father, and adolescents often assume a more responsible role in the family hierarchy. A stepparent may be perceived as a threat to these relationships, especially if step-siblings join the family circle as well. Then there's the matter of split loyalty. Some children worry that they are being disloyal to their other parent if they allow themselves to like or show affection to the stepparent. It is important to

recognize that what may be another chance for happiness for you may, for your children, be more closely associated with more loss, conflict, and overwhelming change.

■ HOW TO RESPOND

When your relationship with a new person becomes serious, tell your children about him or her before you introduce them to each other. Answer any questions, allow them to express negative feelings, and assure them that your relationship with them will not be altered by this new attachment. (It's a good idea to tell your ex-spouse, too, so your children don't worry about having to keep it secret.) At the first meeting, don't expect your children to take immediately to your new friend, who must also be prepared for a cautious, even chilly reception. The relationship should be given time to develop naturally.

When you decide to marry, encourage your children to take a role in the wedding. It is an important ritual for all of you, for it signals the beginning of your new life together as a family. If your children feel a part of the process, the family will be off to a better start.

Then comes the hard part: moving in together. If it's economically feasible, consider moving into a home that's new to all of you. In this neutral territory adolescents are less likely to feel possessive about their space or to feel it's being encroached upon by strangers. Allow a period of time for transition and adjustment as family members get used to each other and learn their roles in the new configuration. Introduce your new spouse to your ex-spouse, if possible; a civil, cooperative relationship among parents and stepparents is not only reassuring to the children but also allows them a more open and relaxed relationship with each adult. Encourage regular visits and communication between the children and their natural parent.

Do not expect miracles of your blended family. Younger children may adjust reasonably quickly, but adolescents have stronger opinions, more established routines, and, at least in their own eyes, more to lose in the disruption of their old life. They may aggressively challenge the stepparent or withdraw emotionally. Keep the lines of communication open with your teen; understand that this behavior may be part of his grieving over his losses; help him articulate and work out negative feelings before they become habitual. But do not tolerate disrespect or blatant disobedience, and don't let rules and standards slide. He still needs the security of familiar structure and boundaries.

If you are the stepparent, you face a somewhat different challenge. You're entering a family with its own style, a structure with set routines, rules, rituals, and expectations. If you keep in mind that you are not a substitute but rather an extra parent; if you respect your stepchildren's privacy and particularly their relationships with both their parents; if you do not force a relationship before it has had time to develop naturally; if you support and share in the youngsters' interests; if you do not assert your authority, at least in the beginning, but rather leave the role of primary disciplinarian to your spouse, then you stand a good chance of being accepted. Do not be a doormat, however. Recognize that

there will be acting out of some kind initially, and do not take it personally.

If tension and conflict do not recede over time, or worsen, consider consulting a professional, perhaps for the whole family. Remember that the best foundation for any family is a warm, solid, mutually supportive marriage. Over time—with lots of patience, understanding, and good humor on your part—conflicts will ease as the youngsters grow more comfortable and learn to trust you.

Foster Families

Foster parents provide an essential service in the child protective system, that of caring for children who require a safe, temporary home away from their biological parents. Most foster parents are motivated by love and compassion, and all are faced with the daunting task of caring for children who may have a history of neglect or abuse or who may have been through several foster homes already.

There is no lack of criticism of the foster-care system, but very little of it is directed at the parents themselves. The social-service agencies in charge of foster care bear the brunt of blame for the success or failure of the system, but ultimately, we all are responsible. As many foster parents can attest, social workers are often inexperienced and always overworked, and too little effort goes into avoiding multiple foster-family placements—nine or ten is not uncommon—which can have a damaging impact on a teenager's emotional development. Foster parents are warned not to become attached to a child, and yet it is the consistent, uninterrupted emotional commitment that gives a youngster a sense of security and stability and the capacity to form other emotional bonds later in life.

Adolescent foster children pose a special challenge. In addition to the usual teenage behavior, they are likely to exhibit a host of negative feelings in response to being uprooted from home and family—however dysfunctional—as well as from friends and neighborhood, and set down in a strange new environment with unfamiliar rules and expectations. Grief may manifest itself as sullenness, withdrawal, belligerence, or antisocial behavior.

■ HOW TO RESPOND

If you are new to the foster care system, certain guidelines may be helpful. Keep in mind that while returning the child to his biological parents is the ultimate goal, that will not happen as long as his original home environment is deemed unsafe. Because it is overwhelmingly in the teen's best interest to keep foster placements to a minimum, try to make your home his last stop before the teen's return to biological parents or his adoption, either by you or another family.

When you've gone through foster care training and are offered a placement, be sure first to ask questions about the child to ascertain whether you can manage the youngster. Don't feel guilty about being selective beforehand; rejecting an adolescent once the youngster has come to you is very damaging to an already fragile sense of self. Ask the social worker about the teen's background and why the placement is necessary; whether the youngster has any special problems or needs; how many foster homes have preceded this placement; whether there are siblings; if parents or extended family have visitation rights. Ask as many questions as will help you feel comfortable about your decision.

Some couples are hesitant about taking in a foster child if they have children of their own. It may be difficult and disruptive for your biological children, but one common strategy is to take in only foster children younger than your own children. Your decision to become a foster parent should depend on how strong and stable your family is and how much time you can realistically devote to an extra child with special needs.

Once the child is in your home, keep written records of calls to and from social workers, visits with the child's parents, observations about the adolescent, and anything else that may be useful to social service agencies, the courts, and adoptive parents. Social workers are often overwhelmed and harassed, so try to remember that they're doing the best they can within a system that is slow, flawed, and overburdened. Maintain contact not only with social workers but with the lawyer who represents the teen's case. Be as specific as possible in your discussions—this is where your notes will come in handy—and try not to get into an adversarial position. If your foster child is having a particularly difficult time adjusting to your home, seek help from social services or from a support group.

Some critics have likened foster homes to hotels for transients, but as a foster parent you can provide much more for an adolescent than room and board. An adolescent needs attention, nurturing, structure and predictability, and a sense, however temporary, of belonging. Understand at the outset that this is no easy task, that your patience and commitment will be tested—but that the rewards are immeasurable. Educate yourself about adolescent development and the special problems of children from dysfunctional homes. You will get training when you enter the foster parent program, but any other knowledge you can bring will enhance your relationship with the youngsters who come under your care and guidance.

Gay Parenting

The number of families in the U.S. in which one or both parents are homosexual is rising. Researchers can only guess how many children belong to gay families, but estimates range between 6 million and 14 million. Gay men and women are adopting children, and members of lesbian couples are having babies of their own. Gay celebrities with children have helped propel the issue into the public forum.

In a society in which many people are still uncomfortable with the idea of homosexuality—and more so with homosexual parents—gay couples face suspicion and outright hostility in their quest to redefine the nature of the family.

For many people the main objection to gay families is the notion that such a setting cannot possibly be "healthy" for the youngsters involved. One unspoken assumption often is that the children of gay people grow up to be gay. What research has been done on this question indicates that the children are no more likely than children of heterosexual couples to be homosexual; they perform as well in school and appear to be no more vulnerable to emotional and behavioral problems.

No matter what the makeup of the family, what ultimately counts most in child rearing is not the sexual orientation of the parents but how well they bond with and nurture their children. That doesn't mean, however, that kids don't have a difficult time coming to terms with having two moms or two dads, with being different in a way that may be harshly judged by their peers and some in society.

■ How to Respond

Fitting into the community and enjoying the life of the neighborhood is a valuable component of the family experience. With this in mind many gay couples choose to live in an area of the country that is more open to differences, thereby allowing their children to feel more at home among various ethnic and sexual variations from the mainstream model of the family. Support groups are more readily found in such communities, and they offer support and assistance to gay couples who must continually battle the perceptions of the outside world. On the other hand, many gay parents are discovering that having children brings them closer to other parents—through school and sports activities especially—in more traditional communities.

Most gay parents encourage openness and

honesty with children and teens from the beginning. Attempts to keep the parents' relationship a secret only suggest that it is something to be ashamed of, an attitude that may be hard to correct later. As with a heterosexual marriage, it is not necessary to explain the exact sexual nature of *your* relationship, but be prepared for questions that are sure to arise when the youngster's friends begin teasing.

But there is no getting around the fact that adolescents living with same-sex parents will have to deal with acts of intolerance, ranging from name-calling by classmates to hostility from their friends' parents, at a time when they are struggling with identity issues and need the acceptance of their peers. It is unrealistic to expect that you can protect your teen completely from the prejudices of society, but you can build his self-esteem and therefore his ability to deal with the biases of others. Be a sympathetic listener—particularly important because he may be angry at you for being the reason he is different. Understand the conflicts peculiar to his situation. But do not apologize; if you accept and take joy in who you are, eventually—possibly not until he is an adult—he will, too.

Your child should know that both his parents love and are dedicated to him in the same way other parents love and are dedicated to their children. Ask your extended family to take an active part in your adolescent's life, not only to expand his sense of belonging to a family but also to enable him to develop relationships with adults of the opposite sex from you. This should alleviate somewhat his feeling of isolation, of being different from his peers and therefore "wrong."

Get to know your teen's teachers, and if you feel comfortable "coming out," discuss the difficulties your adolescent may be facing with schoolmates and perhaps teachers as well. School curricula and textbooks in much of the country are becoming more inclusive of alternative lifestyles and families, but teachers and administrators may still need prodding in the direction of openness and tolerance.

The emotionally turbulent years of your child's adolescence may be complicated by your sexual orientation, but you can reasonably expect that as an adult he will be more tolerant than his peers of differences of all kinds. That alone is a valuable legacy. (See also *Homosexuality*, page 163.)

Cultural Differences

The U.S. has always held out to immigrants the promise of political freedom and economic opportunity, but it also presents a multitude of social and cultural challenges, particularly to those who come from radically different traditions.

Immigrants are caught between two worlds. They face enormous pressure to conform to American culture, yet for the most part feel more comfortable surrounded by the familiar trappings of home—language, religious rituals, food, music, sports, clothing. For many adults, assimilation occurs in academic and professional arenas, but home and social life may still revolve around the traditions of their country of origin. For their children, however, the story is usually quite different.

Immigrants face the same problems in raising children that all parents face, compounded by the fact that the long-held values they brought with them are often discordant with those of the dominant culture. American movies and television present family life that is very different from what many immigrants consider acceptable, let alone proper. In families transplanted from patriarchal societies, for instance, fathers may feel threatened as their wives and children gain more mobility and clamor for greater say in their own lives.

Parents experience culture shock more dramatically with their adolescents, for whom peer approval is so important, than with younger children. Often to their parents' dismay, teens strive for conformity in dress—the right sneakers or hairstyle—to overcome looking different. Learning the language, including the latest slang, is another way to blend in. In fact, immigrant children generally learn English more quickly than their parents and then serve as translators, which gives them a level of power that may be discomfiting to their elders. American dating customs—especially sex before marriage—are often a source of friction between parents and teenage girls.

One path to assimilation that some adolescents unwittingly—and unfortunately—follow is in school performance. A good education is one of the strongest components of the American dream. As a rule, foreign-born children perform better academically than native-born children, spending less time watching TV and more doing homework. But the longer they live in the U.S. and the more time they spend among their U.S.-born peers, the lower their grades tend to slide. Long-term goals often become less ambitious over time.

Hence a question to ponder is how and to what extent to assimilate into a society that offers unlimited educational, economic, and professional opportunities but whose popular values might run counter to yours. Guiding your family through the maze may require tempering the beliefs of your native culture with the spirit of American compromise and flexibility. Your teens may eagerly embrace American ways and values, but they are still children and must be guided by you.

■ HOW TO RESPOND

Nurture those aspects of your life that make it meaningful for you. Your religious beliefs and practices are probably prominent among these; as in any family, they offer solace, support, continuity, and stability, as well as a sense of connection to the community. If you worship outside the home, continue to do so with your family; if daily rituals are part of your worship, try to make sure the children honor and participate in them.

If your teenagers reject the family religion, you may have no choice but to allow them to do so in the name of family peace. Keep in mind that many adults return to the faith of their roots, especially when they have families of their own, often with an appreciation made more profound by their exposure to other forms of worship and ways of life.

Although it may be difficult in the beginning, gradually become more involved in the life of your new community. Your children's school activities and other interests are an excellent place to start. If you are not fluent in English, look into ESL (English as a Second Language) courses at local schools, churches, or service agencies such as the Literacy Volunteers of America. But don't give up your native tongue or insist that your children speak English all the time. Fluency in more than one language is a skill you and they can use to advantage in school and many professions.

Make your teens study. Don't allow TV to usurp time better spent doing homework, reading, or practicing language lessons. On the other hand, be careful not to deprive them of the chance to socialize with friends. Adolescents do not function well under constant pressure to achieve and excel; their emotional development often suffers. Emphasize—by example, especially—the value of hard work and goal-directed behavior, but also remember that they need time to relax, pursue nonacademic interests, and develop the peer relationships that will enrich their lives, help them fit in and belong, and ease the transition all adolescents must make into adulthood. The more flexible you are willing to be in this regard, the less likely your teenager will be to rebel and possibly leave the family fold.

If you or other family members are having difficulties adjusting, take advantage of special programs offered by churches and social agencies that address the problems unique to immigrants. In larger urban areas you may find counselors of similar ethnic background who will understand any concerns you may have about your children. Remember that American parents face many of the same issues you do, and that there is no stigma attached to asking for professional help, particularly when there is the risk of family disintegration. Understand that assimilation is a long, complex, and sometimes painful battle, but it can be won without the loss of ethnic pride and identity.

Sibling Rivalry

Conflicts and disputes between children are a common and inevitable feature of family life. Younger adolescents (ages eleven to fifteen) are more likely to squabble with siblings than are older teens, who tend to be more tolerant and less excitable. While parents may find these battles upsetting and exasperating, they do perform a valuable function in the socialization of children. If you allow your children to work out their disputes themselves, they will learn to negotiate, compromise, share, and respect one another's differences; all are skills that will serve them well in the future. Sibling relationships are usually of longer duration than relationships with anyone else, and that bond is tremendously important throughout one's life.

Tension between siblings may be aggravated by tension between the parents—if the latter are fighting, if they separate or get a divorce—or by the entry of a stepparent, usually a stepfather, into the family. On the other hand, in these stressful situations siblings offer one another support, solace, and understanding.

■ HOW TO RESPOND

While it's probably impossible to prevent sibling rivalry, there are certain principles that may keep it at a manageable level. For one thing, sibling conflicts are exacerbated when parents join the fray. Unless someone is in danger of getting hurt, staying out of the fracas is a good idea. Set basic ground rules—like no hitting, playing fair, and so on. The more you get involved in your children's fights, the more often they are likely to fight.

When you find yourself being tugged into a battle, there are ways to deal with it. Step back, tell them you know they're capable of working out the problem, and leave them to handle their own disputes. Learning how to share, negotiate, renegotiate, and settle differences are important life skills that will serve them well in all their interpersonal relationships. More importantly, it is through conflict resolution that they learn to appreciate and feel responsible for each other. If necessary, serve as a neutral mediator. Don't take sides, but rather ask your teens to give their versions of what happened and what caused the problem. Without getting entangled yourself, try to get them to see each other's viewpoint and come to a settlement themselves. If tempers are running hot, call a "time-out" period first.

Make each feel special. Value each of your children for the individuals they are, support their strengths, and respect their differences. Make sure to schedule regular time with your teen as well as younger children to do things you enjoy doing together. Your love and attention will go a long way toward making life with his sibling more bearable.

Latchkey Kids

With more than half of all mothers working outside the home, the phenomenon known as latchkey kids—children coming home from school to an empty house—is becoming commonplace. What is the effect of children being in self-care?

According to one large study, maternal employment by itself does not have a direct effect, positive or negative, on the emotional development of children. Other studies suggest that the children of two working parents tend to be more self-reliant, independent, and successful in school; when single mothers are employed, their families usually benefit not only from the increased income but from the improvement in the mothers' self-esteem and morale. The research is not definitive, and there appears to be a difference between how well boys and girls adjust. Fortunately, as children enter adolescence, spending a few hours alone is a less worrisome proposition.

If your teen must spend some time by himself at home, be sure he knows how to handle unusual or emergency situations. He should have your work number, the phone numbers of neighbors who are likely to be home in the afternoon, and an emergency plan that you have rehearsed with him, including calling 911 and how to exit the house in case of fire. Consider whether safety means all the doors should stay locked. He should know how to handle phone calls from strangers and unexpected knocks on the door. If he must baby-sit younger siblings, you might consider enrolling him in a baby-sitting course (offered by many YMCAs and other community agencies) that includes cardiopulmonary resuscitation and other emergency training. But be careful not to give him more responsibility than he can handle.

Discuss your expectations, such as doing homework, helping siblings with their homework, or preparing the salad for dinner. Clarify that homework, not television, comes first, and whether friends are allowed to visit when no adults are at home.

Adolescents often have extracurricular activities that keep them at school, such as clubs and sports, and if they're over sixteen they may also have jobs, their own cars, and their own agendas. If you're depending on your older teen to look after young siblings at home, you may have to compromise by letting him pursue his own interests a couple of times a week and make alternate arrangements for the other children.

Be sure your home is safe before you leave children alone for any length of time. If you have guns, they should be locked away, unloaded, and separate from ammunition (also locked away), and only you should have access to the keys or the combination. Alcohol and drugs of any kind should also be stored in locked cabinets.

Physical or Sexual Abuse

In the view of some experts, child abuse in this country has reached almost epidemic proportions. According to a recent report, more than two million children are subjected to neglect and physical, emotional, or sexual abuse every year. There is no standard definition for what constitutes child abuse—different cultures have different notions of the best way to discipline children—but in any case experts agree that the number of abuse cases reported represents a small percentage of the actual number committed.

Sexual abuse all too often occurs within families. In fact, in roughly two-thirds of cases the abuser is a parent or other family member (and is most often a man, although women abuse, too). Often the abuser already has the youngster's trust, so it is fairly easy to manipulate the teen into some kind of sexual act, either as a spectator or a participant. Then the abuser swears the adolescent to secrecy, threatening fearful consequences if the events are reported to others. Sexual abuse may be subtler, too, involving inappropriate language, reading materials, or touching.

Date rape is also sexual abuse, and your daughter should know how to deal with a boy who insists on sex even after she has refused. If you have a son, make sure he understands that no matter how far the petting has gone, if the girl says no to intercourse she means no, and that's where it should end. (See also *Date Rape,* page 93.)

■ CAUSES AND CONSEQUENCES

Most parents prefer to think of child abuse as something that happens to other people's children. While it is evident that certain kinds of stress make abuse statistically more likely—poverty, job loss, marital problems, alcohol and drug use, extremely young and poorly educated mothers—abuse occurs across all economic lines and in seemingly good homes.

Many people blame the prevalence of violence on TV and in the movies, and while that connection has yet to be fully documented, media violence may contribute to our acceptance of physical aggression toward children. It is worth noting that cultures in which corporal punishment is not sanctioned have much lower rates of child abuse.

Without intervention or therapy, abused children grow up into troubled adults, suffering from any of a variety of symptoms such as low self-esteem, depression, relationship difficulties, extreme aggressiveness or passivity, and substance abuse. Many in turn become abusers of children.

■ Identifying the Signs

Abuse of any kind leaves an indelible mark on its victims. The signs of physical abuse, of course, are readily apparent. Sexual abuse is harder to detect if the child does not report it. Some sexually abused teenagers display overtly sexual behavior around their peers. If you notice your teen's behavior changing dramatically, try to find out why. An adolescent who has been sexually abused may be fearful, withdrawn, sad, or angry; may complain often of stomachaches and other physical ailments, including genital pain or rash; and may be more aggressive and disruptive in school and develop academic difficulties. Sexually abused children are often depressed and are at greater risk for suicide.

■ How to Respond

Even well-adjusted, even-tempered parents occasionally experience so much stress that they find themselves screaming at their youngsters or threatening punishments they would never dream of carrying out. But if you find yourself falling into a pattern of snarling, yelling, shoving, or hitting your child—or, at the other extreme, ignoring or neglecting the youngster—stop and take stock of your emotional state. If the demands of your life are simply more than you can handle, particularly if you have to handle them alone, don't be afraid to ask other adults for help.

Call on relatives, friends, or baby-sitters to give you a break now and then. Try to arrange your schedule so that it is less complicated; stick to priorities and drop the frills, at least for a while. If you or your partner feel a constant rage you cannot always control, do *not* take it out on the kids. Get professional help as soon as possible. If necessary, send the children to stay with relatives until you have cooled down and learned better ways not only to cope with stress and anger but also to handle conflicts with children. Family therapy should be considered.

Wise parents understand that the best way to protect their child against sexual abuse is to build self-esteem from early childhood and teach the child to trust his or her instincts in matters of physical intimacy. Begin these discussions in early childhood, refining and adjusting them as your child gets older. The better prepared and self-confident a youngster, the less likely the teen is to fall prey to an abuser.

If your teenager reports abuse, assure the adolescent that it was not the youngsters' fault—abuse of a young person is never the child's fault. If the child was molested within the preceding twenty-four hours, take the youngster immediately to your doctor or a hospital emergency room. (To preserve evidence, do not let the teen take a shower or change clothes.) After the medical examination, you will likely be directed to a mental health clinician and to the police or local child protective agency. Stay with your child during this process and for several days afterward. The youngster has been through a terrible trauma and will need you to help with the passage through the natural rage, fear, and guilt. (See also *Childhood Trauma and Its Effects*, page 205.)

Some cases of abuse are less dramatic and obvious but can be damaging nonetheless. Be sensitive to reports by your youngster about adults or peers making inappropriate sexual remarks or physical contact that may still constitute sexual abuse. Also remember that even a few words can constitute harassment in the eyes of the law and, equally important, can be intimidating to a young person.

If the abuser was the other parent, he or she should leave the house and not be allowed to return until after a successful course of professional treatment, at the very least. The family, especially the abused child, should also undergo counseling with a professional therapist experienced in treating sexual abuse.

Moving

The typical adolescent will usually balk at the idea of moving, particularly to another part of the country. Moving means leaving a beloved home, an old neighborhood, good friends, and a school in which teachers, fellow students, and routines are reassuringly familiar. Adolescents have a harder time than younger children adjusting to a move because peer relationships assume greater importance at this stage in their development, and interruptions in friendships can cause anxiety and insecurity. (See *Diversity of Friends*, page 150.)

Most teens eventually adjust once they have settled into the new home and the new school, but for others the process results in emotional setbacks. This is especially true when the move is part of a larger crisis such as divorce or the death of a spouse, or if the family moves repeatedly. According to statistics, for each relocation, children are 3 percent less likely to graduate from high school.

■ HOW TO RESPOND

If you can, try to plan a major move around one of your child's academic transitions, when he would have to change schools anyway—between elementary and junior high or junior high and high school, however the school system divides the grades. This way your adolescent will feel less conspicuous and may have an easier time making new friends. If possible avoid moving in the middle of the school year; a shy teen in particular will suffer from feeling left out of cliques and friendships already in place. When a teen is entering the final year of high school, some families allow the adolescent to stay behind and live with another family for the school year.

Because the limbo between leaving old friends and making new ones can be demoralizing for adolescents, try to make the transition less abrupt. Get all the information you can about the part of the country you're moving to and share it with your youngster, using pictures, maps, and brochures (generally available from the local Chamber of Commerce). Point out recreational areas, football stadiums, theaters and concert halls, proximity to theme parks—things that make the new town sound more appealing.

Plan the actual move together. Make it an adventure. After you've arrived and settled in, encourage your teen to keep in touch with old friends by telephone and mail, and perhaps arrange visits back to the old neighborhood. In the new community you might encourage your adolescent to get involved in activities at the YMCA or a church or synagogue, particularly if the school year has not yet begun. Many teens, however, prefer to enter the social arena at their own pace and in their own way.

If you yourself are positive and excited by the prospect of moving and meeting new people—and if you can keep the internal life of the family consistent and stable—your youngster will have an easier time adjusting. The experience may even help strengthen social skills, adaptability, and self-confidence.

Unemployment

Job loss has become a distressingly common event. Few across the economic spectrum are immune to it, and when it strikes, the toll on the family is both emotional and financial.

Unemployment tests the strength and health of a family in a way few other crises do. The loss of income and the resulting belt-tightening are certainly painful; the blow to a parent's identity and self-esteem can be even more devastating. But family bonds can be both preserved and strengthened if job loss can be perceived less as a crisis than as an opportunity.

While teenagers generally have a more sophisticated understanding of unemployment than young children, they are also more likely to take a parent's job loss more personally. Your teen's reaction may strike you as shallow or self-centered—the adolescent may be angry that the budget for clothing purchases is suddenly cut—or it may go much deeper. A teen's self-image may suffer; the youngster's sense of stability may be threatened. The symptoms may be indirect: stomachaches, sleep disturbances, or other physical symptoms; withdrawal or depression; perhaps a drop in academic performance. If the unemployed parent becomes depressed or abusive, the teen may exhibit more severe symptoms. Adolescent children of unemployed parents attempt suicide twice as often as other children.

■ HOW TO RESPOND

Your adolescent should be told when a parent loses his or her job. Because teenagers are aware of the ramifications for the family of prolonged unemployment, they may express concern, if not outrage, about suddenly being poor or having to move, maybe to a less acceptable neighborhood or a smaller house, or having to change schools. Try to understand your teen's perspective, which by definition is limited largely to the teen's own needs and the acceptance and approval of friends. For many adolescents, parental unemployment is a stigma, like divorce, that marks them as different from their peers. If job loss or underemployment translates into less money for clothes or skis or a car, then the struggle to belong becomes more difficult.

To the extent that you can, assure your child that you will keep changes to a minimum, that although everyone in the family will have to make some adjustments in spending and expectations for a while, you will try to avoid major disruptions of family life. Don't give in to guilt and continue to spend money on your teen while you scrimp on basic needs. However the teen might object, remember your adolescent will not learn about dealing with life's problems if sheltered from them.

Anyone in a stressful situation benefits from feeling useful. Many teens have summer jobs or part-time jobs during the school year and are used to paying for their own clothes, CDs, and entertainment. Others may be resistant when asked to contribute in this way to the family finances, even if that means nothing more strenuous than a couple of baby-sitting jobs a week. If your teen is willing to cover his own personal expenses, let him know how much you appreciate his help. This early training in budgeting will come in handy in a few years when he has to live on his own.

The best way to protect your children

from undue anxiety is to remain upbeat yourself. This will probably not be easy, because job loss can shatter an adult's self-image as a competent individual who can provide for his or her family's needs, now and in the future. Keep in mind that you are not alone in this situation; nor do you have to go through it alone. You may feel a sense of loss, betrayal, worthlessness, or powerlessness; it helps to voice these feelings with your spouse or a friend, a pastor or a support group.

If your spouse is unemployed, be prepared to listen and support and point out his or her strengths. Avoid giving too much advice or checking up regularly on the status of the job search. Marriages are often strained by the job loss of one partner, so it is vitally important that both partners maintain mutual support and communication in order to spare the children as much tension as possible.

Above all, keep a sense of perspective. Unemployment is not the end of the world. With humor, flexibility, and a commitment to maintaining the children's safety and security, you can pull through.

A Chronic Illness in the Family

By the time children reach adolescence, most are no longer plagued by the common, minor illnesses of childhood, such as colds, ear infections, and strep throat. Health concerns are more likely to revolve around diet and exercise; too many American teenagers are overweight and sedentary. But about 1 percent of adolescents are afflicted with a chronic illness, such as epilepsy or diabetes; an even higher percentage have asthma. These and other chronic illnesses can hamper physical activity and interfere with regular school attendance.

For parents, the challenges of a chronic illness are several: managing the special care these illnesses often require; dealing with their own feelings of anger, guilt, grief, and powerlessness; and helping an adolescent cope emotionally and live as normal a life as possible. (See also *The Adolescent With Chronic Illness,* page 166.)

If chronic disease has struck you or your spouse, you must deal with your own emotions—anger, guilt, grief, and powerlessness—as well as those of your family. In addition to the physical and financial strain, chronic illness may mean constraints on some of the activities you enjoy with your family. Athletic exertion, even just shooting baskets, may have to be limited; if the condition is more severe, you may not have the energy to help with homework.

Whatever the severity and duration of your illness, it's important to help your adolescent understand and not be frightened by it. Teenagers who've studied biology and health in school will grasp basic medical concepts when clearly explained. Give as much information as they can absorb, and answer all questions truthfully. Be as positive as is realistic, emphasizing your strength and all the measures you're taking to get healthier. But also point out whatever limitations apply and must be respected.

Encourage them to express any fears or concerns. Validate their feelings, correct any misconceptions, and reassure them that Mom or Dad is still the same person who loves them very much.

There are practical considerations for a family with a chronically ill parent. Child care is usually not necessary if adolescents are part of the household. The children themselves can be enlisted to help around the house, although you should not expect your teen to shoulder full responsibility for younger siblings or housework. The important thing is to keep family life as normal as possible, and that includes allowing your adolescent the time and space to pursue his own interests and hang out with friends. Respect his needs, and he may surprise you by being more attentive to yours.

If you must be hospitalized, prepare your teen by fully explaining the reason. Even surgery can be described in a matter-of-fact, benign way, without gory detail. The adolescent should be allowed to visit you in the hospital unless you and the doctor have a compelling reason to believe the experience would be more frightening than reassuring. Children, even adolescents, can conjure up horrific visions if the truth is kept from them, so let your teen see you, touch you, talk to you, and do what little things he can to make you more comfortable, such as read aloud from a book or magazine, comb your hair, or bring you flowers. An adolescent needs this time with you as much as you do.

The healthy parent should try to keep home life routine and orderly, with as little interruption as possible, except for the visits to the hospital. He or she should spend time with the adolescent each day to reinforce a sense of safety and normalcy and to make plans for the time when the other parent recovers and returns home.

Aging Grandparents

The American population is aging. Nearly a quarter of the population will reach the age of sixty-five between 2010 and 2030. What will make this generation of seniors different from their predecessors is their relative good health, thanks to advances in medicine and increased public awareness of the benefits of staying fit.

Adolescents can express especially harsh views about older people. Teen culture tends to be obsessed with surface appearances; therefore a deeply lined face is neither beautiful nor worthy of interest or admiration. Wrinkles are less representative of life lived than of simple unattractiveness. A grandparent's inability to remember a grandson's name is not only upsetting but off-putting. It is the parents' job to impress upon their youngsters that aging is part of the natural process of change that occurs in each person's life and to teach them to discern the gifts that come with age: wisdom, patience, a living connection to the past, and more time to share with grandchildren.

■ HOW TO RESPOND

Encourage your teen to discuss his feelings about grandparents and old age, however unenlightened you might find them. Explain the biases in our society against the elderly, and point out the veneration with which more traditional cultures look upon their older members. You might try what one mother did: She showed her daughter a book of photographs of native Americans taken in the late nineteenth century, including several of women with deeply furrowed faces. Predictably, her daughter wrinkled her own nose in distaste, but she returned to the book again and again and eventually conceded that the faces were "interesting" and that she wondered about the lives those women had led.

Be aware of your own feelings about aging. Kids pick up on their parents' unspoken fears and biases. Just as it's unwise to obsess about being thin around your adolescent daughter, so is it unwise to greet each new gray hair with panic and each new wrinkle with loathing. Avoid saying, *Oh, she looks so old!* when an actress who has been around a while comes on screen. Don't yell, *Hurry up, old man!* at the gentleman driving at a leisurely pace in front of you. Such careless comments only reinforce the stereotype that old is bad, slow, useless, or should be retired or discarded.

Maintain a strong relationship with grandparents. Children lucky enough to have a solid connection to extended family, including grandparents, have a decided advantage in their social and emotional development. Most grandparents are eager to be part of their grandchildren's lives—to tell family stories, create memories together, and pass on traditions. If your teen has been close to his grandparents since early childhood, the biases of adolescence will likely not apply to them. Grandparents can provide a more objective and sympathetic ear for concerns and complaints the youngster may not be

RAISING GRANDCHILDREN

The extended family—grandparents, aunts and uncles, cousins, in-laws—is an important resource for both parents and children. Grandparents routinely pitch in with child care and emotional support and sometimes financial assistance. Occasionally they are called upon to provide much more: the full-time care and responsibility for grandchildren.

Different kinds of events precipitate this disruption in family structure, but they are nearly always traumatic, if not devastating, for the children. Parents may die prematurely because of accident or illness. In communities where AIDS has taken a heavy toll on the adult population, families made up of a grandmother and grandchildren are not unusual. Parents may be unable or unwilling to care for their children because of chronic drug or alcohol abuse or other dangerous lifestyles. Some of these parents are abusive to the point of harming their children.

Grandparents are generally ready to simplify their lives, relax, and enjoy the golden years. A grandmother suddenly forced to take over the role of parent must deal with many emotions—grief, loss, anger, resentment, and perhaps guilt—in addition to coping with some of those same emotions in her grandchildren. The transition is never easy for anyone, and yet because of the blood bond, the reassuring familiarity, the feeling the children have of still belonging to someone, a family remains, and for children, that continuity is of great help in the healing process.

If you are raising grandchildren, don't forget your own needs while you are ministering to theirs. The advice that applies to any parent under stress is relevant to you. Ask for help when you need it, from other family members, your pastor or rabbi, a professional, or support groups. If the children are having trouble in school, make sure their teachers and counselors understand your home situation. Ask for their advice. Give yourself a break whenever you can. Dealing with a typical adolescent's needs and problems—much less those of an adolescent who has experienced trauma and upheaval—is a demanding job.

The loss of his parents can severely impair a teen's cognitive, emotional, and social development. For a better understanding of the various disorders that may arise, as well as guidelines on when and how to find help, please refer to *Emotional Disorders*, page 195, and *Disruptive Behavioral Disorders,* page 220.

able to articulate to you. If you live far from your parents, encourage your child to maintain contact through letters, E-mail, regular phone calls, and video and cassette tapes.

Expose your child to older people in your circle who are alert, healthy, and active. Look into community programs that bring together adolescents and the elderly. Many high schools sponsor concerts by their chamber orchestras and choirs in nursing homes, where they are warmly received. By helping your adolescent build a more positive attitude toward and respect for older people, you are not only strengthening the bond between generations that is so important for both, but you're also striking a blow against ageism.

Death and Dying

Just as many grown-ups are unhappy about the prospect of growing old, many more have difficulty coming to terms with the final stage of the life cycle. For some, the easiest way to deal with death is not to discuss it at all, especially with the children. But by skirting the issue, parents do a disservice to everyone and, on a more philosophical level, may be denying themselves the opportunity to enhance their own appreciation of the richness and preciousness of life.

Sharing beliefs about death usually entails sharing beliefs about the meaning of life. For some adolescents, caught up in exploring who they are and what they believe, the topic is a particularly relevant one. For others, death is something that happens to other people and has no relevance to their lives. Ideally, the subject has been openly discussed in your household since your children were young.

An adolescent faced with bereavement may respond in some of the same ways adults do. In addition to grief, he may feel guilt, anger at the deceased (for drinking and driving, for instance, or not following doctor's orders), anger at being abandoned, or fear because of his own mortality. An adolescent who has lost a parent is at risk for severe depression, reckless behavior, and suicide.

Many adolescents hide their emotions when there has been a death in the family. It may be a case of simple denial or, because they are so sensitive to friends' perceptions, they might feel shame at being different. Or they may feel the need to be strong and stoical, so they can take care of the surviving parent or other family members.

■ HOW TO RESPOND

If your adolescent has suffered a loss—friend, teacher, close relative—make sure you are available to support him through the grieving process. Don't let your teen feel stranded or alone. Even a youngster who appears competent and mature in other areas will need your help. If a grandparent, parent, or sibling has died, you may feel devastated yourself, but grieving together will be of great comfort to both of you. Extended family can help out, too.

Encourage your teen to talk about the deceased, to recall good times and special moments. Allow the adolescent to express feelings, however petty or angry or even bizarre they might strike you. We all grieve in different ways before reaching an acceptance of death and moving on. We pass through a range of natural, normal responses.

Help your teen with the grieving process. Make scrapbooks that help remember the person—the goal here isn't to forget, but to integrate the memories of the deceased person into the life of the present and future. Visits to the grave and other rituals and traditions can help this integration process.

People get back into normal routines at different rates. Perhaps your teen wants to "get back to normal" more quickly than you or other family members. Don't stand in his way—but also encourage acceptance rather than denial of the death. And be on the lookout for symptoms that may indicate your teenager is experiencing more than simple grief—prolonged difficulty in school, behavior problems, extreme withdrawal, risky behavior (substance abuse, reckless driving), and suicide attempts. Don't try to handle these alone. Consult a clinician as soon as possible.

Studies of bereaved families suggest that adolescents are at greatest risk for depression when the surviving parent—more often the mother—is herself depressed or otherwise unable to attend to, or even notice, her children's needs. If the death results in other disruptions in family life such as a decline in income, moving, and less time spent with the surviving parent, the adolescent suffers accordingly. As difficult as it might seem, don't let your own grief overwhelm you to the point that your youngster feels unable to come to you. Sharing grief, as well as comfort and support, will help all of you deal with the immediate loss and build a stronger, closer family.

If a sibling dies, the trauma is sometimes greater even than when a parent dies. The surviving child may have lost his best friend, or he may feel guilty about all the fights and the name-calling. The survivor will need a great deal of consoling, support, and understanding. Grieve together for the lost child, but be careful not to idealize him or her, or your surviving child may wonder whether he will ever be good enough to make up for the loss.

6

School-Related Concerns

■ ■ ■

The profound biological and psychological changes that characterize adolescence are accompanied by equally striking changes in the cognitive process—the way a teen understands, remembers, and considers the world.

Another feature of cognitive development is that adolescents increasingly think for themselves. Many adolescents like to engage in discussions of religion and politics and social problems, and while the ideas your teen expresses may sometimes seem wildly idealistic or off the wall, they represent the development of more complex independent thinking.

Many parents of teenagers grow familiar with the impatience, which sometimes borders on contempt, that their children exhibit for adult opinions. Some teens experience less overt rebellion, and the parents observe their children pass through their adolescence in a relatively calm, consistent fashion. Yet it *is* normal for a teenager to question received wisdom, to seek out inconsistencies, to challenge and probe and wonder. One feature of cognitive development in adolescence is learning to think abstractly.

In junior high and high school, this growing intellectual sophistication is met, ideally, with a curriculum and teaching methods that challenge adolescents to think for themselves, solve problems, see all sides of an issue, and begin to master the habits of self-discipline and organization that will serve them throughout their lives. Perhaps more importantly, during these years they also begin the serious business of becoming adults. They learn who they are—their interests, capabilities, and weaknesses—as they complete the task of separating from parents and entering the greater community on their own.

Overachievement

Most parents would love for their children to make the high honors list every quarter and be the darlings of all their teachers. Some teenagers manage that feat easily because they're intellectually gifted, motivated, and enjoy school. Other teenagers succeed, but at some cost to themselves. Adolescents who work too hard tend to obsess over grades, despair over anything less than an A, and have no social life or time to enjoy activities or hobbies. If your teen works too hard, it should be of concern to you.

■ CAUSES AND CONSEQUENCES

The motivation to do well is inborn in many people (see *Motivation,* page 130), but often pressure is exerted by parents whose dreams and expectations bear little resemblance to their adolescent's own interests and abilities. Some parents want their youngster to excel as they did in the same field or to accomplish what they always wanted to but never did—be a doctor, perhaps, or a great stage actress. The teen may react by doing everything she can to please her parents, regardless of her own desires. This can be damaging to her self-esteem and her relationship with you.

Some overachievers are perfectionists who, even without undue pressure from their parents, are overly critical of themselves, intolerant of mistakes, and afraid to try new things because they fear failure.

■ HOW TO RESPOND

Gifted children and overachievers often have difficulty fitting in with their peers. Some are genuinely self-sufficient on their own; others compensate for their lack of friends by focusing exclusively on schoolwork and academic perfection. Gently encourage your teen to seek out peers of similar ability and interest, perhaps in the chess club or the orchestra. Social development is a critical part of growing up. (See *Diversity of Friends,* page 150.)

A truly exceptional child may be happier in a single-sex school or in any school in which high academic achievement is valued and rewarded. This is especially true with achievement-oriented girls who sometimes feel they must hide their talents to impress or to avoid intimidating boys.

For a youngster satisfied with nothing less

than perfection, set an example by not berating yourself for mistakes or setbacks but instead working steadily at a given task until you accomplish it. Attempt to distinguish *your* ambitions from those of your adolescent. Youngsters need to find paths in life suited to their individual gifts and talents; following an avenue prescribed by a parent may not be the best route to finding a fulfilling and satisfying pursuit. You may expose your adolescent to your own business or professional interests, but be sure that you are *supporting* her in pursuing her own best instincts and that you are not *shoving* her in a direction not of her choosing.

Underachievement

There are many, many teens who, though perfectly capable of excelling in school, still flunk tests, hand in careless work dashed off at the last minute, or don't turn in homework at all. If your child works too little, it should be of concern to you.

■ CAUSES AND CONSEQUENCES

Although the motivation to do well is inborn in many people (see *Motivation,* page 130), parents may have expectations that bear little resemblance to their adolescents' own interests and abilities. Parents naturally want their youngsters to do well or perhaps want them to accomplish what the parents always wanted to but never did. Some teens react by doing everything to please their parents—but others rebel by not trying at all. This response can be damaging to self-esteem and even to the youngster's relationship with you. Attempt to distinguish *your* ambitions from those of your adolescent.

■ HOW TO RESPOND

Some teens with undiagnosed learning disabilities find themselves isolated from their classmates who seem to find learning so much easier. Others with high abilities try to mask their capabilities. If you believe your youngster is an underachiever, talk to her teachers and school counselors. Perhaps together you can seek ways to motivate your youngster.

Each child comes with a unique set of talents and interests, and it's your job to honor those and encourage your adolescent to live up to her full potential. Teachers, guidance counselors, or school psychologists can help assess an underachieving child's abilities and determine what program would be best suited for her. She may be more gifted at music than math; she may have a distaste for long reading assignments but display verve and creativity in art class. She may decide that she wants to be a nurse when your plan for her was medical school. Wherever her interests and aptitudes lead her, get out of the way and cheer her on.

Although intended as a challenge to encourage success, the urge to compare your child to siblings or friends is a tactic that rarely, if ever, works. The feeling of not being as good as cousin Amy can be debilitating to a teen who's already on an emotional seesaw, and she'll resent cousin Amy, too. Don't express disappointment or anger that your teen doesn't do any better. Some schools award grades for "application" or "effort," as distinct from academic accomplishments. As a parent, you should reward diligence, good study habits, careful and thoughtful schoolwork, and best efforts, even when they fail to produce an A or a B.

Learning to accept that we all make mistakes and can, in fact, learn from them is an important lesson, too. As a parent you should step back and let your adolescent struggle to accomplish tasks independently. Explain that like everyone else she is better at some things than others, and encourage your youngster to try new activities and hone new skills.

MOTIVATION

Change is the most universal characteristic of adolescence. While biological changes are the most obvious and emotional changes the hardest to ignore, intellectual changes are taking place, too. Teenagers are more capable of complex, abstract thinking than younger children, of setting goals for themselves. For the first time they perceive the future as something they can, and must, prepare for. The high-school years represent their chance to build the foundation for future achievement, during which they need to buckle down and work, to assume full responsibility for their academic performance.

The bright, articulate, straight-A student may be every parent's dream—but if your teen falls somewhere short of that, she may nevertheless possess qualities that will help her flourish in her chosen pursuit. Along with IQ, motivation is a significant predictor of long-term success.

Research on the dynamics of motivation has yielded some interesting results. Apparently the motivation to make good grades is not strictly tied to intelligence or ability but depends on a mix of psychological factors: persistence, a positive attitude, resilience, and the ability to come up with strategies for learning and achieving. A very bright teen who does not have these qualities may not do as well as a less bright teenager who does.

Adolescents who believe that intelligence is a fixed, predetermined quantity—a measurable, unchanging IQ—tend to see achievement in terms of performance; everything they do confirms either how smart or how dumb they are. So they avoid tasks that might prove difficult to avoid confirming that they're not smart; errors are seen as failure.

In contrast, young people who believe intelligence can be increased by effort take errors and other obstacles in stride as part of the process of learning and persist in their efforts to master new material. They are less afraid of taking risks and therefore able to pursue a broader range of subjects; difficulty in a new field is simply something to work through and not an indicator of low intelligence or ability. This holds true as much in sports as in academics, in learning to play an instrument as in learning Chinese.

Needless to say, a positive attitude is essential not only to succeeding in school but also to life success. The caution and anxiety of a performance-oriented adolescent may hamper her progress long after graduation; the optimism and eagerness of a mastery-oriented individual can more often bring success.

The oft-cited disparity in math and science achievement between adolescent girls and boys is due partly to motivational factors. Some girls who feel stereotyped as nonscientific withdraw from more difficult material, because they are worried about performance and prefer being seen as good students rather than risking a low grade. There are other factors, of course; girls still worry about being perceived as "too smart" or at least smarter than boys, and in the classroom it has been documented that teachers tend to expect more from boys than girls and, accordingly, call on and praise boys more often.

How can teachers and parents help?

From early childhood on, make a point of praising hard work and a job well done. Instead of saying *Boy, you're really smart!* try *Boy, this is a well-written paper!* or *You must really enjoy the cello—you've worked hard on that piece.*

Teach your children that success is born of effort and perseverance. Help them understand that challenges that seem insurmountable are often solvable indeed with time and effort—and the satisfaction of meeting a challenge makes effort worthwhile.

Your child needs to learn that mistakes are part of the process of learning. Small setbacks can be put into perspective—gains are made one step at a time, and sometimes the steps are backwards ones.

Most important, don't let your adolescent sell herself short by saying *I'm just not smart enough.* You need to offer her the reassurance that she *is* smart enough.

SETTING EXPECTATIONS, DEFINING CONSEQUENCES

Some parents have continuing battles with their teenagers over schoolwork, homework, and, ultimately, grades. Repeated arguments over school performance wear down everybody involved; confrontations alone are not likely to be effective in motivating the youngster to improve schoolwork.

A better approach is to set goals in such a way that the teenager understands both the *expectations* and the *consequences* for not meeting those expectations. With a framework in place, constant fighting with the parents may be avoided.

For example: The parents and the teenager can sit down and discuss the youngster's school performance. If they agree that it is reasonable to expect her to earn the grade of B on her report card in each subject, then the teen should also understand that there will be a consequence if grades lower than a B are earned. A possible consequence could be that the teen is not allowed to watch television or to drive a family car until all grades meet the standard. In other words, the consequence is put in place for several weeks. It may be six or eight weeks until the end of the marking period.

Just as important as reaching such an agreement is that the parents follow through with the consequence if the expectations are not met. There is no one magic formula for setting expectations and assigning consequences, because any system of this sort needs to be individualized. It may be that the right expectation for your child is to earn Cs or better; it may be that the best consequence might be no bowling or no Walkman. The consequences should relate to the goal—for example, television might be forbidden in order that more time can be devoted to studying. Your teenager should understand that there is a connection between performance and privileges.

Homework

Whatever your beliefs about homework—a commonly discussed issue is what amount is appropriate—it is clear that homework is of value not only in the job of learning but also as a means to develop good work habits, discipline, and perseverance.

Schools that assign a fair amount of homework generally graduate students who perform better academically. Homework reinforces material learned at school, and being prepared gives your adolescent the self-confidence she needs to absorb new material. Homework requires planning, organizing, time, materials, and independent work. If she needs extra help at home, you are there to provide it. If you cannot, suggest that she ask the teacher for help; some teens are reluctant, but they need to understand that their reticence may result in their falling behind and that most of their teachers would much rather assist a student early on than to have to give her a D on her final exam.

In many schools, students are assigned several hours of homework every day. Unless your adolescent is well organized and disciplined, the work may quickly become burdensome. She may stay up late every night and then be exhausted in school; she may not do homework in certain subjects and skip those classes to avoid the teacher, creating a potential disciplinary problem for both you and the school. She may develop stress-related symptoms or withdraw socially, developing an apathetic attitude. She may simply give up and decide to fail the course.

■ How to Respond

Request a conference with the teacher. Most teachers have an understanding of the time involved in the work assigned, and if your adolescent requires longer to complete her assignments, this should be discussed. Consider your expectations, as well as your youngster's and the teacher's.

You can help your teen by encouraging a daily study routine. An assignment notebook is a must for most adolescents. Your teenager should set aside a time and place just for homework, with proper lighting and the necessary materials readily available. While it might seem obvious to you that a quiet environment is the ideal one for studying, your teen may insist she can only work with a CD blasting in the background. We all have different work styles, and as much as it might go against your instincts, you need to respect hers.

If her grades are unsatisfactory, however, she may not truly know how to work efficiently. Try an experiment: Agree that she will do homework one week with music, one week without. Let the adolescent determine which style is more effective based on such criteria as grades received and time required to complete the work.

Work out a schedule with your teen for chores. If your daughter has too many extracurricular activities crammed into the week, she may need to drop one. And if it's *your* desire that the teen take piano or ballet or tennis lessons, take a look at your own priorities. Your adolescent needs some time not to do homework in order to hang out with friends or to sit around and do nothing at all.

Give what help you can with homework when it's requested, but don't do your child's work for her. Try to give suggestions without undermining the teen. Discussing a project can expand her thinking. Rather than telling her what to do, ask questions and offer suggestions. She must do the work, but if you offer feedback (rather than instructions), that's a different matter than doing the work for the adolescent.

For instance, you can help plan a timetable. You may even critique the work or perhaps do minor editing. Your constructive feedback may help direct the teen's energy and, as an added benefit, may allow for lines of communication between the parent and adolescent. But mete out your assistance with care: If you write any of the paper for her, you're giving her the message that she's incapable of doing it herself or doing it well enough to meet your standards. Ownership—of success and achievement as well as mistakes and failure—should be hers and hers alone. As with all tasks, encourage effort, care, diligence, and pride in the finished product.

Student-Teacher Conflicts

When the chemistry is right, the classroom is like a small community. When the spirit of cooperation flows, the adolescent learns how organizations work, valuable lessons indeed for later life, when school has been superseded by the employer, the company, or the corporation.

In some cases, however, there is a genuine mismatch of personalities that isn't solely a product of adolescent boredom. Such a clash of characters may hamper a student's motivation, self-esteem, and therefore her ability to absorb material and be productive. A teacher who is cold or hostile may color a student's perception of the subject matter—she'll hate history forever or be convinced she will never be good at math.

■ IDENTIFYING THE SIGNS

If your adolescent is having problems with a particular teacher, she may complain that she's being picked on or that the teacher doesn't like her or think she's very smart. She may find ways to get out of that particular class, such as feigning illness to go to the nurse's office; she may refuse to go to school altogether. Her grades in that subject may drop, and you will probably hear from the teacher even before report cards are issued. Sometimes the teen is able to talk explicitly about the conflict; in other instances, her complaints may be less distinct and the problem more difficult to understand.

■ HOW TO RESPOND

Most schools schedule times during the school year for parents and teachers to discuss a student's progress. Go, even if your child is doing well, because teachers need to know that parents are actively involved in their children's education, that they care, that they support the teachers and the school. If your child is having problems generally, it would be useful to hear teachers' insights and questions, and the teachers would benefit from learning of any problems at home or recent stresses (such as divorce or the death of a grandparent) that might shed light on possible changes in behavior, absences, missed homework, or other classroom problems.

If it seems clear that your youngster's difficulties stem from a conflict with a specific teacher, first ask the teenager for her input on the situation. Adolescents can be critical of looks, clothes, and mannerisms and may judge someone—particularly a teacher—harshly and unfairly for the smallest "offense." If her complaints seem to have some merit, ask for a conference with the teacher, a guidance counselor, or the principal. Work within the protocol of the school.

Go with an open mind, prepared to listen to the teacher's viewpoint rather than being defensive or accusatory. Share with the teacher your adolescent's concerns as well as your own ideas, expectations, and an assessment of your teen's strengths and weaknesses. You and the teacher are collaborators, not adversaries, and what's best for your child (and the teacher's student) is the ultimate goal for both of you.

It might help to remind yourself that teachers are human and sometimes make the mistake of stereotyping students or favoring some over others. Then there's the question of simple compatibility. Whatever the problem, they must be made aware of your teen's distress. As long as parents are not antagonistic, teachers are generally receptive to an honest discussion.

Guidance counselors sometimes initiate meetings between parents and teachers, although many prefer to call parents in only as a last resort, because they believe adolescents, with a little help, have the tools to think through their own problems and come up with their own strategies for coping. A good counselor mediates between student and teacher in such a way that neither party feels she has lost anything but that each has a better understanding and respect for the other's position. Talking to an experienced, compassionate guidance counselor can be an illuminating experience for both student and parents. Strategies may be devised whereby the teen is helped to make it through the class, learning from the experience.

In extreme cases, when no resolution of the student-teacher conflict can be reached, the student may have to be transferred to another class with a teacher who is more accommodating to that student's particular learning style. It is important, however, that neither you nor your teen come to regard moving from one situation to another as the best solution to a conflict.

Cheating

Cheating is fairly common among young children—when playing games, for example—because at that age rules and the reasons for them are not well understood. Genuine cheating may occur again in junior high, when differences in intellectual ability and academic performance among children are becoming more obvious. In high school it is even more common as the pressure builds to get good grades, be accepted into a good college, or simply to pass a course.

■ CAUSES AND CONSEQUENCES

Some parents expect their children to get A's and only A's. The pressure, both subtle and overt, may become internalized, and the teen may feel the pressure intensely as college application time approaches. Your adolescent may feel you're pushing too hard, possibly expecting a level of work from her that she cannot produce, and cheating of some kind is the only way she knows to satisfy you. Cheating may seem the easiest solution.

Other teens cheat simply because they are poorly motivated and are unwilling to exert the effort to take notes, read, or study. If your child cheats, it is important to distinguish the motivation—is it in response to parental performance demands or is it laziness?

Another kind of cheating involves the overhelpful parent. Perhaps over the years you've gotten into the habit of "helping" her by actually doing some of her work or projects and allowing her to turn it in as her own—all in the interest of impressing the teacher and getting a higher grade. By any measure, whether it's a collaborative effort between child and parent or the child's alone, cheating or plagiarism (presenting the work of others as one's own) is a risky and unacceptable behavior.

■ HOW TO RESPOND

As with most misconduct, cheating is an opportunity to teach an adolescent a good life lesson. Don't lose your temper, especially if your daughter tells you herself about a cheating incident. If it appears to be an isolated event, done during a test, perhaps, in a moment of panic, calmly help the teen come up with strategies to be better prepared for tests in the future. Taking tests may be a fearful experience, but if a youngster can practice and otherwise prepare better for them, the temptation to cheat will be lessened. Help the teen resolve the incident in her own mind, perhaps by discussing it with the teacher.

If cheating occurred more than once, try to figure out the reason and how much your own expectations may have affected it. Be understanding and supportive, but be firm about the ethical issues. Make sure she understands the consequences and fulfills her responsibilities, but do not be too harsh or impose draconian punishment.

As with so many of the difficult areas of parenting, handling this situation well, without rage or hysteria, may help you head off future problems.

Extracurricular Activities

Extracurricular activities enrich your adolescent's life in many ways. Band and orchestra, drama club, chess club, community work, any number of competitive sports—all can round out your youngster's school experience and present her with valuable opportunities to pursue an interest, learn or hone a skill, or engage in vigorous physical activity.

Such activities also provide your teenager with a chance to interact with peers in a setting that is safe, fun, and less charged with the kind of social tension that some teens are prone to find in other group activities. Competitive sports are valuable in that they teach teamwork, commitment, discipline, perseverance in the face of loss, showing up on time, respect for rules, and other qualities that enhance the athlete's character and emotional well-being. Similar goals can be met through involvement with the band, the debate club, and other activities.

In this country too many youngsters are overweight and sedentary, and in spite of all the campaigns publicizing the long-term benefits of exercise, the numbers are not improving. Most schools are conscientious about making kids move and play, and health classes emphasize the importance of diet and exercise, but many students still go home and sit in front of the TV for hours after school. Involvement in sports or other pursuits that get a teen off the couch and out into the world would clearly be of great benefit.

On the other hand, some adolescents throw themselves into extracurricular activities to the detriment of academics. Varsity sports in particular can encroach on study time and, as a result, drag down grades. If your child is too tired to finish her homework or stays up night after night doing it, it could be because of all those varsity volleyball games. If her teachers start complaining about low test scores and missing homework, it's time to talk to her.

A moderate, balanced schedule of after-school activities is beneficial to most adolescents; the danger lies in packing too much into those hours and ending up with an adolescent who is overextended or whose schoolwork suffers. One benefit of extracurricular activities is that they require the teen to establish priorities.

■ HOW TO RESPOND

Not Enough Activity. Parents of couch potatoes can help by setting an example and being physically active themselves. Sports the whole family can participate in, such as tennis, hiking, volleyball, or bicycling, can help get your child in the habit. Any kind of exertion makes everyone feel good, emotionally

as well as physically; if your teen discovers the satisfactions of exercise early, chances are that she'll make it part of her life.

Be careful not to unduly pressure your teenager, which can often backfire, especially when competitive sports have been excessively encouraged. Fathers in particular can get too involved in their children's athletic lives, becoming more intent on winning than on having fun or learning the finer points of game strategy. If winning becomes the driving goal, the pressure on your athlete may be too great and she may refuse to play at all. If she shows no interest in organized sports, she should know that other activities such as swimming, walking, or biking are just as healthy and just as much fun. Dance and other activities not usually regarded as sport may also meet this goal.

A general note about sports: Be sure your adolescent is in good health before she signs up for any sport, and that she is physically mature enough for it. Your family physician is the best judge of whether she is ready for track and field, for instance, or for a rough contact sport. Injuries may result if her muscles, bones, and other systems are not sufficiently developed.

Too Much Activity. If soccer and band and the school paper are the passions of your teen's life, she will have to learn to juggle her responsibilities in both school and after-school arenas. This is an opportunity for her to develop some good work habits, such as organization, discipline, and more efficient use of study time.

In most schools, students are required to

maintain at least a passing grade in all subjects in order to be eligible to participate in organized school activities. Don't challenge this rule. Band teachers and coaches understand the need for balance and will actively support their musicians' and athletes' efforts to keep up with schoolwork (except in the occasional school system where sports have assumed exaggerated significance). If your teen is truly overextended, ask her to decide which activity she can't live without and cut back on the rest. There's always the summer for catching up on other interests.

Be sure your teenager is getting involved in things that are of interest to her, not things *you* think will look good on a college application. No matter how good a case you might make for the latter, she won't enjoy it if her heart's not in it.

Learning Difficulties

It is estimated that some 10 to 30 percent of youngsters have learning differences of some kind, ranging from fairly mild spelling or concentration problems to more severe disabilities in reading, comprehension, expression, and arithmetic.

Most of these teens exhibit at least average intelligence. One of the criteria for diagnosing developmental disorders or learning disabilities is a large discrepancy between IQ and achievement test scores. Learning disabilities are most often diagnosed when a student's achievements are significantly lower than what is expected based on her assessed intellectual potential.

Most children exhibit adequate motivation and average intelligence, earning A's, Bs, and Cs. When a teen experiences difficulty with a subject (for example, in the transition from basic arithmetic to algebra or geometry), that's probably a normal variation. But learning disabilities are more serious. They can involve any step in learning, from receiving information for processing to processing and expressing it. The problems can be related to reading, sequencing, writing, language, and math skills.

If your maturing child is not doing as well as her teachers expect based on their assessment of her intelligence, try to ascertain the exact nature of her trouble: Is she reading well below grade level? Does she have trouble understanding what she hears or reads, following instructions, paying attention, or focusing on one task at a time? Is she easily excited or distracted, and does she have trouble sitting still? If so, request that she be evaluated by a team of professionals. Two of the most common reasons for a child to have difficulty learning are *dyslexia* and *attention-deficit/hyperactivity disorder.*

Dyslexia. This developmental disorder is generally thought to be a congenital disorder of brain function, manifested in reading, writing, and spelling problems, often with letter reversal. It is hard to identify without diagnostic tests. The child with dyslexia is often of normal intelligence and has no visual or hearing problems. Dyslexia affects more boys than girls, and symptoms begin to appear by about the age of seven. Because reading is so fundamental to learning and

WORKING WITH THE SCHOOL

Your responsibility for your youngster's education doesn't begin and end with making sure your teen arrives at the bus stop on time. You need to establish and maintain contact with the school. Meet with your adolescent's teachers at parent-teacher conferences and open-school nights; seek out other opportunities to establish lines of communication with them. Get involved with your local parent-teacher organization by attending meetings or perhaps volunteering for one of its many committees. Be a booster for the school band or athletic teams.

If your teenager is having problems with school, keeping an open dialog with teachers and school staff becomes even more important, whether the difficulties are performance-related or behavioral. Request an appropriate evaluation; a neuro-psycho-educational evaluation may identify learning disabilities or specific developmental disorders and determine whether your youngster is eligible for added services, ranging from special education consultation, special tutoring, access to the resource room, or other approaches.

Seek to understand how the school addresses such problems. Understand their policies and try to work within the system. Ask the guidance counselor whether other services are available. She may know about various support groups or specific interest advocacy groups that may be helpful to you and your family.

Make sure that you and your youngster know the rules in your local school system. Many school systems are becoming very strict and have policies of "zero tolerance." That means that absolutely no weapons (even small pen knives on key rings are forbidden) and no drugs (even aspirin) are allowed. Very serious consequences, such as suspension for one year, can occur after the first offense. These rules may apply even to official school activities that take place elsewhere, such as athletic events at competing schools or field trips.

---

getting along in the world and the workplace, early diagnosis and therapy are essential.

Attention-Deficit/Hyperactivity Disorder. ADHD is diagnosed in a child with a pattern of symptoms, including inattention, hyperac- tivity, and impulsiveness over a period of at least six months, with demonstrable ill effect on school performance.

Some child experts find such criteria too subjective, especially when applied to young children (one observer's "fidgety" may be

WHAT YOU CAN DO AT HOME

There are a number of ways in which parents can ensure that their teen's home and school life are in productive harmony. Consider these suggestions:

■ Encourage your teenager to talk about school. Don't be dissuaded by one-word answers. Go beyond the routine, open-ended question *How was school today?* Initiate more meaningful, deeper conversations about school and the subjects being studied. *Tell me about your day today.* Show your interest by asking follow-up questions. *How did that test you were studying for go?* Try sharing your own school experiences with your adolescent.

■ Find time regularly to review—together—the work your teenager brings home. Take an active interest in schoolwork. Suggest ways to supplement the work. Drive your youngster to the library or other places that offer complementary learning experiences. Be open to learning new facts or theories from your teenager.

■ Make sure your teenager has adequate space and material to work. Also, help your teen establish priorities and learn how to balance schoolwork with other activities, including sports, television, computer games, and talking on the telephone.

■ Support your teenager's interest in extracurricular activities. Such activities will enhance her natural interests and talents and provide the opportunity for her to cultivate friendships with others who share her interests. Help her learn how to keep these activities from interfering with schoolwork or burdening her with an overly demanding schedule.

■ Help your teenager regard success or good grades as its own reward. Don't link academic accomplishments to a system of bribes of money or material things.

■ Continue to visit the school—even when there's not a problem. Stay in touch with your teenager's teachers, and when necessary, serve as her advocate. Attend open houses and special programs at the school. Keep informed about your teenager's school, its curriculum, and the school system.

■ Being calm at home can help a teenager handle difficulties at school. Make a special effort to maintain a stable, supportive home environment, particularly during times that are more stressful, such as the beginning and end of the school year, during exams, and transitions from elementary school to middle school or on to high school.

■ Make a point of knowing your youngster's friends and the people with whom she is spending time.

Your role in your youngster's education continues beyond the early years, both at school and in the home.

another's "normally active"). In fact, in early surveys, as many as 20 percent of American schoolchildren were thought to be hyperactive; now estimates are much more conservative, at about 3 percent. As with dyslexia, the danger exists of attaching the ADHD label to children who merely lag behind their peers in development, have a learning difficulty, or display other behavioral problems. Again, an evaluation by a team of professionals may be needed. For a more detailed discussion of dyslexia, see page 248, ADHD, see page 225, and other learning disabilities, see *Learning Difficulties,* page 138.

School Refusal, Truancy, and Dropping Out

Every parent is familiar with the occasional stomachache or other symptom that suddenly strikes children on the morning of a test or presentation. This kind of specific complaint is quite different from a more generalized failure to attend school, which in adolescents may take the form of school refusal, truancy, or dropping out.

School Refusal. Although anxiety about school is seen most often in younger children, for whom separation from parents may be difficult, it sometimes affects adolescents entering junior and senior high. Schoolwork is usually more demanding, and in this case a little nervousness is natural. There may also be social demands, and the teen may feel self-conscious. The adolescent may want to retreat from school to home or another environment that is seen as safe and less intimidating. In such cases, the anxiety may develop into *school phobia* or *school refusal* and become so overwhelming that the teen may refuse to go to school altogether. She may also develop psychosomatic symptoms that keep her home day after day. Her anxiety may stem from a number of causes—a fear of doing poorly and not meeting your expectations, poor relationships with peers, or disillusionment with a system that does not satisfy her needs.

Truancy. This term is usually reserved for absences of which the parents are unaware. Adolescents may get on the school bus in the morning but leave the campus for the rest of the day; teens who drive themselves to school have even more mobility. Although many schools have systems for monitoring attendance, many adolescents find that it is not that difficult to be truant.

Most teens who skip school are not doing well academically and may even have learning problems that make the classroom experience frustrating and humiliating. Their truancy may be occasional or extended; in the latter cases, delinquency may also occur.

Dropping Out. In most families, education is held in high esteem, and completion of high school is taken for granted. Most jobs require at the minimum a high-school diploma, and a college degree opens up considerably more opportunities. But an adolescent who has experienced chronic school failure or simply isn't interested in learning, who wants to get a job or get married, or whose home environment does not support academic achievement may turn a deaf ear to all pleas to finish school.

■ How to Respond

School Phobia. This should be dealt with as speedily as possible, because the longer the adolescent is out of school, the harder it is for her to return. Listen to your teen and take her complaints seriously, but remind her that school attendance is compulsory and that what may be a temporary emotional problem may escalate into a legal one. Seek help as soon as possible, and work with teachers and school counselors to identify the problem and work out an acceptable solution.

Truancy. Recurrent truancy is a serious problem, particularly if it is part of a general pattern of school failure or delinquency. It will likely be handled by social services agencies as well as by school personnel and administrators. Depending on the severity of the case, juvenile court may become involved as well. If you don't get your teen back in school and keep her there, the adolescent is at greater risk for a continued escalation of antisocial behavior and the development of a conduct disorder. (See *Conduct Disorders,* page 236.)

Dropping Out. Discuss with your adolescent her reasons for wanting to leave school, the probable consequences of her decision, and her various options, preferably before she stops attending. If it's more money she wants, suggest a part-time job. (But limit working to weekends, because after-school jobs take up time that should be spent on homework or extracurricular activities. When a teen tries to juggle too much, it's generally the schoolwork that suffers.)

Seek the advice of guidance counselors, who may have special insights into your teen's difficulties. Perhaps her education needs to be reorganized. A vocational track may be more appropriate to her needs. But in the end, *respect her decision*. To force her to stay in school beyond the requirement of the law (typically, age sixteen) might only alienate her and cause more serious problems.

Encourage responsibility in other areas. Getting a job, holding onto it, and being successful at it can help develop confidence. Paying rent—even while living at home—can add a real-world perspective to the adolescent's sense of responsibility for making decisions about her life.

Dropping out of school needn't be the end of the world if a strategy for the future can be worked out. For a teenager who's tired of doing badly in school (and probably getting into trouble with teachers and administrators), a job may be more rewarding, a boost to self-esteem. You can help the youngster keep in mind the option of returning to school or of pursuing a graduate equivalency degree. Many successful entrepreneurs in this country left school at sixteen or even earlier and have demonstrated again and again that good business sense, hard work, and motivation can more than make up for a lack of formal education. Vocational school and apprenticeships also offer the chance to learn a useful and satisfying trade.

SCHOOL SUSPENSIONS

If your teenager is suspended from school, try not to react with anger. Begin by listening carefully to the school counselors and administrators, as well as to your youngster. Attempt to understand exactly why suspension is the chosen punishment for your teen's misbehavior.

In most instances, students are suspended for good cause and the best course for their parents is to support the decision made by school personnel. If you accept the appropriateness of the punishment, you can better help your teenager learn something from the experience. This may be the best course even when you disagree with some aspects of the school administrator's position. Many adolescents need to learn that their moms and dads are not always going to be able to rescue them from the consequences of their misbehavior but also take heart from knowing that their parents are their advocates in the school. If you choose to fight vehemently on your youngster's behalf when the punishment in fact suits the misdeeds, you will send the wrong message to your teen.

Don't allow your youngster to regard a suspension as vacation time or an opportunity to catch up on television reruns. The days of suspension should spent in a disciplined fashion—reading, doing school-related work, working, but not just hanging around the house or, worse yet, hanging out at the mall or around town. For some teens, this means direct supervision during the suspension. Teens need to understand the effect their behavior has on others—including the parents who may have to miss work during the suspension.

On the other hand, you may feel strongly that school personnel have seriously misread the situation and are unfairly punishing your youngster. If, after due consideration, you want to appeal your teen's suspension, inquire as to the proper channels, most likely via the school principal or perhaps directly to the board of education. Take your youngster with you—your adolescent has the most to lose from this decision. Gather all the facts you can, including school records, teachers' statements, and psychological assessments. If the student is being punished for an educational or emotional handicap, changes in your teen's educational plan may be indicated, possibly even attending another school.

7

The Adolescent and the Community

■ ■ ■

Our society has become a different place from the one the baby-boom generation remembers from childhood. The stereotype then was mom as June Cleaver, vacuuming in high heels and pearls; today's mom is more likely to borrow her teen's jean jacket. A delinquent used to be a kid who stole a pack of gum on a dare and prayed he wouldn't be caught because the shame would be so great. Kids still steal gum, of course, but some of today's delinquents are more likely to hustle guns for drive-by shootings. If risk takers used to be kids who smoked cigarettes behind their parents' backs, those guilty smokers have been joined by more than a few youngsters who experiment with which drug cocktail will give them the best buzz.

The very idea of community has changed. "Community" used to be the place where we belonged, the place where we were linked not just by location but by our common concern and involvement, a place where everyone knew and cared about the neighbors. Today a community seems to be only the place where we come from, a place where we often don't even know our neighbors, much less have concern for their welfare. A recent poll asked teenagers what they wanted most from life. The overwhelming choice was "happiness." Far down on the list was making "a personal contribution to the community."

The idea of doing things for the greater good or even thinking that matters has become an alien notion to us. But judging by the amount of fear and violence reported in the papers, by the numbers of teens committing suicide, having children, or joining gangs, isolation is not the answer.

If there are any constructive generalizations to be made, one is that what children learn at home will be reflected in their attitudes toward the community. A corollary is that how the community reacts toward its youngsters can have an impact on them for the rest of their lives.

The purpose of this chapter is to understand, anticipate, and deal with behaviors and events that are a consequence of the complex interrelationship between the individual adolescent and his community.

Boundaries

Total obedience and regular punishment were once the standard for what was expected from and what was meted out to teenagers. The approach didn't always work, of course, and in many communities today corporal punishment is no longer condoned because of the potential for negative effects. We also understand that unquestioning obedience can create fearful, submissive teenagers who, to their disadvantage, may grow up to be unquestioning adults.

■ How to Respond

Certainly parents need to set limits for their teenager. Adolescents need structure and rules to guide their behavior. A household would be nothing less than chaotic (and messy) if no one put anything away in the kitchen, if everyone wanted dinner at a different time, and if the family dog was left to fend for itself. But teenagers, like the rest of us, won't respect, much less obey, rules if they seem arbitrary and unfair. So here are some rules about making rules.

BE CLEAR ABOUT WHAT YOU WANT AND WHY. Parents do not always have to explain their actions; on the other hand, "because I said so" isn't a good reason. Your teen should understand that your rules are reasonable, established for a purpose, that there are areas of flexibility and you will, within reason, negotiate. Yet the negotiation shouldn't be endless—some teens will negotiate and argue until they get what they want. The challenge is to negotiate and yet be firm.

IF IT ISN'T IMPORTANT, LET IT GO. Some of your adolescent's irritating behavior will undoubtedly push you to the limits of your tolerance. But in the larger scheme, a teenager's sloppiness, musical tastes, and endless phone use are relatively minor annoyances, so try to be tolerant. If it will help, remember how you were when you were a teenager and the fights you got into with your parents over, say, *your* clothes.

"DO AS I SAY, NOT AS I DO" ISN'T VALID. Hypocrisy and double standards won't work. How could you expect your teenager to observe a rule if you don't observe it yourself? This is not to say that the rules are the same for parents and teenagers, but respect for rules should be equivalent.

MAKE SURE WHAT YOU ASK FOR IS REASONABLE. If you tell your teenager to do something that doesn't match *his* principles—perhaps you disapprove of his friend Joe, but he really likes Joe—you create a real moral dilemma for your adolescent: Does he give up his friendship just because you say so, or does he stay true to himself and his feelings and be regarded as disobedient?

ALLOW FOR NEGOTIATION AND FLEXIBILITY. Give a teenager the opportunity to have some input, as long as it isn't unreasonable. There may be a way to achieve compromise between the parent (who wants some degree of tidiness and order) and the teenager (who may seem to desire total chaos and anarchy in his room) as he seeks to assert his growing independence. Learning to make responsible decisions, and learning about compromise, will be of great help to your teen out in the "real" world. Work out deals: Perhaps his weekly allowance will depend on having his room picked up. If the room meets minimal standards at the designated time—say, at noon on Saturday—the teen gets his allowance (or the car keys or whatever the deal stipulated). It is essential that this deal not produce argument. Both parties need to negotiate, reach understanding, and then honor their agreement.

THE OLDER THE TEENAGER, THE FEWER THE RULES. You have to let go eventually, and trying to maintain control of your teenager not only hinders independence, but also it hinders building judgment and self-confidence.

NOT ALL RULES HAVE EXCEPTIONS. Where health and safety are concerned, rules need to be strictly followed: No bike riding without a helmet, for example. Otherwise, rules should be flexible enough that your teenager isn't automatically looking for a way around them or a way to break them altogether.

Firm, consistent limits established earlier in childhood need to be maintained, and your disciplinary approach should also continue to be based on love and nurturing. At times, conflicts between a parent and teenager arise because the parents' values may not agree with the teen's values. Does that mean the teenager is wrong? Or does it mean the parents are inflexible? As a parent of a teenager, these are important questions for you to review time and time again.

Build on your earlier disciplinary approach; those patterns will evolve but can still be maintained during the teenage years. Gradually, you are enabling your teen to make his own decisions—about his personal possessions and much else in his life. Respect and cooperation are bywords here as your teen assumes decision-making responsibility for himself. That's an intrinsic part of growing up in preparation for leaving the nest.

TEENAGE FADS

Although the known etymology doesn't confirm this, the word *fad* may have its roots in some ancient word meaning "something that adolescents do to drive their parents crazy." It certainly seems that every generation has a new capacity to surprise and even upset their parents when it comes to fads.

Take dancing. Once wild dancing was the jitterbug. Then it was the limbo. Now it's diving into a mosh pit and, if you're lucky, not breaking your nose.

Or consider hair (usually a surefire way to annoy one's parents while proclaiming your difference from them). A couple of generations ago most men had short hair and were clean shaven. Then their flower-powered sons were bearded and long-haired. Now we have adolescents with hair that's spiked, mohawked, dyed green and orange, or shaved off completely.

Or take other forms of expression. During World War II it was considered by some to be manly and patriotic to get a tattoo (of an American flag, say) on an arm. Then hippies, reveling in psychedelia, painted flowers on their bodies, and some guys pierced their ears. Now some of *their* teenagers have taken body adornment to a whole new level by getting multiple tattoos—big ones, literally from head to toe—and piercing not just their earlobes (in as many as twelve places) but also tongues, eyebrows, belly buttons, and nipples.

Weird hair and earrings pose no particular danger, while tongue-piercing can be dangerous. Tattoos, as well, have health risks, and in some jurisdictions it is illegal to tattoo a minor without parental permission.

Rebelliousness may be acceptable (and even healthy) within certain boundaries; but limits may also be required. An ongoing discussion of what's hot and what's not (and what is acceptable and what isn't) is one way to avoid rude surprises.

Remember, too, that the very nature of a fad is that it's transitory—one minute a hip, hot concept flashing brightly across the adolescent universe; the next, just a cold, burned-out ember, leaving only some embarrassing traces behind.

Curfews

As many adolescents reach their middle and late teens, conflicts over curfews become common. In some places local governments are enacting curfew ordinances for teenagers as a "tough" response to increased juvenile delinquency and decreased parental supervision—whether the parents approve of curfews or not. (See *The Community's Role*, below.)

While such ordinances are becoming more widespread, you as the parent should still set the rules. Again, making your teen a responsible partner is the best approach. Especially when driving is involved, a curfew should be established and honored (perhaps eight o'clock on school nights, midnight on weekends).

Why draw the line at curfews? Because parents usually don't know what happens when their teens are away from home, who they are with, exactly where they're going, and so on. The only way to measure the teen's responsibility is on the basis of his arrival home—*on time*. To abide by the curfew also means that the teen must *plan* his evening. He must take into consideration weather, traffic, and who needs a ride home.

Your teen needs to understand the reciprocal nature of the deal: You are placing your trust in him with the car; in return, he needs to live up to the timeline established for him.

■ HOW TO RESPOND

A Parent's Role. In establishing a curfew, as with any other limit or boundary, be reasonable—establishing rules that makes sense, that the teen can respect, that don't seem arbitrary and unfair. Give the teenager the opportunity to have some input, as long as it isn't unreasonable; wanting to finish a volleyball game, for example, before coming home to set the table is a conflict of interests, not one of disobedience. (See also *Boundaries*, page 146.)

The Community's Role. If juvenile crime is on the rise in your neighborhood, some comprehensive community-based curfew programs might need to be implemented. Many of the cities that have enacted curfews have found that curfews have had a significant impact on both juvenile crime and juvenile victims of crime.

As of the middle of the 1990s, nearly 150 of the 200 largest U.S. cities had curfews in effect for juveniles. Typically, curfews are in effect from 10 P.M. to 6 A.M. and apply to adolescents under sixteen because statistics show that most offenses by juveniles occur between those hours. Though law-enforcement personnel generally view a juvenile curfew as an effective means to combat late-evening crime, it's also intended as a way to protect youth from becoming victims of crime themselves.

Such programs vary, but many approaches incorporate curfew centers or recreation centers and churches to which juveniles who have been picked up by the police for violating curfew are taken. These centers typically are staffed with social service professionals and community volunteers.

Juvenile curfew violators and their families are often referred to social-service providers and counselors, while repeat offenders may be subject to fines or community-service sentences. Recreation and jobs programs as well as antidrug and antigang programs may be fundamental parts of the package, too.

The communities that have enacted curfew ordinances and attendant programs like these have seen a significant reduction in juvenile crime. Denver, Colorado, for example, saw its rate of repeat offenders drop from 56 percent to 7 percent over a period of less than two years after putting their Safe-Nite program into effect.

Diversity of Friends

As children make the transition to adolescence, the focus of their social relationships moves from their parents and family to their peers. The ability to form close, satisfying friendships is a critical element of emotional growth and maturity.

Your adolescent will share with a close friend secrets that he may no longer feel comfortable bringing to you. With such friends, a teen can openly explore feelings about the opposite (or the same) sex, dating, jobs, and friendship. Friends offer each other understanding and acceptance and the chance to be themselves. The intimacy of many adolescent friendships allows teens to explore and define who they are and what their place is in the world. For that reason parents must encourage and support these important relationships.

Close adolescent friendships are beneficial in several ways. They bolster self-esteem, social skills, and a sense of connectedness and belonging. They have academic benefits, too; teens with solid friendships tend to be motivated to do well in school and receive higher grades.

Yet some relationships may be detrimental. When the interactions are with peers who engage in dangerous behavior or who have negative opinions about school, a vulnerable teen may adopt those attitudes in order to be part of the group.

For many parents one of the hardest things to face about adolescence is that they no longer have the same influence over their child's choice of friends as they did when he was younger. By junior high, teens are selecting new friends almost exclusively on the basis of their own criteria—and *not* their parents'.

■ How to Respond

Before you pass judgment on your teen's friends, you should consider one important point. A major task of adolescence is to create a sense of identity, one that is separate from parents and family. Clothing, hairstyles, and music are ways the teenager expresses his individuality, his separation from you. So if, for example, your primary objection to his friends is the way they look, relax. Fads pass, and it's more important that you, and your adolescent, look beyond and beneath attire and hairdos.

"Bad" Friends. If your teen's friends express opinions or display behavior that concerns you, evaluate how serious these are and if they pose a threat to his well-being.

Don't criticize the friends or forbid your child's association with them. Instead, consider inviting them into your home, making them feel welcome, and trying to get to know them. You may be pleasantly surprised by what you discover; you may also realize that if your own child is basically trustworthy he will tend to choose equally trustworthy friends. (According to one study, 98 percent of delinquent children, but only 7 percent of nondelinquents, have delinquent friends.) By accepting his friends, you may defuse tension and invite trust and acceptance. At the very least you'll know what the group is up to while they're hanging out at your house.

If your teen's friends exhibit antisocial or delinquent behaviors, discuss what you know with your child. His good sense may prevail, and he may back out of these relationships himself; if he does not and seems determined to follow a potentially dangerous path, enlist the help of a professional. Talk to other parents with similar concerns and, if necessary, to school counselors and administrators. (See also *Antisocial and Delinquent Behavior*, page 154.) If your adolescent abruptly shifts from spending his time with one group of peers to another, more negative group, it may be a signal of drug use.

No Friends. While most teenagers manage to make friends fairly easily, about one in five does not. For some, solitude is their natural and preferred state; for others, it is a bitter, miserable experience.

There are many possible reasons for friendlessness—extreme shyness, lack of social skills, physical unattractiveness (remember, teenagers can be harsh judges), even being "too smart." Whatever the problem, as you try to help your child, keep in mind that even if popularity in high school seems paramount, it simply isn't that important in the long term.

If your teen is truly miserable, try to figure out with him some strategies for overcoming his difficulty. Is he overcritical of others? Is he a good listener? Can he keep a secret and is he loyal? Does he initiate conversations, particularly with other shy people, or does he hang back and wait to be approached? Does he participate in after-school activities or sports that would bring him in contact with other kids? His honest answers to these questions could establish a good basis on which to build lessons in the art of making friends.

Drinking and Driving

Despite the fact that the legal drinking age in all fifty states is twenty-one, many teenagers get access to alcohol, usually beer but sometimes hard liquor. Far too often they drink and drive.

The combination of an inexperienced teenage driver with alcohol is often lethal—and often not just for the teens themselves but also for those sharing the road with them. Adolescents usually don't realize the extent to which alcohol impairs reflexes and clouds judgment.

If a teen smokes marijuana as well (which by itself can affect his reflexes for at least four to six hours afterward), the combination produces a "multiplier effect," making for extremely hazardous driving.

■ HOW TO RESPOND

A Parent's Role. One of the most important things you can do to ensure that your teen doesn't drink and drive is to set a good example: *Never drink and drive yourself.* If you set a poor example, don't expect your teen to listen when you tell *him* not to get behind the wheel after drinking.

Other ways parents can combat teen drinking and driving are:

- A DEFENSIVE DRIVING COURSE.
  Not only will his taking such a course lower your auto insurance rate, but it may also give him the edge he needs to avoid other drunk drivers.

- EDUCATE YOUR TEEN.
  Make sure your adolescent knows about the consequences of driving drunk or drugged: Accidents, death, loss of license, and increased insurance rates are only a few of the potential consequences of driving while drunk. Impress on him as well that "drinking and driving" and "driving drunk" are the same, and both can result in suspended driver's licenses. Too many adolescents think that as long as they aren't drunk, it's okay to drive—not realizing that their driving skills are impaired by even small amounts of alcohol in their bodies.

- LAY DOWN THE LAW.
  Set up clear rules about speeding and irresponsible driving, and firmly enforce them.

- AVOID OTHER DRINKING DRIVERS.
  Your teen should ride with responsible drivers and *never* ride with someone who has been drinking (including you or the parent of a friend). If your teen needs a ride home but you're not available, have him call a cab, and you'll reimburse him.

- DESIGNATED DRIVERS.
  Encourage teens to get in the habit of choosing a designated driver *before* going to a party. After they get there (or even on the way there) it may be too late. Some parents and teens have arrangements that the parent will come to pick the teen up if the youngster feels uncomfortable about his ride and calls home. The pick-up is done without lecturing. Issues are then discussed the next day, after everyone has slept on them.

- JOIN MADD.
  The national organization Mothers Against Drunk Driving is a clearinghouse for additional information and guidance.

Parents can also network with other parents to ensure teens won't drink in their homes.

The Community's Role. If your school doesn't already have a chapter of SADD (Students Against Driving Drunk), encourage the students to organize one. SADD takes advantage of peer pressure by promoting a positive image of teens who don't drink and drive and has been very effective in getting tougher laws passed.

An important aspect of the SADD program is its *Contract for Life*. The contract is mutually entered into by parents (or guardians) and their adolescents. The document states, in part, the following: "We view this contract as a means of opening the lines of communication about drinking, drug use, and traffic safety to ensure the safety of all parties concerned."

Since this reciprocity acknowledges that drinking and driving is also an adult problem, it may lessen a teen's defensive attitude on the subject. Talking over the *Contract for Life* may also allow you to begin talking about this important issue.

Thrill-Seeking Behaviors

Many teenagers take risks. They need to find out what they are capable of, to test their limits, to try new things. On the flip side, it's natural that as a parent you want to protect your teenager from harm. Unless you keep adolescents under lock and key, it isn't possible to protect them from everything, nor should you try. Only by making mistakes do we learn—and sometimes those mistakes are painful, literally and figuratively.

Now that your teenager is old enough to be involved with the world at large, not just his little world at home, you worry about how he behaves out in the community, about the risks he may be taking when he is out of your sight. You worry about his health and his safety, about drug experiments, unsafe sex, driving too fast, or even in-line skating in traffic. If it's a teenager's biological imperative to take on the new and

unknown, it's the parent's to be concerned about the risks.

■ HOW TO RESPOND

A Parent's Role. If your adolescent sets a physical challenge for himself; if the risks are within reasonable limits; and if your teen has demonstrated that he's prepared for that challenge, then you would do best to step back and let him try. To forbid his attempt is to risk squashing his spunk and create an unnecessary conflict.

The key, however, is *reasonable limits*. If you feel the risk is too great—snowboarding on a difficult slope, say, when your teenager is a novice at the sport or making homemade fireworks—you may need to set limits. Working as a team, parents need to find creative ways to say no, to explain the balance of safety and risk. Discuss the challenge rationally, and give advice on how he can experiment yet still be safe.

Some teenagers are thrill seekers for whom extreme sports, driving too fast, experimenting with drugs, unsafe sex—risky behaviors in general—have great appeal. (Several studies, in fact, suggest that some individuals have naturally diminished levels of brain serotonin—one of the natural chemicals that make us feel good—and that by engaging in risk-taking activities these individuals increased their serotonin concentrations.)

Impulsive risk-taking and sensation-seeking behaviors are also characteristic of persistent delinquents. If your teenager seems to live for danger and impulsiveness, this is a teenager who needs careful observation and who may need professional intervention.

Antisocial and Delinquent Behavior

Serious delinquent behavior is escalating at a shocking rate: In 1994, juveniles accounted for nearly one in five of all violent crime arrests, a 54 percent increase from 1988. In the same period juvenile arrests for weapons law violations increased 62 percent.

In a national sample of sixth through twelfth graders surveyed in 1993, more than one student out of three reported gangs in their school. (See *Gangs,* page 158.) Nearly half knew of other students bringing weapons to school, more than half had witnessed violence in their schools, and one-quarter of students worried about becoming a victim of violence at school.

They worry with good reason. Current statistics show that adolescents twelve to seventeen had up to double the risk of being a victim of a violent crime—murder, rape, robbery, aggravated assault—than adults twice their age. Adolescent homicide victims were most often killed by a friend or an acquaintance, usually with a gun. The death rate among seriously delinquent adolescents is roughly *fifty* times greater than for nondelinquent teens.

Many teenagers break the law at one time or another. Usually their lawbreaking takes a fairly petty form, like sneaking into a movie theater or making prank phone calls. But some teenagers' behavior is objectionable— to their parents, teachers, and their community—*and* self-destructive. In some cases, these behaviors are destructive to others or even criminal.

What causes such antisocial behavior?

And what should you do if your adolescent gets into trouble? An isolated act of vandalism, such as throwing a rock through the window of an abandoned building or spray painting graffiti on a wall, may not lead to a pattern of delinquency. But if a young person repeatedly breaks the law or commits a serious crime, he will be considered a delinquent. Part of the challenge is knowing the difference between isolated events and a developing pattern.

Who Is at Risk? There is a complex interplay of risk and protective factors that result in some adolescents becoming delinquents and others not. There is no simple cause-and-effect explanation, although evidence suggests that delinquent behavior is more likely in an adolescent whose parents have inflicted inconsistent or harsh punishment. Giving youngsters mixed signals of what is right and what is wrong or responding to bad behavior with ruthless discipline are factors that promote delinquent development.

Not surprisingly, another often cited factor in research into delinquent behavior is a family life that is neglectful, intolerant, and unloving. Genetic factors, too, may play a part in development of conduct problems.

Young people labeled rebellious and defiant may be expressing, in the only way they know how, extreme emotional pain. Bad behavior may be a signal that a teen is having a hard time coping with life. If his parents are constantly fighting or are divorcing, or if parents are neglectful, distant, not giving love or attention, or failing to monitor the adolescent's day-to-day activities, a brush with the law may give a teen the attention he has been craving. It will also divert attention away from other family problems that may be weighing on him, such as spousal abuse or parental alcoholism.

Outside influences, too, play a part. Exposure to violence desensitizes children, and television and movies clearly shape an adolescent's behavioral responses. (See *Violence in the Media,* page 156.) In other cases, peer pressure is a factor. Some adolescents will shoplift on a dare by a friend, perhaps being unaware of the moral and legal implications.

Teens who have fallen into a pattern of delinquency are often also doing poorly in school, adding to their already low self-esteem, and are uncommunicative at home. Their risk for suicide is also greater (see *Teenage Suicide,* page 213) as is the likelihood that they'll run away from home (see *Running Away,* page 96).

■ HOW TO RESPOND

A Parent's Role. If your teen exhibits antisocial behavior, getting to the cause is essential; a harsh reaction on your part will only compound the problem. Often antisocial behaviors are secretive, so clearly demonstrating your interest in your adolescent's welfare is important.

Being loving and supportive can be difficult when you're angry over your teen's misdeeds, especially if he's in trouble with the law. Suddenly having a delinquent for a son can wreak havoc on a family; for a family already in crisis it can be devastating. But you must look beyond the conduct itself and try to understand the cause.

Parents should encourage their teens to act responsibly. Making the consequences disappear by denying them or arranging for the police to minimize them tends to reward irresponsible and antisocial behavior. Encouraging responsibility includes admitting the infraction and paying the consequences for the action. (See *Conduct Disorders*, page 236.)

Professional Intervention. A thorough evaluation is appropriate for adolescents who exhibit a pattern of delinquency. An evaluation may be arranged by your teen's physician or a local social service agency. The evaluation by a child and adolescent psychiatrist or other clinician will help develop a comprehensive biological, psychological, and social treatment plan. When there are persistent or serious delinquency problems, the juvenile court will also be involved.

Therapy may be part of the comprehensive treatment and can help in some instances. The therapist must attempt to keep lines of communication open with both the teenager and the parents. In fact, the entire family may benefit from family therapy, because one youngster's problems affect every family member. The therapist's neutrality may also offer you perspective, an important tool that might otherwise be missing. (See *Family Therapy,* page 326.)

Various other therapies may be tried, including individual therapy (see *Individual Psychotherapy,* page 320) and group therapy (*Group Therapy,* page 328). A teen with untreated attention-deficit/hyperactivity disorder or other emotional or behavioral difficulty may need comprehensive treatment (see *Attention-Deficit/Hyperactivity Disorder,* page 225). When these other difficulties are successfully treated, this often results in a decrease in the delinquent behavior.

The Community's Role. According to the Office of Juvenile Justice and Delinquency Prevention (OJJDP) of the U.S. Department of Justice, effective delinquency prevention calls for community action and commitment. Collaborative efforts must be made between parents, schools, social welfare agencies, and the juvenile court system, with communities assessing their delinquency problem in relation to known risk factors and then implementing programs to counteract them.

Young people need to have certain "protective factors" enhanced. Especially important are strengthening resiliency and a positive outlook; fostering positive relationships that promote close bonds; and promoting healthy beliefs and clear standards.

Violence in the Media

Television broadcasters and filmmakers continue to insist that there's no proof linking TV and movie violence to aggressive behavior in teens. But hundreds of studies overwhelmingly argue to the contrary. TV and movies do influence value systems and shape behavior. Given that much TV and movie content today is violent in nature, the effect on adolescents can be profound—even in families with no pattern of violence whatsoever.

The impact of TV and movie violence may be immediately evident, or it may surface years later. The negative influence on vulnerable adolescents is critical—as a result of seeing violence depicted, adolescents can become immune to the pain and suffering of others and the horror of violence. Or they may become more fearful of the world around them.

More worrisome, adolescents may come to imitate the violence they observe, behaving in aggressive or harmful ways toward others. Violence can be seen as a way to solve problems. A teen may come to identify with certain characters, victims, and/or perpetrators.

The effects may not only be cumulative, but also in susceptible teens, watching a single violent TV program or movie can increase aggression. In fact, adolescents who have viewed violent shows, films, or videos are more aggressive for a number of days following the viewing, although already aggressive adolescents are more prone to such influence.

■ HOW TO RESPOND

A Parent's Role. Parents have tremendous power to moderate the influence of the media. That begins with exercising control over what your kids watch.

ESTABLISH SOME GROUND RULES (E.G., NO R-RATED MOVIES). Network with parents of your child's friends to establish the same rules. Talk and set limits. The teen must understand that when a limit is violated, there are consequences. Yet even if the rule is broken, parent and adolescent should continue the discussion—of the movies *and* the rules. Negotiate what the ground rules are to be, especially as the adolescent gets older.

Try to help your teen gain some perspective on the violence seen on television and at the movies. You can have some influence over his perceptions and can exercise considerable control over what he views at home. Try to close the distance between the unreality of actors and real life, helping the adolescent to see the violence, suffering, and danger of the screen more clearly for what it is: dangerous and cruel.

WATCH AT LEAST ONE EPISODE OF A TV PROGRAM. Then at least you'll know about what your teenager is watching, and if you're unhappy with his choice, talking to him about what he sees and feels may help to sharpen his judgment.

DISCUSS A CHARACTER'S AGGRESSIVE/VIOLENT BEHAVIOR WITH YOUR TEENAGER. Point out how that kind of behavior doesn't solve problems and shouldn't be tolerated. Get your teen's input on how the character could have found a nonviolent solution to his problem.

ENCOURAGE VIEWING OF TV SHOWS AND VIDEOS THAT DEMONSTRATE HELPING, CARING, AND COOPERATION. Studies show that just as viewing violence can foster aggression, seeing humane conduct influences kind and considerate behavior. In contrast, go to a movie in which violence occurs but in which the violence is not glorified. Movies about the Holocaust, for example, deliver the message that violence and cruelty are disgusting and horrible.

LIMIT VIEWING HOURS. Since there's a great deal of violence in both adult and youth-oriented programming, just limiting the number of hours your adolescent watches TV or videos can reduce the amount of aggression and violence he sees. Develop rules: For example, the TV goes *off* at a given hour on school nights. Discuss the problem with other parents, too. It is vital that parents get involved and, at selected times, take charge.

Shoplifting

Most teens who admit to shoplifting usually say their action was stupid and irresponsible, and until they were caught—which generally happens to repeat shoplifters—they never thought of it as a serious crime. It was just something they did impulsively, without thinking about the possible repercussions of their actions.

Causes and Consequences. Immediate gratification is one explanation for shoplifting—if a teenager doesn't have the money for something he wants, he simply takes it. But shoplifting can also be a "social" activity: A friend will dare his buddy to pilfer something, or one friend will see another shove something up a sleeve and do the same thing.

Unfortunately, getting away with petty theft can make a teen feel invincible. To an adolescent wondering at his feeling of awkwardness and who desperately wants to be viewed as cool, shoplifting sometimes makes him feel good about himself—for the wrong reason.

■ HOW TO RESPOND

A Parent's Role. If you discover that your teen has shoplifted, make him deal with the consequences of his crime. If he has stolen a CD or a T-shirt, insist that he return it to the store he stole it from—with you accompanying him. Facing the store owner and facing up to his wrongdoing may be a powerful enough lesson to keep such behavior from being repeated. If it seems like a bad idea to return the item in person, the teenager can mail the item or payment anonymously.

Talk to your teen and find out what motivated him to steal. If he stole a CD to give himself an emotional lift, try to figure why. You also need to impress upon him how serious stealing is, and why it is wrong and its consequences. Getting caught shoplifting can mean a police record, and having even a juvenile record could drastically affect his later life options.

Gangs

Because gangs first appeared in economically depressed urban areas, the misconception is that gangs are an inner-city phenomenon. Yet today gangs can be found anywhere, and any teen is a potential gang member.

There is no typical gang member profile, according to the U.S. Department of Justice. They are male and female; they have poor parents and rich parents; they have broken, dysfunctional homes and ideal, loving families; they live in decrepit urban tenements and neat suburban split-levels—in short, gangs are a cross-gender, cross-country, cross-cul-tural problem that occurs in all socioeconomic groups. As of the mid–1990s gangs in upscale communities are skyrocketing. Unlike crowds of social friends from school, gangs tend to have a leadership structure, may have initiation rituals and specific clothes ("colors"), and often identify geographic areas that are regarded as the gang's personal "turf."

A 1996 first-ever nationwide survey of gang activity, which tallied data from all fifty states, found more than 650,000 gang members were part of 25,000 gangs, with gang problems worsening in 48 percent of the communities and improving in only 10 percent. The survey made it all too clear that gangs have spread to virtually every corner of America.

Compared with nongang juvenile offenders, gang members tend to be younger when they first commit crimes, more violent in public, and more likely to use guns.

Teens join gangs for a variety of reasons. The age when most adolescents are attracted to gangs—between twelve and seventeen—is the age at which they're the most emotionally vulnerable, grappling with uncertainty about their identity and where they fit in. Some adolescents are seeking in a gang the unconditional affection and emotional support their families don't provide at home; some need to get a sense of belonging, of being a part of something. Respect can be an issue, too, along with the normal developmental need to feel in control of their lives. Some seek the excitement.

■ HOW TO RESPOND

A Parent's Role. Parents must ensure that their teen receives the loving support he needs so that he doesn't need to go in search of compassion and acceptance elsewhere. Yet even a full and satisfying home life isn't enough—teenagers *do* need healthy relationships with other teens.

Encourage your teen to take part in school sports or other extracurricular activities. Taking a job or pursuing hobbies or other interests can provide your teen with the companionship of his peers. If there are gangs in your neighborhood or your teen's school, talk with your adolescent about what his options are in selecting company and pastimes.

Parents should also encourage other parents, school boards and PTAs, and local law enforcement agencies to devise community strategies either to prevent gangs from emerging and/or to combat existing gangs. Parents can help develop community centers for sports and other social activities. Parent networks in which parents keep in touch with parents of other kids may also increase supervision.

Guns and Adolescents

In the hands of adolescents, firearms can produce tragedy—and gun-related tragedies occur often. Consider that four times as many juveniles were killed with a gun in 1994 as in 1984. Gunshots are the cause of one in four teenage deaths, and more than 70 percent of teenage homicide victims are shot to death. Firearms were used in six out of ten suicides among fifteen- to nineteen-year-olds.

These numbers are explained, in part, by simple access: Evidence shows that the availability of guns is associated with youth suicide risk. (See *Teenage Suicide*, page 213.) More than 100,000 students are thought to carry guns to school, and one in twenty admits to carrying a gun somewhere other than school at least monthly. Some schools have taken strict steps, such as installing metal detectors like those found in airports and establishing mandatory school suspension for those students found carrying guns.

Guns do indeed kill people—more and more of whom are adolescents.

■ HOW TO RESPOND

A Parent's Role. If you have a firearm in your house, you may want to consider getting rid of it. At least make certain that it's kept in a locked cabinet at all times. "Playing" with a gun can have terrible consequences—your teen or another youth could be accidentally shot. A depressed or intoxicated teenager could commit suicide; a "game" of Russian roulette can be deadly. Since most adolescents are able to find even carefully hidden objects—padlock keys included—police recommend that you use a combination lock and avoid using an obvious number for the combination (so no birthday or anniversary dates).

An interest in guns isn't by definition dangerous, as it may take a variety of forms. But a parent needs to understand the teen's motivation regarding his guns. Interests in target-shooting or hunting can be safe hobbies when the teen is given thorough instruction and supervision regarding appropriate procedures and precautions.

On the other hand, a much greater danger is posed by the teen who has a weapon because he feels the need for self-defense or in order to threaten others. In either case, discuss why your teen has a gun. Try to understand the fear that makes the teen feel the need. Guns acquired for such purposes should be confiscated. In many communities, police will dispose of such weapons, no questions asked. The fear must also be dealt with through discussion and problem-solving, perhaps in consultation with local school or police authorities.

Children Having Children

Though parents like to believe that their teenage son or daughter isn't having (or wouldn't think of having) sex, the odds are they're wrong. Though parents like to believe that their daughter won't get pregnant or their son won't get someone else's daughter pregnant, they may be wrong about that, too. (See *Pregnant and a Teen?: The Odds Are Against You,* page 162.)

If, despite sex education and contraception, the unthinkable happens, what do you do?

■ HOW TO RESPOND

A Parent's Role. If your daughter tells you she's pregnant, your first response is likely to be, *You're WHAT?!* followed closely by *What were you thinking?* or *We raised you better than that.*

Even if you don't know but only suspect, try to keep calm. Your daughter has no doubt agonized for weeks about telling you before finally getting up her courage, and she's already scared to death—both for herself and about your reaction. She knows she has to make one of the most difficult decisions of her life—*Have an abortion? Carry the pregnancy to term and keep the baby? Give the baby up for adoption?*—and she needs to be able to decide wisely and carefully. Your job is to help *her* make that choice, which means giving her unwavering love, support, and guidance, but not coercion.

Depending on which side of the abortion issue you come down on, avoid saying things like *You realize that if you have an abortion, you'll be a murderer* or *Don't expect me to take care of your baby for you if you decide to keep it.* Don't make this almost impossibly difficult decision any harder for your daughter.

If your son tells you he has gotten a girl pregnant, try not to let both barrels loose with *How could you be so stupid?* Yes, he may have been irresponsible, but at least he's acknowledging his role in the situation and isn't just walking away from it as many young men do. This event may be as traumatic for your son as it is for the girl, and he will need your love and support. He may also need some legal counsel, since he does have a financial obligation. If he denies allegations of paternity, he may have to resolve the dispute in court.

Whatever you do, don't pressure your son or daughter into an unwanted marriage for the sake of "doing the right thing." Some 75 percent of teenage marriages fail within a couple of years, and some teens are so resentful of being forced into being a family and so ill-equipped to be parents that they take it out on their infant.

The importance of parent-teenager communication is seldom greater than when a family is facing an unwanted teenage pregnancy, and even the strongest family may be tested to its limits.

First Things First. Has your daughter taken a pregnancy test? If she has and the result was positive, have it performed again by a laboratory, which offers complete accuracy. Assuming your daughter is pregnant, help her find out what her options are. If you don't have a pediatrician or family doctor who can help your daughter make an informed decision about what's best for her, Planned Parenthood is an excellent resource, and most communities have an office nearby.

If your daughter chooses to terminate her pregnancy, she needs to do so as quickly as possible. First-trimester abortions (10 to 12 weeks) are medically simple procedures, usually done in a doctor's office, with few complications. Second-trimester procedures (after the thirteenth week) are considerably more complicated and need to be done either in a hospital or a clinic. Most doctors won't perform abortions beyond the second trimester, and some states have made them illegal.

If your daughter decides to carry her baby to term, prenatal care is essential, and your daughter needs to be under the care of a doctor as soon as possible. Because girls are usually in denial about being pregnant for a number of weeks before taking a pregnancy test, they're also denying their developing

fetus the prenatal care required during this important early period. This is the stage where alcohol and drug use can most profoundly affect the developing fetus. For a range of reasons—youth, poverty, or substance abuse—teenagers are more likely to have premature, stillborn, or low-birth-weight babies (who are at risk of severe developmental and emotional problems) or have serious complications themselves during delivery.

If your daughter has made the decision to carry her baby to term, she must then decide whether to raise the baby herself or give the infant up for adoption (although only 4 percent of unmarried teen mothers put their babies up for adoption).

Start by asking her some simple questions. Try not to be confrontational, but lead your daughter to see her situation in a realistic way. Will she be able to manage financially, since with changes in the welfare laws, governmental support will no longer be automatic? Does she realize should she drop out of school, the statistics suggests she'll likely end up with a low-paying job? On a more personal note, does she realize that there will be no more hanging out at the mall or going to parties, because an infant will demand virtually all of her time, nonstop? Will she be able to handle the stress of a colicky baby that cries all night for nights on end? Does she realize that this is for keeps, that the job of parenting will last longer than she has been alive?

Most teenagers and, particularly, young and immature teens don't have the emotional maturity it takes to be a good parent, and

PREGNANT AND A TEEN?
The Odds Are Against You

According to the National Center for Health Statistics, almost one million girls under twenty get pregnant every year, some 29,000 of them under fourteen.

Beyond such fearsome statistics, pregnant and parenting teens and their babies usually face lasting hardships in the form of health risks, academic failure, and poverty. Consider:

- Most teenage mothers drop out of high school (more than 40,000 every year) and never complete their high-school education.

- Most teenage mothers live below the poverty level, earning about half the lifetime income of women who first give birth in their twenties.

- Only about one in five unmarried teenage mothers ever receive support from the teenage fathers.

- Teenage fathers are less than half as likely to complete high school as are their nonparenting peers.

- Teenage mothers are at much higher risk for serious medical complications while giving birth than older women and have a 60 percent higher death rate than women who give birth in their twenties.

- One-third of teenage mothers sixteen and younger have a second child within two years.

As the war on welfare policy in the United States is undergoing a major overhaul, the adversity faced by teens and especially their children is likely to get even worse, as will the impact on the community. As it is, the number of children placed in foster care has increased a staggering 64 percent in only ten years, and the number of homeless single teen mothers has increased fivefold. What will happen to teens and their children when the safety net is weakened or no longer available to them?

To date, efforts to reduce teenage motherhood have had little success. Perhaps faced with ever-increasing numbers of homeless teenage mothers, communities will take a more energetic, creative, and comprehensive stance in combating teenage pregnancy.

according to one recent poll some 91 percent of teens agree. If your daughter is leaning toward adoption, reassure her that she's not rejecting her baby; she's giving the infant a chance for a good life by providing a loving set of parents who are emotionally and financially secure. Having her baby adopted may well be the most loving thing she can do for her baby. Other options may be considered as well—aunts and uncles, grandparents, the mother- (or father-) to-be's own parents may want to care for the child. Help her think creatively about what is the best solution for everyone.

Getting Counseling. Sometimes a teenager gets pregnant not by accident but by design: She believes a baby will give her something to love and be needed by or she thinks it will make her boyfriend commit to her or a pregnancy will force her parents to give her more attention or independence. If this is the case, your daughter needs to have professional help before she can decide about her pregnancy. Even if your daughter's pregnancy was unplanned, a therapist or counselor can help her handle the emotional stress she will undoubtedly be going through.

If your son unintentionally got a girl pregnant, he'll have problems himself—guilt, fear, and anger among them—that a therapist can help him deal with.

In either situation, your teenager will be counting on you to be there to lean on and to listen to his or her other fears and to bolster the teenager's courage. But since your emotional resources might be stretched a bit thin, don't hesitate to seek help for yourself (and the rest of the family) during this difficult time.

Homosexuality

It isn't unusual for adolescents—particularly young adolescents—to find themselves attracted to a friend or a teacher of the same sex. Pleasurable erotic contact with someone of the same sex is almost as common. Typically teens are dismayed by their reactions and wonder *Am I gay?* Such thoughts are usually transient and don't mean the youngster is gay or lesbian, but merely that the teen's sexual orientation is crystallizing.

In contrast, an older teen who has been questioning his sexual orientation for some time may resolve that he's gay, and he is basing it on more than a fleeting attraction. Because of the social stigma, though, few gay teenagers come out of the closet during adolescence; some may stay closeted their whole lives out of fear of reprisals or rejection.

Researchers feel that for many, the development of a homosexual identity goes through several stages, although different people get through the stages at different rates and many don't complete the development until they are in their twenties or thirties.

• STAGE 1: FEELING DIFFERENT.
Having social experiences in the middle teen years that made them feel different from other adolescents, such as a boy's

sharing few interests with other boys or a girl's feeling unfeminine.

- **STAGE 2: IDENTITY CONFUSION.**
Reaching physical maturity and realizing that they are attracted to members of the same sex, causing emotional turmoil and questioning their heterosexuality.

- **STAGE 3: IDENTITY ASSUMPTION.**
Moving from private acknowledgment of sexual preference to admitting it openly, if only to other homosexuals.

- **STAGE 4: IDENTITY INTEGRATION.**
Adopting homosexuality as a way of life, both emotionally and sexually.

■ HOW TO RESPOND

A Parent's Role. If you begin to suspect your teen is gay or he tells you straight out, your first reaction may well be denial (*This is just a phase you're going through*) followed by dismay, disappointment, perhaps shame, anger, repugnance, and guilt (*What did I do wrong to make you turn out this way?*). Knowing that many happy and successful people are homosexual doesn't soften the shock for parents whose dreams for their teenager probably included a traditional marriage and family—or who may themselves harbor negative feelings and stereotypes about homosexuals.

For your teen's sake, try to step back from those feelings. If you only suspect, ask the question. If the answer is yes, recognize the courage it took for him to be honest with you, and be pleased that the nature of your relationship is such that he felt he *could* tell you. Don't deny your pain, which you're entitled to, but don't let it cut you off from your teenager. And don't cut him off from your love.

Of course you'll be worried for him. Despite more progressive social attitudes, homosexuality is still very much stigmatized in our society, and somewhere along the line your teenager will run into intolerance, maybe even physical hostility. Many young men—perhaps fearing latent homosexuality themselves—aren't above gay bashing.

Accept that your teen can't help being gay; if he could choose a different course, he might for no other reason than that his life would be so much easier. Homosexuality is not a disease, illness, or mental disorder. Both the American Psychiatric Association and the American Psychological Association consider it an alternative form of sexual expression.

Adolescence is an emotional minefield to begin with, filled with trepidation and insecurity and shaky self-esteem. Knowing that he is homosexually oriented compounds a teen's angst to a degree that's hard to imagine.

What your teen needs most from you is loving acceptance and support. Gay teens are reluctant to come out to their parents, because the vast majority of parents either react negatively or outright reject them. Couple this parental rejection with verbal or physical abuse by their peers and it's no wonder that many gay teens have problems in school, start using drugs, or run away from home. Homosexuality is a risk factor for adolescent suicide; some teens find the anguish, shame, guilt, and fear that often comes with the realization that they're homosexual so unbearable that, lacking parental love and support, they consider suicide.

It will no doubt take you time to adjust to the fact that your teenager is gay. But your teenager is still your teenager and still needs your love, your support, your acceptance, and your guidance.

8

The Adolescent With Chronic Illness

■ ■ ■

Every parent wants good health for his or her teen. Growing pains, curiosity about sex, and sprained ankles are inevitable; even so, as parents, we want our adolescent sons and daughters to be healthy and to be able to enjoy the ever-enlarging world of opportunities and challenges before them.

Unfortunately, many adolescents and their families are confronted by chronic diseases. Some diseases are passing challenges that, after a few months or years, resolve themselves and can be forgotten. Others are life-long facts of everyday life.

A chronic disease lasts by definition three months or more (as distinct from an acute ailment such as the flu or a minor infection that comes and goes in a matter of days or, at most, weeks). The adolescent must cope with the physical discomfort, disability, and anxiety associated with the illness. The chronic disease becomes a day-to-day factor in the teen's life, and in the life of the family. School, sports, and social and family time may be affected. A range of emotional and behavioral consequences may also result.

Adolescents with a chronic disease—and

their families—adapt to the life changes required by the diagnosis. The love and support of parents and siblings are basic to the support mechanism. The role of the parents in normalizing life for the ailing adolescent and the rest of the household is also critical, as is working to enable the young person to continue sampling her expanding universe.

This chapter focuses on specific illnesses. Each is different and presents unique challenges; common, chronic illnesses such as diabetes and epilepsy are discussed, as are cancer and cystic fibrosis. The experiences of dealing with these and other chronic disorders have much in common. In addition to consulting the entry devoted to the disease with which you are concerned, see also *Coping With Chronic Disease, Part I: A Parent's Role* (below) for strategies in dealing with the issues you face and *Coping With Chronic Disease, Part II: Challenges for the Adolescent* (page 170) for a better understanding of what your teenager may be experiencing.

COPING WITH CHRONIC DISEASE, PART I
A PARENT'S ROLE

The chronic diseases discussed in this chapter vary widely in symptoms, severity, and treatment regimens. Yet whatever the long-term prognosis, the goal is the same: to help the young person grow and mature as normally as possible with a minimum of disruption to the life of the family.

ACKNOWLEDGE YOUR RESPONSE.
Before you can help your adolescent deal with her ailment, you must first recognize and control your own feelings.

Anger, disappointment, fear, and guilt are predictable parental responses to the news an adolescent is chronically ill. A cloud of concerns may seem to envelop you—the emotional turmoil every parent experiences; confusion at dealing with the specialists and the complexities of the medical system; and financial worries. It is perfectly normal and understandable for a parent to rail at the Fates, *Why does it have to be my kid?*

You may find yourself questioning your ability to care for your adolescent, blame yourself or your spouse for your child's illness, or mistrust your teen's physician. Some parents become overprotective and others detached from their child. Be aware of your emotions and how they affect your behavior and your interactions with others. For example, anger may be directed inappropriately onto others—the ill adolescent, the physician who delivered the bad news, or other family members.

Keep Your Cool.

Stay calm or, at least, let your teenager know and see that, even though you are upset, you are still in control. A parent's attitudes can have a significant impact on the youngster's reaction. Your anxieties can translate in your son or daughter to increased worry or even panic (*If Mom's that upset, it must be hopeless or worse than I thought!*). At the same time, be honest with your adolescent about your emotions. It is unrealistic always to be happy or to pretend there is nothing wrong. Let her know it is difficult, but that you will be there to support her.

Don't take your teen's illness personally. You don't have the disease, your adolescent does. You play a supporting role, but the principal performer is your teenager.

Identify Your Responsibilities.

You will need to establish relationships with the necessary medical professionals who will provide the help your teenager requires. Your health-care team should educate you about the disease. You may need to do additional reading about it or perhaps seek sources of new information on the Internet. Find other parents who have experienced some of the challenges you now face, and meet with physicians and ask questions. You may want to share your knowledge with your teenager—and, in turn, learn from her.

Depending on the age and maturity of your child, you may have sole responsibility for making treatment decisions. As your child grows, however, you will gradually need to share the responsibility with your adolescent, finding a balance between making, discussing, and eventually turning over treatment decisions and management to the maturing adolescent. You may have a continuing role in the delivery of care and will need to provide the physical, emotional, and financial support your adolescent requires.

Establish a committee of command. In most cases, the best approach involves both parents meeting with physicians and helping to make decisions. The adolescent must have an ever-growing voice, too, if she is well enough. As the adolescent matures, if she feels excluded or does not agree with the treatment regimen, she may not cooperate fully.

Take advantage of the guidance offered by your teen's physician. A doctor with a specialty in your adolescent's disorder may also be a key counselor. Prominent roles can be played by therapists, nurse practitioners, other physicians, family members, teachers, and trusted friends. Consider the advice of the professionals you encounter at special schools, camps, and counseling facilities, too. In the case of many chronic disorders, there are national organizations with local branches. Ask for help—it may come in the form of information, referrals, or support groups where, as parents, you can meet others who are confronting what you are.

UNDERSTAND AND UTILIZE THE SCHOOL CONTEXT.

As well as being the focus for academic and intellectual development, your adolescent's school exercises a powerful influence on her emotional and social life. An effective partnership with your adolescent's teachers needs to be established.

Be sure teachers, administrators, the school nurse, and even bus drivers have a clear understanding of the illness and its impact on the teen. Arrange a meeting to ensure that the school staff understands the nature of the chronic disease and its affects on your adolescent. In some instances, the presence of the teen's physician can be invaluable in answering specific questions about the adolescent's capabilities as well as the disease, and attendant myths and fears.

REMEMBER THE REST OF THE FAMILY.

Caring for an ailing teenager may require sacrifices on the part of other family members. Prolonged hospital stays, continuing therapies, and other demands and changes produced by the disease and its treatment can throw the routine of a family out of balance. Spend extra time with your other children, who may harbor many feelings toward the sick sibling ranging from guilt to anger.

Initially, the illness may take center stage in your family. Be careful not to allow your life to be consumed by the illness to the exclusion of other family members, activities, and established patterns. No one—not you, the sick youngster, nor anyone else—will benefit. In the short run, the focus may be inevitable; but over the longer term, your goal should be to reestablish day-to-day patterns that incorporate the treatment regimes and necessary lifestyle adjustments into the mainstream of the household as soon as possible.

In the case of a diabetic teen, for example, the best approach is to focus more on her during the initial period of diagnosing and controlling the diabetes. Gradually, however, the spotlight should fade and the lights come up on the larger drama of the family as a whole, in which the diabetic adolescent is but one player, the diabetes one factor in her life. For the teen with epilepsy, a seizure lasts only a few minutes—at most other times, the epilepsy is ordinarily a secondary issue. Try to maintain a larger perspective.

Keep in mind, as well, that your response and your adolescent's in dealing with a chronic disease will alter over time. Learning to live with a chronic disorder requires changing speeds, shifting gears, and stops and starts. It's an ongoing process of adaptation.

Live a life of your own, too. Seek respite care. Maintain a social life, individually and collectively as a family. Call upon friends and family members to help you. Normal life must go on—it's better for you *and* your adolescent.

COPING WITH CHRONIC DISEASE, PART II
CHALLENGES FOR THE ADOLESCENT

Adolescence is about expanding horizons. It's an exhilarating but difficult time for a healthy teenager. She is looking increasingly to peers rather than parents for a sense of belonging. The adolescent is beginning to exercise control over her life and is becoming more independent in her school and social life. There is a new premium on privacy, as the adolescent comes to regard more and more of her thoughts and her private space as hers and hers alone.

The onset of a chronic disease presents a whole new set of challenges that complicate the teen's growing independence. For younger children, chronic disease can be bewildering. The maturing adolescent, however, is able to comprehend more completely the altered circumstances. For most teens, a clear understanding can be reached—but that takes time and may involve anxiety, panic, and denial before acceptance.

Another normal response is anger at this obstacle to emerging independence. The lifestyle restrictions that accompany the illness—dietary limitations, for example, or the need to recuperate from surgical procedures or the side effects of medications—may result in immaturity, passivity, and overdependence on parents. On the other hand, the adolescent may respond with behaviors that are reckless or hostile to parental authority. The teenager wants to fit in, to be *normal*—yet a chronic disease may set her apart from her peers. The diabetic can't eat what her peers eat, asthmatic teens may need to refrain from certain physical activities, and seriously ill adolescents may have to deal with periods of hospitalization, surgery, and drugs with side effects. Some illnesses and treatments change a youngster's appearance—at a time when other people's perceptions seem terribly important. An adolescent's self-image can be altered by the difficulties posed by disease.

HONESTY AND ACCEPTANCE.

To help your teen deal with her disease, you need to be honest with the youngster—and with yourself. Children and adolescents alike have a remarkable capacity for sensing when they are being told less than the truth. Leaving your teen uninformed of her condition can foster fears and risk alienating the teen.

An adolescent is struggling with control, wanting to resist her parents' control and exercise her own. Concerns about fairness and honesty are never far from the surface, but open, honest dialogue about her illness can actually be used to foster normal adolescent development.

There's another reason for being candid. The clearer an understanding an adolescent has of her disorder, the more she will be able to feel in control and to assume responsibility for her treatment and disease management. Illness can actually offer a child a chance to experience mastery as she manages aspects of her disorder or its treatment.

AVOID BEING OVERPROTECTIVE.

The adolescent who is shielded by a parent learns less about taking care of herself. A teenager, particularly one with a chronic disease, should be mastering more and more of the skills necessary to be independent. Too much involvement by the parent in her life may also be perceived by the adolescent as interference. The struggle between openness and privacy is a normal part of adolescent development.

Understand the adolescent's limitations and help her work within them. Challenge the teen to extend herself, to excel in areas where she can. Don't overindulge. In general, the family rules should apply equally to the teen with a chronic illness. There's no parallel universe for the sick; they must live in the world, too. The young woman with chronic illness must still learn the dos and don'ts at home and school, with friends and with herself.

THE ADOLESCENT'S SELF-IMAGE.

Teenagers are very self-conscious of their bodies. Puberty can be difficult for many adolescents. The significant physical changes of puberty focus their attention on changes in height and weight, sexual development, and other physical characteristics. Teens with chronic health problems have additional stress to manage during puberty that can affect their self-image.

Attaching a label to a youngster is often necessary. If she has cancer or cystic fibrosis, teachers, caregivers, and others in the family and out in the world may need to know. Yet labeling also has its risks. A young person can be reduced from a unique individual to merely a function of a disease.

Try not to think of your teen with a chronic disorder as a patient, and don't confuse her identity with the illness. To put it another way, don't let the illness stand between you and your daughter. The teen mustn't sense you see her as the weak link who is letting the rest of the family down.

Being sick isn't a character flaw. On the other hand, it isn't a badge of honor to be rewarded like an act of bravery. Keep a balanced view of your child. Don't let the disease take over, as the focus shouldn't be the sickness but on the adolescent's normal development.

DON'T ISOLATE THE TEEN.

A chronically ill adolescent has different experiences than other teenagers. She feels lonely in a unique way because she may not share their experiences, because her illness limits her ability to do things other kids are doing.

Understand your adolescent's strengths and weaknesses, her health in the context of her chronic illness. Then help your adolescent do the same. Don't establish limits in your mind—or the adolescent's. Your child, like any other, needs your expectations and hopes, your dreams and your discipline to help shape her future.

Asthma

Asthma is a disorder in which breathing difficulties occur due to hyperactive airways. It is often triggered by allergens, though symptoms can also be caused by exercise, viruses, or pollution. Asthma is the most common chronic disease of childhood. While asthma usually develops prior to adolescence, the wheezing and coughing of asthma may first appear during the teen years.

■ IDENTIFYING THE SIGNS

If your teenager has been diagnosed with asthma, you know the symptoms all too well. During an *asthma attack,* as the episodes are called, breathing becomes labored, resulting in a wheezing or whistling noise on breathing out. Exhaling is more difficult, with a tight feeling in the chest.

Any discussion of asthma necessarily concerns *allergies,* though other potential causes include a viral respiratory infection such as a cold, a sinus infection, some medications, or emotional stress. Sudden exposure to cold or dry air or to physical exertion can also bring on an asthma attack.

Allergies are an overreaction by the body to the presence of substances such as mold, pollen, or smoke to which the allergic person is sensitive. The presence of the allergen produces an immune system reaction. The allergen—often an innocent environmental substance such as animal dander, dust mites, or mold—deceives the body into thinking it is a dangerous invader. One response is that blood plasma cells produce a protein called gamma globulin IgE.

Each time the allergen is identified, more IgE antibodies are released. In the mucous membranes, the IgE cells initially produce such allergic symptoms as weepy eyes and runny nose. As more IgE antibodies are released, they accumulate in the body.

■ CAUSES AND CONSEQUENCES

During an asthma attack, the tiny airways in the lungs called bronchial tubes are narrowed because the smooth muscles that surround them constrict. The membrane that lines them also swells, and the mucus there becomes thick and sticky. Air has more difficulty passing through the tubes and produces wheezing.

Asthma is an organic disease—its symptoms are very real and can even be life-threatening. Yet there is a *somatization* element, too, meaning that the mind has an effect on individual attacks and influences the overall course of the disease. Typically, this is more pronounced in younger children, creating an exaggerated effect on individual asthmatic attacks and the overall course of the disease.

With the advent of adolescence, some children may experience a change in allergic symptoms, including the lessening or cessation of all allergy symptoms in some teenagers.

■ HOW TO RESPOND

Asthma attacks can be life-threatening, involving rapid respiration, cough, increased heart rate, and vomiting. In emergency cases, constant coughing is accompanied by *hypoxia* (oxygen deficiency), which causes the lips and nails to begin to turn blue from the lack of oxygen in the blood. This is a medical emergency, requiring emergency medical assistance.

Medications. Inhalers can be used to dispense several types of medication simply by inhaling and should be used to *prevent* attacks. The same medications are used *during* attacks but are best administered with a *nebulizer*, a device that transforms liquid medications into tiny particles so that they can be introduced into the lungs as a fine spray.

Some medications (called *bronchodilators*, including albuteral and metaproternol) release the muscular tension around the bronchial tubes. These medications are usually used along with drugs that reduce the swelling and inflammation of the tubes (corticosteroids) or that prevent future asthma attacks (cromolyn sodium, Intal). In emergency cases, adrenaline may be administered by injection, but in most cases medications are inhaled as mist from a nebulizer. If the attacks are precipitated by exercise, an inhalant may be employed prior to physical activity.

Eliminating the Allergens. Asthma medications are important, but a second, equally essential component of any treatment regime for an asthma sufferer involves identifying and, if possible, eliminating allergens that trigger asthma attacks.

Secondhand smoke in the home from cigarettes, pipes, or cigars must be eliminated. If you or anyone in your family smokes, a child with asthma is a good reason to quit. At the very least, take your habit outside. Discourage the teen from smoking.

The Adolescent's Role. Be sure the teen understands what is happening to her body and the workings of any medications. Help her assume responsibility for managing her asthma.

It is not uncommon for a teenager to feel indestructible—but, for the adolescent with asthma, that can be an especially dangerous notion. The teen who hasn't had a dramatic attack for some time may become lax in following the prescribed inhalant therapies (*I haven't had a problem and I feel great, therefore why do I need this?*). That can set the stage for more serious asthma attacks.

The teen must understand the importance of adhering to the treatment regime. Try to help the adolescent take responsibility for the inhalant therapy, but avoid establishing a pattern in which a parent has to remind the teen daily (*Have you taken your medicine, dear?*). If she manages her asthma herself, less parental and medical interference in her life is required.

Minor asthma can be exacerbated by a reliance upon the use of inhalants only when wheezing occurs. A careful, preventive medication approach is more likely to minimize or eliminate dramatic asthmatic attacks—attacks that can be life-threatening. The teen's physician should be consulted periodically to monitor the adolescent's lung function.

Diabetes

A few generations ago, diabetes was virtually untreatable and fatal. In 1921, insulin was discovered and diabetes became manageable. Today, diabetes remains a lifelong challenge, but the youngster with diabetes can expect to live a satisfying and productive life.

■ IDENTIFYING THE SIGNS

In most cases, the undiagnosed diabetic becomes ill, loses weight, urinates frequently, and is constantly thirsty, usually with an overall sense of lethargy. In girls, severe vaginal yeast infections may also occur. In many instances, the diagnosis of diabetes is made in childhood or the early years of adolescence, but it can be diagnosed at any age.

■ CAUSES AND CONSEQUENCES

Diabetes mellitus, as the disorder is formally known, occurs when the pancreas fails to produce an adequate supply of the hormone insulin. One possible explanation for the failure of a previously healthy pancreas is a viral infection in genetically susceptible children that gradually destroys the cells in the pancreas that make insulin.

Insulin controls the amount of sugar or glucose in the blood. Insulin is necessary for the energy-producing sugar to enter the cells of the body. Too little insulin results in hyperglycemia, an excess of glucose in the blood but not enough in the cells. If left untreated, this surplus of blood glucose produces the symptoms of diabetes and its potentially life-threatening complications, in particular *diabetic ketoacidosis*, in which the changes resulting from elevated blood glucose levels lead to symptoms of rapid respiration, dehydration, and eventually unconsciousness or coma.

The type of diabetes found in adolescents, juvenile-onset diabetes, is also referred to as insulin-dependent diabetes mellitus, IDDM, or Type 1 diabetes. It must be treated with both diet and insulin.

■ HOW TO RESPOND

Managing diabetes is an almost mechanical process involving the replacement of the absent insulin in the blood in a manner that closely copies the balance of the normal body. The insulin, administered as shots, must be delivered in the right quantities and at the proper times. By glucose monitoring, dietary discipline, and other approaches, the body's blood sugar can be maintained at proper levels.

Establishing appropriate routines and adhering to them are more than a mechanical matter. For a teenager, the required regimen can feel like martial law. The adolescent years are a time when the youngster feels strong needs to be independent and may rebel against parents, teachers, physicians, and other authority figures. Thus, the day-in, day-out discipline of shots, diet, and tests can seem suffocating. Treating diabetes is a two-fold challenge for the teen and her parents. The diabetic must master the routine *and* agree to accept and submit to its daily demands.

Insulin Shots. In younger children, parents typically administer the shots, but after age eight or nine, the child is usually able to manage the injections. Most often, the shots are given twice daily, before breakfast and dinner. Tests of blood glucose levels must be done frequently to be sure the diabetes is well controlled. Again, too much blood sugar can result in ketoacidosis. *Hypoglycemia*, which occurs if blood sugar levels fall dangerously low from too much insulin, produces symptoms of tiredness or fainting.

In some youngsters, diabetes proves more difficult to manage than in others. "Brittle" or "unstable" diabetes may require three or four daily insulin shots, the installation of a diabetic insulin pump, and even periodic hospitalization to bring blood sugar levels under good control.

Dietary Controls. Insulin for the diabetic teenager is a matter of life and death. A less dramatic component of any treatment regimen is the management of your teen's diet. The goal is to maintain levels of glucose in the blood within a normal range. The adolescent with well-controlled blood sugars will feel better and grow better and will be less likely to have early medical complications from her diabetes. These long-term complications may include atherosclerosis, high blood pressure, and circulation problems.

This means there are forbidden foods, namely those rich in simple sugars, such as candy, cookies, and other sweets. The availability of sugar substitutes has made it much easier for diabetics to tolerate these necessary restrictions. Meals should be balanced, consisting of a range of healthy foods, with an emphasis on foods high in fiber, such as fruits, vegetables, and whole grains. Alcohol will also elevate blood glucose, and the ado-

lescent should be advised normal experimentation with drinking alcohol may be dangerous and should be avoided.

The adolescent's diet must also be regimented according to a strict schedule. The three meals should be consumed at regular intervals and may be supplemented by regularly scheduled snacks, perhaps at mid-morning, mid-afternoon, and bedtime. An exercise program may also be prescribed, because physical activity can help control diabetes.

Emotional Intervention. Managing diabetes—especially in adolescents—presents challenges in helping the teenager accustom herself to its regimens and social challenges. Self-discipline, emotional support, and reassurance from parents and others are almost as crucial as the lifesaving insulin.

The teenage years can be a challenging time for the parent of a diabetic. The adolescent with diabetes may understand perfectly well that her good health—in fact, her very survival—depends upon maintaining stable levels of blood sugar. Yet the need for autonomy, independence, and experimentation that are a natural part of adolescence may interfere with the diabetic regimen and medical management of the disease.

Some teenagers go through a phase of denial, where they refuse to comply with dietary limitations or injection schedules. Others will misrepresent the results of their glucose tests in order to cover up binges on sweets or the consumption of alcohol, both of which significantly raise the blood sugar.

The diabetic adolescent has a chronic disease that will remain with her as long as she lives—and how long and how well she lives may be a direct consequence of how clearly she understands and manages her diabetes. Over many years, elevated blood sugars can, again, accelerate the development of atherosclerosis or high blood pressure and lead to other severe health problems, including blindness, kidney failure, and heart problems.

While maintaining blood glucose within healthy limits is important, the diabetic adolescent should also understand that there is no guarantee she will experience no complications. Learning and accepting this as a teenager may help in coping with any complications that may occur as an adult.

In explaining the lifetime risks, be careful not to overwhelm the adolescent. Timing is important, and the long-term dangers shouldn't be off-loaded on the youngster all at once. Since establishing healthy habits must be a lifelong goal and responsibility of your teen, repeated discussions may be necessary so that the adolescent will understand the consequences of her actions. As the child matures, the process becomes less a parent-child partnership and more the adolescent's sole responsibility as she assumes control over the shots and the blood glucose monitoring.

Coping with diabetes is a unique challenge, but it has similarities to the process of living with other chronic diseases or disorders. For some general guidance, see *Coping With Chronic Disease*, pages 167 and 170.

Emotional Factors Producing Illness

Some adolescents complain of pains or discomforts for which a physician is unable to identify a cause. In other cases, a recognizable physical disease is accompanied by symptoms that are exaggerated or unlikely consequences of the disease. When pains or other symptoms cannot be explained by physical findings or appear exaggerated, the problem is classified as a *somatoform disorder.*

■ IDENTIFYING THE SIGNS

In teens, somatoform disorders may accompany the menstrual cycle in girls, the changes of puberty, as well as a variety of other acute and chronic illnesses. Anxiety and worry, fatigue, loss of appetite, aches, and pain are frequent symptoms. The frequency of these somatic symptoms is slightly higher in girls than in boys.

In certain cases, an adolescent may develop symptoms of blindness, double vision, deafness, poor balance and coordination, paralysis, seizures, or other specific symptoms that mimic a neurologic disorder. In such instances, when no physical cause can be identified, the problem is classified as a *conversion disorder.*

A related problem, *hypochondriasis* or *hypochondria,* is characterized by anxiety and worry about having a disease that is not explained by identifiable physical causes. This condition often occurs with depression. *Body dysmorphic disorder* is diagnosed when the adolescent becomes preoccupied with imagined physical deformities or defects.

Academic problems, school refusal, social withdrawal, and emotional and behavioral problems often accompany somatoform disorders.

■ CAUSES AND CONSEQUENCES

In cases of somatization disorders, the symptoms are not intentionally produced. Rather than a physical cause, psychological and emotional factors—mood changes, anxiety, or psychological conflicts—are underlying these disorders.

■ HOW TO RESPOND

Pain is subjective regardless of the cause. A toothache that one person finds debilitating is a nagging distraction to someone else. The perception of pain depends on a variety of factors, including an individual's experience, physiology, and psychological state.

The expression of and reaction to pain vary with the age of the child. Infants and toddlers are likely to react strongly to pain by crying and physical gestures. As a child grows older, she may cope differently. For example, the child may tolerate an injection because she is able to understand the idea that short-term discomfort may have long-term benefits. She may also have more experiences and coping skills (such as the ability to distract herself). By adolescence, however, a mature understanding of pain and its significance is usually present. Even so, new and unfamiliar discomforts such as the periodic cramping of menstruation initially can overwhelm an adolescent. Given time, experience, and support,

the exaggerated response to the symptoms may lessen or even disappear.

Before concluding your adolescent's pain or other symptoms arise from changes triggered by emotional and psychological causes, consult your adolescent's physician to attempt to rule out possible organic, physical explanations.

If your child has menstrual, gastrointestinal, neurologic, or other physical complaints of unidentifiable cause, especially if the discomforts are interfering with the teen's ability to perform in school or to function socially, attempt to identify potential causes of emotional or psychological distress.

Among them may be academic pressures; a recent change in school; a move to a new neighborhood; grieving over the death or illness of a friend or family member; difficulty in adapting to the physical and emotional changes of adolescence; or physical or sexual abuse. There are many sources of stress for teenagers. Are there problems in the home between the parents or with a sibling? Have there been other recent changes in the adolescent's life?

Prescription and over-the-counter medications may have side effects even when used as directed. If your adolescent is taking medication daily and develops unexplained physical symptoms, check with your family physician to determine whether the cause could be side effects from the prescribed drug.

Abuse of medications is another potential cause of physical complaints. Alcohol abuse, the inappropriate use of toxic household chemicals (such as glue, aerosols, or gasoline for sniffing), or illicit drug use may be causing emotional and behavioral problems.

If your daughter's stomach problems frequently involve vomiting with no organic cause, discuss her eating patterns. Such symptoms may indicate an eating disorder. (See also *Eating and Nutritional Disorders,* page 260.)

Does the adolescent have trouble sleeping? If the complaints are accompanied by a recent change in eating habits or a sudden disinterest in friends or activities she previously enjoyed, the teenager may be depressed. Teens who have sleeping problems may try to self-medicate with alcohol. If you suspect sexual or physical abuse, see *Physical or Sexual Abuse*, page 117.

If you can find no explanation or the symptoms worsen, have your adolescent evaluated by her physician to rule out any physical cause. The doctor may decide to refer you to a child and adolescent psychiatrist to help determine the cause and appropriate course of treatment. A careful evaluation may identify depressive, anxiety, or other disorders that are causing the unexplained physical discomforts in your teenager. (See also *Emotional Disorders,* page 195, and *Disruptive Behavior Disorders,* page 220.)

If you are able to identify the source of the stresses, take steps to alleviate your teen's worry. Explain that the physician has found no physical explanation for the pain. Be gentle in explaining that taking medicine won't help the pain get better. Reassure the adolescent that ways can be found to make the discomfort go away. Acknowledge that the pain is real. Your adolescent's physician may be helpful in counseling your child, too.

Devise strategies, and attempt to give your adolescent a sense of control. By recognizing the problem, by developing stress-reducing strategies, the complaints can be managed. If a social situation is intimidating, encourage your adolescent to take a friend along; if an academic problem looms large, arrange for tutoring to enhance confidence as well as her skills. Such strategies will help reduce anxiety and the associated physical complaints.

Your adolescent must also understand that her complaints are not punishment; they're not her fault. Be careful not to reinforce the behaviors. Explain to the adolescent how the problem occurs and what steps can be taken to address it.

Delayed Puberty

Puberty is a normal part of growing up. However, there is no "normal" schedule for an adolescent's physical and emotional changes. On average girls begin puberty with the development of breast buds at age ten or eleven. Rapid overall growth and menarche follow about two to two-and-a-half years later. In boys, the growth of testes, accelerated overall growth, and other signs of puberty begin on average at age twelve or thirteen. Some children go through the physical changes quickly, while in others the changes may not be complete for four or five years. For a teen, differences between her rate of maturing and that of her schoolmates can be a cause for concern.

When a child begins to mature much earlier than is usual, the term *precocious puberty* is applied; when much later than average, the term is *delayed puberty*.

■ Identifying the Signs

The term delayed puberty is generally applied to girls who have not developed breast buds by age thirteen and boys whose testicles have not enlarged by thirteen and a half.

■ Causes and Consequences

The largest single factor in delayed puberty is an adolescent's genetic inheritance. The child of parents who matured late are more likely to experience delayed puberty. In general, however, improved nutrition has resulted in the earlier onset of puberty in all adolescents throughout the twentieth century.

In rare instances, a endocrine gland abnormality may produce delayed puberty.

■ How to Respond

If you or your teenager is concerned at the absence of indications of puberty—the development of breast buds or testicular enlargement followed by an increase in height—consult your adolescent's physician. Bone X rays will reveal bone growth and the progress your adolescent is making toward physical maturity.

The "treatment" for delayed puberty, in most cases, is to provide emotional support for the anxious teenager. Reassure the adolescent that the development of physical characteristics and the growth spurt that result from the body's increased endocrine activity will happen, probably very soon. The adolescent may feel isolated as classmates seem suddenly older and more mature, yet the late onset of puberty does not mean that full adult height or other physical developments will be any less on average than those of adolescents who entered puberty earlier.

Help the teen manage the stress; guide her into activities consistent with size and development. High-contact sports that emphasize strength and stature, such as football or basketball, may be less appropriate than those, such as tennis and swimming, for which sheer size and strength are not paramount.

A Parent's Role. Make sure your adolescent understands that nothing is wrong; some people mature earlier, some later. The range of normal is very wide and includes the nervous and gawky nine-year-old girl and the sixteen-year-old boy embarrassed by his short stature. Your adolescent doesn't want to feel different. Assure her that it's just a matter of timing.

Strike a balance between noticing that your child isn't physically developing at the same rate as her peers and not overreacting. Drawing attention to the already self-conscious adolescent will not help. The contrast between her and a taller, heavier friend whose figure is beginning to assume an adult shape shouldn't become a focus of family discussion. That will only add to her self-consciousness. At an appropriate time, talk calmly with your adolescent about her concerns and the changes that are anticipated.

As she develops, don't confuse physical development with emotional maturity. Girls with breasts and boys with burgeoning muscles don't necessarily know how to behave in

TOO SHORT OR TOO TALL?

Height is a consequence of a number of factors, among them nutrition and the absence (or presence) of disease. There is, however, one overriding factor that strongly influences how tall (or short) an adolescent will grow up to be: a child's genetic inheritance, the genes shared with parents. Thus, tall parents are more likely to have tall children. Shorter mothers and fathers typically have relatively shorter children.

Certain diseases affect height. An insufficiency in pituitary gland function (hypopituitarism) will delay growth and sexual development. Hypopituitarism is treated with growth hormone replacement. Too much of the human growth hormone secreted by the pituitary gland produces acromegaly and gigantism, disorders in which the skeleton becomes enlarged. Medical evaluation and treatment are available. Other chronic disorders may interfere with normal growth, such as poorly controlled diabetes, certain bowel disorders, and sickle-cell disease.

In the absence of a physical disease or condition, there are medical steps to be taken by an adolescent dissatisfied with her height. Human growth hormone, which can now be synthesized in a laboratory, is used to treat short children and adolescents. Medical intervention with hormone therapy for short and tall adolescents is controversial. The long-term consequences are unclear; the debate is fueled by a lack of guidelines for use (and misuse) of these expensive, unproven therapies.

No matter what approach is taken to help your teenager, help her develop self-confidence. Short and tall people alike can be successful, popular, creative, and happy. Your tall daughter may discover that increased sports opportunities for girls have changed the stigma of being tall into an advantage; for the fourteen-year-old boy concerned at being the shortest kid in his class, there's every chance he will get taller, that his growth spurt is yet to come.

Reassure your adolescent. A tape measure indicates less about a person than ability to achieve and succeed. One of your jobs as a parent is to help the adolescent develop a self-image that balances her physical, emotional, intellectual, and social attributes. Curiosity, cleverness, kindness, humor, and other humanizing characteristics are available to tall and short alike—and mean more than whether one is shorter or taller than her prom date.

ways that are as mature as their bodies might suggest. Conversely, the child who is less mature physically isn't necessarily slower to mature emotionally. Physical and emotional maturity tend to parallel each other, but do not proceed in lockstep.

Menstrual Problems

The reproductive phase of a girl's life begins with menarche, her first menstrual period. On average, menstruation begins at thirteen.

Puberty can be both an exciting and a challenging time for the adolescent, involving the need for a new appreciation of the body and its potentials. The accompanying adjustments—which include new responsibilities—are emotional as well as physical. The ebb and flow of changing hormonal patterns must be integrated into daily life. With the love and support of her family, self-consciousness of her new shape will gradually give way to confidence and familiarity with her new maturity. Yet, for some adolescent girls, there are added challenges, when menstruation is accompanied by extreme emotional and physical discomfort or its arrival is delayed.

The following are among the menstrual problems a teenage girl may encounter:

Premenstrual Syndrome. Some women experience unpleasant symptoms prior to or during their periods. The normal hormonal changes can cause a teen's skin to break out a few days before her period. Some women have bloating and a slight weight increase due to fluid retention. Others may notice breast tenderness or have pelvic pain. Some adolescents find themselves feeling depressed, irritable, or anxious around the time of their periods.

In most cases of premenstrual syndrome (PMS) with pain, an over-the-counter medication such as ibuprofen is effective in relieving the discomforts. Some women have more severe premenstrual syndrome, which may require additional therapy. PMS tends to develop in women in their twenties and thirties.

Painful Menstruation. More severe discomfort during menstruation, termed *dysmenorrhea*, is not uncommon. *Primary dysmenorrhea,* menstrual pain unrelated to another physical condition or disease, typically begins in adolescence. Though the causes are multiple, recent research suggests the explanation may be an excess of prostaglandins, a group of hormone-like chemicals that may cause cramping and body aches during menstruation.

Failure to Menstruate. The majority of adolescent girls begin to menstruate by age fourteen, yet delays until sixteen or even eighteen years of age occur. Thin or very athletic adolescents may often develop menses later, yet in most situations they reach menarche without treatment.

Primary amenorrhea is, simply put, delayed menarche. The causes for the delay vary—primary amenorrhea is found in teens who pursue intense athletic activity, such as competitive swimming, gymnastics, dancing, or running. Anorexia nervosa, an eating disorder involving a fear of becoming fat, leads to dieting, weight loss, and malnutrition. Anorectic prepubescent girls often fail to begin menstruating, or if menstruation has already begun, it ceases with development of the dieting behavior. Anorexia nervosa is a serious psychiatric illness requiring appropriate treatment. (See *Anorexia Nervosa,* page 260.)

Other causes of delayed menarche include too many miles run (normal menstrual patterns usually result when the athlete eases her training schedule) as well as hormonal or physical abnormalities that interfere with the menses. Chromosomal disorders can impede ovary development and ovulation.

■ **HOW TO RESPOND**

If your daughter fails to begin menstruating by age sixteen, consult her physician or gynecologist. Select a gynecologist who has a good reputation in dealing with teenagers—a girl's first pelvic exam should be conducted with sensitivity to her fears and sense of personal privacy.

Pain during menstruation is another reason for consulting your teen's physician. A physical examination and history will determine factors that may cause the pain. Strategies such as hot baths, heating pads, pelvic exercises, deep breathing, and massages may ease the discomfort. Medications that block prostaglandins may be prescribed to reduce pain and ease cramping.

Regardless of the cause or seriousness of the menstrual problem your daughter experiences, your reassurance is essential. Make

yourself available to talk. Your daughter may need to discuss this, including her fears and concerns regarding her developing body.

Her emerging sexuality—or the failure of her body to assume some of the sexual characteristics her friends may exhibit—can be disconcerting. Help your daughter develop positive feelings about herself. Such conversations can be a means by which parents and adolescents establish new lines of communication. These exchanges shouldn't simply lay out guidelines for sexual behavior; the focus should be on affirming the child's health. Reassure her that her problems are not unusual, and discuss your experience with similar situations. In this way, a parent can buttress the youngster's self-esteem and foster a positive parent-adolescent relationship.

Chronic PID in Girls

When bacteria invade the vagina and cervix and travel upward into the pelvic cavity and reproductive organs, infections can occur. This infection is called *pelvic inflammatory disease,* or PID. Long-term infection of the fallopian tubes will result in scarring that can obstruct the passage of eggs down the tube and produce sterility.

■ **IDENTIFYING THE SIGNS**

A dull pain in the lower abdomen and pelvis may be accompanied by foul-smelling vaginal discharge or bleeding. Pain during sexual intercourse and heavy bleeding during periods are also common symptoms. When not treated effectively, nausea and vomiting may also occur.

A troublesome characteristic of PID is that there may be few or no symptoms—and only later in life when a woman tries to become pregnant will she discover her fallopian tubes are obstructed as a result of past infection.

■ Causes and Consequences

Teens generally contract PID from sexual activity because the bacteria that produce PID can be sexually transmitted. The bacteria may also enter the reproductive tract during childbirth, gynecological surgery, miscarriage, or when using an intrauterine device (IUD). The infections responsible for PID include chlamydia and gonorrhea.

■ How to Respond

If your daughter suspects she has pelvic inflammatory disease, consult her physician. An analysis of cervical secretions will determine whether gonorrhea or chlamydia are present. Another procedure, a *laparoscopy*, may also be done to determine whether PID is present. This minor surgical procedure involves the insertion of a tiny lighted instrument through a small incision in the abdomen so that the pelvic organs can be examined.

When identified early, pelvic inflammatory disease can be successfully treated with antibiotics.

As important as treating the infection is—in order to prevent permanent damage to your daughter's reproductive organs—she also needs information about how to avoid getting the infection again. Douching increases the likelihood of PID and should be avoided. The sexually active teenager must be helped to understand what constitutes "safe sex" (at a minimum, the preventive use of both a condom and a spermicide *every time*).

Not all cases of PID in teenagers occur as a result of sexual behaviors, but most do. Consequently, your daughter needs to understand the risks of sexual behaviors. You may not want to believe that your daughter is having a sexual relationship, but it is essential that you help her learn how to take responsibility for this aspect of her life. In teens who *aren't* sexually active, the presence of PID may suggest that sexual abuse has occurred. (See *Physical or Sexual Abuse,* page 117.)

She may need your help. She may need information about contraception and sexually transmitted diseases. You can help your daughter by giving her the information she needs to protect herself. For a further discussion of sexual experimentation in teenagers, see *Sexual Experimentation,* page 90.

Seizure Disorders

Seizures have often been described as lightning storms in the brain, and the description fits. Epileptic seizures result from abnormal electrical activity in the brain, which may produce unexpected, intense physical movements or loss of consciousness.

■ IDENTIFYING THE SIGNS

Seizures vary considerably. *Focal seizures* (also referred to as *partial seizures*) involve a specific part of the brain and may or may not be associated with visible movements or sensory stimulation. There is no loss of consciousness in simple partial seizures, but there may be confusion following complex partial seizures.

Generalized seizures involve a sudden and unexpected loss of consciousness, followed by a physical collapse and rhythmic contractions of the arms and legs. After a few minutes, the teen will return to consciousness, though usually she will be disoriented.

Because your adolescent is unlikely to have a seizure when in the presence of the doctor, the physician will depend upon you to observe exactly what happens before, during, and after your teen's seizures. Your teen's reports of the sensations and the experience are also very important. This data can help the physician identify which kind of seizure activity occurred.

If seizures are recurrent, the child is said to have *epilepsy*.

■ CAUSES AND CONSEQUENCES

Seizures may result from injury or infection in the brain, lead poisoning, or chemical imbalances in the blood. In many cases, there is no identifiable cause.

A specific type of generalized seizure called *petit mal seizures* ("staring spells") may be mistaken for daydreaming. Lasting ten to twenty seconds, these are episodes of impaired consciousness, and an adolescent who experiences them is not simply a dreamer. When her attention cannot be attracted by calling her name or gesturing within her line of vision or if the teen does not recall the events of the preceding moment once she does respond, the episode may well have been a seizure.

■ HOW TO RESPOND

If your adolescent experiences a seizure, it will likely pass without immediate medical intervention. During a generalized seizure, however, you should protect the teen from injuring herself. Position the adolescent on her side to allow saliva to drain and to prevent choking if vomiting occurs. If the teenager is eating when the seizure strikes, remove any food in the mouth with your finger if possible. Remain with the teen for the duration of the seizure and offer comfort when the adolescent is responsive. Consult your physician immediately afterward.

If a seizure lasts more than two or three minutes or if a second seizure follows immediately, call for emergency medical assistance.

In some adolescents who experience focal seizures, the disorder poses a challenge that is the opposite of a medical emergency. Often the seizures go undiagnosed, and the adolescent is categorized by parents or teachers as a daydreamer or as uncooperative. Such teenagers may have academic difficulties in school that are attributed to disinterest, lack of motivation, or other emotional or behavioral factors.

The search for the cause is the first approach. There should always be a careful medical evaluation of seizures in an adolescent. You and your physician may also seek consultation with a neurologist. Blood tests, X rays, brain wave examinations (*electroencephalograms*), or other tests may be ordered to determine the cause. If an explanation is found, such as fever, infection, or injury, it will be given appropriate treatment.

If seizures recur, an anticonvulsant medication may be prescribed. When taken in appropriate doses, these drugs prevent further seizures in the majority of cases.

Seizures usually occur less often with age. Children are five times more likely to have a convulsive episode than an adult.

Emotional Intervention. Reassure your adolescent first: She isn't abnormal, handicapped, or disabled just because she has had a seizure. Although it may feel shameful for the teenager to lose control in a seizure, her seizures should not be a shameful secret. In fact, educating your teen's teachers and peers to the nature of the condition is the best way to get past outmoded notions about epilepsy.

Your adolescent may be hesitant or apprehensive after having a seizure. She may wish to avoid taking part in physical activities with her peers for fear of losing consciousness. She may tend to isolate herself to avoid the negative reactions of her peers. She may feel left out because seizures prevent her from driving and make her feel as if she doesn't fit in.

Your job—as a parent, as a family—is to bolster your adolescent's self-image. Self-esteem may be shaken by worries about future seizures. Tell the adolescent that she is perfectly normal prior to a seizure and returns to normal afterward. It's just for moments that the teen is not herself—and you will work with the teen and her physician to eliminate those moments altogether in the future.

Your adolescent does, however, need to be given the opportunity to express her anxiety and concerns about the disorder. Her seizures may alarm you, but you can help her adjust to them if you keep your anxiety about the seizures under control and if you emphasize her successes in other aspects of her life.

The adolescent with epilepsy who takes anticonvulsant medication daily shouldn't be made to feel it's a sign of a problem in her life. The medication helps her stay healthy, and she can feel she is taking control by taking the drug, assuming responsibility for adhering to her medication regime. A medic-alert bracelet is a good idea.

Beware of being overprotective; don't allow fear to prevent your adolescent from taking on new challenges. On the other hand, don't overindulge the teen. Help your adolescent appreciate that her primary goal should be to strive to enjoy, grow, learn about, and expand her universe just as her peers are doing—and not to worry about when her next seizure may occur.

Epilepsy is a disorder that presents unique challenges to the epileptic adolescent and her parents; as with any chronic disease, however, there are common challenges to parent and teen. For a discussion of some of those challenges, see *Coping With Chronic Disease,* pages 167 and 170.

Cancer and Other Life-Threatening Diseases

When an adolescent has an illness—whether it's minor or major—she needs special treatment. Any teenager with a serious or potentially life-threatening disease suffers a wide variety of emotional as well as physical pains. This circumstance presents parents, siblings, and friends with opportunities as well as burdens. Cancer, cystic fibrosis, and sickle-cell anemia are three life-threatening diseases that are a great challenge to any family. (Much of the same guidance applies to the child and family facing life-threatening diseases as to those confronting chronic diseases; see *Coping With Chronic Disease,* pages 167 and 170.)

Cancer. Cancer isn't a single disease; there are more than 200 kinds of cancer. Each type of cancer, however, results from uncontrolled growth of certain cells that, over time, will destroy healthy tissues if the cancer is not treated.

A variety of cancers occur during adolescence. Some of them are highly curable, including certain leukemias (cancers of the blood) and lymphomas (cancers of the lymph nodes). Brain and bone cancers also occur in adolescence. The very word *cancer* still brings with it fear—and a sense of fatality. Despite good news about cures, however, cancer *is* a leading cause of death among teenagers, along with accidents, homicides, and suicides.

Cystic Fibrosis. This inherited disease affects certain glands and their secretions. Cells in the lungs, pancreas, and sweat glands are most often affected, though the sinuses, reproductive organs, liver, and intestines may also be affected.

Cystic fibrosis is often confirmed by a *sweat test,* in which the quantity of salt lost in perspiration is measured. Adolescents with cystic fibrosis secrete excessive amounts of salt in their perspiration; their skin may have a salty taste, and salt crystals may be visible on the surface of their skin. The adolescent with cystic fibrosis tends to be underweight and to grow slowly. By adolescence, the disease has likely become a fact of life.

Insufficient amounts of certain enzymes needed to properly digest fats and protein result in stools that are foul-smelling and bulky. The lungs, too, are often seriously affected, as thick mucus tends to accumulate in the airways, producing a persistent cough in the adolescent with cystic fibrosis. The primary goals of treatment are to manage lung secretions so as to improve lung function; to replace or supplement inadequate digestive enzymes; and to replace salt lost through perspiration or excretion.

Sickle-Cell Anemia. This blood disease is found primarily among persons with African-American or Mediterranean ancestry. In some states, a blood test is conducted at birth to determine whether a newborn has the disorder. A genetically inherited abnormality, sickle-cell anemia is passed on to a child only if both parents carry the sickle-cell defective gene.

Sickle-cell anemia results from abnormally structured hemoglobin molecules in the red cells. The abnormal red cells are vulnerable to changing shape, becoming sickle-shaped instead of round. When this happens under some conditions, the sickled cells obstruct small blood vessels. This can cause intense pain and precipitate a pain crisis in which medical intervention may be required. The cells are destroyed and anemia results, with a range of potential complications. Over time, repeated severe episodes can result in irreversible damage to one or more internal organs, including the kidneys, lungs, or liver.

■ HOW TO RESPOND

Parents may blame themselves for a child's disease, especially if the disease has a genetic component. Some parents may also experience a kind of mourning, a *grief reaction*, when the diagnosis of one of these life-threatening disorders is made. The challenge looms of dealing with the frequent hospitalizations, surgery, or chemotherapy or other medications and their serious side effects.

For teens with cystic fibrosis, there are the added challenges presented by such special treatment approaches as a mist tent and the need for postural lung drainage, in which the teen positions herself such that gravity will drain fluids from the lungs. There is also a powerful odor to the stool of an adolescent with cystic fibrosis.

Anxiety and depression are common emotional reactions in adolescents with cancer, cystic fibrosis, sickle-cell anemia, or other life-threatening diseases. These emotions can exaggerate the aches and pains that accompany the diseases.

Helping the adolescent deal with her anxiety and depression is an important part of the parent's role. A teenager is old enough to master a variety of strategies to manage stress and pain. Breathing exercises and stress-reduction techniques can help. The presence of a parent, sibling, or friend during a procedure to distract the adolescent can help, too. The adolescent should be allowed to develop her own set of strategies to deal with the physical and emotional components of the illness. Support groups for teenagers with specific chronic illnesses can be important in helping an adolescent cope with the course of a chronic illness.

In an adolescent, the knowledge that she has a chronic or terminal disease can produce various reactions. The adolescent's cognitive and emotional maturing allows a growing understanding of what death and mortality mean. The teen will struggle with denial, anger, depression, and anxiety. With time and support from family, friends, and professionals, your adolescent can be allowed the opportunity to find resolution and acceptance of the burden she faces. But it will take time, and there may be moments when the teenager rebels against the treatment being offered. The need for autonomy and independence are normal developmental struggles.

Be cautious not to overreact every time you get word of some new disease breakthrough or treatment—it may not be a lifeline at all but a cruel false promise.

To the greatest degree possible, look to your adolescent's strengths and health. Don't establish limits in your mind—or the teenager's. The sick adolescent, just like any other, needs parents' expectations and hopes, their dreams and their discipline to help shape her future.

TALKING TO AN ADOLESCENT FACING DISEASE OR DEATH

Even after years of experience, most physicians feel anxious and helpless in dealing with a dying youngster. It's no wonder that most parents find the prospect of discussing an adolescent's impending death with her hard to imagine. The teenager with a chronic disease isn't a great deal easier to comfort.

UNDERSTANDING DEATH.
A teenager is likely to understand what death represents as well as you do. You probably won't need to devise extensive explanations of the concept. Your adolescent will understand such straightforward statements as *death is irreversible; when a person dies, she no longer breathes, speaks, or eats;* and *death isn't temporary.*

Death is a natural part of the life cycle. That doesn't mean, however, it is easy to accept—especially as an immediate destiny for a young person—and for some parents, denial and not discussing the issue with the adolescent offers a kind of emotional protection. With young children, parents have a right to decide whether the child is to know her disease is a fatal one.

With a teenager, the situation is different. An alert adolescent—one who is conscious and not so medicated she is unable to think clearly—probably knows without being told how grave the situation is. Even so, some parents elect not to tell the teenager.

TELLING THE ADOLESCENT.
In general, a better strategy is to be honest. Initially, the adolescent may not be willing to confront the truth. Some teens cannot or refuse to understand; there is no need to insist. There's nothing to be gained by insisting upon instantaneous understanding and acceptance.

Before telling a teenager of her condition, think through how it is to be done. Talk the issue over with your physician and clergyman. Determine who is the best person to open the discussion of the subject, whether the young person will be most comfortable first hearing the news from a parent, the physician, or someone else. If a person other than a parent tells the adolescent, a parent should be nearby to participate.

When talking about a teenager's impending death, do not offer the information as a pronouncement. Rather, the prognosis should come in the course of a conversation. The adolescent may need to talk at length about death's meaning; the subject may come up again and again. Understanding and acceptance may emerge in the teen's mind only after repeated conversations. Religious beliefs and rituals, if part of the family's culture, can be invaluable in assisting a young person in coping with death.

Be Prepared for a Denial.

The adolescent may refuse to accept what you are telling her. An emotional eruption may result. That reaction is difficult yet understandable. Don't try to talk her out of how she is feeling. She needs understanding, time, and support.

Emphasize Life, Not Death.

Even having been diagnosed as having a terminal disease, the adolescent may have months or even years to live. The adolescent's curiosity can still be exercised; an appetite for new experiences can still be satisfied. The focus shouldn't be on closing doors but on opening up the adolescent's mind and maintaining as active a school, social, and family life as possible.

The adolescent must be allowed to maintain hope. Even when death is inevitable, the teen should be assured that her parents and physicians will do everything possible in fighting the illness. Dignity, too, is critical. The adolescent's wishes and desire for privacy should be honored.

Put Them in the Picture.

The adolescent needs to be able to trust her caregivers, parents, and medical professionals. One way to foster a trusting relationship is to give honest explanations of treatments, medications, and the likely outcomes. Be truthful: A lie, as innocent as it may seem, will probably have to be unlearned later. If a procedure is going be uncomfortable, don't pretend it's painless. Be honest with yourself, too.

Keep the adolescent informed about the treatment. The child should know what is being done, why, and what to expect. Answer her questions, too. If you don't know the answer, say so.

SEEKING COUNSELING.

Don't be surprised if, over a period of weeks or months, your child experiences mood swings. Hopelessness, alienation, anger, and depression are all common responses. If any such emotional stage seems serious or prolonged, a good strategy may be to reach outside the family and seek consultation. Your treatment team should consist of professionals who support the physical and emotional aspects of sickness and health. Support groups and family and individual therapy can provide understanding, solace, and an outlet for your feelings and those of the adolescent.

Every adolescent is different; there is no standard reaction to facing death. The manner, however, in which the news is given, the support offered the teen by parents and others around her, have an effect on the reception of the news. Young people can be astonishingly brave in the face of death; some are overcome with fear or anger. But all adolescents require the support and affection of their families to help them accept the truth.

Part 3

SERIOUS PROBLEMS AND ABNORMALITIES

■   ■   ■

In the each of the seven chapters that follow are a number of disorders that can represent serious obstacles to an adolescent's development and family life. These emotional, behavioral, and developmental problems usually require professional intervention, but the information provided in these chapters will help you understand what is going on with your teenager so that you can ask a child and adolescent psychiatrist or other mental health clinician the right questions and get the right kind of help for your youngster and your family.

9

Emotional Disorders

■ ■ ■

For many years, adolescence was depicted as a time of raging hormones, emotional upheaval, and embittered battles between teenagers and their parents. Indeed, some suggested that an adolescent who did not go through a serious and prolonged identity crisis during the second decade of life was at risk for psychological maladjustment and significant emotional problems as an adult.

A more contemporary view of adolescence suggests that most youngsters pass through these years with little emotional turmoil and manageable levels of rebelliousness and confusion. Intergenerational battles—like those for a shift in personal power within the fami-

ly—are, in most cases, mild and developmentally appropriate. Far from churning up endless conflict, adolescence represents for most an important transition to a productive adulthood.

On the other hand, the greater complexity and stress of modern life—including the higher divorce rates, more intense competition for jobs, and continuing geographic mobility—do make this passage more perilous than it was in the past.

The amount of emotional upheaval a teenager and his family experience will be influenced by a number of factors, including the way the changes of puberty play out in the individual youngster; the degree to which becoming a teenager marks him as different; his height in relation to other teens; the depth of a boy's voice; the size of a girl's breasts; the age at which menstruation begins; and the existence of emotional, behavioral, or general medical problems. How the family responds to and supports the maturing child, however, will have a significant impact on the tone and outcome of his adolescent passage.

Given the often seismic shift in behavior, it is not always easy to tell when a teenager is navigating the teenage years successfully and when he is having serious problems. Adolescents tend at times to report greater distress and describe even the most commonplace life-events in more extreme terms than they did as children. While most teenagers do not experience serious psychiatric disorders, a parent today must judge changes in his or her child against an awareness that there is, in general, a greater prevalence of emotional and behavioral disturbances during adolescence.

This chapter will look at some of the major emotional problems that teenagers experience and consider ways to evaluate the seriousness of these problems and the need for professional help.

Anxiety and Avoidant Disorders

Everyone experiences anxiety. It is a natural and important emotion, signaling through stirrings of worry, fearfulness, and alarm that danger or a sudden, threatening change is near. Yet sometimes anxiety becomes an exaggerated, unhealthy response.

Given the array of changes and uncertainties facing a normal teenager, anxiety often hums along like background noise. For some teenagers, anxiety becomes a chronic, high-pitched state, interfering with their ability to attend school and to perform up to their academic potential. Participating in extracurricular activities, making and keeping friends, and maintaining a supportive, flexible relationship within the family become difficult. Sometimes anxiety is limited to generalized, free-floating feelings of uneasiness. At other times, it develops into panic attacks and phobias.

■ IDENTIFYING THE SIGNS

Anxiety disorders vary from teenager to teenager. Symptoms generally include excessive fears and worries, feelings of inner restlessness, and a tendency to be excessively wary and vigilant. Even in the absence of an actual threat, some teenagers describe feelings of continual nervousness, restlessness, or extreme stress.

In a social setting, anxious teenagers may appear dependent, withdrawn, or uneasy. They seem either overly restrained or overly emotional. They may be preoccupied with worries about losing control or unrealistic concerns about social competence.

Teenagers who suffer from excessive anxiety regularly experience a range of physical symptoms as well. They may complain about muscle tension and cramps, stomachaches, headaches, pain in the limbs and back, fatigue, or discomforts associated with pubertal changes. They may blotch, flush, sweat, hyperventilate, tremble, and startle easily.

Anxiety during adolescence typically centers on changes in the way the adolescent's body looks and feels, social acceptance, and conflicts about independence. When flooded with anxiety, adolescents may appear extremely shy. They may avoid their usual activities or refuse to engage in new experiences. They may protest whenever they are apart from friends. Or in an attempt to diminish or deny their fears and worries, they may engage in risky behaviors, drug experimentation, or impulsive sexual behavior.

PANIC DISORDER. More common in girls than boys, panic disorder emerges in adolescence usually between the ages of fifteen and nineteen. Feelings of intense panic may arise without any noticeable cause or they may be triggered by specific situations, in which case they are called *panic attacks.* A panic attack is an abrupt episode of severe anxiety with accompanying emotional and physical symptoms.

During a panic attack, the youngster may feel overwhelmed by an intense fear or discomfort, a sense of impending doom, the fear he's going crazy, or sensations of unreality. Accompanying the emotional symptoms may be shortness of breath, sweating, choking, chest pains, nausea, dizziness, and numbness or tingling in his extremities. During an attack, some teens may feel they're dying or can't think. Following a panic attack, many youngsters worry that they will have other attacks and try to avoid situations that they believe may trigger them. Because of this fearful anticipation, the teen may begin to avoid normal activities and routines.

PHOBIAS. Many fears of younger children are mild, passing, and considered within the range of normal development. Some teenagers develop exaggerated and usually inexplicable fears called *phobias* that center on specific objects or situations. These intense fears can limit a teenager's activities. The fear generated by a phobia is excessive and not a rational response to a situation. The objects of a phobia usually change as a child gets older. While very young children may be preoccupied with the dark, monsters, or actual dangers, adolescents' phobic fears tend to involve school and social performance.

Several studies have revealed an increase in *school avoidance* in middle-school or junior-high years. With school avoidance, excessive worries about performance or social pressures at school may be at the root of the reluctance to attend school regularly. This leads to a cycle of anxiety, physical complaints, and school avoidance. The cycle escalates with the worsening of physical complaints such as stomachaches, headaches, and menstrual cramps. Visits to the doctor generally fail to uncover general medical explanations. The longer a teenager stays out of school, the harder it becomes for him to overcome his fear and anxiety and return to school. He feels increasingly isolated from school activities and different from other kids. (See also *School Refusal, Truancy, and Dropping Out,* page 141.)

Some youngsters are naturally more timid

than others. As their bodies, voices, and emotions change during adolescence, they may feel even more self-conscious. Despite initial feelings of uncertainty, most teens are able to join in if given time to observe and warm up. In extreme cases, called *social phobia*, the adolescent becomes very withdrawn, and though he wants to take part in social activities, he's unable to overcome intense self-doubt and worry. Gripped by excessive or unreasonable anxiety when faced with entering a new or unfamiliar social situation, the adolescent with social phobia becomes captive to unrelenting fears of other people's judgment or expectations. He may deal with his social discomfort by fretting about his health, appearance, or overall competence. Alternatively, he may behave in a clowning or boisterous fashion or consume alcohol to deal with the anxiety.

Because so much of a teenager's social life gets played out in school, social phobia may overlap with and be hard to distinguish from school avoidance. Some teens with social phobia may try to sidestep their anxious feelings altogether by refusing to attend or participate in school. Classroom and academic performance falls off, involvement in social and extracurricular activities dwindles, and, as a consequence, self-esteem declines.

Some teens may experience such a high level of anxiety that they cannot leave the house. This disorder, *agoraphobia*, seems to stem from feelings about being away from parents and fears of being away from home rather than fear of the world. In fact, a number of children who demonstrate severe separation anxiety in early childhood go on to develop agoraphobia as adolescents and adults.

■ Causes and Consequences

Most researchers believe that a predisposition towards timidity and nervousness is inborn. If one parent is naturally anxious, there's a good chance that their child will also have anxious tendencies. At the same time, a parent's own uneasiness is often communicated to the child, compounding the child's natural sensitivity. A cycle of increasing uneasiness may then be established. By the time this child reaches adolescence, his characteristic way of experiencing and relating to his world is tinged with anxiety. Some research suggests that children who are easily agitated or upset never learned to soothe themselves earlier in life.

In many cases, adolescent anxiety disorders may have begun earlier as *separation anxiety*, the tendency to become flooded with fearfulness whenever separated from home or from those to whom the child is attached, usually a parent. Adolescents can also have separation disorders. These teens may deny anxiety about separation, yet it may be reflected in their reluctance to leave home and resistance to being drawn into independent activity. Separation anxiety is often behind a teen's refusal to attend or remain at school.

School avoidance can follow a significant change at school, such as the transition into middle school or junior high. It may also be triggered by something unrelated to school, such as a divorce, illness, or a death in the family. Some youngsters become fearful about gang activities or the lack of safety in school.

A worried teenager performs less well in school, sports, and social interactions. Too much worry can also result in a teenager's failing to achieve to his potential. A teen who experiences a great deal of anxiety may be overly conforming, perfectionistic, and unsure of himself. In attempting to gain approval or avoid disapproval, he may redo tasks or procrastinate. The anxious youngster often seeks excessive reassurance about his identity and whether he is good enough.

Some teenagers with anxiety disorders can also develop mood disorders (see *Depressive Disorders,* page 209, and *Bipolar Mood Disorders,* page 217) or eating disorders (see page 260). Some teenagers who experience persistent anxiety may also develop suicidal feelings or engage in self-destructive behaviors; these situations require immediate attention and treatment. (See *Teenage Suicide,* page 213.) Anxious teens may also use alcohol and drugs to self-medicate or self-soothe (see *Experimenting With Alcohol and Drugs,* page 94) or develop rituals in an effort to reduce or prevent anxiety (see *Obsessive-Compulsive Disorder,* page 201).

■ HOW TO RESPOND

If your teenager is willing to talk about his fears and anxieties, listen carefully and respectfully. Without discounting his feelings, help him understand that increased feelings of uneasiness about his body, performance, and peer acceptance and a general uncertainty are all natural parts of adolescence.

By helping him trace his anxiety to specific situations and experiences, you may help him reduce the overwhelming nature of his feelings. Reassure him that, although his concerns are real, in all likelihood he will be able to handle them and that as he gets older, he will develop different techniques to be better able to deal with stress and anxiety.

Remind him of other times when he was initially afraid but still managed to enter into new situations, such as junior high school or camp. Praise him when he takes part in spite of his uneasiness. Point out that you are proud of his ability to act in the face of considerable anxiety. Remember, your teenager may not always be comfortable talking about feelings that he views as signs of weakness. While it may seem at the moment as though he's not listening, later he may be soothed by your attempts to help.

If fearfulness begins to take over your teenager's life and limit his activities, or if the anxiety lasts over six months, seek professional advice. His doctor or teacher will be able to recommend a child and adolescent psychiatrist or other professional specializing in treating adolescents.

Managing anxiety disorders—as with any adolescent emotional disturbance—usually requires a combination of treatment interventions. The most effective plan must be individualized to the teenager and his family. While these disorders can cause considerable distress and disruption to the teen's life, the overall prognosis is good. (See also *Emotional Factors Producing Illness,* page 177.)

Treatment for an anxiety disorder begins with an evaluation of symptoms, family and social context, and the extent of interference or impairment to the teen. Parents, as well as the teenager, should be included in this process. School records and personnel may be consulted to identify how the teen's performance and function in school has been affected by the disorder.

The evaluating clinician will also consider any underlying physical illnesses or diseases, such as diabetes, that could be causing the anxiety symptoms. Medications that might cause anxiety (such as some drugs used in treating asthma) will be reviewed. Since large amounts of caffeine, in coffee or soft drinks, can cause agitation, a clinician might look at the youngster's diet as well. Other biological, psychological, family, and social factors that might predispose the youngster to undue anxiety will also be considered.

If a teenager refuses to go to school, a clinician will explore other possible explanations before labeling it school avoidance. Perhaps the teen is being threatened or harassed, is depressed, or has an unrecognized learning disability. He may also be skipping school in order to be with friends, not from anxiety about performance or separation.

If the teenager has engaged in suicidal or self-endangering behavior, is trying to self-medicate through alcohol or drug use, or is seriously depressed, these problems should be addressed immediately. In such cases, hospitalization may be recommended to protect the youngster.

In most cases, treatment of anxiety disorders focuses on reducing the symptoms of anxiety, relieving distress, preventing complications associated with the disorder, and minimizing the effects on the teen's social, school, and developmental progress. If the problem manifests in school avoidance, the initial goal will be to get the youngster back to school as soon as possible.

Cognitive-Behavioral Therapy. In many cases, cognitive-behavioral psychotherapy techniques are effective in addressing adolescent anxiety disorders. Such approaches help the teenager examine his anxiety, anticipate situations in which it is likely to occur, and understand its effects. (See *Cognitive-Behavioral Therapy*, page 323.) This can help a youngster recognize the exaggerated nature of his fears and develop a corrective approach to the problem. Moreover, cognitive-behavioral therapy tends to be specific to the anxiety problem, and the teen actively participates, which usually enhances the youngster's understanding.

Other Therapies. In some instances, long-term psychotherapy (see *Individual Psychotherapy,* page 320), and family therapy (see *Family Therapy,* page 326) may also be recommended.

Medications. When symptoms are severe, a combination of therapy and medication may be used. Antidepressant medications, such as nortriptyline (Pamelor), imipramine (Tofranil), doxepin (Sinequan), paroxetine (Paxil), sertraline (Zoloft), or fluoxetine (Prozac), or anxiety-reducing drugs, such as alprazolam (Xanax), clonazepam (Klonopin), or lorazepam (Ativan) may be prescribed in combination with cognitive or other psychotherapy. When tricyclic antidepressant medications such as imipramine are prescribed, your teen's physician may want to monitor for potential side effects by conducting periodic physical exams and occasional electrocardiograms (EKGs).

Obsessive-Compulsive Disorder

As many as 2 percent of the adolescent population suffers from obsessive-compulsive disorders (OCD). Usually appearing around age ten, this disorder affects more teenage girls than boys.

While most people use some rituals and routine to establish some degree of order and calm in our lives, the uncontrolled rituals and repetitive worries of teens with OCD become means by which they attempt unsuccessfully to decrease anxiety. The symptoms drive their lives, significantly compromise their functioning, and, in severe cases, can disrupt their emotional, social, and cognitive development.

■ IDENTIFYING THE SIGNS

An adolescent with OCD usually experiences both *obsessions* and *compulsions.* Obsessions are unwanted intrusive thoughts, images, or impulses that the person recognizes as senseless or unnecessary. Obsessions push their way into a teenager's mind involuntarily, producing distress and interfering with the adolescent's ability to go about his day-to-day activities. The adolescent may ruminate over dirt, germs, and contamination; harm happening to him or his loved ones; exactness or symmetry; and religious

scruples. Frequently, obsessions center on bodily functions and sexual or aggressive preoccupations.

Compulsions are repetitive and ritualistic actions, carried out in response to a perceived internal obligation. They regularly follow certain rituals or rules, for which the teen can often recite elaborate and precise chronology, rate, order, duration, and number of repetitions. These rituals may be motivated directly by obsessions or an effort to ward off certain thoughts, impulses, or fears. An adolescent may, for example, wash his hands dozens of times a day, even to the point where the skin becomes chapped and raw, to reduce his anxiety about dirt. Compulsions commonly seen during adolescence include other such repetitive behaviors as ordering or checking or such mental acts as praying, counting, or repeating words silently.

Rather than providing a soothing influence or directly relieving anxiety, obsessions and compulsions tend to increase anxiety or distress in the teen with OCD. The obsessions go beyond excessive worries about real-life problems. Seldom is there a logical connection between the rituals and the situation or object they are intended to address. Moreover, they don't even make sense to the person himself. In most teenagers suffering from OCD, the worries and behavior tend to change over time with various obsessions and compulsions occurring simultaneously.

■ CAUSES AND CONSEQUENCES

OCD has a biochemical component, with similarities to depressive disorders. (See

Depressive Disorders, page 209.) It is more likely to occur in children and adolescents whose parents also have (or previously had) OCD.

In most cases, academic achievement is not severely affected by OCD, but peer relationships often are compromised. Severe symptoms can consume an adolescent and his family. Cleaning rituals, doing and undoing of various tasks, and checking rituals can consume hours in the day, interfere with sleep, and prevent completion of even simple tasks.

Early on, as the obsessions and compulsions are emerging, parents often try to convince themselves that their youngster is only involved in peculiar habits or passing through a phase. The teen may acknowledge that he, too, sees the odd nature of his behavior, leading his parents to believe that the symptoms are within his control. The teen who suffers from OCD has lost some control over his thoughts and actions and his pleading, extorting, or bargaining may involve the parents.

■ HOW TO RESPOND

If your adolescent's OCD seriously limits his activities and interferes with your life and his daily routines, seek professional advice. Your teen's physician will be able to recommend a child and adolescent psychiatrist or other professional specializing in treating teenagers with OCD. The evaluating professional will involve parents and may include other family members, as well as your teen. The treatment process will likely begin with an evaluation of symptoms and the family

and social context and a careful review of the teen's development.

Managing OCD—as with all adolescent emotional disorders—usually requires a combination of treatments. Just how the problem is approached depends on the teen, the family, and the specific treatment setting chosen. While OCD can cause considerable distress and disability, effective treatment can enable the adolescent's healthy development to continue.

Treatment will center on reducing the symptoms; relieving distress; preventing complications associated with the disorder; and minimizing the effects on the teen's social, school, and developmental progress. If the problem manifests in school avoidance, the initial goal will be to get the youngster back to school.

Parents may feel embarrassed and secretive about the content of and limitations imposed by their teen's symptoms. Once parents recognize the symptoms, which is usually early in the development of OCD, prompt professional evaluation is crucial, as effective treatment can relieve the teen's symptoms. The symptoms won't abate without help, and giving in to or assisting in the enactment of these symptoms is rarely helpful to the teen. Despite a youngster's awareness that the thoughts and acts are unnecessary, obsessive-compulsive behavior is not just a phase. These teenagers have lost some control over their thoughts and actions. They have a biological disorder and need the help of a child and adolescent psychiatrist or other qualified professional.

Effective treatment of OCD should combine a number of elements over an extended period of time, including medication and family and individual therapy. Learning about the disorder is also an important part of treatment. The task for parents and teen is to learn how to live with this biological susceptibility and get treatment when symptoms are severe.

Psychotherapy. Because adolescents with OCD are likely to be apprehensive, the ability of the clinician to establish a solid relationship is critical to success. A good therapeutic relationship can absorb much of the teen's anxiety and promote open discussion. Many teenagers feel uneasy when asked to describe their thoughts and rituals, especially if the subjects involve bathroom or sexual material. Psychotherapy can help teens deal with their emotional conflicts and reactions to their obsessive-compulsive behavior. Psychotherapy can also address related problems: anxiety about family problems or divorce; loss of self-esteem; unrealistic expectations; perfectionistic striving; regulation of sexual or aggressive impulses; and the general effects of having a chronic psychiatric illness during one's development. Because OCD is often chronic, effective therapy can require months or even years.

Family Therapy. This approach addresses the way in which symptoms affect family life. It provides an opportunity to identify ways in which family members unwittingly perpetuate symptoms as well as other problems that could be promoting symptoms. It also offers support to family members as they learn about this disturbing illness and ways in which they can help the teenager. (See also *Family Therapy,* page 326.)

Cognitive-Behavioral Therapy. Found effective in treating OCD, cognitive therapy focuses on changing the irrational beliefs and distorted thoughts at the root of the disorder. Behavioral techniques may include, for example, a method to reduce the youngster's anxiety so that obsessive-compulsive behavior is prevented. (See also *Cognitive-Behavioral Therapy*, page 323.)

Medication. Certain medications in combination with psychotherapy are helpful in reducing symptoms of OCD. Among medications prescribed are antidepressant medications, such as fluvoxamine (Luvox), fluoxetine (Prozac), paroxetine (Paxil), sertraline (Zoloft), bupropion (Wellbutrin), desipramine (Norpramin), imipramine (Tofranil), nortriptyline (Pamelor), and venlafaxine (Effexor). When tricyclic antidepressant medications such as imipramine are prescribed, your teen's physician may want to monitor for potential side effects by conducting periodic physical exams and occasional electrocardiograms (EKGs).

Hospitalization. In most cases, an adolescent child with OCD can be effectively evaluated and treated as an outpatient. Admission to a hospital is not necessary unless the family's capacity to support the teenager is thoroughly depleted or overwhelmed, or the OCD symptoms cause the teen to become self-destructive or dangerous.

Tics and Tourette's Disorder

A tic is a rapid, repeated twitch of a muscle that produces a quick, sudden, and uncontrollable movement. The affected muscles will begin to twitch for no apparent reason. Parts of the body most frequently involved include the face, neck, shoulders, body trunk, and hands. Sounds that are made involuntarily are called vocal tics.

Teens who have tics usually developed them between the ages of six and ten. Tics are three times more common in boys than girls. Tics can be voluntarily suppressed for brief periods, and most are mild and hardly noticeable. In some cases, however, they are frequent and severe and can affect many areas of an adolescent's life.

■ IDENTIFYING THE SIGNS

The most common tic disorder is called *transient tic disorder*. Affecting up to 10 percent of children during the early school years, it is less common during adolescence. Tics that last one year or more are called *chronic tics*. Chronic tics affect less than 1 percent of children and may be related to a more unusual tic disorder called *Tourette's disorder*.

Tourette's disorder usually appears by the age of fifteen. Teens with Tourette's disorder have both body and vocal tics. Some tics disappear by early adulthood, and some continue. Teens with Tourette's disorder may also have problems with attention and concentration. They may act impulsively, may develop obsessions and compulsions, and may blurt out certain words or phrases, including, in rare instances, obscenities. Tourette's disorder sometimes occurs along with obsessive-compulsive disorder. (See *Attention-Deficit/ Hyperactivity Disorder,* page 225.)

■ CAUSES AND CONSEQUENCES

Transient tics can occur in bright, highly sensitive youngsters. Teens who are overly shy or self-conscious are more likely to have tics than those who are more relaxed. Transient tics disappear by themselves over time. The tics associated with Tourette's disorder, however, do not simply disappear.

Although the precise cause of Tourette's disorder is not known, it appears to run in families. There is some evidence that certain stimulants used to treat attention-deficit/ hyperactivity disorder in children (for example, methylphenidate) may worsen or exacerbate an existing tic. The symptoms of Tourette's disorder often become less evident over time, but the course of the syndrome is unpredictable.

■ HOW TO RESPOND

Teens with tics or Tourette's disorder cannot control these sounds and movements and should not be blamed for them. Punishment by parents, teasing by classmates, and scolding by teachers will not help the teen control the tics and may damage the teenager's self-esteem. This can be a major source of stress and shame for a teen who is seeking acceptance and approval from peers.

The best approach to transient tics is to

ignore them. In the vast majority of cases, they go away on their own. Helping your teenager become more relaxed may help speed their exit. You can help do this by making sure your youngster is not overscheduled and has free time to unwind and by not being overly critical.

If the tics become frequent (more than ten a day), last for more than a year, interfere with school or friendships, or involve coughing, sounds, words, or profanity, see your teen's doctor. Through a comprehensive medical evaluation, often involving pediatric and neurologic consultation, a child and adolescent psychiatrist or other professionals with expertise in adolescent disorders can determine whether a youngster has Tourette's disorder or some other tic disorder. The professionals can also advise the family about how to provide emotional support and the appropriate home environment for the youngster with persistent tics.

Treatment for a teen with a tic disorder may include medication such as clonidine (Catapres), haloperidol (Haldol), or pimozide (Orap) to help control the symptoms. In most cases, it is easier to control the teen's vocal tics than to eliminate all the body tics. In addition, individual psychotherapy or family therapy is often necessary to address the anger, depression, and other behavior problems sometimes associated with the adolescent with Tourette's disorder. Family therapy may also help provide support and lessen stress in the home for all family members.

Childhood Trauma and Its Effects

An adolescent who is referred to a school guidance counselor or a mental health clinician for a specific problem—disruptive behavior, truancy, or threatened suicide, for example—may reveal that, at some point in his life, he has suffered through a horrible event that has left him traumatized.

Such experiences as violent crimes, natural disasters, plane crashes, or long-term abuse within the family can cause trauma in children. Children or adolescents may then develop acute and, at times, chronic emotional disturbances.

Trauma is defined as an event more overwhelming than a teen would be expected to encounter. While a divorce in the family is upsetting, it would not constitute psychic trauma; in contrast, a child witnessing one parent knifing the other would. Children who experience such horrible events may also experience emotional harm or develop emotional difficulties as a direct result of the trauma. Left untreated, all but the mildest of psychic trauma can resonate throughout a person's life.

Researchers have identified two basic types of psychic trauma: one episode or *single-blow trauma,* which results from one sudden and unexpected event such as a rape, a bad car accident, or a devastating tornado; and *repeated trauma,* which arises from long-standing offenses to a person's integrity, such as sexual or physical abuse. Each type of psychic trauma has characteristic signs.

SINGLE-BLOW TRAUMA. Also called Type I posttraumatic stress disorder (PTSD), single-blow trauma produces a number of characteristic symptoms. Children or adolescents who experience single-blow trauma usually retain detailed memories of the event for a long time. No matter how much an adolescent may try to forget, these memories remain vivid. Unlike regular memories, these are uncontrollable, intruding into daily activities and interfering with day-to-day routines.

Teenagers often attempt to gain mastery over the randomness and lack of control evidenced in a sudden disaster by asking *Why me?* They become preoccupied with finding reasons, a purpose, and ways in which the event could have been averted. When this reworking and rethinking is not successful, a teen can become pessimistic about the future and feel little purpose in life. Some young people also experience visual hallucinations both immediately following and long after the single-event trauma. After watching a sister die, for example, a youngster may see her revisit him as he tries to go to sleep.

REPEATED TRAUMA. Also called Type II posttraumatic stress disorder, repeated trauma occurs in teenagers who have been abused often and for a long time. Chronic trauma is also common in children who have been reared in war zones. Many of the same symptoms that accompany Type I occur, as well as additional ones with Type II. Because the trauma is repeated or prolonged, the youngster develops a sickening anticipation and dread of another episode. After being repeat-edly traumatized, youngsters may have a confusing combination of feelings, at times feeling angry, at others sad or fearful. Often these children or teens appear detached and seem to have no feelings. Such emotional numbness is a hallmark of this type of trauma.

■ IDENTIFYING THE SIGNS

Immediately following any kind of traumatic event, young people commonly experience brief and usually limited denial and emotional numbness. They will often try to stop thinking about the experience. Teens who have suffered through repeated traumatic horrors develop and use a variety of psychological mechanisms to cope.

Some teens (such as youngsters who are regularly abused physically) may develop a type of self-hypnosis that enables them to deaden and escape, at least in their minds, the pain of the trauma. This self-hypnosis is called *dissociation*. Reliance upon dissociation as a coping mechanism can have negative effects on a teenager's development.

Long-standing or repeated abuse also produces rage. Anger festers, occasionally exploding in tantrums and violent behavior. A teen may turn this rage against himself, engaging in self-endangering behavior. He may direct his anger through aggressive or delinquent behavior, or he may identify with the aggressor, turning the rage toward others, victimizing and humiliating them. On the other hand, the adolescent may also experience aggression as dangerous, so his behavior may become extremely passive, leading to victimization.

Internal changes may occur as the teen

tries to adapt to both the trauma and the loss caused by the trauma. For example, psychic numbing may minimize the pain. Holding tenaciously to the specific memory of the trauma may be an effort to master the experience. Developing a belief in omens—attaching meanings to unrelated occurrences such as an eclipse or a sudden thunderstorm, for example—may be an attempt to reduce the adolescent's sense of helplessness. The resulting state of unresolved mourning and continuing grief, however, interferes with the teen's ability to live and learn.

In cases where the event has led to disfigurement, disability, or prolonged pain, a teen may feel guilt, shame, self-revulsion, or rage if his peers shun or tease him. Suicide attempts or self-mutilating behavior may also occur with these teenagers. (See *Teenage Suicide,* page 213.)

RELIVING THE TRAUMATIC EVENT. Traumatic events may be repressed but are not fully forgotten. The teenager may re-experience the trauma through any of his senses. He may experience vivid and unwelcome flashbacks, most often during quiet, unfocused times, when the youngster is bored in class, falling asleep, listening to the radio, or watching television.

In the adolescent's activities or behavior, he will recall and attempt to rework the event. Drawings, writings, and stories may incorporate and reflect the traumatic event(s). Although this may be referred to as "play," repetitive posttraumatic behavior is more often grim work that resembles slave labor. Reliving the event represents an attempt to master fears that continue to haunt the teenager.

Typically, trauma shatters the natural sense of invincibility and trust basic to normal youngsters. This shakes the teen's confidence about the future and can lead to limited expectations. Traumatized teenagers often have a pessimistic future view of career, marriage, children, and even life expectancy.

Other signs common to those who suffer posttraumatic stress syndrome include sleep problems; panic; deliberate avoidance of trauma reminders; irritability; immature or regressed behavior; and overvigilance and depression.

■ CAUSES AND CONSEQUENCES

Psychic trauma (PTSD Type I and PTSD Type II) occurs as a result of overwhelming and horrible external events over which the child or teen has no control. The experience renders the young person temporarily helpless.

Childhood trauma can also mimic a number of other serious emotional disorders, both in childhood and later in adolescence or adulthood. It is not uncommon to find that a teen brought to a mental health professional for other problems—conduct disorder (see *Conduct Disorders,* page 236), a major depression (see *Depressive Disorders,* page 209), attention-deficit/hyperactivity disorder (see *Attention-Deficit/Hyperactivity Disorder,* page 225), obsessive-compulsive disorder (see *Obsessive-Compulsive Disorder,* page 201), panic disorder (see *Panic Disorder,* page 197), antisocial or violent behavior (see *Oppositional Defiant Disorder,* page 232)—

has also experienced an intense, terrible trauma or series of traumatic events.

Childhood trauma darkens the teen's vision of the future as well as attitudes about people. Young people who have been traumatized will voice cautious, one-day-at-a-time attitudes. They may say they can't count on anyone. Sexually traumatized girls may shrink from men (using avoidance to cope with the trauma) or approach them with overly friendly advances (if they attempt to master the trauma by trying to relive it). Teenagers who have been traumatized tend to recognize the profound vulnerability in all people, especially themselves.

Trauma-related fears often persist into adulthood. While many anxious teenagers express some apprehension about growing up or getting married, sexually abused teens may grow up fearing sexual contact.

Passing fears—of strangers, lurking objects, the dark, being alone—are not uncommon at certain developmental stages of childhood and with other emotional disorders. Extreme panic and avoidance of these situations, however, may be the result of earlier exposure to severe trauma.

Within the traumatized teen, internal changes may occur, which can affect him later in adult life. Without treatment, some childhood trauma can result in later problems characterized by violent behavior, extremes of passivity and victimization (people who were raped or incestuously abused as children are often raped again), self-mutilation, suicidal or self-endangering behavior, multiple-personality disorder, and a variety of anxiety disturbances.

■ How to Respond

Early intervention in psychic trauma is important. Families that offer support, understanding, and a sense of safety as close to the time of the traumatic event as possible can effectively limit the negative effects of the trauma. Your adolescent's physician may also recommend consulting a child and adolescent psychiatrist or other mental health professional for evaluation and treatment.

Psychotherapy. Group or individual therapy that allows the teen to talk about the trauma in his own words over a period of time can help him move through the posttrauma stages and get beyond the pain, mastering the experience, and develop better coping skills.

Therapy will support the youngster as he describes feelings. In time, he may be able to understand his symptoms, behavior, and characteristic ways of dealing with the trauma. Moreover, talk and directed creative expression (perhaps including music and drama) eventually give the teenager the opportunity to look at the event or series of events in context and to gain perspective. Gradually, the teen is helped to see that what happened to him was an encapsulated experience, a personal disaster that occurred in a moment in time, rather than as a fate that determines and controls the rest of his life.

Medication. Occasionally, medication is prescribed to treat symptoms of posttraumatic or acute stress disorder. Among the medications that might be prescribed are antidepressants, such as doxepin (Sinequan), imipramine (Tofranil), nortriptyline (Pamelor), and anxiety-reducing agents, such as clonazepam (Klonopin) or lorazepam (Ativan).

Adolescents who experience severe psychic trauma can be helped and are responsive to treatment. With the sensitivity and the support of his family, a teenager can accommodate the memory of the trauma as someone who survived. The adolescent who has experienced a trauma can go on to lead a healthy, productive, satisfying life.

Depressive Disorders

Depression is a term used to describe a common condition characterized by feelings of sadness, gloom, misery, or despair. Most people experience temporary depression at various points in their lives. Teens with a depressive disorder, however, experience disturbing symptoms that are beyond the range of normal sadness or depression.

The teen years are often a time of brooding and melancholy, but some adolescents are especially prone to frequent and very distressing periods of depression. Your teenager may have a depressive disorder if his mood is consistently sad or if he sees his life and future as grim and bleak.

■ IDENTIFYING THE SIGNS

There are two basic types of depression: *major depression,* which lasts at least two-weeks, and the milder but chronic *dysthymic disorder*, in which a long-standing depressed mood seems to be connected with the teenager's temperament or disposition. Teens with depression may also have anxiety or exaggerated fears. (See *Anxiety and Avoidant Disorders*, page 196.) Not all youngsters with severe depression appear depressed. Instead, they may seem irritable or moody, swinging from great sadness to anger.

Usually there are other clues or signals that a youngster is depressed. He may lose interest or pleasure in many activities. He may sleep or eat too little or too much and may have difficulty concentrating or making decisions. Feelings of worthlessness, guilt, or anger may find expression in suicidal thoughts or ruminations about death.

During a period of depression, a teenager may look sad, tearful, withdrawn, uncharacteristically listless, and dull. He may seem to lack initiative or may appear agitated. He may neglect his appearance, looking dirty, with mismatched clothes and disheveled hair. This is not a fashion statement. His movements are slow; his voice sounds monotonous; his speech reflects hopelessness and despair. He frequently says things such as *I'm stupid* or *No one loves me* or *I'm bad.* While sensitive at these times to rejection by others, the depressed teen often has a negative or depressing effect on others, causing them to avoid him.

Teens with *dysthymic disorder* have milder symptoms of depression—a depressed, irritable, volatile mood; appetite and sleep changes; diminished energy; low self-esteem; feelings of hopelessness; poor concentration and indecisiveness—for a year or longer. This chronically depressed mood colors every experience, impression, and response, and the teen experiences most things negatively.

■ CAUSES AND CONSEQUENCES

Depression is a complex and multifaceted condition. Likely rooted in a genetic and/or biochemical predisposition, depression also can be linked to unresolved grief, possibly in response to early real or imagined losses of nurturing figures. Depression may also reflect that the adolescent has learned feelings of helplessness rather than feeling empowered to seek solutions for life's problems. Depressed thinking tends to be negative, hopeless, and self-defeating—reinforcing further feelings of depression.

Some seriously depressed adolescents have experienced early life and environmental stresses, including childhood trauma (see *Childhood Trauma and Its Effects,* page 205), such as the death of a parent or other significant person. They may live in families where they regularly witness or are victims of parental aggression, rejection or scapegoating, strict and punitive treatment, and parents abusing each other. Such family pressures may contribute to the development of depressed mood disturbance in a teenager.

Girls appear to suffer from feelings of depression during adolescence more often than boys (this continues into adulthood with women experiencing more depressive episodes than men). Complex neurobiological and sociocultural factors are the likely explanation for this difference. Because boys are often encouraged to translate feelings into actions, their depression is more likely to produce external behavioral disturbances and acting out. Girls, on the hand, are more often focused on or preoccupied by their internal feelings. As a result, they may be acutely self-conscious about their bodies and performance.

Depression usually interferes with a teenager's social and academic functioning. When an adolescent is depressed, school performance usually deteriorates. While depressed, a teenager cannot concentrate. He believes himself to be hopelessly unable to finish schoolwork, and he may skip classes and see his grades drop. Feeling depleted, listless, and incompetent, he may lose interest in extracurricular activities and drop out.

While teenagers are naturally more likely to sleep late in the morning whenever possible, a depressed teen will nap excessively throughout the day or go to bed early in the evening. He may complain of headaches or stomachaches, especially before attending a new social event. (See *Emotional Factors Producing Illness,* page 177.)

Hopelessness, despair that things will never change, and a general feeling of deadness may be expressed in suicide attempts or dangerous and self-injurious behavior. In addition, depressed teenagers may use drugs or alcohol, in some cases as self-medication to try to relieve their depression. (See *Teenage Suicide*, page 213.)

During adolescence, teens with severe depression may also have other emotional disorders, including delinquent behavior (see *Antisocial and Delinquent Behavior,* page 154), school attendance problems (see *School Refusal, Truancy, and Dropping Out,* page 141), anxiety disorders (see *Anxiety and Avoidant Disorders,* page 196), substance abuse (see *Substance Abuse Disorders,* page 279), and eating disorders (see *Eating and Nutritional Disorders*, page 260).

■ HOW TO RESPOND

In trying to decide whether symptoms are serious enough to seek help, talk with your teenager. Let him know that you see his sadness. By showing interest and the desire to help him understand his feelings, you bring hope to the teen. Parents often have difficulty understanding why a teen feels such a catastrophic sense of loss or perceived failure, so it's important to listen carefully to the teen and to try to imagine yourself in your youngster's position. Without pressuring him, point to activities he enjoys and handles successfully. Help build self-esteem by recognizing small triumphs and admiring his competence.

At the same time, try to determine whether the teenager seems capable of handling the feelings on his own or whether he seems overwhelmed. If the symptoms persist, particularly if they begin to interfere seriously with multiple areas of his life, ask his doctor or his school for the name of a child and adolescent psychiatrist or other professional trained to work with adolescents.

Treatment should begin with a full evaluation, which usually includes all members of the family. The assessment must include an evaluation of the risk of suicidal behavior and will seek to rule out substance use or an underlying physical disease or illness that could also produce depressive symptoms, as well as distinguish depression from simple bereavement.

Parents will be asked to describe symptoms and such behavioral changes as irritability, moodiness, and sleep and appetite changes and to report the duration of symptoms as well as any possible precipitating event.

Many parents who are also seriously depressed may have trouble accurately describing their teenagers' symptoms. They may either view everything in negative terms, therefore exaggerating problems, or be so preoccupied with their own depressive symptoms that they fail to observe their adolescent accurately. In such families, it is not uncommon for parents to be unaware of their teenager's sadness, suicidal thoughts, and sleep disturbances.

Individual Psychotherapy. Therapy offers support and empathy while encouraging exploration of the depressed feelings and symptoms. While creating a sense of safety by setting limits on dangerous behavior, a therapist will encourage a teenager to express his upsetting feelings, usually a sense of loss, powerlessness, aggression, or danger. Therapy helps the adolescent deal with these feelings rather than act them out. If a teenager's self-esteem seems particularly low, therapy may work to improve confidence and competence through skills training.

If a specific circumstance or event has precipitated the depression—divorce, for example—therapy gives the youngster a chance to resolve some of his feelings and accept even an unhappy reality.

Cognitive-Behavioral Therapy. Often effective in treating depression in adolescents, cognitive therapy focuses on the irrational beliefs and distorted thoughts that are part of depression, such as a negative view of the self, the world, and the future. Usually a depressed teen personalizes failure, magnifies negative events, and minimizes positive events and attributes. Sometimes these negative thought patterns have been formed or reinforced by the teen's home environment. Cognitive therapy focuses on identifying negative thought patterns or distortions and on helping the adolescent change his thinking. (See also *Cognitive-Behavioral Therapy*, page 323.)

Group Therapy. Group therapy for depressed teens can help them develop or improve social skills, which can lead to a greater sense of mastery and improved self-esteem. Teens may find it easier to express feelings in a supportive peer-group environment. This can be especially helpful during a developmental stage when peer groups are an increasingly important resource. Support groups for parents can help them manage specific problem behaviors, use positive reinforcement, better communicate with adolescents, and become better listeners for their youngster. (See also *Group Therapy*, page 328.)

Family Therapy. If the teenager is willing and able to work within a family context, family therapy can address certain problems that may worsen depression in teens: lack of generational boundaries; severe marital conflict; rigid or chaotic rules; and neglectful or overly involved parent-child relationships.

Family therapy can also help parents manage specific problem behaviors, use rein-

forcement correctly, listen and communicate with their teenager in an age-appropriate manner, and support the teenager as he prepares to move beyond his family structure. In addition, other family members with psychiatric disorders may be identified during family sessions, and they can be assisted in getting their own treatment. (See also *Family Therapy*, page 326.)

Medication. In moderately and severely depressed adolescents, antidepressants, such as bupropion (Wellbutrin), desipramine (Norpramin), fluoxetine (Prozac), imipramine (Tofranil), nortriptyline (Pamelor), paroxetine (Paxil), sertraline (Zoloft), and venlafaxine (Effexor), may be prescribed in combination with psychotherapy. Before the teen begins taking a medication, specific target symptoms should be identified in a discussion between the youngster, the parent, and the physician. Possible side effects and other aspects of the medication should be fully discussed; when tricyclic antidepressant medications, such as imipramine, are prescribed, your child's physician may want to monitor for potential side effects by conducting periodic physical exams and occasional electrocardiograms (EKGs).

Hospitalization. Any seriously depressed adolescent at risk for suicidal or self-endangering behavior must be immediately assessed. If he is preoccupied with suicide or has a well-thought-out plan, this constitutes an emergency situation, and his safety should be assured. (See *What to Do in Emergencies*, page 316.)

Teenage Suicide

That a teenager could be so unbearably unhappy that he would choose to kill himself is something that's almost too painful for a parent to examine. But with the increasing prevalence of teen suicide, no parent can afford to ignore the possibility.

Before the mid–1970s, suicide by adolescents appeared to be a rare event; now one out of ten teens contemplates suicide, and nearly a half million teens make a suicide attempt each year. Sadly, suicide has become the third leading cause of death for high-school students. Indeed, the actual rate of death by suicide may be higher, because some of these deaths have been incorrectly labeled "accidents."

◾ CAUSES AND CONSEQUENCES

One reason for the increased risk of death by suicide among teens is that the means of committing suicide are now so readily available: Firearms, pills, and other potential weapons of self-destruction can be easily obtained. Although more girls attempt suicide than boys, more boys than girls die by their own hand. This is partly related to the methods: Boys frequently use guns, which are more likely to have lethal consequences than an overdose of pills, a common method used by girls.

Underlying Factors. Researchers agree that life today brings greater pressures and stresses, and many adolescents have difficulty dealing with them by virtue of age, temperament, and upbringing. Other contributing factors include an increase in turmoil within families, societal violence, and feelings of despair.

Essentially, a suicide attempt results from the teen being completely overwhelmed and unable to cope. This might occur after a single catastrophic disappointment such as the breakup of a relationship; sometimes it's the result of a long decline, such as continual failure in school with unbearable feelings of frustration, anger, and shame. Other trigger factors can include profound changes within the nuclear family, such as divorce, remarriage, or the death of a parent; intense family discord; unreasonable parental expectations; a troubled relationship with parents; moving to a new community; a history of losses; and the suicide of a peer or family member.

◾ IDENTIFYING THE SIGNS

Young people under extreme stress often exhibit signs of depression. Since most adolescents experience mood swings, it can be difficult to distinguish serious depression from normal emotional lows. Duration of the lows is a very good clue: If your teenager's gloomy mood lasts for longer than two weeks, and he can't seem to shake it off and have fun, you have good cause to be concerned.

You need to be watchful for other symptoms of depression:

- Have his eating and sleeping habits changed?
- Has he undergone a marked personality change, either exhibiting angry actions or rebellious behavior or becoming suddenly shy and withdrawn?

- Has he stopped seeing his friends and enjoying his regular activities?

- Is he using drugs or alcohol or exhibiting other risky behaviors such as reckless driving?

- Has his schoolwork declined?

- Has he endured a recent humiliating experience?

- Does he have difficulty concentrating?

- Is he persistently bored and/or lethargic?

- Is he suddenly neglecting his appearance?

- Is he complaining about physical symptoms often related to emotional distress, such as headaches, stomachaches, and fatigue?

- Is he giving away his possessions or throwing away important belongings?

- Is he intolerant of praise or rewards?

- Is he writing about death, perhaps in songs or poems?

- Does he make comments such as *I can't take it anymore* or *nobody cares* or *nothing matters* or *I wish I was dead?*

Some people are at higher risk for making a suicide attempt than others. Those who are at higher risk tend to be withdrawn, impulsive, either aloof or aggressive, and overly perfectionistic. They are often black-or-white thinkers for whom a humiliation such as a poor grade, a bad showing on the basketball court, or a romantic rejection is catastrophic. They feel they can't or won't recover and that things will never get better. To a perfectionist, an embarrassment can't be laughed off; it

is devastation. Some teen suicide attempts may closely follow the death by suicide of a peer. (See *The Suicide of a Friend,* page 216.) If your adolescent has been depressed and an adolescent peer commits suicide, be particularly watchful.

■ How to Respond

A Parent's Role. If an adolescent says he is going to kill himself, *take it very seriously.* The overwhelming majority of suicide attempts closely follow such expressed threats of self-destruction. Even if your teenager doesn't appear depressed, if he has clearly given up on his future, you should be concerned. The problems a teen encounters during adolescence can trigger suicidal thoughts and impulses.

When you are concerned, talk to your teenager. It's a myth that talking to people about suicide will put thoughts in their heads. Instead, talking will reassure them that others truly care and, most importantly, will give them the opportunity to express feelings and their sense of helplessness or desperation.

Tell him you love him, and ask him to tell you what is troubling him. Remind him that although his problem may seem catastrophic right now, it can be worked out, and you'll help him to do so. Remove any weapons—guns, pills, ropes, and the like—from your house. Decreasing accessibility to means of destruction can lessen the risk of a serious attempt or even death.

Don't assume that your teen's situation will improve by itself, and don't dismiss your teen's problems, no matter how insignificant they may seem to you. To your despondent teenager his difficulties seem insurmountable. Reacting negatively or ignoring his worries out of your own fear or anxiety will stop any communication, increase his feelings of isolation and despair, and add to his burden.

Fortunately, many teenage suicide attempts don't succeed. Some suicide attempts aren't really meant to succeed ("parasuicide"), appearing to be a misguided cry for help or a means of getting attention. Any suicide attempt, however, means a teenager is in crisis and needs psychiatric help (and usually his family does, as well). He is clearly suffering, and his family must get him professional attention and do everything they can to relieve his suffering and pain.

Since many of us at one time or another have felt hopeless and helpless, we assume we can identify with a teenager who is feeling this way. But depressed adults know from experience that such feelings are only temporary; an experienced adult can usually conjure up reassuring memories of being in control of their lives and can use this knowledge to make adjustments. By contrast, when an adolescent sees his life as bleak, it's hard for him to realize that it's a transitory state.

Professional Intervention. Whether your teenager is in immediate danger or not, many communities have suicide prevention hotlines and professionals who can help you. Or ask your pediatrician, school counselor, or county social service agency to recommend a child and adolescent psychiatrist or other profes-

sional who can provide a comprehensive evaluation and treatment plan. Even if your teen shrugs off his actions (or words) and says he was only trying to scare you and didn't intend to kill himself, the fact that he had to resort to such tactics suggests that he needs to learn better communication and coping skills. An outsider can be objective; that distance can be helpful in getting a depressed teenager to talk.

With antidepressant medications such as fluoxetine (Prozac) getting so much press, parents may think that a prescription may be enough to get their youngster out of a funk. While researchers know that depression has a biochemical component that is often responsive to medication, treatment should begin with a comprehensive evaluation. Therapy will then focus on what is causing the depression, anger, or inability to cope. An antidepressant medication then may be prescribed in *conjunction* with such therapy.

Lessening the Risks. Some teens easily handle problems and bounce back from them; others are crushed by stressors and feel that suicide is their only option.

For the lucky ones, the individual's emotional resiliency acts like a protective barrier. Though we don't yet have all of the answers about neurochemical responses to stress, we do know that two important factors help a stressed individual overcome adversity—family climate and personality traits.

Affectionate, involved, and supportive parents help their teenagers develop and refine their social, cognitive, and intellectual abilities. Increased confidence and self-

THE SUICIDE OF A FRIEND

When an adolescent commits suicide—particularly if the event is discussed by the media—other teens may be at increased risk by virtue of what has been labeled the contagion effect. To a vulnerable peer, the dead teen's use of suicide as a quick and easy solution to life's difficulties may seem glamorous, since it was on the evening news or the front page of the newspaper.

Experts agree that communities should avoid romanticizing or overly memorializing a teenager who has killed himself. In fact, most experts favor a reduction in media coverage of youth suicide, because studies have found an increase in adolescent suicide deaths following both actual and fictional media presentations of suicides.

Suicide prevention programs have been developed as a means of responding to the suicide of a student within a community. The aim of such programs is to contain the potential for imitative suicidal behavior among the suicide's peers. Intervention efforts are specifically geared to minimizing the contagion effect. If your local media devotes extensive coverage to teenage deaths, consider approaching them and explaining why they should consider changing this practice.

Talk to your own teen about what happened. Listen to his thoughts on why a peer committed suicide. He's trying to understand what happened, and perhaps you can help him appreciate that committing suicide isn't an heroic act but a desperate failure to adapt to the world. If your youngster seems to identify closely with the peer's decision, he may be at risk himself. (See "A Parent's Role" in *Teenage Suicide*, page 214.)

esteem in the teen fosters greater resiliency to stress. Consistency and good communication between parent and teenager reinforce and strengthen resilient behavior. Applying too much pressure to succeed or being overly critical can produce stress and problems for your teen. Whether households have one parent or two, teenagers are more likely to develop resiliency tools with loving, supportive, and flexible parents.

We don't enter the world as perfectly blank slates, and temperament plays a large part in a person's ability to cope with stress. Clearly, self-esteem, self-confidence, and adaptability are a combination of genetic and environmental factors.

Experience is a critical influence on behavior. Teenagers can be helped to temper their responses to situations and to control impulses, which are crucial tools in handling stress. Teens can also learn to be responsible and sensitive to others, giving them a better understanding of their place in the world. Academic and scholastic performance in school also imparts a measure of personal power and a sense of control, both of which are protective barriers against stress.

Bipolar Mood Disorder

Some teenagers are trouble by both depressed and elevated or euphoric moods. The youngster's mood may shift suddenly from one extreme to the other; sometimes there is a rapid cycle between high and low moods. Teens with these severe mood changes may have a *bipolar mood disorder.*

■ IDENTIFYING THE SIGNS

In bipolar disorders, manic episodes usually alternate with periods of depression and relatively normal moods. The manic element of bipolar or *manic-depressive* disorder is signaled by an elevated, expansive, angry, suspicious, or irritable mood lasting at least one week.

During a manic episode, a teenager irrationally distorts his view of himself and has inflated self-esteem. He may talk constantly and rapidly and have difficulty sticking to one idea or subject at a time.

He is easily distracted, appears agitated and restless, and sleeps very little. Most alarming, he may engage in reckless and dangerous activities. Bipolar disturbance usually interferes with school functioning or peer and family relations.

During manic episodes, adolescents often experience psychotic symptoms such as hallucinations and delusions. They may report hearing voices or seeing visions. Intense paranoid thinking can result in belligerent or aggressive confrontations. Delusions of grandeur—during which the teen believes he has special powers or importance—can lead to dangerous behavior, such as driving fast and recklessly or jumping off roofs.

Manic teenagers tend to externalize their problems. They perceive themselves to be fine, blaming conditions or people in their environment for their difficulties.

Their behavior and appearance may make them extremely hard to tolerate. Their hygiene may suffer, and they can refuse to eat and sleep. Hyperactive, silly, giggly, or aggressive in their verbal communications, they may use profanities and make sexual comments freely during a manic episode.

In children and younger adolescents, manic episodes are often characterized by irritability and moodiness. By the time a child reaches puberty, distinct signs of euphoria, elation, paranoia, and grandiose delusions may become more apparent. As bipolar disorder is developing or evolving in a teen, sadness, mania, and agitation are often intermixed. With time, the teen may show more evidence of severe depression and mania. Other features of a manic episode may include hyperactivity, talkativeness, and excessive distractibility. When the disorder is milder, the mood disturbance is called *cyclothymic disorder.*

■ CAUSES AND CONSEQUENCES

Bipolar disorders tend to occur in families. In addition to the genetic component, parenting can also have a role in the disorder. As a result of their own intense moods and feelings, some parents with mood disorders have difficulty being consistent and effective in their parenting.

■ HOW TO RESPOND

Treatment of bipolar disorders (manic-depressive illness) should begin with a full evaluation by a child and adolescent psychiatrist or other qualified professional. Due to the frequent occurrence of psychotic symptoms such as delusions and hallucinations in combination with social withdrawal, poor hygiene, irritability, and temper tantrums, bipolar disorders may be mistaken as schizophrenia in a teenager. (See also *Psychotic Disorders,* page 270.)

Individual Psychotherapy. Since bipolar disorder is a lifelong condition, it is crucial that the young person learn about the disorder and how to live with it. When identified, symptoms can be successfully treated and controlled. In addition, stressors that might precipitate symptoms can be avoided, reduced, or coped with. When coping skills are learned, these teenagers and their families can lead emotionally rich and productive lives.

Cognitive-Behavioral Therapy. Often effective in treating the ups and downs of bipolar disorder in teens, cognitive therapy focuses on the irrational beliefs and distorted thoughts that are part of the mania or depression. In dealing with periods of depression, the therapy may address the youngster's negative view of self, the world, and the future. Such negative thought patterns may have been formed or reinforced by the family environment. Cognitive therapy focuses on identifying and correcting negative distortions and on helping the teen change his thinking. (See also *Cognitive-Behavioral Therapy*, page 323.)

Group Therapy. Group therapy for adolescents helps them develop or improve social skills, which can lead to better feelings of mastery and improved self-esteem. Teenagers may find it easier to express feelings in a supportive peer-group environment. Support groups for parents can help them manage specific problem behaviors, use appropriately positive reinforcement, communicate with their teens in an age-appropriate manner, and become better listeners for their adolescent. (See *Family Therapy,* page 326.)

Family Therapy. Family therapy can address problems that may worsen or exacerbate bipolar disorder in adolescents: a lack of generational boundaries, severe marital conflict, rigid or chaotic rules, or neglectful or overly involved parent-child relationships. In addition, family sessions may help identify other family members with psychiatric disorders and assist them in getting their own treatment. (See also *Family Therapy*, page 326.)

Medication. Once other possible causes such as substance abuse, a medication reaction, another medical condition, or another behavioral disorder have been ruled out, a mood-stabilizing medication may be prescribed. Lithium, carbamazepine (Tegretol), or valproic acid (Depakene/Depakote) are commonly prescribed. Before a teenager begins taking a medication, specific target symptoms should be identified in a discussion between the teen, the parent, and the physician. Possible side effects and other aspects of the medication should also be discussed. In some teens, antidepressants may be needed in addition to the mood stabilizer during the depressed phase, and antipsychotics may be used with the mood stabilizer during the manic phase.

Hospitalization. If recognized early, manic-depressive episodes can be treated on an outpatient basis or in a partial hospital program. When there is self-endangering behavior or aggressive behavior toward others, hospitalization may be necessary. Some teens with mania may require hospitalization to ensure their safety.

10

Disruptive Behavior Disorders

■ ■ ■

As parents, we often measure our youngsters' well-being by their behavior. We notice how they act and interact within the family, at school, in the community, and with their peers. At times we are reassured by what we see, and at other times, we wonder if their behavior may give cause for concern. At different developmental stages, we expect different degrees of self-control. We also tend to see their behavior as a reflection of ourselves as parents, and frequently worry whether we are being good enough parents.

By the time your child reaches her teen years, you will have a fairly detailed picture of her temperament, personality traits, and behavioral style. By now, you can probably anticipate how she will behave, learn, and interact with others. Adolescence, however, is a perplexing and complicated transitional time for both you and your child. As you look at your changing and changeable teenager during this time, you may often wonder if you aren't actually dealing with a stranger. As teenagers undergo dramatic transformations in their physical, emotional, social, and cognitive development, they can experience considerable stress. Concurrently, their behavior may seem uncertain and erratic—both to you and to them.

In the process of evolving a relatively stable adult identity, your teenager will experiment. In the course of a day, she may test out one behavior, discard it, and assume another. In addition, teenagers may express themselves in a volatile and provocative manner. During adolescence, the concept of "normal behavior" stretches to accommodate the teen's natural responses to the physical, sexual, emotional, cognitive, and social changes that she is experiencing. During adolescence, teenagers are struggling with issues regarding dependence and independence. The parent-child relationship must change to allow the youngster greater independence. Parents gradually relinquish the control they exert as their teenager takes on greater autonomy and responsibility for herself, her actions, and her decisions.

Occasionally, however, when parents see that their teen is growing away from them, that the teen is no longer so compliant or eager to please and is less reasonable, they may interpret this as direct rebellion or provocation. If parents then intensify efforts to control the youngster's behavior or impose their own structure on her, the teenager may well intensify her resistance. While such power struggles are common during adolescence, many parents find them troubling and wonder whether they may be symptomatic of an underlying emotional problem. Rarely do the power struggles of adolescence signal a cause for great concern. In the vast majority of instances, even when

a teenager acts rebellious, the behavior is transient and short-lived.

There are some teenagers, however, who communicate through their behavior a more constant state of internal distress. These teenagers may have one of the *disruptive behavior disorders*. It is almost as if they are trying to demonstrate to the world their internal feelings of distress and upset through outward actions of disruptive behavior. As a teenager's behavior ripples out in disruptive waves, others in her life are likely to be distressed. Adolescents with these externalizing disorders are both troubled and troubling to others.

In some instances, a behavior unequivocally signals serious emotional problems. When a teenager repeatedly gets into serious fights, tortures small animals, or sets damaging fires, there can be little doubt that something is wrong. Adolescents with disruptive behavior problems seldom report their own distress. Instead, they are identified by adults, typically parents and teachers, and sometimes by law enforcement and legal officials. Since disruptive behaviors usually have a direct and negative impact on other people, it is not uncommon for these teenagers to be viewed as being "bad" rather than emotionally troubled or mentally ill. Labeling, however, can be misleading and sometimes damaging, because disruptive behaviors may be symptoms of larger, underlying emotional problems that have been overlooked and gone untreated.

Behavior disorders are by their nature both disruptive and confusing and, according to some studies, account for as many as two-thirds of all referrals to adolescent psychiatrists and other professional mental health clinicians. Chances are that when a teenager has a disruptive behavior disorder, signs have existed throughout childhood. Many of these children have been involved in the mental health system prior to adolescence. Some have been treated for depressive disorders, separation anxiety, panic attacks, and other emotional disorders. Still others appeared slightly troubled, although the nature of the trouble was never actually explored or diagnosed. Some youngsters who did not appear particularly troubled as children and were able to navigate the demands of childhood and function reasonably well respond to the changes of adolescence with disruptive behaviors that may well suggest the existence of deeper problems.

How then do parents judge when their teenager's behavior signals a larger problem? How do they gauge the feedback from others, from teachers, other parents, and adults in the community? When does teenage rebellion or misbehavior cross the line into disordered behavior?

In this chapter, we will look at a group of disorders in which a teenager's distress is expressed primarily in the way she acts. These include *attention-deficit/hyperactivity disorder* (ADHD), *conduct disorder,* and *oppositional defiant disorder* (ODD). Since school is a larger part of the world in which adolescents generally conduct themselves—both in terms of socialization and achievement—we will start by discussing school problems that may be related to disruptive behavior disorders.

School Problems

Whether a teenager has learning disabilities, emotional disorders, behavioral disturbances, or a combination of problems, they are often expressed in her social interactions, academic accomplishments, and attendance at school. In the classroom, a troubled teen might act up and disrupt the class or act in an antagonistic or seductive manner with teachers. The adolescent may not complete assigned work and may fail to achieve according to her potential. She may be habitually late, cut classes, or simply not show up. Each of these school problems has important academic and social consequences, and each may speak of an underlying emotional problem. Whenever youngsters have serious difficulties at school—especially if they drop out—their emotional, behavioral, cognitive, and social development may be seriously compromised.

After the family, school is the most important socializing influence on children. During the adolescent years, the role that school assumes in a youngster's life expands. School is where the teen spends the greater part of each day, where important interactions and accomplishments are played out, and where she tests herself out as a social, competent, accomplished human being.

School is frequently the place in which adolescents assert their independence, establish a sense of self, find their places in the world, deal with their emerging sexuality, and consider career choices. School offers adolescents the opportunity to attain skills that they will need for success in the adult world.

During adolescence, the practical demands

of school become increasingly complex and rigorous. There is growing pressure for youngsters to perform in school—so that they can compete for colleges and jobs. Sometimes alcohol and illegal drugs are widely available and are used by peers. Pressure to fit in, to date, and to make decisions about sexual activity are also part of an adolescent's school experience.

All this happens at time when teenagers are likely to feel alienated from their usual sources of support. While teens rightfully insist on more responsibility, privacy, and autonomy, parents feel they exert less influence on their teens. Many parents tend to be less directly involved in their teenager's school experience. Some parents are largely unaware of what is going on with their youngster at school—as long as all goes well. At home, parents may be puzzled by their teenager's occasionally rude, isolated, moody, provocative behavior. In many instances, it is only when a disappointing report card comes home or a phone call comes from a teacher or school counselor that serious problems come to light.

A youngster's problems at school can produce problems for both parent and teen. Often parents personalize their teenager's successes and failures at school. Because a teenager is trying to diminish her dependence on her parents and increase self-mastery, attempts by a parent to understand or help with school problems can be experienced as controlling or intrusive. This may create tension, frustration, or antagonism between parent and teenager.

Troubles at home can also affect the teen's school experience. Divorce, remarriage, illness or death in the family, a job change, financial difficulties, or a move can all cause a teenager significant turmoil. This turmoil can affect the teen's ability to concentrate, to sit in class, to complete schoolwork, or to comply with school rules and expectations. Frustrations and worries that stem from home may be acted out with teachers and peers, causing behavioral problems.

From an earlier base of emotional support and understanding at home, most teens are able to manage stress within the family as well as the increasingly sophisticated, rigorous, and complicated social and academic demands of school life. When, however, early experiences or current home circumstances do not adequately support the teenager, she may develop serious problems in handling the social and academic demands of middle school, junior high school, high school, and college. Teenagers who are struggling with both troubled school lives and chaos at home are doubly vulnerable to anxiety, depression, loneliness, frustration, anger, fear, and despair.

When a youngster is upset by tensions at home, schoolwork is often affected. If this results in poor academic performance, tensions at home may increase. Teenagers who have learning or social problems at school might conceal them at home. As time passes, a chasm of silence, deception, and anxiety can widen, causing tensions. Sometimes when a teen has problems at school, instead of expressing her feelings to others, she may become withdrawn and sullen or belligerent and irritable at home.

Parents' attitudes toward school, academics, and teachers continue to be important during adolescence, whether the youngster acknowledges it or not. Parents who continue to reinforce appropriate school-related behaviors, such as regular attendance, completing homework, reading, and studying, are less likely to have youngsters with school problems.

On the other hand, parents can also impose expectations that are unreasonably high. When that happens, a teenager may feel overwhelmed by pressure to achieve, compete, and please. Occasionally youngsters respond to such pressure by developing serious problems such as eating disorders (see *Eating and Nutritional Disorders,* page 260), depressive symptoms (see *Depressive Disorders,* page 209), self-destructive behaviors (see *Teenage Suicide,* page 213), or disruptive behavior disorders (see *Oppositional Defiant Disorders,* page 232).

Many parents believe that once their youngster reaches middle school or junior high, there's no longer a need to be involved in the school, especially since their teenager seems embarrassed or irritated by their presence and participation. Yet, recent studies have shown that teenagers with parents who are involved through high school are most likely to succeed. Those whose parents are consistently uninvolved are at highest risk for dropping out. Although it may be tempting to lessen your involvement in your teenager's education, it is important not to underestimate the value of your continued participation. (See also *What You Can Do at Home,* page 140.)

When teenagers are having school problems, parents should attempt to understand underlying reasons. If your teenager is habitually late, skips classes or a particular class, or fails to attend, ask why. There may be very real reasons, for example, that a teenager refuses to go to school or fabricates excuses for avoiding school. Instead of criticizing, ask what she does when she is not in school. Hanging out with friends creates a very different picture and is done for different reasons and feelings than lying on the couch watching television.

For some teenagers, school does not feel like—and, in fact, may not be—a safe place. Many teenagers feel ill-equipped to deal with the conflicts and aggression that they face daily. Whether there is a school bully, concerns about gangs, or trouble with a particular teacher or coach, a teenager may respond to such conflicts by avoidance.

Some schools have trouble keeping out the violence that surrounds them. Gangs, assaults, extortion, intimidation—these experiences are all too real for some students. As a result, some teenagers are afraid to go to school because they fear for their physical safety. When students feel anxious and menaced at school, they may refuse to go. Even when they do attend, there's a good chance that they will act out their anxiety in some way.

Some schools are less sensitive and less supportive of students' individuality than others. When schools squelch individuality by demanding rigid uniformity, some students may feel that being themselves is bad, inadequate, or unacceptable. Such a negative self-perception can lead to distorted perceptions of social situations as well as diminished intellectual efficiency and motivation.

Some schools seem unintentionally to communicate inappropriate expectations for troubled students. Sometimes, by labeling students as emotionally disturbed or behaviorally disordered, they set up the expectation of failure. In other cases, schools set classroom standards that are either too low or too high. Schoolwork that is too demanding leads to frustration, which can cause aggression, regression, or resignation. Schoolwork that is too easy can lead to boredom and lack of focus, which can result in disruptive behavior or the teenager may avoid school altogether.

Some schools or classrooms fail to manage behavior with consistency. When a student cannot predict a teacher's responses, the youngster may feel anxious and powerless to figure out appropriate behavioral alternatives. It is confusing when a specific misconduct is punished at one time and overlooked at another. The lesson learned may be that favorable consequences following good behavior cannot be relied upon. This lowers the incentive to behave properly.

At the same time, it is crucial that schools provide reinforcement for desirable behavior and avoid reinforcing inappropriate behavior. If a student who is always acting up in class gets all the attention, however negative that attention may be, other students may rightly feel passed over and ignored. The lesson could be that good behavior and high achievement are hardly worth the effort.

Occasionally, teachers do not provide teens with optimal models. Teachers whose attitude toward academic work is cavalier, who treat others unkindly or disrespectfully, or who are disorganized tend to foster similar attitudes and conduct in their students.

Given that school is a child's springboard to adulthood, it is crucial that parents take an active part in their teenager's academic pursuits and maintain regular contact with the teachers. In this way, potential school problems can be identified early enough to devise strategies and appropriate interventions. Finally, parents can demonstrate their belief in the value of the education by being consistently involved in school.

Attention-Deficit/Hyperactivity Disorder

Once called *hyperkinesis* or *minimal brain dysfunction*, attention-deficit/hyperactivity disorder (ADHD) affects between 3 to 5 percent of all children, perhaps as many as two million American youngsters. Two to three times more boys than girls are affected, though the disorder is being identified increasingly in girls. On the average, at least one or two teens in every classroom in the United States need help for the disorder. While it appears that some of the symptoms of ADHD disappear by adolescence, some teenagers continue to have difficulties in their social relationships and school performance. In some teens, attention-deficit/hyperactivity disorder may coexist along with antisocial or delinquent behaviors.

Teens with ADHD are inattentive, overactive, impulsive, and disorganized. These behaviors may resemble normal teen behavior. They are, however, persistent, extreme, and truly outside the control of the teen with ADHD. Adolescents with attention-deficit/hyperactivity disorder have a harder time keeping their minds focused on individual tasks for even short periods of time without becoming bored or distracted. And even more impulsive than their non-ADHD peers, these teens seem incapable of curbing their automatic reactions, of thinking before they act. During stressful situations, these already exaggerated behaviors become more extreme. Because of these troublesome symptoms, the adolescent may have trouble developing a sense of mastery and positive self-esteem.

In most youngsters with ADHD, the signs have been noted and the condition diagnosed long before the teens reached adolescence. Therefore, many have received treatment and symptoms have been controlled. Moreover, research suggests that by adolescence almost 50 percent of all children diagnosed with ADHD no longer have symptoms.

■ IDENTIFYING THE SIGNS

Although signs of this disorder are often evident during toddlerhood or even earlier, most children would have been seen by their pediatricians or mental health clinicians in elementary school. Occasionally, the disorder is first diagnosed in the teenager. Like other behavioral disorders, ADHD is most often identified by people other than the youngster. Adults have varying tolerances for excessive activity, so the same behavior may be accepted as exuberant by one teacher but considered more serious by another. Some parents do not know what level of activity, concentration, and compliance to expect from their children, especially during the teen years.

Sometimes problems may be present at school but not in the home, or at home but not at school. Some youngsters are bored, discouraged, restless, and unable to follow instructions at school not because they have ADHD, but because they don't find the type of structure or challenge they need. Other teenagers may have undiagnosed learning disabilities and may express their frustration through behavior. They may have difficulty concentrating and, ultimately, become disruptive in the classroom. In addition, because anxiety, depression, and other emotional problems can produce symptoms that resemble ADHD, the need for accurate diagnosis is important.

ADHD is a chronic disorder most often diagnosed in the elementary-school years with symptoms varying from mild to severe. Some teenagers with ADHD have more problems in large groups but do better one-on-one. A teen with severe symptoms of ADHD will have problems in all settings: at home, at school, and at play. If ADHD goes unrecognized and untreated, a teenager can develop low self-esteem, frustration, academic underachievement, even failure, and social isolation, which can follow her into adulthood.

While most teenagers are impulsive at times, those with ADHD are impulsive to a degree that can be not only distracting but occasionally dangerous. Teenagers with ADHD may talk inappropriately in class or may blurt out answers before questions are completed or while classmates are attempting to answer. Their schoolwork often is messy, showing a lack of thought and focus, or assignments are lost. Homework papers and assignments are frequently incomplete or full of errors. Such teenagers may act recklessly: driving too fast and dangerously or stealing, sometime on a whim without considering the consequences.

Yet, paradoxically, the very same youngsters may be able to concentrate for considerable stretches of time on certain activities that they enjoy or that come easily, such as drawing cartoons or watching television. Such selective attention seems related to motivation and pleasure in the task.

It is still not clear whether hyperactive teenagers have difficulty perceiving and understanding social cues or whether they perceive them correctly but fail to respond appropriately. In normal circumstances, most teens adjust behavior intuitively and through learning so that, for example, they can join a group activity smoothly and without interrupting. Teens with ADHD, however, have problems in monitoring their behavior, reflecting upon its impact, and adjusting to specific social situations. They are more likely to barge in and disrupt the process. As a result, teenagers with ADHD have difficulties in social situations and frequently have few friends.

In sports activities they might run into others, pushing, hitting, shoving, ignoring the rules and structure of the game. Often they lack the concentration to succeed in learning a sport. While there may be no particular anger, hostility, or malicious intent in the intrusive physical contact, it often results in quarrels and fights. At other times, teenagers with ADHD may be oppositional and argumentative with parents, teachers, and peers.

■ CAUSES AND CONSEQUENCES

Despite years of research, the cause of ADHD is still not fully understood. Evidence to date indicates that there are many things underlying ADHD, among them genetic and neurobiological vulnerabilities. A child's environment may contribute to the development of the disorder or worsen the symptoms. Some cases of hyperactive behavior are linked to levels of lead in the blood; fetal alcohol syndrome (in which alcohol consumed during pregnancy has a range of effects on the unborn child); exposure to other drugs in utero; or serious head injury. In the 1970s, speculation centered on ADHD being a result of food additives; later it was concluded that additives were not a significant cause of the syndrome. In the 1980s, public attention turned to sugar in its search for an explanation for ADHD. Many parents still limit dietary sugar, but follow-up research studies have discounted the sugar theory.

Stressful circumstances in the youngster's home, coupled with neurological vulnerabilities, seem to increase the likelihood of problems related to ADHD. The prevalence of teenagers with hyperactivity, impulsiveness, and inattention is greater in disadvantaged, large inner-city environments. This may be due to such related factors as poverty; malnutrition; lead poisoning; poor prenatal and neonatal health care (which can lead to prematurity or low birth weight); drug or alcohol abuse during pregnancy; and family disturbances, including violence and drug and alcohol abuse. Any one or a combination of these factors can play a significant role in developing and perpetuating ADHD symptoms.

While the exact degree to which a chaotic environment contributes to ADHD symptoms is still unclear, it does appear that parents who are able to provide support, stability, educational stimulation, and hope can help their adolescent partially compensate for her vulnerabilities. The symptoms of ADHD make parenting more challenging. Dealing with ADHD symptoms, and the inevitable frustration that results, may cause many parents to doubt their parenting skills. Parents of teenagers with ADHD report greater stress, social isolation, and self-blame and demoralization. These factors can translate into a parenting style that is more intrusive, controlling, and disapproving. As a result, the teen's emotional development, competence, and self-esteem can be negatively affected.

From time to time, every teenager appears to live in her own world, and parents complain that the teenager is uncooperative or doesn't listen. Parents of teens with ADHD, however, have often experienced years of the frustration and exasperation that comes from trying to establish limits and discipline for children who seem consistently unable or unwilling to listen. Because all adolescents naturally strive toward assuming more responsibility and independence, the frustration of parenting a teen with ADHD may well intensify during this period of development.

A cycle of negative interaction, stress, and failure can also occur in the classroom between teachers and teens with ADHD. Teenagers who are disruptive, fidgety, and impulsive can be singled out by the teachers and labeled as disciplinary problems. Academic settings with multiple periods, large classes, teachers who have differing styles, and complex schedules present additional problems for the teenager with ADHD.

In addition to classroom conduct, your teen's schoolwork will likely show the effects of the disorder. Unable to give close attention to details, your teenager may make careless mistakes. It might appear that she does not follow through on instructions or finish schoolwork. Most hyperactive youngsters avoid, dislike, or refuse to engage in tasks that require sustained attention. As a result, homework and schoolwork often go unfinished or are sloppily executed, especially when the work is boring, repetitive, or difficult. At home, they typically don't finish chores or fail to remember weekly tasks.

While some teenagers with ADHD function well in the classroom, especially if they are bright, others tend to underachieve at school. Some fail to achieve up to their potential because they have trouble paying attention, find it hard to organize their thoughts, or actually have trouble processing and remembering information. The less successful that teens with ADHD are with their schoolwork, the less motivated they may be to succeed in academics. With many youngsters with ADHD, it seems that even their most concentrated efforts bring little success. Not unexpectedly, truancy and dropout rates are high among these youngsters.

It is hardly surprising that adolescents with ADHD tend to have low self-esteem. Many find themselves in constant trouble, and many feel socially isolated. Most lack the feelings of mastery and competence that other adolescents gain from social and academic successes. Therefore, many of these youths feel demoralized within a cycle of failure and criticism that is perpetuated both at school and in the family.

There has been considerable debate in recent years about whether children outgrow ADHD and whether it becomes less active a problem in adolescence and adulthood. Many researchers believe that the syndrome itself never really disappears but rather that adolescents learn to control or compensate for it to some degree. For those who receive the diagnosis early, medication in combination with other treatments may have stabilized the condition.

In one study, most youngsters between the ages of eleven and seventeen experienced less severe symptoms. Nevertheless, these very same teenagers were more easily distracted and had more difficulties than those teens without the disorder. In fact, another study found that after the age of sixteen, nearly half of these teenagers had some problem behaviors. They tend to be more combative and argumentative and are more likely to engage in vandalism or truancy. According to the same study, about one-third of these youngsters also used and abused drugs.

ADHD commonly exists with other problems, such as specific learning disabilities, depression, or anxiety disorders. (See *Learning Difficulties,* page 138, *Depressive Disorders,* page 209, and *Anxiety and Avoidant Disorders,* page 196.) Almost half of those diagnosed with ADHD are also diagnosed with oppositional defiant disorder or conduct disorder. (See pages 232 and 236.)

■ HOW TO RESPOND

ADHD is a treatable condition, that requires a comprehensive approach. More than 200 studies have shown that medication can produce beneficial results. During adolescence, however, some youngsters may be unwilling to take medicine that they took in childhood because they feel ashamed or controlled by the medication. Other treatment approaches, singly or in combination with medication, include cognitive therapy, behavioral therapy, social skills training, parent education and support, and remedial education.

If attention-deficit/hyperactivity disorder is diagnosed in your teen, learn about the condition. Talk to your teenager's doctor, child and adolescent psychiatrist, and teachers. Stay involved in her school to see that she is getting appropriate *remedial education* or special tutoring whenever necessary. Parents of adolescents with ADHD continue to be their youngster's best advocates. They need to be involved in getting their teens the help they need.

Cognitive-Behavioral Therapy. Behavioral therapy can help control aggression, modulate social behavior, and regulate attention and physical movements. This approach encourages and rewards teens for proper behaviors. Cognitive therapy ideally teaches those with ADHD greater self-control, self-guidance, and more thoughtful and efficient problem-solving strategies. (See *Attention-Deficit/Hyperactivity Disorder,* page 225.)

Social Skills Training. When coupled with cognitive therapy and medication, social skills training helps teenagers understand and smooth out difficult social behaviors. Social skills training uses reinforcement strategies and rewards for appropriate behavior. Through this approach, teens learn to *generalize* behavior, that is, to apply one set of social rules to other situations.

Social skills training can help adolescents learn to evaluate social situations and adjust their behavior accordingly. This can also be learned through group therapy, because youngsters of this age are especially likely to benefit from such group interactions with their peers. Despite such programs, however, youngsters with ADHD may continue to have socialization problems, which can be quite painful for the adolescent who is seeking acceptance from peers.

Parent Training Programs. Some parents are helped through parent training programs. In these sessions, parents learn practical strategies for managing their youngster's behavior. In this type of training, the emphasis is on observing the youngster and communicating clearly. Furthermore, parents are often helped through such training to appreciate and respond appropriately to their teenager's changing developmental needs. Parents are taught new and age-appropriate negotiating skills, techniques of positive reinforcement, and other strategies to assist a teen with ADHD to manage her behavior. (See *Parent Management Training,* page 240.) Parents may also benefit from participating in programs run by local and national support organizations that help advocate for their teenagers. These programs can help lessen parents' feelings of isolation, frustration, and demoralization, which can occur when parenting a child or teen with ADHD.

Family Therapy. When teenagers are willing to participate in therapy along with their families, this approach can address the family stress normally generated by living with a youngster who is struggling with the symptoms of ADHD. Sometimes, when ADHD has been diagnosed in childhood, parents understandably become closely involved with their child's disorder and care. As the child matures, it is necessary to continue to shift greater responsibility for monitoring and managing the disorder to the youngster. Family therapy can help parents make the appropriate shifts and adjustments to accommodate their teenager's changing needs and to shift more control to the teen.

Occasionally in the course of family treatment, a parent may be identified with the same disorder, and treatment of that parent may be considered. Family therapy can also help other members—siblings and grandparents, for example—adjust to and accommodate the changing, increasingly independent youngster and her needs. (See *Family Therapy,* page 230.)

Medication. Since the 1930s, *psychostimulants* have been used to treat what we now call ADHD. Stimulant medications include methylphenidate (Ritalin), dextroamphetamine (Dexedrine), and pemoline (Cylert). These medications increase a person's attention and reduce excess fidgeting and hyperactivity, allowing the youngster to focus more effectively. They increase nervous system alertness by stimulating the brain to produce more dopamine and norepinephrine, two of the many neurotransmitters (chemical messengers). When used judiciously and appropriately, the beneficial results from medication can be dramatic.

Some believe that the diagnosis of ADHD is used to justify medicating children who are perceived as active, expansive, or difficult by adults who lack the patience and willingness to tolerate them. The rapid increase in the use of methylphenidate worldwide has resulted in concern about the overuse of medication.

Using stimulant medications to treat a teen with ADHD is a serious decision. There are a variety of factors to consider, among them the duration of the disorder, the short-term and long-term benefits of medication, and the potential side effects. During adolescence, it is also important to review the effectiveness of your teenager's medication and to insure that she has a growing participation in the review. If medication is being recommended for the first time, ask how the decision to prescribe medication was arrived at and the kind of follow up needed to monitor its use. If your teenager has been taking medications since childhood, discuss the advantages and disadvantages of continuing the medication with your teen's physician.

In many cases, medication enables youngsters to concentrate for longer periods, to complete tasks, and to comply with requests. The most common side effects of stimulant medication are reduced appetite and difficulty falling asleep. Some youngsters report stomachaches and headaches, especially during the first few days of treatment. If these side effects continue, they can often be controlled by reducing the dosage.

In rare cases, stimulant medication is thought to have interfered with a child's growth, although some researchers dispute the point. There is, however, general agreement that once medication use is discontinued, normal growth will resume. It is crucial that the treating physician carefully monitor height and weight.

When stimulants fail to effectively modify the symptoms, or cause problematic side effects, other medications may be helpful. The most commonly used are bupropion (Wellbutrin), fluoxetine (Prozac), guanfacine (Tenex), imipramine (Tofranil), nortriptyline (Pamelor), and sertraline (Zoloft).

In general, youngsters with ADHD are at higher risk for academic failure, social isolation, accidents, low self-esteem, demoralization, and disruptive behavior (including antisocial behaviors). For some, ADHD can be a lifelong disorder, but for those children diagnosed and treated early, the condition can be effectively managed, and their lives can indeed be productive, successful, and fulfilling.

Oppositional Defiant Disorders

At times, all teenagers are oppositional, argumentative, and inattentive. Absorbed in their own thoughts and concerns and more interested in their peer group, teenagers frequently turn a deaf ear to the adult world. Even when the demands are reasonable, a teenager may respond with belligerence or passivity. Because the thrust toward separation is especially intense, adolescence is a time when oppositional behavior is sometimes expected.

Disrespectful, defiant, and hostile behavior, however, must be carefully examined in a teenager when it begins to affect the youngster's social, family, and academic life or seems extreme compared to the teen's peers.

■ IDENTIFYING THE SIGNS

It's not always easy to distinguish oppositional defiant disorder (ODD) from normal, age-appropriate oppositional behavior. Symptoms of the disorder tend to mirror, in exaggerated form, problems common to most families with teenagers. In addition, different families have various levels of tolerance for negative behavior. In some, a minor infraction of the rules produces major consequences, while in more tolerant homes, oppositional behaviors are largely ignored unless they cause practical difficulties.

In teenagers with ODD, there is a pattern of uncooperative, defiant, and hostile behavior toward authority figures that seriously interferes with their day-to-day functioning. They regularly lose their tempers, argue with adults, actively defy adult rules, refuse adult requests, and deliberately annoy others.

Blaming others for their mistakes, these teens may appear touchy, angry, resentful, spiteful, or vindictive, even to their peers. Although aggressive behavior tends to be limited, some youngsters engage in mild physical aggression, and their language tends to be more aggressive and obscene than the average teenager's. Though particular stresses of adolescence may significantly increase oppositional behavior, the symptoms usually represent a behavioral style that has been present for many years.

Teenagers with ODD were, in many instances, fussy, colicky, difficult-to-soothe infants. During the toddler and preschool years, when a certain degree of oppositional attitude is considered normal, ordinary points of contention in the family became battlegrounds for intractable power struggles. These oppositional episodes were typically centered around eating, toilet training, sleeping, and speaking. Temper tantrums were usually extreme.

In childhood and then in adolescence, youngsters with ODD consistently dawdle and procrastinate. These teens may agree to perform tasks but later claim ignorance of the responsibilities, much to their parents' chagrin and frustration. They may say that they do not hear and, as a result, are often referred for hearing evaluations, only to be found to have normal hearing. The issue is *listening* rather than hearing. By adolescence, parents and their oppositional teen usually have established patterns of interaction that contribute to stress and problems at home.

During these years, struggles with teens commonly center on keeping their rooms neat, picking up after themselves, taking baths or grooming appropriately, using obscene language, complying with curfew, doing homework, and attending school. In all instances, winning becomes the most important aspect of the struggle for the teen. At times a teenager with ODD will forfeit cherished privileges rather than lose the argument.

In milder forms of ODD, open conflicts are limited to the home environment, while at school, the adolescent may be quietly resistant and uncooperative. More severe forms involve overt defiance toward other authority figures such as teachers, coaches, and other adults in the community. Teenagers with ODD may get into trouble with police—most often for a disrespectful, provocative, or belligerent attitude.

Teenagers with ODD typically have little insight and ability to admit to their difficulties. Rather, they tend to blame their troubles on others and on external circumstances. They are always questioning the rules and challenging those perceived to be unreasonable.

Before puberty, the rate of ODD is higher in boys than in girls. In adolescence, the incidence of the disorder is roughly the same.

■ CAUSES AND CONSEQUENCES

It appears that oppositional defiant disorder arises out of a circular family dynamic. A baby who is by nature more difficult, fussy, and colicky may be harder to soothe. These parents often feel frustrated and as though they are failures. Parents who perceive their child as unresponsive or "bad" may come to anticipate that the child will be unresponsive or noncompliant. They may then become unresponsive or unreliable in return, adding to the baby's feelings of helplessness, neediness, and frustration.

As parents attempt to assert control by insisting on compliance in such areas as eating, toilet training, sleeping, or speaking politely, the young child may demonstrate resistance by withholding, withdrawing, or refusing to cooperate.

As a child matures, increasing negativism, defiance, and noncompliance become misguided ways of dealing with normal separation issues. In this way, the disorder may represent unresolved separation anxiety, a tenacious drawing out of the "terrible twos."

The more a child reacts in defiant, provocative ways, the more negative feedback she elicits from the parents. In an attempt to achieve compliance, the parents or authority figures remind, lecture, berate, physically punish, and nag the child. But far from diminishing oppositional behavior, these kinds of responses toward the child tend to increase the rate and intensity of noncompliance. Ultimately, it becomes a tug-of-war and a battle of wills.

When such patterns typify parent-child relationships, discipline is often inconsistent. At times, parents may explode in anger with efforts to control and discipline. At other times, they may withhold appropriate punishments and consequences so that these soon become hollow threats. As the child continues to provoke and defy, parents lose control. Then, feeling regret and guilt, especially if they've become verbally or physically explosive, the parents may become excessively rewarding in order to undo what they now perceive to have been excessive discipline or harsh consequences.

When a child starts school, this pattern of passive-aggressive, oppositional behavior tends to provoke teachers and other children as well. At school the child is met with anger, punitive reactions, and criticism. The child then argues back, blames others, and gets angry.

By the time a youngster with ODD reaches adolescence, she may have had years of difficulty at school. Her behavior and attitude regularly cause disruption in the classroom and interfere with social and academic functioning. When her behavior and defiance affect her schoolwork and behavior, she will have experienced school failure and social isolation. This, coupled with chronic criticism, can lead to low self-esteem. Usually, ODD youngsters feel unfairly picked on. In fact, they may believe that their behavior is reasonable.

In many cases, oppositional disorders coexist with ADHD. (See *Attention-Deficit/Hyperactivity Disorder,* page 225.) Symptoms of ODD may also occur as part of a major depressive disorder (see *Depression Disorders,* page 209), obsessive-compulsive disorder (see *Obsessive Compulsive Disorder,* page 201), or an attack of mania (see *Bipolar Mood Disorders,* page 217). In some

teenagers, ODD may represent a remnant of separation anxiety disorder (see *Anxiety and Avoidant Disorders,* page 196), in which oppositional defiance reflects a reaction to feelings of ambivalence and anxiety that arise from the developmental move toward independence. There also seems to be a correlation between ODD in a teen and a history of disruptive behavior disorders, substance abuse, or other emotional disorders in family members.

■ HOW TO RESPOND

Although ODD is often diagnosed in childhood, there are many youngsters who continue to have behavioral difficulties well into their adolescent years. If you are concerned that your adolescent may have ODD, you should seek a professional evaluation. This is important as a first step in trying to identify the various factors that may contribute to ODD in your adolescent.

During the evaluation process, parents recognize the interactive aspects of this disorder and begin to look for new ways to relate to their teen. Books and parenting workshops given under the auspices of churches, schools, and community agencies may also help parents respond better to the needs of their youngsters. Once ODD has been diagnosed, the child and adolescent psychiatrist or other professional may recommend a combination of therapies for ODD. Among the options your clinician may recommend are the following:

Parent Training Programs. Some parents are helped through formal parent training programs. In these sessions, parents learn strategies for managing their adolescent's behavior. These are practical approaches to dealing with an adolescent with ODD. The emphasis is on observing the adolescent and communicating clearly. Parents are taught negotiating skills, techniques of positive reinforcement, and other means of reducing the power struggles and establishing more effective and consistent discipline. (See *Parent Management Training*, page 240.)

Individual Psychotherapy. The therapeutic relationship is the foundation of successful therapy. It can provide the difficult adolescent with a forum to explore his feelings and behaviors with a nonjudgmental adult. The therapist may be able to help the youngster with more effective anger management, thus decreasing the defiant behavior. The therapist may employ techniques of cognitive-behavioral therapy to assist the teen with problem-solving skills and in identifying solutions to interactions that seem impossible to the teenager. (See *Cognitive-Behavioral Therapy,* below.) The support gained through therapy can be invaluable in counterbalancing the frequent messages of failure to which the adolescent with ODD is often exposed. (See also *Individual Psychotherapy,* page 320.) When conducted by a child and adolescent psychiatrist, individual psychotherapy may be accompanied by the use of antidepressant and antianxiety medications. (See *Medications,* page 329.)

Family Therapy. Problems with family interactions are addressed in family therapy.

Family structure, strategies for handling difficulties, and the ways parents inadvertently reward noncompliance are explored and modified through this therapy. This approach can also address the family stress usually generated by living with an adolescent with ODD. (See *Family Therapy,* page 326.)

Cognitive-Behavioral Therapy. Behavioral therapy may help adolescents control their aggression and modulate their social behavior. Teenagers are rewarded and encouraged for proper behaviors. Cognitive therapy can teach defiant teens self-control, self-guidance, and more thoughtful and efficient problem-solving strategies, especially as they pertain to relationships with their peers, parents, and other adults in authority. (See *Cognitive-Behavioral Therapy,* page 323.)

Social Skills Training. When coupled with other therapies, social skills training has been effective in helping teens alter their difficult social behaviors that result from their angry and defiant approach to rules. Social skills training incorporates reinforcement strategies and rewards for appropriate behavior to help a teenager learn to *generalize* positive behavior, that is, apply one set of social rules to other situations. Thus, following the rules of a game may be generalized to rules of the classroom; working together on a team may generalize to working with adults rather than against them. Through such training, adolescents can learn to evaluate social situations and adjust their behavior accordingly. The most successful therapies are those that provide training in the teen's natural environments—such as in the classroom or in social groups—as this may help them apply what they learned directly to their lives.

Medication. Medication is only recommended when the symptoms of ODD occur with other conditions, such as ADHD, OCD, or anxiety disorder. (See *Attention-Deficit/Hyperactivity Disorder,* page 225, *Obsessive Compulsive Disorder,* page 201, and *Anxiety and Avoidant Disorders,* page 196.) When stimulants are used to treat teens with attention-deficit/hyperactivity disorders, they also appear to lessen oppositional symptoms. There is no medication specifically for treating symptoms of ODD when there is no other accompanying emotional or behavioral disorder.

Conduct Disorders

By the time a person reaches adolescence, she likely knows what type of behavior is expected of her and which behaviors are unacceptable. Yet all teenagers misbehave from time to time, for a variety of reasons. Perhaps they feel that they need to assert their own autonomy. Maybe they wish to test the limits imposed on them. Teenagers sometimes misbehave because they are experiencing internal distress: anger, frustration, disappointment, anxiety, or hopelessness.

There are also teenagers whose behavior is consistently troubling to others. In these cases, the teen's behavior is clearly outside the range of what is considered normal or acceptable. Perhaps most alarming is that many of these teenagers show little remorse, guilt, or understanding of the damage and the pain inflicted by their behavior.

Increasingly, we read stories in the newspapers of teenagers who routinely set fires, torture animals, or torment other people. We hear of teenagers who join gangs and cruise the streets, terrorizing others. In extreme cases, there are those who physically, sexually, or murderously assault people.

When their behavior is this disturbed, the temptation is to dismiss these adolescents as scary, lost, or bad to the core. Increasingly, there is a tendency to relegate them to the criminal or juvenile justice system. Yet, by doing so, we may overlook the fact that some of these youngsters have underlying psychiatric disorders that can help explain some of their behaviors. For some of these teens, psychiatric treatment is more effective than correctional incarceration.

Conduct disorders are among the most frequently diagnosed childhood disorders in outpatient and inpatient mental health facilities. It is estimated that 6 percent of all children have some form of conduct disorder. The condition is far more common in boys than in girls in early childhood, but adolescent girls are increasingly diagnosed with the disorder.

The earlier a child displays extremely disturbed behavior, the worse the prognosis. The teen with a conduct disorder has moved from being disobedient and disrespectful (behaviors characteristic of oppositional defiant disorder) to violating the rights of others with aggression or illegal activity. Some studies report that high levels of activity and unmanageable behaviors at the age of four presage behavioral problems in later school years. Behavioral problems at eight are reliable predictors of adolescent aggression. Some of the underlying causes of severe behavioral problems, including family violence and abuse, can be prevented or successfully managed. It's important to look beyond the obvious negative behaviors to identify underlying biological, emotional, or social vulnerabilities that might be present. These vulnerabilities may be treatable.

■ IDENTIFYING THE SIGNS

Teenagers who are diagnosed as having a conduct disorder are physically and verbally aggressive beyond what is seen among their peers. Their aggression typically is expressed toward people and animals, in the destruction of property, in deceitfulness and theft, and in serious violation of society's rules.

In order to diagnose a conduct disorder, a clinician will evaluate the teen for the presence of a repetitive and persistent pattern of behavior that violates the basic rights of others. Usually, teenagers with serious conduct disorders engage in a number of unacceptable activities. Almost invariably, they seem to have little or no remorse, awareness, or concern that what they are doing is wrong.

For example, teenagers with conduct disorders might bully, threaten, and intimidate others. Routinely, they initiate physical fights, sometimes using weapons such as bats, bricks, broken bottles, knives, and guns. They get involved in muggings, purse snatching, armed robbery, sexual assault, animal torture, and rape.

Teenagers with conduct disorders might break into other people's homes, buildings, or cars. They might systematically lie to obtain goods or favors or to avoid obligations. They might con others, shoplift, or get involved in forgery. They repeatedly violate rules, break curfew, run away from home, or become truant. The severity of these negative or problem behaviors vary from youngster to youngster.

Clinicians distinguish between types of conduct disorder. Children younger than ten years of age, especially those previously diagnosed with oppositional defiant disorder (see *Oppositional Defiant Disorders,* page 232), are said to have *childhood-onset conduct disorder.* When the symptoms and behaviors of conduct disorder are not evident until after the child has reached ten years of age, the diagnosis is *adolescent-onset conduct disorder.* Youngsters with childhood-onset CD are typically more aggressive; they are likely to have few or no friendships with their peers. They are also at greater risk of persistent conduct disorder or of developing antisocial personalities as adults. Few girls demonstrate childhood-onset conduct disorder; girls are at greater risk for adolescent-onset conduct disorder.

■ CAUSES AND CONSEQUENCES

The diagnosis of conduct disorder implies a multitude of potential criminal behaviors as well as numerous possible biological, psychiatric, and social problems. Teenagers who have not developed an adequate repertoire of behaviors and language skills to express their discomfort, misery, and confusion seem to be at highest risk for conduct disorders. Therefore, the same undesirable or antisocial behavior in different adolescents can indicate very different underlying problems.

It is likely that biochemical underpinnings and genetic vulnerabilities interact with environmental forces and individual characteristics to produce conduct disorders. When there are serious problems during pregnancy, delivery, and the postnatal period, for example, youngsters may demonstrate a variety of neurobiological problems during development. These include slowed development of gross motor coordination (required for throwing a ball or skipping), fine motor skills (handwriting, card playing), and impaired short-term memory. It is not uncommon for children with these kinds of problems to show poor judgment and to have trouble controlling their actions. They have difficulty modulating their behaviors, feelings, and even their biological rhythms of sleep and appetite.

Many teenagers with conduct disorders have learning problems, especially in the area of verbal skills. Since many come from homes in which actions speak louder than words, however, lack of parental stimulation and modeling may account for these weaker verbal skills. Difficulties in reading and language contribute to academic difficulties, especially in the higher grades when understanding and using the written word is a crucial skill. Language deficits may also contribute to an inability to articulate feelings and attitudes, so a teenager might resort to physical expression out of frustration.

In many instances, unrecognized and untreated learning disabilities and cognitive deficiencies create deep frustration for a youngster. Thus, the entire school experience gets filtered through defeat and humiliation. An adolescent may then stop attending school or skip challenging classes. Teens who leave the structure of school, which should offer some opportunity to experience success, may then engage in delinquent behavior. For some, delinquent behavior, however unlawful or unacceptable, provides them with both the status among peers and the opportunity for some reinforcement that they are unable to find at school.

Antisocial behavior abounds in poor inner-city areas together with high rates of family instability, social disorganization, infant morbidity and mortality, and severe mental illness. These class and cultural conditions may well cause and perpetuate severe conduct disturbances in a youngster's behavior.

More and more, child and adolescent psychiatrists and other professionals are recognizing the role played by prior physical, sexual, and emotional abuse in the genesis of certain kinds of aggressive and inappropriate sexual behaviors. Mental illnesses in parents—schizophrenia, severe depression, or manic-depressive disorders—can have a grave impact on the children in the family.

Recently, there seems to be a significant increase in such nonaggressive aspects of conduct disorders as running away, truancy, and substance abuse. (See *Substance Abuse Disorders,* page 279.) It is common for troubled teenagers to use drugs and alcohol. Drugs and alcohol may be used by the teenager in an attempt to self-medicate for symptoms of anxiety, depression, thought disorders, and hyperactivity. They may wish to blot out memories of abuse or treat insomnia. Some think they need drugs or alcohol just to be able to face another day in a violent, abusive household. (See *Substance Abuse Disorders*, page 279.)

Some of the most violent youngsters are likely to be those who have been the most severely abused themselves. Their way of dealing with the abuse is to dissociate their feelings from action. (See *Childhood Trauma and Its Effects,* page 205.) They thus appear to be cold, detached, and lacking in empathy. Yet, because it is the most deeply disturbed teenagers who tenaciously maintain their bravado, boast of their offenses, and threaten others with further violence, they are often passed over to the justice system without effective psychiatric evaluation and intervention.

Conduct disorder can also occur along with psychiatric conditions such as ADHD (see *Attention-Deficit/Hyperactivity Disorder,* page 225), major depression (see *Depressive Disorders*, page 209), and bipolar disorder (see *Bipolar Mood Disorder,* page 217). Though depression is more often associated with withdrawal than aggression, its symptoms can include irritability and rage. Furthermore, episodic destructive behaviors or sporadic episodes of robbery and burglary may represent the manic phase of a bipolar disorder in the presence of a euphoric or expansive mood state. Suicidal behavior and self-mutilating behavior are not uncommon with teenagers who have conduct disorders. Rather than dismiss such attempts as manip-

ulative behavior, adults must take them seriously, not only in terms of the immediate danger but as desperate expressions of frustration, pain, anger, and impulsiveness. Conduct disordered adolescents are usually not very articulate about their feelings and may demonstrate their pain with self-destructive behaviors.

■ HOW TO RESPOND

No single treatment approach has been shown to be effective in addressing antisocial behavior. Because youngsters with conduct disorders may have a myriad of biological, psychological, and social vulnerabilities, a combination of treatment methods targeting each area is most effective.

When a teenager with severe behavioral problems is brought to a child and adolescent psychiatrist or other professional, treatment usually begins with a comprehensive evaluation. This will likely include a detailed medical history, family profile, and psychological testing. A neurological examination sometimes accompanied by an EEG or MRI (see *Medical Tests,* page 353) is often valuable in detecting any central nervous system dysfunction that could contribute to the youngster's problems. A psychoeducational evaluation may uncover intellectual and learning problems that could cause academic and behavioral problems that, in turn, put the adolescent at risk for truancy and disruptive behaviors. The clinician will probably try to determine the degree to which the teenager has control over her aggressive acts and can anticipate a violent episode before it happens. An attempt is usually made to ascertain whether she feels any remorse or concern after such episodes and has the capacity for empathy.

It is often difficult to tap into the inner world of these disturbed youngsters. Turning off questions with a face of bravado or sullenness, many of these teenagers have become so unaccustomed to empathy or concern that they reject it when it is offered. They may brag of their brutality or denigrate their victims. Yet, sometimes, when left alone or in the company of an adult whom they trust, some may let down their defenses and share their agonies, talking about how distraught they really are.

Parent Management Training. Many times, treatment for conduct disorders is family-focused. Parent management training has been used with considerable success with aggressive youngsters, especially when parents themselves are not significantly unstable or disorganized. The degree of alienation that the teenager has experienced in the family is an important variable in family-based treatment. When they can participate fully, this method helps parents recognize and encourage appropriate behaviors in their teenager and discipline the teen more effectively. In order to interact with their teenager in new ways, parents learn to use positive reinforcement. They learn to link misbehavior to appropriate consequences (see *Setting Expectations, Defining Consequences,* page 132) and develop better ways of negotiating with their teenager. Once the parent-child relationship improves, many youngsters are better able to navigate their social and acade-

mic worlds without getting as upset and disruptive. Often, however, teenagers are resistant to this kind of treatment and feel that adults are ganging up on them.

Family Therapy. When teenagers are willing to work with their parents in therapy, this approach can help family members learn less defensive ways of communicating with each other. It can foster mutual support, positive reinforcement, direct communication, and more effective problem-solving and conflict resolution within the family. (See *Family Therapy,* page 326.)

Social Skills Training. Skills training focuses on teenagers in an effort to enhance their problem-solving abilities. Through such programs, a youngster can learn to identify problems, recognize causes, appreciate consequences, learn to verbalize feelings, and consider alternate ways of handling difficult situations. Because most teenagers with conduct disorder feel alone and alienated from the adults in their lives, efforts are made to diminish mistrust of others, especially adults. This type of training helps the youngster seek and become receptive to support and encouragement.

School-Based Treatment Programs. These are in wide use throughout the country, whether in special residential treatment environments, designated community-based schools, or specific programs in mainstream schools. These programs can reintegrate the student into regular classes as the youngster's behavior allows. Successful school-based programs often assess the teenager's strengths, interests, and potential and provide special programs to help the youth achieve skill in a particular area.

Cognitive-Behavioral Therapy. Behavioral therapy may help adolescents control their aggression and modulate their social behavior. Teenagers are rewarded and encouraged for proper behaviors. Cognitive therapy can teach defiant teens self-control, self-guidance, and more thoughtful and efficient problem-solving strategies, especially as they pertain to relationships with their peers, parents, and other adults in authority. (See *Cognitive-Behavioral Therapy,* page 323.)

Medication. Since conduct problems tend to arise from a tangle of biological, emotional, and social stresses, there is no single class of medication that has been found especially useful. Even when another psychiatric problem has been defined (such as ADHD, depression, manic-depressive illness, or schizophrenia), medication is seldom sufficient to alter significantly the conduct disorder symptoms. If the teenager has underlying ADHD (see *Attention-Deficit/Hyperactivity Disorder,* page 225), the use of stimulants may help reduce negative behaviors and impulsiveness. Lithium, a mood stabilizer, has also been shown in some studies to reduce aggression. In some case, anticonvulsant medications such as carbamazepine (Tegretol) have significantly curbed aggressive outbursts. Used judiciously to address specific clinical findings in each individual case, appropriate medication can enhance the success of other treatment modalities.

Given the rather dramatic and disturbing quality of the conduct disorder symptoms, it is important to keep in mind that not all behaviorally disturbed teenagers go on to become antisocial or criminal adults. On the other hand, more often than not, ongoing, adequate medical, emotional, educational, and social supports are required for many years if teenagers with severely disturbed behavior are to go on to live meaningful lives and become productive members of society.

11

Developmental Disorders

■ ■ ■

The first wish of expectant parents is, *Please let my child be born healthy.* In the moments after the baby's birth, you seek to reassure yourself that everything looks perfect and that your baby is healthy. Most of the time, that's the case.

Sometimes even at birth there are signs that there is a problem that might impede the child's development. Initially these signs are mostly physical. We know that an infant born with certain physical characteristics such as those seen in children with Down's syndrome, for example, will have some degree of mental retardation. More often than not, however,

developmental problems are not apparent for many months or even years. The parent who takes home a physically healthy baby may find that the child later lags behind other youngsters of the same age in the development of language or motor skills. Or, as is often the case, everything seems normal until the child is well into elementary school and unable to read with proficiency or demonstrate other academic skills. Most serious developmental problems, however, are usually identified before the start of adolescence.

In some cases, the developmental problem doesn't surface until the teenage years. For example, a slight learning disability might increasingly affect the teen's ability keep pace with peers and the more rigorous demands of middle school or high school. In addition to the consequences of poor academic performance or failure, the adolescent with developmental or learning disabilities also is likely to experience lowered self-esteem. This combination of failure and poor self-esteem can lead to other problems for the teen, such as drug or alcohol abuse, conduct disorders, or sexual promiscuity.

In this chapter we will discuss several developmental disorders. Some, such as autistic disorder and mental retardation, can be very debilitating, although certain individuals with these disorders are capable of functioning at a higher level and may learn more than was once thought possible. We also will explore less severe learning disorders that may be frustrating for both the adolescent and his parents and can threaten academic and social success. The chapter will also focus on how to recognize these developmental disorders and how to respond to them.

Mental Retardation

Mental retardation is the currently accepted term for a disability in which intellectual abilities are significantly below average. Such limited intellectual capabilities can cause problems with an adolescent's social adaptation, in the teenager's ability to communicate with others, to manage self-care, social adjustment, and personal relations, and,

eventually, to succeed in school. Usually mental retardation is identified early in life or by the time a child starts school. In children with severe mental retardation, delays in development are apparent in infancy. With others, their limited intellectual ability may not be evident until the child enters school and begins having difficulty meeting academic and social expectations.

Roughly one in a hundred adults are thought to have mental retardation, but as many as 3 percent of school-age children are diagnosed as mentally retarded. The higher prevalence during the school years may reflect the fact that some children with mild mental retardation improve their adaptive abilities during the school years and function well enough that the diagnosis no longer applies when they are teens or young adults. The disorder is more common in boys than girls, perhaps because congenital anomalies and prematurity is more often seen in boys.

How is a diagnosis of mental retardation reached? Sometimes it is apparent at or soon after birth. An infant born with Down's syndrome, for example, has certain physical characteristics easily identified by the physician, and one of the elements of this genetic disorder is mental retardation, which can range from mild to severe. Other children may show physical differences that suggest mental retardation, such as an abnormally small head, low-set ears, a flattened nose bridge, a wide or high-arched palate, unusually short or long limbs, or abnormally shaped fingers or toes. The presence of such physical characteristics does not necessarily mean that a child is mentally retarded, but it does suggest the need to evaluate the child further and closely monitor development.

The degree or severity of mental retardation is classified by IQ (intelligence quotient) test scores. The average IQ is 100. A child or adolescent with an IQ between 51 and 70 is considered to have mild mental retardation; those with an IQ between 36 and 50 have moderate mental retardation; a level between 20 and 35 indicates severe mental retardation. An IQ below 20 would be termed profound mental retardation. IQ levels suggest the types of interventions and evaluation required and give clues to the long-term outcome.

Many schools classify children with mental retardation by levels of academic functioning. A child who masters the skills of a typical third grader may be referred to as *educable.* If the maximum skills are those of first grade, the child is termed *trainable.*

The diagnosis of mental retardation is made by measuring IQ, but this is not an easy task when a young child has limited language or motor skills. Other developmental tests may be used to measure language, motor, thinking, and social skills. While developmental delays are often identified in this testing process, such delays may or may not be the consequence of mental retardation.

■ Identifying the Signs

As most new parents know, it's easy to suspect a problem when the younger baby next door is doing something that your child hasn't mastered yet. No matter how many times you study the developmental charts that assure you that not all babies are walking at twelve months, you can't help but wonder if something is wrong when your child isn't toddling around. A parent's fears can also be aroused by the adolescent who barely got by academically in elementary school and shows further academic difficulties when faced with the more rigorous demands of middle or high school. No matter how old your child is, trust your intuition and seek help if you are concerned. Always talk with your adolescent's physician about any problems he is having in school or socially. If your doctor cannot help or his response is *He'll grow out of it,* seek a second opinion.

■ Causes and Consequences

There are many causes of mental retardation. Sometimes the cause is readily apparent, while in many instances, especially in individuals with mild retardation, no cause is discernible.

Most cases of mild mental retardation are due to environmental and psychosocial factors, such as lack of stimulation, inadequate nutrition, and exposure to toxins such as lead. About 25 percent of cases of retardation are due either to a chromosomal or metabolic abnormality. The most common chromosomal abnormalities contributing to mental retardation are Down's syndrome and fragile-x syndrome.

DOWN'S SYNDROME. This is the most common form of mental retardation. Approximately 7,000 infants are born in the United States each year with Down's syndrome, representing roughly one in 700 live births. It is due to an extra chromosome.

FRAGILE-X SYNDROME. This the most common form of inherited mental retardation and second only to Down's syndrome in frequency as a known chromosomal cause. It is estimated to occur in about 1 of every 1,250 male births and in 1 of every 2,500 females. Unlike most cases of Down's syndrome, it is carried from one generation to the next.

An example of a metabolic disorder that leads to mental retardation is phenylketonuria (PKU), a congenital deficiency of a particular enzyme (phenylalanine hydroxylase). Infants born with this rare disorder have normal brains that quickly begin to deteriorate due to the absent enzyme. Because a special diet can prevent the severe brain damage linked to untreated PKU, various states in the United States require a simple blood test at birth to screen for this disorder.

Certain conditions during pregnancy can increase the risk of mental retardation. These include toxemia, exposure to radiation during the first trimester, the ingestion of certain harmful drugs during pregnancy, alcohol use by an expectant mother, and maternal malnutrition. In addition, intrauterine infections, complications of premature birth, and birth trauma can also result in an increased risk of mental retardation. Sometimes infants who are born with average intellectual potential develop diseases such as meningitis and encephalitis that damage the brain and nervous system and result in mental retardation.

The consequences of mental retardation depend upon its severity. It is estimated that 30 to 70 percent of adults with IQs between 60 and 80 and adequate adaptive skills live independent lives without special help from outside agencies. On the other hand, people with a more severe level of mental retardation generally require supervised living arrangements and support throughout life.

■ HOW TO RESPOND

When a child—no matter what his age—shows signs of developmental delay or mental retardation, a thorough evaluation should be done to determine the extent and cause of the problem. Don't be afraid to discuss your concerns with your family doctor. You may wish to consult an evaluation service, but all public school systems are required to have services available to evaluate children in need. These evaluations may involve consultations with specialists such as a pediatrician, child and adolescent psychiatrist, clinical psychologist, audiologist, and speech pathologist. Teens with mental retardation need much support and specialized treatment to help them cope with the complex changes and demands of puberty and adolescence.

Getting Help. For any child or adolescent with mental retardation, the goal is to help him reach his full potential and learn to cope with his disability as effectively as possible. Treatment must address the complex interplay of neurobiological and psychosocial matters. A comprehensive approach involving several disciplines is often appropriate. Speech and language therapy, occupational therapy, special education services, environmental changes, skills development, behavioral intervention, psychological services, social skills training, medical care, and psychotropic medications are all possible interventions.

Federal law gives your adolescent the legal right to an education from birth through age 21. The majority of teens with mental retardation can be helped through special education classes in public schools. Most adolescents with less severe levels of mental retardation are "mainstreamed" (included in regular classrooms) for at least part of their school day. This concept of inclusion is likely to expand in the future in public schools, because it has proven to be helpful to all students. Teens with more severe retardation may require schools, or even residential programs, specifically designed to meet their needs. In addition, most communities have some resources and supports, such as recreational and social programs, for teens with mental retardation.

PARENTAL ADJUSTMENT. The diagnosis of mental retardation can be difficult for parents to accept and understand. Most parents have high hopes for their children. Hearing that a child's potential is limited can be painful. Parents often feel angry, sad, betrayed by nature, and they may take on a burden of guilt, feeling that it's all their fault and that somehow they failed their child.

Allow yourself the pain of hearing the diagnosis and the confusion when thinking about your child's future. Seek help through your family doctor or the professionals who evaluated your child. Parent support groups are available in most areas. Health-care and school personnel can refer you to resources in your community for appropriate help and guidance.

In planning for the future, find a professional team that can both inform you of your adolescent's current needs and help you plan for the near and long-term future. Since planning for more than six months at a time is often frustrating, learn to think in six-month units of time: For example, each spring, plan for the following fall.

THE CHANGES OF PUBERTY. If you have an adolescent with mental retardation, with the onset of puberty, new issues will arise. One of the more important ones is sexuality. As with other adolescents, their bodies are changing, and they are beginning to have sexual feelings. Teen sexuality can be difficult for many parents under the best of circumstances. But when teenagers have intellectual limitations that make it difficult or impossible to exercise normal judgment over their bodies, sexuality can become even more of a parental concern and burden.

Communication with your teen is important during this time of major change. Talk to him about the changes his body is undergoing and about the feelings he may have in terms he can understand. Explain the consequences and risks of sexual intercourse without proper safeguards. The subject of controlled sexuality among teens and adults who are mentally retarded is a controversial one. Because of the risk of being sexually abused or taken advantage of, some parents give their daughters birth control pills or have intrauterine devices inserted as a precaution against pregnancy. Some parents consider sterilization for the teen with mental retardation. You should consider your adolescent's sexuality in a way that is consistent with your own beliefs and develop a plan that addresses the health and safety of your teen.

YOUR ADOLESCENT'S ADULTHOOD. Another major concern for parents is where and how your teen will live when grown to adulthood. Even if you choose to keep an adult with mental retardation at home indefinitely, you must acknowledge that there will come a time when you are no longer able or available to care for him. Moreover, as many adolescents with mental retardation move into adulthood, they may feel, like any other person their age, a need to be more independent and separate from their families.

Many adults with mild mental retardation are capable of living independently or semi-independently. They can hold jobs and be productive members of society and in most ways are indistinguishable from those without mental retardation. Those with more limited mental abilities are often able to live in supported living or group homes where, with some supervision, they can care for themselves. These adults can often be trained for jobs that use only skills within their abilities. Employment in the community with supports provided to the employer and employee to ensure success is a reasonable goal for many young adults with mental retardation.

Learning Disorders

In classrooms across the country, there are adolescents struggling to learn. They are of at least average intelligence—some, in fact, are extremely bright—yet for a variety of reasons, they have difficulty learning in our schools.

The terms *learning disorders, learning disabilities,* and *learning differences* have been used to describe various impairments in academic skills. In order to help the adolescent, however, it is important to distinguish clearly which skill is (or skills are) impaired. The disorders that we will discuss in this section are not due to physical disorders, such as a hearing loss or visual impairment. A teen with a learning disorder processes information differently from other youngsters as the result of neurological changes in the brain. Learning disorders interfere with the adolescent's ability to learn or to express what he knows. Most learning disorders have become apparent during elementary school and should have been identified and worked with before the teenage years.

Learning disabilities may run in families and are often preceded by delayed development of language during the preschool years. Perhaps one in ten school-age children has such problems. Boys and girls are likely to be equally affected, though boys are more prone to become frustrated and to misbehave and, as a result, are more often referred for testing and thus are more frequently diagnosed than girls. Teens who have had an undetected learning disorder can be very frustrated and may have experienced failure at school. This can often lead to other emotional, social, or family problems during adolescence.

READING DISORDER. Proficiency in reading is often considered *the* key to success in other academic areas. Reading achievement is closely linked with mastery of spelling and mathematics, and reading difficulties may make mastering other basic skills more difficult as well. Poor readers are invariably poor spellers, although the converse is not necessarily true.

A teen with a reading disorder will read significantly below expected levels. Recent research has found that difficulty with reading is related to the ability to distinguish subtle differences in sounds. There are forty-four units of sound or *phonemes* in the English language, and the first step in reading is to connect the proper sound to the symbols of the alphabet on the page. An adolescent who is far behind in reading skills may have problems in associating these sounds with the symbols he sees, as well as with interpreting words, tracking words, visually discriminating between similar letters (mistaking d's for b's, for example), and various other cognitive problems that impede mastery of reading. These may include difficulties in sounding out words and, eventually, reading comprehension.

Delays in learning to read may be the result of one of a combination of cognitive, emotional, and social factors. The most frequently associated diagnosis with reading disorder is attention-deficit/hyperactivity disorder. (See *Attention-Deficit/Hyperactivity Disorder,* page 225.)

(Note that the term *dyslexia* also refers to a reading disability in which a teen has difficulty in learning to read. This problem is identified when the child has difficulty in identifying words—*word blindness*—or a tendency to reverse letters and words in reading and writing. The name dyslexia was once common, but since its narrower definition includes only certain signs of reading difficulties, the term dyslexia more recently has been superseded by the broader category of *reading disability*.)

SPELLING DISORDER. There is considerable overlap between reading and spelling difficulties, but the processes involved in learning to read and spell are different. It is sometimes thought that if an individual learns to read, then spelling will naturally follow. That is not necessarily true.

An adolescent may read words he cannot spell and may spell other words without being able to read them, further suggesting that reading and spelling skills are independent of each other. Spelling problems tend to last longer than reading problems. Unlike more visual skills, phonics are important in the development of spelling, although visual memory for spelling patterns may play a major role in spelling proficiency.

DISORDER OF WRITTEN EXPRESSION. The emphasis on expressing one's thoughts or ideas in writing is established relatively late, typically in late elementary or early middle school. Adolescents who have difficulty expressing themselves in written compositions may have isolated or multiple problems.

In learning to write, children need to master two tasks. First, they must have control over the muscles of their hands. A child who had difficulty learning to color, use scissors, button or zip clothing, or tie shoelaces may have difficulty learning to control the pencil and to form letters. Those who have major difficulties with these tasks may have increasing difficulty as they grow into adolescence and the need to write increases. Second, early in his school years a child must begin to master the language of writing, that is, the ability to put thoughts on paper using the correct words in the proper order and to be able to spell and use correct grammar, punctuation, and capitalization. Children with problems of written expression may also have handwriting problems.

Adolescents with this disorder are particularly at risk because writing problems tend to be given less credence by teachers than reading disabilities. It is not uncommon for parents and teachers to blame writing problems on the adolescent, ascribing the difficulty to laziness, noncompliance, or poor motivation. Consequently, adolescents with writing disorder are particularly vulnerable to frustration, academic failure, and low self-esteem.

MATHEMATICS DISORDER. Four basic factors are involved in math achievement: language, conceptualization, visual-spatial ability, and memory. Some teens with language disabilities cannot relate math concepts to everyday situations, which may make it difficult for them to calculate word problems. For example, a boy who is failing math may have a visual processing problem that makes recognizing numbers difficult. Difficulty concentrating and excessive impulsiveness, common traits among children with attention-deficit/hyperactivity disorder (see *Attention-Deficit/Hyperactivity Disorder,* page 225), may impair an individual's ability to organize mathematical details. Some adolescents who fail math have memory problems and actually forget what they are doing or what numbers they are using for computation, a problem that is especially noticeable during mental arithmetic.

Disability in mathematics is not as well understood as other types of learning disabilities. The diagnosis of a math disorder is often not made until late in elementary school or in early middle school. Since math is learned, math difficulty can also be due to poor teaching or to long periods of absence from school.

SOCIAL-EMOTIONAL LEARNING DISABILITY. Teens with this disability usually have both social and academic problems. Their social disabilities are often attributed initially to persistent school failure, isolation from peers, and the high prevalence among them of behavioral patterns associated with attention-deficit/hyperactivity disorder that provokes disapproval of peers and teachers. It is now recognized, however, that some youngsters also have serious problems with social skills acquisition.

Such learning disabled teens often have chronic difficulties with interpersonal relationships. They fail to interpret appropriately the emotional responses of others and do not make correct inferences about other peoples' emotional behaviors. Sometimes these relationship learning disorders are referred to as *nonverbal learning disabilities.*

Parents commonly observe their teen's inability to make friends. The youngster may not be invited to parties or to join in social activities. Frequently excluded from the group, the teen may feel isolated. Although an adolescent with social-emotional learning disability may be intelligent and have good general academic knowledge, he may be unaware that others are not interested in his particular preoccupations. In this sense, he appears to be insensitive to the wishes and desires of others and may be considered a "nerd."

MOTOR SKILLS. The ability to control one's movements is important to school success and acceptance by peers. An adolescent who is exceptionally uncoordinated may avoid physical activities, be shunned by peers, and develop poor self-esteem. All of this can adversely affect the youngster's performance and attitude toward school. When fine motor skills (abilities in using the hands for detailed tasks) are poor, the teen may not be able to write legibly or draw an acceptable picture in art class. A teen with poor fine motor skills may also have hand-eye coordination problems. He may know what he wants to do but can't execute the appropriate sequence of motor movements. Many individuals with motor skills deficits also have problems speaking clearly.

■ IDENTIFYING THE SIGNS

Most learning disabilities become apparent during elementary school when a child fails to keep pace with classmates, although in some cases the disability is not recognized until adolescence. Poor school performance is one general symptom of a learning disorder, although not all teens who do poorly in school are learning disabled.

In young children, signs of a possible reading disability include excessive use of fingers to follow words on a page (an indication that the child may have problems visually tracking words), the inability to instantly recognize familiar words, difficulty in sounding out unfamiliar words, and problems with remembering and retelling a story that the child has just read or that has been read to him. Errors are made because words are remembered by features such as their initial letters or length. Individuals with reading disability read words by sight recognition and have difficulty with new words. They tend to spell dysphonetically (in a manner inconsistent with the sounds of the syllables in a word).

A youngster with a motor skill deficiency may have an awkward pencil grasp. When writing, he frequently hesitates and crosses out errors, which often makes his work illegible. Those with mathematics disorder may also have difficulty forming numerals and putting them in proper sequence. They may also have trouble applying computational skills to problem-solving. Although younger children learn to count, it is ordinarily not until formal math instruction is begun that the diagnosis is made.

■ CAUSES AND CONSEQUENCES

It is often unclear what causes a learning disability. In some cases a learning disability may be apparent in several family members, indicating a genetic component. Some children with learning disabilities appear to have a difference in the way their brain functions and processes information, although the brain does not show evidence of damage. For others the cause is never apparent, leading some experts to speculate that these disorders are the result of developmental delays or immaturity.

Although the causes may be unclear, the consequences are not. If a teen has a learning disorder that has not been recognized and treated, this can lead to academic failure and possibly to social and emotional problems.

■ HOW TO RESPOND

If you suspect that your adolescent has an undetected learning disorder, talk to the teacher and the school principal. Public schools can assemble a diagnostic team, or as parents, you may elect to have a private evaluation done. The evaluation team may include a developmental pediatrician, child neurologist, child and adolescent psychiatrist, clinical psychologist, and an educational specialist.

There are three parts to an evaluation for learning disorders. First, an intelligence test helps to identify the level of ability and specific difficulties. Next, achievement tests measure reading, writing, and math abilities. The third part of the evaluation measures how your adolescent specifically processes information, integrates and understands it, stores information, and retrieves it by talking or writing. This psychoeducational evaluation will identify whether there is a learning disorder and, if so, the specific nature or type of disorder and the appropriate remedial interventions necessary.

The impact of a learning disorder is often reduced if the disorder is diagnosed and treated early in a child's school career. When learning disorders are first identified during adolescence, however, there may be other issues that have to be addressed, such as poor self-esteem and social maladjustment. Treatment will involve working with professionals and developing a plan (called an *Individualized Education Plan* or IEP) to fit the individual needs of your adolescent. In some cases this may involve a change in schools or class or a special education class for part of the day. Some teens with slight disabilities may be capable of staying in their regular classroom as long as they have extra tutoring after school.

Reasonable success in school is essential for an adolescent's feelings of self-confidence and self-esteem. Poor school performance can be responsible for secondary emotional or social problems, which affect behavior in school or at home. Adolescents with severe learning disorders may become anxious or depressed and have difficulty relating to their classmates; family stress also is often exacerbated by a youngster's poor school performance. Treatment may be advised to address such emotional, social, or family problems. A teen whose learning is hampered because of the signs and symptoms of attention-deficit/hyperactivity disorder (a limited ability to concentrate and/or hyperactivity) may benefit from the use of medication as well. (See *Attention-Deficit/Hyperactivity Disorder,* page 225.)

Language and Speech Disorders

One of the most fascinating things you do as a parent is watch as your child's ability to communicate develops. The birth cry of the newborn soon evolved into the coos and babbles that became simple words. Now that your child is an adolescent, he may be able to hold his own in any dinner table debate you care to suggest.

The acquisition of language is one of the first learning tasks we expect of our young children. It is also one of the most important, because failure to master one's native language and speak it correctly can lead to social and academic problems for the child. Difficulties in verbal expression can be the result of speech or language problems or both. Speech is defined as the ability to communicate through sounds; language is the ability to communicate through speech.

In order for your adolescent to have developed normal speech and language, four systems must have been intact when they were younger.

- **ENVIRONMENT**
  A youngster must have adequate interaction and stimulation to learn to speak. Quite simply, babies who are spoken to often begin to speak earlier. Learning to speak includes mastering rhythms, inflections, and sequencing. Those who live in homes where people talk little to each other typically have a more difficult time developing language skills.

- **INPUT SYSTEM**
  In order to learn language, a child must be able to hear clearly and not be hearing impaired.

- **THE CENTRAL SPEECH AND LANGUAGE SYSTEM**
  The acquisition of a language depends upon an intact and functioning central nervous system. Although the neurological basis of language processing is not fully understood, it is believed to be principally a function of the left side of the brain in right-handed persons.

- **THE PRODUCTION SYSTEM OF SPEECH**
  Clear speech depends upon the ability to shape correctly the sounds of language. A person who has a defect of the larynx, throat, nasal, or oral cavity will have difficulty being understood.

There are two basic types of language that we must learn in order to communicate. *Receptive* language denotes our ability to decode words and sentences. In order to be able to do this, a child must be able to interpret what he hears and to assign a meaning to words and sentences. This requires that he be capable of applying selective attention to speech sounds. He then must discriminate between similar sounds he hears. From there, he learns to identify basic units of sound as words with meaning.

The second basic type of language is *expressive* language. Used to express ideas, expressive language involves the ability to call up relevant words from one's repertoire, arrange them in phrases that conform to our standards of grammar, and then be able to incorporate the ideas into sentences in a manner that can be understood by others.

■ IDENTIFYING THE SIGNS

Your adolescent, like most, probably began to speak between the ages of one and two. By age two, many youngsters have a vocabulary of about fifty words and can combine two or three words in a statement. Subsequently, both vocabulary and the ability to speak in longer and more complex phrases develop rapidly. *Speech problems* can include delayed speech, articulation problems, and stuttering. *Language problems* may involve difficulties receiving, processing, or expressing language.

Although many speech and language disorders are detected during the preschool or early school years, sometimes they don't become apparent until adolescence when increased writing demands make a firm grasp of language more imperative than ever. In elementary school, for example, the content of the average book passage that a child would be asked to read is generally below the level of what he is capable of understanding at a conversational level. By eighth grade, however, this changes; the content of school texts surpasses the sophistication level of normal conversation. Thus, a teen with even a slight receptive language deficit may find himself falling further behind the rest of the class. Even as late as high school, a problem may surface, often when a teen fails a foreign language course. This is often because the teen does not have enough mastery over his native language to be competent in a second one.

Most of the time a child's mastery of language proceeds unevenly. Between the ages of eighteen months and five years, words form in the young mind faster than they can be expressed. As a result, about 30 percent of preschoolers have difficulty pronouncing certain words or sounds, although almost all children can be completely understood by the time they are in first grade. Stuttering is also common during these early years. Many young children stutter at one time or another for a few weeks or months. About 1 percent of children have stuttering as a long-term problem, which can continue into adolescence and even into adulthood.

There are certain milestones or signposts that speech development is proceeding on course. If a child's development lagged well behind this general timetable, there may have been a speech and language problem.

- At about one month of age an infant's activity should stop when he hears a sound, and he should be making sounds himself.

- Generally the three-month-old looks in the direction of a speaker, smiles in response to speech, and coos.

- Usually the normal five-month-old responds to his name and is beginning to mimic sounds.

- A seven-month-old will respond with gestures to words such as *up* or *bye-bye*.

- At ten months, most infants speak their first words and can accurately imitate pitch variations.

- A twelve-month-old will respond to certain verbal requests and gestures (for example, *Come here* or *Give it to*

Mommy) and is beginning to attach names to certain objects.

- A twenty-one-month-old should be able to identify pictures of familiar objects and should be using words more than gestures to express what he wants.

- By age two, young children should be able to combine words such as *We go* or *Push me.* A child this age should be able to understand fairly complex sentences and refer to himself by name.

- Most three-year-olds are able to sustain a conversation, putting two or three sentences together and moving from topic to topic.

- By the time a child is four, his speech should be clear enough to be understood (for the most part) by a stranger.

■ CAUSES AND CONSEQUENCES

There are many things that can cause a child to have problems developing speech and language skills. Sometimes there is a physical cause for a speech and language problem, such as a hearing loss. A person whose hearing is impaired will be slow to develop language, and the words he does say may not be spoken clearly. Delayed speech and language acquisition are common in those with mental retardation, brain damage, and pervasive developmental disorder (see *Pervasive Developmental Disorder,* page 255), while cerebral palsy and an abnormality such as a cleft palate can result in speech disorders. In many cases, however, there is no physical cause for a speech or language disorder.

Language disorders may be of receptive or expressive language or of both. Think of the last time you tried to conduct a telephone conversation over a bad connection. An individual with a receptive language disorder spends every day as though he were trying to do just that. Many find it hard to distinguish the forty-four different units of sound or *phonemes* in the English language and have difficulty blending them together into words. Adolescents with impaired receptive language often have problems sounding out words phonetically. Not surprisingly, these teens typically have problems in school, especially with reading, spelling, and writing. They tend to be restless and inattentive in class and slow to adapt socially.

Expressive language disorders include problems with resonance and voice, and fluency disorders such as stuttering, articulation disorders, and problems in language formulation. The adolescent who knows what he wants to say but just can't seem to get it out, who can't tell a story, or who commonly can't think of the words he wants may have an expressive language disorder.

RESONANCE AND VOICE DIFFICULTIES. Disorders of resonance and voice include pauses in conversation, repetitions or prolongations of sounds, and lapses in responding to others. These disorders typically require the services of a speech therapist.

STUTTERING. The most common fluency disorder is stuttering, a problem that usually begins when a child is around three or four, although it can first appear in adolescence. The vast majority of preschoolers who stutter outgrow the problem. The most productive course of action is to ignore the stuttering. Don't make the child repeat his words or constantly correct him. About 1 percent of stutterers, however, require speech therapy.

Over the years there have been many theories as to the cause of stuttering. Currently many speech therapists believe that the vocal cords in a stutterer are prone to spasm as a reaction to stress, which interrupts the air flow required for normal speech. Therapy is geared toward teaching techniques that help minimize this disruption.

ARTICULATION DISORDERS. These are the most common disorders of expressive language. Examples include the substitution of one sound for another, the inability to produce a certain speech sound, and sound distortions. In some people with an articulation disorder, the problem occurs infrequently; in others the disorder may be so severe that speech is consistently unintelligible. A youngster with an articulation disorder may have an abnormality in the oral cavity that interferes with proper speech. Hearing loss is sometimes linked to an articulation disorder.

A teen with an expressive language disorder is typically shy in class and may, to avoid talking, rely on gestures or on single words or phrases to get the message across. It is common for these adolescents to be quiet in class so as not to attract the attention of the teacher. Even when they know the answer, they resist raising their hand to avoid having to talk. Some of these adolescents may have a history of delayed language development. Many, although not all, also have reading difficulties. The problem often becomes more apparent as the adolescent advances in school and the writing demands of school intensify.

▪ HOW TO RESPOND

If you suspect your teen has a speech or language problem, talk to his teacher or counselor at school, then consult his doctor. A speech-language evaluation can help clarify the nature of the difficulty and prescribe appropriate therapy.

The first step in an evaluation may be a hearing test. If there is a history of ear infections as a young child, for example, a mild hearing loss could be interfering with speech development. The doctor will also ask you questions about your youngster's early development to determine whether there were any problems or delays. A speech therapist may be consulted for further evaluation and to suggest treatment.

Pervasive Developmental Disorder

The term *pervasive developmental disorders* (PDD) includes a group of disorders characterized by impairments in the development of social interaction, communication skills, and imaginative activity. Two types of PDD are autistic disorder and Asperger's disorder. (See *Asperger's Disorder*, page 258.)

Infants are social creatures who need contact with others to thrive as much as they need food and water to survive. The parent does nothing more than enter the room and the baby smiles, coos in delight, and with every muscle in his body indicates his wish to be picked up. But perhaps when your child was a baby he did not respond in this expected manner. Instead, he seemed to exist in his own world, a place characterized by repetitive routines, odd and peculiar behaviors, and a total lack of social awareness and interest in others. This behavior is characteristic of the pervasive developmental disorder called *autistic disorder.*

Autistic disorder is one of the most severe developmental disabilities of childhood and adolescence and has a prevalence of between two and five per 10,000 children and perhaps higher. This disorder occurs three to four times more frequently in boys than girls and is fifty times more common in the siblings of children with autistic disorder than in the general population.

■ IDENTIFYING THE SIGNS

If your teenager has autistic disorder, you probably detected problems during infancy, since this serious disorder is typically identified by the time a child is thirty months old. The disorder is commonly discovered when parents consult the youngster's doctor, having become concerned that the infant is not yet talking, resists cuddling, and avoids interactions with others.

Upon questioning, the parents of a child with autistic disorder often recall that even as an infant the child did not want to be cuddled. The social smile that we've come to associate with babies was absent or extremely delayed, and the child did not respond with the anticipatory excitement that the normal infant shows prior to being picked up by a trusted loved one.

A person with autistic disorder is generally withdrawn, aloof, and fails to respond to other people. Many children with autistic disorder will not even make eye contact. When hurt, the child may not seek the comfort of a parent's arms. Children with autistic disorder do not play with others, nor will teens with the disorder socialize with their peers but instead tend to spend their time in solitary activities.

Certain behaviors suggest that persons with autistic disorder may have abnormal responses to sensory stimuli. The person with autistic disorder may place his hands over his ears to avoid the stimulation of loud noises. Conversely, at other times he may be unresponsive to sound and even appear to be deaf. He may lick or smell objects that he picks up.

A youngster with autistic disorder may engage in odd and ritualistic behavior that reflects a need to maintain a constant environment. Your teenager may have certain routines that must be followed to prevent him from erupting into a rage. He may, for example, have to touch objects in a certain order or have his food presented in a certain way. He may demonstrate strong taste aversions and thus eat only a very narrow range of foods.

It is common for individuals with autistic disorder to engage in odd body movements such as constant rocking, whirling, and headbanging. Sometimes the behaviors are carried out to the point where injuries are sustained, suggesting an insensitivity to pain.

Many children and adolescents with autistic disorder do not speak at all or may only mimic sounds made by others. Those who do speak may reverse their pronouns, referring to themselves as he or she or you. Nonsense rhyming and other idiosyncratic language also is common.

The severity of autistic disorder varies widely, from mild to severe. Some teens with autistic disorder are very bright and do well in school, although they have problems with effective thinking and social adjustment. Others function at a much lower level. Intelligence tests conducted on young people with autistic disorder reveal the majority to be in the mentally retarded range with particular problems with verbal skills. IQ testing should be performed by professionals with expertise in evaluating youngsters with developmental delays. Occasionally, a person with autistic disorder may display an extraordinary talent in art, music, or another area.

■ CAUSES AND CONSEQUENCES

The cause of autistic disorder remains unknown, although current research indicates a problem with the function and possible structure of the central nervous system. Some conditions such as maternal rubella, encephalitis, and meningitis appear to predispose a child to autistic disorder, though these are not considered to be causes. There is now substantial evidence that autistic disorder is a genetic disorder, although the specific mode of inheritance remains unclear. We do know,

however, there is no support for the theory that autistic disorder develops because of the parents' behavior toward the infant.

Some parents of children with autistic disorder notice a worsening of the condition as the child moves into adolescence, although a small number of youngsters with autistic disorder actually improve during the teen years. About 40 to 50 percent of those diagnosed with autistic disorder develop some degree of speech. Many have some improvement in their ability to interact socially, but it is rare for a person with autistic disorder to have a sexual relationship based on intimacy or to marry.

■ HOW TO RESPOND

The first step in the diagnosis of autistic disorder is to obtain a thorough evaluation by the child's physician as soon as problems are detected. This evaluation usually includes a clinical history, hearing test, language evaluation, neuropsychiatric interview, and observational assessment. Several psychometric instruments are available for the assessment of children with autistic disorder, such as the *Childhood Autistic Disorder Rating Scale* (CARS), the *Autistic Diagnostic Interview* (ADI), and the *Autistic Disorder Diagnostic Observation Schedule* (ADOS). A few children may require more extensive testing of the blood, urine, and brain, but such additional studies are usually conducted in order to confirm that the condition is not the result of another brain or metabolic disorder.

While strides in the treatment of autistic disorder have been made in recent years, this is a very difficult disorder to treat. The suc-

ASPERGER'S DISORDER

In the past, children with Asperger's disorder were often diagnosed as having autistic disorder. While this disorder does share some characteristics with autistic disorder, there are important distinctions.

In general, an adolescent with Asperger's disorder functions at a higher cognitive and intellectual level than a teen with autistic disorder. While about three-quarters of children and teens with autistic disorder test in the mentally retarded range, those with Asperger's disorder typically fall within the normal range of intelligence. While autistic disorder is associated with a lack of language or, at best, a severe language delay, children with Asperger's usually are talking by the age of two. As the child grows, however, he develops odd speech patterns and may speak in a monotone. Some traits of Asperger's disorder may be found in other members of his family.

Like the teen with autistic disorder, one with Asperger's disorder has limited social interactions with his peers. Individuals with this disorder tend to be loners. They lack empathy for others and generally are highly egocentric, displaying eccentric behaviors. An adolescent with Asperger's, for example, may spend hours each day preoccupied with counting cars that pass on the street or watching only the weather station on television. Coordination difficulties, as well as speech delays, are also common with this disorder. Some research has shown Asperger's disorder clustering in families.

The treatment of Asperger's disorder follows the same general guidelines as that for autistic disorder. Teens with Asperger's disorder also have an increased vulnerability to psychiatric disorders such as mood disorders (see *Depressive Disorders,* page 209), brief reactive psychosis (see *Brief Reactive Psychosis,* page 276), and obsessive-compulsive disorder (see *Obsessive-Compulsive Disorder,* page 201).

The outcome for adolescents with Asperger's disorder is generally more promising than for those with autistic disorder, probably because of their higher intellectual and communication abilities.

cesses are limited and depend upon the severity of the problems. Currently, the most effective treatments involve a combination of special education, behavior modification, and sometimes the use of medications. There is no specific medication for autistic disorder, so before prescribing medications, the doctor will seek to identify target behaviors and symptoms, such as aggression, compulsiveness, hyperactivity, social withdrawal, and depression, and then monitor these behaviors to gauge the medication's effect. Any treatment program must be carefully tailored to the needs of the individual. Treatment may lead to broad and positive changes in the adolescent's development and produce an overall reduction in autistic symptoms and behaviors.

12
Eating and Nutritional Disorders

■ ■ ■

For many of us, eating is one of life's simple pleasures. We do it, three or more times a day, usually out of hunger, sometimes to treat ourselves after a stressful day. Sometimes we overeat, particularly foods that we should stay away from; at other times we're too busy to think about eating. But for most people, the consumption of food is a normal and essentially healthy part of life.

There are people, however, for whom food represents more than a basic necessity or simple pleasure. These people have eating disorders. To an adolescent girl, food may unconsciously be the one weapon she can use to gain control over her life, so she stops eating and almost dies in the process. The college girl next door may be eating—but she's eating in secret binges during which she consumes large quantities of foods only to vomit them all at the end of what is an actual food orgy.

In this chapter, we will explore disorders in which people do not use food in a healthy manner to satisfy true hunger. Anorexia nervosa, bulimia nervosa, and obesity will be discussed.

Anorexia Nervosa

In our society, thinness has somehow become equated with beauty—that's part of the explanation for why three-quarters of adolescent girls reportedly are dissatisfied with their weight. It's hardly surprising that few adolescent girls reach adulthood without at least one foray into fad dieting. Luckily, in most cases, these diets are short-lived, and the teen goes back to eating a more normal—and healthy—diet.

For some teens, though, the diet doesn't end once a couple of pounds have been shed. Even though every time she steps on the scale, the number she sees is lower than the day before and her clothes are starting to hang, the dieter only sees fat when she looks in the mirror. The result is that she eats even less. Even after she is skeletal thin, she cannot stop denying herself food.

Anorexia nervosa is a puzzling eating disorder that typically affects adolescent girls and young adult women, though it may occur in preteens and occasionally in boys. While more prevalent in white, middle- and upper-class intact families, anorexia nervosa, contrary to popular opinion, does occur in all socioeconomic groups and in rural as well as urban settings.

Anorexia nervosa is a condition that should not be dismissed as a harmless diet adopted by a teen preoccupied by the way she looks. This is a potentially life-threatening medical illness, a psychiatric disorder, and sometimes a signal that something may be wrong within the family environment.

Some behavior patterns are observed in the first years of life in individuals who later develop anorexia nervosa. Notably, when those who know the teen with anorexia recall her as a toddler, a commonly mentioned characteristic is significant anxiety and fear-fulness. In general, the adolescents who develop anorexia were the girls who at a much younger age appeared to be overly compliant and insecure. As teens, girls with anorexia frequently have problems with depression or have obsessive-compulsive personality traits or the disorder itself. (See *Obsessive-Compulsive Disorder*, page 201.)

■ IDENTIFYING THE SIGNS

Anorexia frequently begins as a seemingly innocent diet. Although the typical girl who develops anorexia is of normal weight (or only slightly overweight), she decides she wants to be thinner and begins restricting her food intake. In interviews with girls who have anorexia, a common recollection is that the diet began after a family member or peer made a disparaging remark about some aspect of the girl's body.

At first most teens with anorexia simply skip desserts and other high-calorie foods. But before long the teen is skipping meals or she may sit with you at the table to give the pretense of eating when she's really doing little but pushing the food from one side of her plate to the other.

Although it may seem as though she cares nothing about food, on the contrary, the youngster with anorexia often spends most of her day thinking about eating. She may beg to take over duties in the kitchen, bake treats for the family, collect exotic recipes. She may encourage everyone else to eat, while taking only the tiniest taste herself. After a while, most teens with anorexia say they feel no hunger, but they continue to be preoccupied with and guilty about eating.

To help speed the weight loss, many youngsters adopt strenuous exercise regimens. Perhaps she has never done anything more vigorous than take a slow stroll around the block; suddenly she's running five miles a day. She also may start using laxatives and diuretics to increase her rate of weight loss. Some teens with anorexia will also induce vomiting after they do eat, to rid their body of the calories.

Associated with her weight loss, the teen may stop menstruating, become constipated, and develop sleep problems. Because they have little body fat, youngsters with anorexia typically are cold and may appear over-dressed for the weather conditions.

At some point, it usually becomes clear to parents that this is not a normal diet. In many households, bargains are struck between parents and their teenager. The girl promises, for example, that she will only lose two more pounds and then she'll start eating again. Once this goal is met, however, she doesn't start eating but sets a new, lower goal.

Even though she may have lost 10 to 40 percent of her body weight and her skeleton is prominent when she looks in the mirror, the adolescent with anorexia only sees an ugly, fat person. The rest of the world sees a starving person. Her image of her body has become distorted.

■ CAUSES AND CONSEQUENCES

We don't know for certain what causes anorexia nervosa, but almost certainly there is no single cause. The strongest motivation for excessive dieting may be the desire to be healthy and fit, especially as reinforced and sometimes distorted by the media. There may be difficulties in family relations, such as when girls with authoritarian parents rebel by controlling what they believe is the one thing within their power, their food intake. Other important issues can be a high-achieving temperament; perfectionism; early sexual development, when girls see themselves (incorrectly) as overweight; low self-image, which can produce exaggerated responses to remarks about being overweight; and early sexual trauma, which can result in girls sometimes unconsciously seeking to make their bodies unattractive in order to protect themselves from sexual advances.

Genetic and biological circumstances may also contribute. Chemical abnormalities in the brain, specifically changes in the neurotransmitters (chemical brain messengers) serotonin or norepinephrine, which regulate mood, have been found in youngsters with eating disorders. A strong commitment to athletics such as gymnastics or wrestling or to artistic endeavors such as ballet or figure skating where body shape or size is paramount to success also seems to be a major contributing factor in many teens of both sexes who develop the disorder. In the same way, the stress of making the transition to a new environment such as college and being away from home may be another factor for vulnerable teens. Finally, the power of the media—magazines, television, and movies—place an unrealistic premium on thinness, which may influence susceptible youngsters.

Although there may be disagreement as to what causes anorexia, no one will argue that this is a dangerous and sometimes fatal disorder that must be treated promptly and completely. Today, there are many adolescents who have recovered from anorexia nervosa who are healthy and at or near normal weight, but in most cases this is achieved only after much time and treatment. With early identification of their eating problems and comprehensive treatment, however, a significant number of teens make good recoveries.

Signs that are equated with a poorer prognosis include late age of onset; long duration of the disease; large weight loss; an accompanying history of bulimia (binge and purge; see page 264); and severe depression. An estimated 6 percent of youngsters hospitalized with anorexia die within ten years. Amazingly, the cause of death is rarely starvation. The most common killers are suicide and electrolyte imbalances, which can produce irregular heartbeat and cardiac arrest.

■ HOW TO RESPOND

Denial is common among teens with anorexia nervosa and often their parents, too. In one study, 25 percent of girls had had symptoms for over a year before they were diagnosed with the disorder.

When should you worry that your teen's diet is really something more than she's telling you? If she loses five or ten pounds and seems to be eating a healthy diet, you probably don't have anything to worry about. But if she is becoming obsessive or secretive in her eating habits, expresses guilt about eating, exhibits some of the symptoms discussed earlier, and loses a substantial amount of weight (more than 10 percent of her body weight), seek professional advice.

The first step of treatment, after a general medical evaluation to rule out other causes of weight loss, is education about normal adolescent growth and nutrition. This may be done by the family physician or pediatrician with the help of a dietitian.

Your teen's physician will be able to recommend a child and adolescent psychiatrist or other mental health professional specializing in the treatment of adolescents with anorexia nervosa. Treating this complicated disorder involves a combination approach that addresses both the medical symptoms and emotional causes. The evaluating professional will involve parents as well as the adolescent and perhaps other members of the family. The treatment process will likely begin with an evaluation of symptoms and family and social context and a careful review of the teen's development. Just how the problem is approached depends on the adolescent and the family, but individual psychotherapy (see *Individual Psychotherapy,* page 320) or family therapy (see *Family Therapy,* page 326) are usually recommended. If depression (see *Depressive Disorders,* page 209), obsessive-compulsive disorder (*ODD;* see page 201), or other psychiatric diagnoses are made, medication may also be prescribed.

Hospitalization. If your daughter is still well enough physically, she may be able to remain at home as long as she undergoes psychotherapy, including family therapy, and nutritional counseling and has her weight monitored. Many adolescents with anorexia nervosa, however, because of their weakened condition, require hospitalization for more intensive treatment. Important treatment issues include gaining back lost weight, improving eating habits, and helping the youngster make social adjustments. For adolescents sick enough to need such intensive intervention, the two- to three-week maximum stay that insurance companies now allow is often insufficient. An alternative to hospitalization during this acute phase of treatment is an intensive, structured program such as day treatment along with partial hospitalization.

Bulimia Nervosa

Bulimia nervosa, like anorexia nervosa (see above), is an eating disorder. Unlike the youngster with anorexia nervosa, however, the teen with bulimia nervosa does not shun food but instead indulges in food binges. Bulimia nervosa is often called the binge-and-purge disorder, because after the teen has stuffed herself until she can hold no more, she induces vomiting.

This disorder is more common than anorexia nervosa. Some studies have found that, on occasion, as many as 18 percent of all college women binge and purge, although roughly 3 percent would be diagnosed as actually having bulimia nervosa. It is rare in males.

Bulimia, which means "ox-hunger," is a disorder in which the person, usually an adolescent girl or young woman, has a morbid fear of becoming fat. Many teens with bulimia nervosa also have or have had anorexia nervosa; in some cases, teens develop eating disorders in which their behavior alternates between anorexia nervosa and bulimia nervosa.

■ IDENTIFYING THE SIGNS

Unlike the teen with anorexia nervosa, who often becomes emaciated, most adolescents with bulimia nervosa are close to normal weight or even slightly overweight, although there is often some fluctuation in weight because of the food binges.

When she is eating at the table with her family or friends, the youngster with bulimia nervosa may seem to have a normal appetite, consuming neither too little nor too much food. Typically, binges occur when the person is alone. Often binges occur every day, the average binge time being slightly over an hour, although some binges may last eight or more hours. During this time, the teen literally stuffs herself until she is full, often to the point of physical pain. Adolescents with bulimia nervosa have been known to consume as many as more than 10,000 calories a day, although the average caloric intake during a single binge is around 3,500, or roughly two-and-a-half times a normal daily diet. The foods binged on vary, but the most frequently eaten binge foods are ice cream, bread, candy, doughnuts and soft drinks. Dental cavities are common among youth with bulimia nervosa because of the high sugar content of their binges and the loss of tooth enamel caused by the acid from vomiting.

A teen with bulimia nervosa may gorge on

food until she feels guilt or acute physical discomfort. Then she will induce vomiting. Initially, most youngsters with bulimia nervosa stick their fingers against the backs of their throats to trigger the gag reflex (some may even have noticeable cuts, abrasions, or calluses on the knuckles as a result of the fingers being driven against the teeth by the vomiting reflex). After a while, most teens with bulimia nervosa do not need to gag themselves and can vomit automatically. Laxatives also are commonly used to help purge the body after an eating binge, and diuretics may also be employed to lose weight. The teen with bulimia nervosa may also engage in periods of excessive exercise or abuse diet pills.

Unlike a girl with anorexia nervosa who does not believe she has a problem, the girl with bulimia nervosa understands that her eating habits are far from normal, and this contributes to her sense of guilt, self-loathing, and lowered self-esteem. Rarely, however, do parents observe their teens with bulimia nervosa engaging in acts of bingeing or purging. These youngsters act secretively, and friends, if anyone, are more likely to be aware of their suffering. Some signs of bulimia that parents might become aware of are missing food (not a few cookies, but a whole box); secretive eating; hoarding food; evidence of vomiting; and over-the-counter emetics and laxatives.

Stealing and other impulsive behaviors, such as overspending and sexual promiscuity, are common with this eating disorder. As you might suspect, food is the object most often stolen. Youngsters with bulimia nervosa also have a high rate of drug and alcohol abuse, and their families have been found to have a higher incidence of depression and substance abuse than the general population.

In contrast to women with anorexia nervosa, most girls with bulimia nervosa continue to menstruate, though their periods frequently are irregular. Because the appearance of the teen with bulimia nervosa may not radically change (unlike the appearance of a teen with anorexia nervosa), the youngster with bulimia nervosa may be able to keep her family and close friends entirely unaware of her problem. The adolescent's weight, however, may fluctuate.

■ CAUSES AND CONSEQUENCES

As with anorexia nervosa, the exact cause of bulimia nervosa is unknown. Evidence points to both emotional and physical causes. The desire to be thinner than one's natural body build, and normal compensatory hunger after days of starvation, are common causes. Because these eating disorders typically surface during puberty, many researchers regard them as defenses against a girl's emerging sexuality, in which the body changes and increased weight that accompany puberty are confused in her mind with her sexuality.

Bulimia nervosa may also be a sign of problems in adolescent identity development or of a mood disorder. Family dynamics are also thought to be a factor in the development of eating disorders, as a girl with an eating disorder may be attempting to get a sense of control over, or to find comfort despite, a hostile family environment. Personally traumatic events may also be contributing factors.

Although the typical teen with bulimia nervosa appears healthier than one with anorexia nervosa, this disease can also have serious, even life-threatening health consequences. Dangerous electrolyte imbalances often occur as a result of frequent vomiting and laxative abuse and can cause dangerous irregular heartbeats and even cardiac arrest. Other risks are pneumonia (due to aspirating vomit) and gastrointestinal and dental problems. Girls with bulimia nervosa may also suffer from depression and substance abuse and may become suicidal.

■ How to Respond

If you detect that your daughter has a tendency to go on eating binges or purges by vomiting or laxative use, seek professional advice. Your teen's physician will be able to recommend a child and adolescent psychiatrist specializing in treating adolescents with eating disorders. As with anorexia nervosa, education about healthy nutritional habits is the first step in treatment.

Bulimia nervosa is a difficult disorder to treat. Though no single treatment has proven to be optimal, treatment designed to help the teen learn to control her impulses seems to be the most effective. A combination approach that addresses both the medical symptoms and the emotional causes is best, and the evaluating professional will involve parents as well as the adolescent and perhaps other members of the family. The treatment process will likely begin with an evaluation of symptoms and family and social context and a careful review of the adolescent's development.

Just how the problem is approached depends on the child and the family, but individual psychotherapy is one proven approach. A good therapeutic relationship can absorb much of the teen's anxiety and promote open discussion of important issues such as identity and body image. (See *Individual Psychotherapy,* page 320.) Cognitive-behavioral therapy, which focuses on identifying and correcting negative distortions and on helping the teen change her thinking, can also be helpful. (See *Cognitive-Behavioral Therapy,* page 323.) Group therapy, in which youngsters with similar problems can meet and talk in a supportive group environment, can offer a way to understand and control behaviors such as overspending, sexual promiscuity, and drug and alcohol abuse, as well as the symptoms of the eating disorder. (See *Group Therapy,* page 328.) In the same way, family therapy can provide to the parents and other siblings, as well as the youngster with bulimia nervosa, an opportunity to explore the family context for the binge-and-purge behavior and some of the stresses and anxieties that may have led to it. (See *Family Therapy,* page 326.)

Medication. Several research studies have shown that antidepressant medications may reduce the binge-and-purge cycle in adolescents with bulimia nervosa, but the results may not be long-lasting. While some medications may benefit some individuals when combined with psychotherapy, medications are generally not as effective as therapy alone.

Obesity

Despite the known health risks of being overweight, Americans in general weigh too much. As a society, we tend to eat too much, prefer the foods that make us fat, and exercise too little.

We know that eating a diet high in fat and calories puts us at increased risk for life-threatening diseases that range from heart attack to some cancers. Yet many of us ignore the evidence and plunge into yet another hot fudge sundae or make room for one more burger. Unlike anorexia nervosa and bulimia nervosa, obesity is very prevalent in males as well as females.

In many cases the seeds of obesity are sown early in life. While obesity can occur any time, the most common ages in childhood are between the ages of five and six and during adolescence. This isn't to say that every child who carries some excess weight is destined to be obese. As their bodies change, teens, especially girls, may go through a period where they are slightly overweight. A few extra pounds do not indicate obesity, although they may indicate a tendency to gain weight easily and necessitate some dietary changes. Generally, a person is not considered obese until her weight is at least 10 percent higher than what is recommended for her height and body frame. In children and teens, doctors often use a simpler rule: If children look obese, they are.

How prevalent is obesity during childhood and adolescence? Statistics indicate that anywhere between 16 and 33 percent of children and adolescents are obese. For many, childhood obesity is a precursor of lifelong weight problems. Research has shown that a child who is obese when she is between the ages of ten and thirteen has an 80 percent chance of becoming an obese adult.

■ IDENTIFYING THE SIGNS

A teen who is a few pounds overweight or carries a small spare tire around her middle is not necessarily obese. But if the teen's normal weight, according to weight tables, should be 100 pounds and she weighs 120, she probably has a problem. More importantly, does she look fat? When you pinch the skin of her upper arm, can you grab more than an inch?

■ CAUSES AND CONSEQUENCES

The causes of obesity are complex and include genetic, biological, behavioral, and cultural factors. At its simplest, however, obesity occurs when a person eats more calories than her body burns up through normal activities and exercise. This excess is then stored as fat.

There are, of course, some people who seem able to eat all day and not gain weight. Others may eat relatively little and put on extra pounds. What determines whether a teen is prone to obesity appears to be partly a matter of genetics. If one parent is overweight, there is a 50 percent chance the teenager will also be overweight. When both parents are obese, their offspring have an 80 percent chance of following suit. Conversely, if neither parent has a weight problem, youngsters are only at a 10 percent risk of becoming seriously overweight.

Oftentimes people say they are obese because of health problems. Although certain metabolic disorders can cause obesity, fewer than 1 percent of obese people can attribute their excess weight to a physical cause.

There are both physical and emotional consequences of obesity. The physical problems such as increased risk of heart disease, high blood pressure, and diabetes become more of a problem as the body ages. Then, too, the obese person tends to be more sedentary than one of normal weight. This lack of exercise not only makes it harder to lose weight but also can contribute to ill health.

The emotional problems associated with child or adolescent obesity are more immediate. Teens with weight problems tend to have much lower self-esteem than their normal-size counterparts. Young people who are obese often tend to be unpopular with their peers, which can contribute to depression and other emotional problems. In part, this is a result of the strong cultural bias against obesity that begins in childhood. Many negative labels are given to overweight teenagers—they may be unfairly railed against as being ugly, stupid, or lazy.

Some overweight young people also develop troublesome symptoms of binge-eating and purging rituals and may exhibit other problems in controlling their impulses. They may also go on unhealthy diets, develop unhealthy weight-loss behavior, and experience weight cycling, in which their body weight yo-yos up and down over time.

■ HOW TO RESPOND

If your child is obese, she should have a thorough medical examination to rule out the rare possibility of a physical cause.

In the absence of a physical disorder, the only way to lose weight is to reduce caloric intake while at the same time increasing the teen's level of physical activity. Losing weight is difficult under the best of circumstances. You can't make your teen lose weight; she has to develop her own motivation to change. Fortunately, many appearance-conscious teens—much more so than children—are motivated to embark on a self-improvement campaign. In many instances of teens with obesity, there is also one or two obese parents in the home. Making healthy eating and regular exercise a family affair improves the teen's chances of success at weight control. Sometimes family therapy may be appropriate to change family-wide patterns of eating and exercise. (See *Family Therapy,* page 326.)

The Proper Diet. Ask your doctor to recommend a diet that still enables your teen to receive adequate nutrition while lowering her fat and calorie intake. If she is at the beginning of her growth spurt, the goal should be to keep her from gaining weight, not to lose weight. As she adds inches in stature without gaining pounds, you will notice a slimmer figure.

If the doctor recommends weight loss, set realistic and safe goals; for instance, one pound a week. Have her weigh herself no more than once a week, since frequent weigh-ins are often discouraging when the pounds refuse to budge. To help her lose the weight and firm up her body, you may want to encourage her to join a gym or start jogging, swimming, bicycling, walking, or some other form of exercise. Some teens are helped by weight-loss support groups where they can get the support of other overweight teens and adults.

Behavior Modification. As she diets, remember that you are not only trying to help her lose weight but are attempting to teach her a new way of eating and exercising. The reason most overweight people gain back their lost pounds is that after they've reached their goal, they go back to their old ways of eating and not exercising. An obese person must learn to eat and enjoy healthy foods in moderate amounts and to exercise regularly if she is to lose weight and keep it off.

13

Psychotic Disorders

■ ■ ■

Psychotic disorders, which are also referred to as *thought disorders*, are among the most serious of mental disorders. The symptoms of schizophrenia, psychosis due to a mood disorder, brief reactive psychosis, and toxic psychosis are upsetting and often frightening to both the parents and the adolescent. In most cases, a teen with one of these disorders requires psychiatric treatment as soon as symptoms develop.

Imagine the fear of the parents of an adolescent who suddenly starts behaving in a bizarre manner. The teen admits that voices are telling him to do bad things or are threatening to cause him harm. The youngster warns his parents that there is poison gas leaking into his bedroom or that the police are watching their home because aliens have landed there. He is unable to answer his parents' questions, yet he continues to ramble, often incoherently, and his parents have trouble following his thinking. Such experiences are terribly frightening for adolescent and parents alike.

Psychotic disorders are characterized by an impairment of the thinking processes that renders the adolescent unable to perceive thoughts, actions, and even the world as they really are. When so impaired, the person is incapable of thinking logically. The disorganized or unusual behavior and emotional reactions of a teen with psychosis follow no particular pattern but rather can be described as illogical; inappropriate to the situation; puzzling to the observer; uncharacteristic of the adolescent; or making no sense. A teen with a thought disorder may speak in a disorganized, incoherent, or incomprehensibly vague manner. He may speak rarely or in torrents of words that have little to do with reality. The concept of "conversation" may not be applicable, as there is an absence of the mutual perception, awareness, and understanding basic to a normal conversational exchange.

The perception that one has heard or seen something that is not present, a *hallucination*, is common to some psychotic thinking disorders, as are *delusions,* false and often bizarre beliefs that a person clings to despite overwhelming evidence to the contrary.

Unusual, distorted, or impaired thinking can also be caused by other disorders.

During adolescence, alcohol and drug abuse can produce disordered thinking. (See *Toxic Psychosis,* page 277, and *Substance Abuse Disorders*, page 279.) Occasionally, teens with severe developmental disorders that result in impaired communication skills may appear to think illogically when the difficulty is actually a result of their deficit in language skills. (See *Pervasive Developmental Disorder,* page 255.) These symptoms may be misdiagnosed as thought disorders.

Hallucinations also occur in some adolescents with seizure disorders (see *Seizure Disorders,* page 184) and in some with post-traumatic stress disorder (see *Childhood Trauma and Its Effects,* page 205). The obsessions of teens with obsessive-compulsive disorder and the body image distortions characteristic of the adolescent with anorexia nervosa clearly interfere with the ability to think logically, yet these are not psychotic disorders.

The subject of this chapter is the mental disorders that seriously impair an adolescent's ability to function in reality. These disorders of thought process include schizophrenia, severe mood disorders of depression and mania, brief reactive psychosis, and toxic psychosis. Any teen with disordered thinking or behavior should be evaluated immediately by a clinician who has expertise in these serious mental disorders.

Schizophrenia

Schizophrenia is a chronic psychotic disorder that typically begins in late adolescence or early adulthood. An estimated 2.5 million Americans have been diagnosed with this severe mental illness. This disease is found in about 1 percent of the world's population but is rare in children under twelve years of age. Schizophrenia is a disorder that affects both males and females equally.

While it's most likely to emerge during the college years or in early adulthood, in adolescence the problem may appear slowly, with gradually increasing symptoms over a number of months.

■ IDENTIFYING THE SIGNS

A person with schizophrenia is impaired in his ability to understand reality in a manner consistent with his age, development, intellectual capability, education, and culture. Adults, teens, and children alike who develop schizophrenia have difficulties in the *form* of their thinking, which may involve illogical thinking, difficulty in organizing thoughts, or loose associations. They may also have an impairment in the *content* of their thinking, exemplified by hallucinations and delusions.

Illogical Thinking. An adolescent with schizophrenia frequently speaks in a manner that makes it difficult to piece together the elements of what he is saying. The word *because* may be used inappropriately. Assertions made in a single sentence may contradict one another. Unnecessary or inappropriate reasons may be given for statements. A teen might justify forgetting something because of something else utterly unrelated—*I left my books at school because the teacher wore a blue hat.* Another verbal example of illogical thinking might be *I didn't like the cake, but I like it as a cake.*

Loose Associations. Loose associations are defined as unconnected shifts from one topic or thought to another. In an adolescent with schizophrenia, the elements in his conversation seem unrelated. The listener is often confused, puzzled, and unable to follow the thread of the conversation, because the adolescent with this symptom has offered no verbal connections for changes in the topic.

Hallucinations. When teens hallucinate, they usually assert they are hearing or seeing something or someone that doesn't exist in

reality. Their brains process "experiences" in a manner similar to dreaming. Thus, the "experiences" are strictly internal events and are not based on information from their environment.

Hearing voices is a common auditory hallucination in schizophrenia. A teenager with schizophrenia may describe these voices as telling him to *hit my sister, run away from home,* or *do bad things.* Some teens with schizophrenia report hearing voices that called them derogatory names. Sometimes they recognize the voice as a relative's or friend's; at other times it is described as a stranger's voice; sometimes there are multiple voices.

Delusions. A delusion is a belief that appears false or bizarre yet cannot be changed by logical argument and is outside the realm of what is acceptable for a specific community, culture, or religion. A teen's conviction that certain foods are radioactive and will poison him is an example of a delusion, as is the belief that an adolescent's actions are controlled by messages from the television.

The symptoms and effects of schizophrenia don't always follow a set pattern. Some individuals with schizophrenia will become withdrawn, others boisterous; some are fearful, others unexplainably angry or aggressive. Teenagers with schizophrenia have severe problems relating to their environment and to the people around them. They have difficulties maintaining social relationships with peers, communicate poorly, and misunderstand verbal and nonverbal social cues from others. They behave in bizarre ways, which causes them to be increasingly rejected by those around them. A deterioration in their ability to function socially will both isolate them and lead to a drop in school performance. Teens who develop schizophrenia may also have unusual fears, may experience puzzling or fluctuating emotional states that go well beyond the normal realm of teenage mood swings, and may have developmental delays.

■ CAUSES AND CONSEQUENCES

No one has as yet been able to identify the cause or causes of schizophrenia. Abnormalities in brain development play a role. Genetic factors are involved—this is supported by the higher incidence of the disorder within families where one or more members have schizophrenia. The malformation or changes in the brain may also be the result of a viral infection during the second or third trimester of pregnancy. A variety of studies provide data to support each of these theories, but most researchers believe that ultimately a constellation of several conditions and factors will be identified as the cause of schizophrenia.

Schizophrenia is a lifelong disease that can be controlled but not cured. Over the years great gains have been made in controlling the disease with medication, therapies, and family education. Typically the adolescent with schizophrenia has periods with severe symptoms, but with treatment, he can improve considerably. Unfortunately, each episode of severe symptoms may result in some loss of capacity, which makes it difficult for the teen to regain functioning at his previous ability level in both cognitive and social areas.

■ HOW TO RESPOND

If your adolescent is having any of the psychotic symptoms discussed earlier in this section or is severely withdrawn and emotionally unresponsive, you should seek help. Start with his doctor, who will then refer you to a child and adolescent psychiatrist or other physician if schizophrenia or another psychotic disorder is suspected. Both you and your teen will need support as you struggle to accept and deal with this serious and frightening psychotic disorder.

Treatment of schizophrenia should begin with a comprehensive evaluation. The child and adolescent psychiatrist will ask you about your teen's developmental history and symptoms and interview both you and your adolescent. The clinician will then spend time observing the teen's behavior. A neurological examination determines whether any central nervous system dysfunction is contributing to the symptoms. A psychoeducational evaluation uncovers intellectual and learning problems as well as problems the adolescent may be having in getting along with his peers. As part of this evaluation, a battery of tests may be administered to assess not only intelligence but also his ability to think logically. During the comprehensive evaluation, careful consideration will also be given to other possible disorders before reaching a diagnosis of schizophrenia.

Hospitalization. During periods of acute illness, hospitalization may be necessary to provide a safe and structured environment. The immediate goal when an adolescent with schizophrenia is hospitalized is to control the acute psychotic symptoms. It is important to work closely with your adolescent's psychiatrist, nursing staff, and education specialists to construct a treatment and follow-up plan that will best meet his needs. Once he leaves the hospital, the plan should take into account ways to help him learn as much as possible in school and reach his highest level of functioning.

Medication. If your adolescent is diagnosed with schizophrenia, medication will treat his particular symptoms. Antipsychotic medications may help decrease excitability, improve his ability to think in a logical manner, and reduce hallucinations. These medications have greatly improved life for many people with schizophrenia by apparently blocking certain chemical receptors in the brain. Among the antipsychotic medications are chlorpromazine (Thorazine), haloperidol (Haldol), and thioridazine (Mellaril).

Antipsychotic medications may cause side effects such as sun sensitization, loss of bladder control, weight gain, blurred vision, dry mouth, the feeling of faintness, severe muscle spasms, and tremors. Newer antipsychotic medications seem to have fewer side effects and seem to improve significantly problems with motivation, attention, and aggression. These include risperidone (Risperdal), olanzapine (Zyprexa), and clozapine (Clozaril).

Other Therapies. While antipsychotic medications are effective in controlling or reducing some of the acute symptoms of psychosis, they may not address the social withdrawal that is so common in people with schizophrenia. Thus, psychotherapy and family counseling usually are key components of treatment in both the effort to help the adolescent with schizophrenia live as normal a life as possible and to help the family cope with his illness.

Psychosis Due to a Mood Disorder

A few teenagers with mood disorders develop psychotic symptoms. While most adolescents with depression or mania don't have psychotic symptoms, some severe forms of these emotional disorders are accompanied by such symptoms as disorganized thinking, hallucinations, and delusions.

■ IDENTIFYING THE SIGNS

While adolescents with schizophrenia may show signs of a depressed mood, more often their moods are numbed or apathetic. Thus, the youngster with schizophrenia is typically depressed in response to the grave impairments in their abilities.

In contrast, severely depressed adolescents with mood disorders are persistently and extremely sad. They feel truly hopeless. Often their eating and sleeping patterns are disrupted. At the opposite extreme, teenagers with mania feel euphoric, and their energy seems endless. With both depressive and manic moods, however, the adolescent seems mired in the mood state and does not experience varying moods in the context of daily activities and relationships.

Psychotic depression can produce hallucinations that compound the hopelessness. These teens may hear voices making derogatory remarks about them, calling them insulting names or telling the young person to take his own life, that he is a hopeless burden and to go ahead and end it all. Psychotic delusions may be similarly extreme: Despite evidence to the contrary, the teen may believe he himself is the cause of a variety of ills, anything from the death of a loved one to racial conflicts at his school.

Psychotic mania may produce hallucinations that, again, compound and confirm the mood. Voices may tell the euphoric adolescent that he is the strongest, most attractive, and most powerful person alive. Voices may urge him to do things such as try to fly off a rooftop, stop six lanes of traffic, announce a cure for AIDS, or proclaim himself the messiah.

Thinking is disturbed in other ways, too. These teenagers with mania describe their thoughts as racing at high speed and their communications reflect this. Their speech is loud and fast and often lacks complete thoughts or sentences. The rapid stream of loosely connected thoughts that results is sometimes described as a "flight of ideas."

■ CAUSES AND CONSEQUENCES

The causes of psychotic mood disorders are unknown, but there is evidence of a genetic predisposition that makes some teenagers vulnerable to disturbed moods, depression in response to overwhelming stress, and psychotic symptoms. While there are no consistent patterns in teens with psychosis due to mood disorders, full recovery from acute episodes is usual. During the episode itself, the disrupted thinking can be incapacitating, but unlike psychosis due to schizophrenia, there is usually no permanent deterioration in communication or social skills following an episode.

■ HOW TO RESPOND

If your adolescent has psychotic symptoms, seek immediate help. Distinguishing whether the psychosis is due to a mood disorder or to schizophrenia is sometimes difficult, but it is important that the understanding be reached, because the treatment approaches to each disorder is distinct. You may want to begin with the youngster's physician who may refer him to a child and adolescent psychiatrist for a complete evaluation.

The psychiatrist will interview both parent and teen, inquiring about current and any earlier symptoms. The details of the symptoms themselves will help the clinician determine whether a mood disorder may be responsible for the thought disturbance. Psychological testing may also be done to help understand the emotional and cognitive status of your teenager.

Hospitalization. If your teen is thought to be a danger to himself or others or is unable to care for himself, hospitalization may be recommended. The goal, however, will be to devise a treatment approach that will enable the youngster to return to his family and home. Intensive treatments can also be done on an outpatient basis or through a partial hospital program after the issues of safety have been resolved.

Medication. If your adolescent is diagnosed with a mood disorder with psychotic features, treatment will address the impaired thinking and the mood disorder. For psychotic depression, antidepressant medications, such as imipramine (Tofranil) or fluoxetine (Prozac), may be used in conjunction with antipsychotic medications, such as haloperidol (Haldol) or risperidone (Risperdal). Psychotic symptoms associated with mania will likewise be treated with combinations of medications, perhaps including mood stabilizer medications such as lithium along with antipsychotic medications. Once the psychosis has been effectively treated, the antipsychotic medication may be discontinued, but the antidepressant or mood stabilizers may be continued.

Other Therapies. After insuring safety and controlling the psychotic symptoms, therapies may be recommended such as those used with other types of emotional disorders. (See *Bipolar Mood Disorder,* page 217, and *Depressive Disorders,* page 209.) These various forms of treatment offer support for the teenager and his family, who will be faced with learning about the mood disorder, exploring ways to resolve the problems effectively, and preventing future episodes.

Brief Reactive Psychosis

Occasionally adolescents suddenly develop psychotic symptoms that last for a few hours or days. This disorder is called brief reactive psychosis. Such an episode generally occurs when a young person has been under great stress. He may face an important adjustment, having just experienced a death in the family, left home for college, witnessed acts of violence, or suffered sexual or physical abuse. Some teens whose emotions tend to fluctuate wildly, who are impulsive, and who have difficulty maintaining stable relationships also experience periods of brief reactive psychosis. Unlike schizophrenia, in which symptoms typically worsen over a period of weeks, brief reactive psychosis seems to arrive abruptly, producing disturbed behavior in a teen who previously had functioned satisfactorily.

■ IDENTIFYING THE SIGNS

Sudden disorganization of behavior, speech, and emotional reactions are the key symptoms of brief reactive psychosis. The adolescent may appear agitated and confused and may adopt bizarre behavior or dress. For no apparent reason, he may suddenly start screaming, or he may adopt the opposite approach and withdraw into a silent shell. When he does talk, his speech may be nonsensical, full of incomprehensible and repetitive phrases. Hallucinations or delusions sometimes occur in brief reactive psychosis but are usually brief.

■ CAUSES AND CONSEQUENCES

Brief reactive psychosis appears to be linked to extremely stressful events in the adolescent's life. Other causes have not been identified or extensively studied in young people. The acute psychotic symptoms often resolve quickly, with total recovery in a few days. After the episode, however, some adolescents may feel depressed, have lowered self-esteem, and feel anxious about future attacks.

■ HOW TO RESPOND

Support and safety are two primary concerns in helping a teen who is experiencing a reactive psychosis.

Medication. Antipsychotic medications are often effective in treating acute psychotic symptoms; among those that may be prescribed are chlorpromazine (Thorazine), haloperidol (Haldol), and thioridazine (Mellaril).

Other Therapies. While medications will modify the symptoms, they will not eliminate the problem that caused the psychosis in the first place. Thus, individual psychotherapy (see *Individual Psychotherapy,* page 320) is often recommended to help the teen learn to cope with the emotional stresses that precipitated the episode and his particular vulnerability to stress. (See also *Childhood Trauma and Its Effects*, page 205.)

Hospitalization. During periods of acute illness, hospitalization may be necessary to provide a safe and structured environment. The immediate goal is to control the acute psychotic symptoms and treat them as quickly as possible.

Toxic Psychosis

Toxic delirium or toxic psychoses occur when a medication, illicit drug, alcohol, medical condition, or head injury results in a person developing temporary psychotic symptoms.

■ IDENTIFYING THE SIGNS

Unlike schizophrenia or other psychotic disorders in which impaired thinking and communication are major symptoms, toxic psychosis is more likely to cause vivid, disturbing hallucinations or other perceptual problems. These sensory experiences may be extremely frightening and may be accompanied by agitated, uncontrolled, and even aggressive behavior. An adolescent with this condition appears to suddenly "lose his mind" and become disoriented, unable to identify who or where he is or why he is behaving in a certain manner. The youngster may also have signs of fluctuating alertness.

■ CAUSES AND CONSEQUENCES

The most common causes of toxic psychoses are the use of certain drugs such as hallucinogens and amphetamines, an overdose of over-the-counter medications such as sleeping pills, antihistamines, and cold preparations, and alcohol abuse or withdrawal. Teens with substance abuse disorders have a higher risk of developing toxic psychosis. (See *Substance Abuse Disorders*, page 279.)

Some teens hallucinate when they have high fevers. Medical illness that alters the balance of body chemicals may also result in a toxic psychosis. For example, a person with kidney or liver disease may hallucinate and become disoriented because of the toxic effects of a buildup of waste products in the body.

Teens who develop a drug-induced psychosis will generally recover once the drugs are out of their systems. The gravest danger occurs during the psychotic episode, when the adolescent may inadvertently cause serious harm to himself or others.

■ How to Respond

A toxic psychosis requires immediate medical intervention to identify the cause and provide appropriate treatment. Consult your family physician or take your teen to the local emergency room quickly.

Hospitalization. Persons experiencing acute symptoms of toxic psychosis or toxic delirium may need to be protected so that they will not harm themselves or others. A quiet place and the presence of a trusted person may be the best environment. Continual verbal support and encouragement can be very helpful. Some may require a brief stay in the hospital.

Medications. In some cases, antipsychotic drugs are administered to control the distorted perception (hallucinations) and decrease the teen's agitation.

As part of the diagnosis, your doctor may advise laboratory tests to determine whether a particular medication, illicit drug, or chemical did indeed trigger the psychosis. If the cause of the psychotic episode was drug or alcohol abuse, a substance abuse evaluation and treatment program may be appropriate.

14

Substance Abuse Disorders

■ ■ ■

I t is a rare teen who goes through adolescence without some exposure to drugs or alcohol. Even if your teen has no intention of drinking or using drugs, she will probably at some point be in a situation where drugs and alcohol are being abused by her peers. Will she be able to say no? Or will she succumb to the will of the crowd and take that drink, inhale that smoke, or pop that pill in the interest of belonging or simply out of curiosity? Surely, that very question has to enter the minds of the parents who, late on a Saturday night, anxiously await the sounds that signal their teen's safe arrival home.

Statistics tell us that most teens are unable to resist the lure of drugs and alcohol. Today, roughly two out of three teens try marijuana at least once before they graduate from high school; some start experimenting with drugs as early as grade school. In practice, the most common pattern is for teenagers to begin experimenting with cigarettes, wine, and beer. Next they try marijuana. Public drinking typically follows, then use of LSD, pills, cocaine, and even heroin. Most teens don't have to look very long and hard to gain access to cigarettes and alcohol, which can start them on this dangerous spiral of substance abuse.

Why do teens drink or take drugs? Adolescence is a challenging time for most teens and their families. The need to separate from one's parents, the need to form a sexual identity, and the increasing sense that impending adulthood with all its responsibilities is just around the corner all can lead to great inner turmoil. If your teen has friends who drink or use drugs, peer pressure is an added factor to the equation, particularly to those teens who are easily influenced by their peers. Teens also use drugs and alcohol simply for the fun of it, as recreational drug abusers routinely report experiencing a sense of exhilaration, euphoria, or release.

Some adolescents feel the need to escape the struggle that is taking place inside them. Some find that by downing a few drinks or smoking a joint or two the tensions seem to lift. The so-so student gets high and comes to think it doesn't matter that she's not getting into the college she wanted. The loner who takes drugs at a party because everyone else is doing it may feel like he belongs, that he is part of a group. Suddenly, the shy girl becomes the life of the party or finds the nerve to finally talk to the boy she has been eyeing from afar. The use of substances to deal with stress, however, is often not the initiating event but a learned response at later stages of abuse.

As difficult as they may be to face, the challenges of adolescence cannot be successfully met when one's psychological vision is clouded by alcohol or drugs. Moreover, there are the liabilities that come with viewing the world through a distorted lens. Drugs can adversely affect one's ability to retain information, which translates into substance abusers earning lower grades. Teens under the influence shed their inhibitions—and their judgment. The result can be sexual indiscretion, which can result in pregnancy or disease, not to mention damage to one's self-esteem once the alcohol wears off. Those who drink or do drugs are also more likely to put themselves into dangerous situations, especially in motor vehicles.

Obviously, not all teens who try drugs or alcohol develop problems, just as not all adults who enjoy alcohol are alcoholics. Most teens who use drugs and/or alcohol will experiment for a while and then stop altogether or continue to use them casually without any significant problems. Others, however, will become regular users and suffer varying kinds of physical, emotional, and social problems. Some of these heavy teenage abusers will discontinue use as they mature, typically in their middle twenties, but the dependence will continue in others. We also know that some adolescents who become dependent will die as a result of drug or alcohol use or cause the death of others. There is much research regarding why some teens become dependent and some do not. The factors that seem related to adolescent substance abuse include a family history of substance abuse, parental attitudes toward use, parental modeling, peer influence, chronic exposure to drugs—which changes brain chemistry producing the drive to use them—extreme shyness, physical or sexual abuse, and chronic mild depression.

In this chapter, we will examine substance abuse. Within the next pages, we will acquaint you with risk factors that may make a teen more prone to a substance abuse problem, tell you what signs to look for to determine whether your teen is using drugs or alcohol, and consider treatment.

Alcohol Abuse

An estimated 20 million adults in the United States abuse alcohol. More than half of these alcoholics started drinking heavily when they were teenagers.

There's no question that drinking is a problem in most high schools. Alcohol is our most pervasive drug. Teens have access to it at parties, can obtain it from older friends who are of legal age to buy it, or may simply raid their parents' liquor cabinets. Moreover, unlike drug use, the moderate use of alcohol is considered perfectly acceptable in most adult social circles. Teens see their parents enjoying a cocktail after work or having a glass of wine at dinner. Drinking comes to represent a very sophisticated and adult thing to do. *Mom and Dad do it . . . why shouldn't I?* the teen may reason. Parental acceptance of moderate to heavy use, however, may send the message that alcohol use has little inherent danger.

What *is* so bad about teenage drinking? Aside from the fact that it's illegal, one major concern is that some teens who drink heavily can become addicted to alcohol. An adult who is a heavy drinker may take years to become a full-fledged alcoholic—that is, someone who is physically and psychologically addicted to alcohol. A teen can make the transition from the party drunk to alcoholic in a matter of months.

Which teen at the party will develop a drinking problem? That is impossible to predict. Denial, however, that alcohol has negative consequences is a key in helping you know whether your youngster may have a problem. Consider the example of a teen who does not eat all day, then gets drunk and has an automobile accident. A youngster who is able to acknowledge the alcohol as the cause of the accident and never drinks again is, obviously, at lower risk for developing a problem. A teen who associates not eating before drinking as the cause of the accident is at much greater risk for developing a problem. This teen is denying the seriousness of alcohol and her use of it.

All alcohol use by teens should be regarded as dangerous, not only because of the risk of alcoholism but because teen drinkers put themselves in harm's way. Each year more than 10,000 young people in the United States are killed and 40,000 injured in alcohol-related automobile accidents.

■ IDENTIFYING THE SIGNS

The signs of alcohol intoxication are easy to spot. If your teen comes home with slurred speech, uncoordinated movements, and an altered mood—she may be giddy or depressed—she probably has been drinking.

The problem in detecting alcohol or drug abuse is often that those who chronically abuse substances become adept at covering their tracks. A teen who has spent the evening drinking, for example, may make sure you're in bed before she comes home.

There are, however, warning signs that may signal a problem. These include chronic fatigue, repeated health problems, a personality change, apathy, depression, low self-esteem, withdrawal from the family or a troubled relationship with parents, a drop in grades at school, and a change in friends.

You know that your teen is drinking, but how can you tell when she's crossed over the line from social drinker to problem drinker? The following drinking patterns indicate alcohol abuse or alcoholism:

- **Preoccupation with drinking.**
  Those who are alcohol-dependent are always thinking about their next drink. They may even choose their social activities according to the likelihood that alcohol will be served.

- **Symptomatic use of alcohol.**
  No matter what the problem, alcohol abusers view alcohol as the cure-all. If she can't sleep, she'll take a drink, the same cure she'll prescribe for her aching neck or case of pretest nerves.

- **Increased tolerance.**
  One symptom of alcoholism is the brain's ability to tolerate higher concentrations of alcohol. Whereas the occasional drinker may feel the effects of alcohol after one drink, a person who consistently abuses alcohol may have to drink three or four drinks to get the desired high. Children of alcoholics may have inherited an increased tolerance and may be able to drink several beers or glasses of wine before feeling the high, even without their having a history of chronic use.

- **Loss of control.**
  A person with an alcohol problem can't limit herself to one or two drinks, although that may be her intention. Instead, the intended one drink leads to several, and she ends up intoxicated.

- **Solitary drinking.**
  Most people who enjoy alcohol drink in social situations. But an alcoholic's focus is not on her drinking partners but on the alcohol itself. If you find your teen drinking alone in her room, she probably has a serious problem.

- **Drinking to feel "normal."**
  The teen who is drinking frequently and who must get drunk in order to feel good, less shy, less depressed, or even to feel "normal" is misusing alcohol.

- **Making excuses.**
  Alcoholics typically rationalize their drinking. She got a bad grade on a test, so she gets drunk, or she and her boyfriend have an argument and the only thing that will make her feel better is a bottle of wine.

- **Blackouts.**
  Some alcoholics suffer memory lapses after drinking bouts, perhaps passing out but at least not remembering what they did while drinking. Following the blackouts, the alcoholic may feel guilty and anxious over what may have transpired during those missing hours.

■ CAUSES AND CONSEQUENCES

Conventional wisdom once held that alcoholics were simply weak human beings who couldn't muster up enough willpower to stay away from their source of ruin. We know now that it isn't so simple. Alcoholism is a disease that is found throughout our society.

There are many factors that contribute to the likelihood that a given individual will become addicted to alcohol. A teen's susceptibility to advertising campaigns that make alcohol use look very attractive, her role models, the age at which she begins to drink, and the way she feels after she drinks all contribute to whether she begins to abuse alcohol. Moreover, we know that there is a genetic component at work. Alcoholism tends to run in families. At least seven million American children have an alcoholic parent. Statistics tell us that these children are four times more likely than the offspring of nonalcoholic parents to develop a drinking problem. Most children of alcoholics also live in turbulent households. The child may feel guilty, blaming herself for her parent's problem. She may live in a constant state of anxiety, be embarrassed of her parent or seething with anger. Depression, confusion, and the inability to form close relationships are common among the children of alcoholics. All of these youngsters are intermittently neglected, and some are physically or sexually abused. At some point, these elements may coalesce to contribute to the teen's own drinking problem. The consequences of alcohol abuse are more clearcut than the reasons behind the abuse.

A teen who drinks, even only occasionally, exposes herself to potential danger. Alcohol is involved in more than half of all accidental deaths, suicides, and homicides—and in nearly half of all automobile fatalities. A teen who drinks at a party becomes more vulnerable to sexual advances because of her impaired judgment and may do things that, when sober, she would never consider. Moreover, because alcohol is a depressant, it may cause a depression-prone individual to become extremely depressed and even suicidal. Finally, a teen who drinks alcohol frequently and in excessive amounts risks becoming alcohol-dependent.

■ HOW TO RESPOND

As with most health problems, it is easier to prevent alcohol abuse than to cure the problem once it has taken hold. Perhaps the first step in the process involves fostering an environment in which your child feels good about herself—low self-esteem is common among young substance abusers. Communication between parent and teen also is essential. Many young alcoholics admit to therapists that it was impossible to talk with their parents about their worries.

Talk to your children about alcohol and drugs, the effects and potential dangers. Although schools have become more involved in drug and alcohol education, parents also should have a strong voice in shaping their children's attitudes. Remember, too, that your actions are even more important than your words. Many child and adolescent psychiatrists believe that as early as fifth grade, children form their attitudes toward alcohol based on what they see at home and on television. Thus, children who routinely see their parents abusing alcohol (or drugs) are more likely to follow suit.

If your teen is using drugs or alcohol, the sooner you are aware of it, the sooner you can find the help necessary to prevent the problem from escalating. Don't hesitate to call other parents to make sure there will be no alcohol at a party. Upon discovering your teen has a drinking problem, the treatment options will depend upon the severity of the problem. A good starting point is usually your child's physician, who can answer questions you may have and recommend a child and adolescent psychiatrist or another treatment approach. The recommendation will likely depend on the seriousness of the problem. (See *The Four Stages of Substance Abuse*, page 285.)

If the alcohol abuse appears to be a one-night-only event—a graduation party, perhaps, or a post-game celebration where your teenager joined her peers in their "partying"—then an open discussion, an appropriate consequence (a Saturday night at home or an earlier curfew), and ongoing conversations and monitoring may be appropriate. If, however, the problem is a more serious one, other strategies may be in order.

Alcohol Abuse Treatment. Getting both the teen and the family to commit to a program of treatment is the first goal. As parents, you must be willing to invest the time and energy to participate in your teenager's treatment. Other family members, too, may need to be included in the process.

Establishing firm parental limits is critical in dealing with early adolescent alcohol abuse, although as the teen grows older, the degree to which the late adolescent is willing or able to control the impulse to drink is also a major factor in determining the appropriate treatment approach. Outpatient care can be successful if the youngster acknowledges the problem, indicates a desire for help, and is willing to abstain from all substance abuse. This means, as well, a willingness to attend regular therapy sessions. More intensive and restrictive inpatient care may be appropriate for teens who have other psychiatric problems; who continue friendships with peers who are substance abusers; who are not motivated to change their behaviors; or who have failed in previous attempts in outpatient settings.

While twelve-step programs such as Alcoholics Anonymous are often the model for alcohol treatments, other strategies may also prove valuable. Among them may be social skills training, in which youngsters are helped to master social behaviors and adjust their own behavior accordingly; behavioral therapy that targets impulsiveness and attempts to help the teen to learn to manage the impulse to drink or to manage anger by learning to use alternative behaviors (see *Cognitive-Behavioral Therapy,* page 323); and family therapy, in which problems in the home that may contribute to the teen's impulse to abuse alcohol (for example, severe marital conflict or other family members who are depressed or themselves alcohol or drug abusers) can be identified and addressed (see also *Family Therapy*, page 326).

Many teens have other problems, such as attention-deficit/hyperactivity disorder (see *Attention-Deficit/Hyperactivity Disorder,* page 225) or depression (see *Depressive Disorders,*

THE FOUR STAGES OF SUBSTANCE ABUSE

There are four stages of substance abuse. In the first stage, the adolescent uses drugs—typically beer, marijuana, or inhalants—with friends, mostly on the weekends. You likely will notice no changes in behavior. When confronted, most teens at this stage deny that they are using drugs.

In the second stage, often called drug misuse, the teen actively seeks the mood swing delivered by drug or alcohol use. The adolescent may feel slightly guilty but not enough to stop the abuse. The drugs used may include stimulants, tranquilizers, or hallucinogens. A teen in this stage may start using drugs when alone. Frequency of use increases to four or five times a week. Schoolwork declines, extracurricular activities fall by the wayside, old friends are replaced with new ones, and changes in dress may appear, as do rapid mood changes and dishonesty.

A teen in the third stage has mood swings from high euphoria to such lows that suicide becomes a risk. Many teens at this stage—termed the drug or alcohol abuse stage—sell drugs to help support their habit. Lying, fighting, stealing, and school truancy or failure are all signs. Despite such adverse consequences, the teen continues drug use. The mood and behavior changes you see in the teen are frequently due to withdrawal from the abused substances.

In the fourth stage, the teen may need drugs every day to prevent the physical and psychological symptoms of withdrawal and won't be picky about which drug is used. Anything available may be consumed; the teen may do whatever it takes to get high. During this stage, the teen becomes preoccupied with using and acutely uncomfortable when unable to use.

The most important aspect of this stage, called drug dependence, is the loss of control. The teen is unable to stop using drugs. When the teen tries to use in moderation, the adolescent still finds herself using until drunk or stoned. The teen will use larger and larger amounts of drugs or alcohol. Guilt, shame, depression, and thoughts of suicide are common. A teen at this stage of addiction may have dropped out of school. Frequent overdoses occur and overall physical health deteriorates badly. Some physical signs to look for include recurrent bronchitis, nosebleeds, red eyes, chest pain, high blood pressure, fatigue, memory loss, tremor, confusion, hallucinations, and delusions. At this stage of dependency, inpatient treatment is usually necessary.

page 209) that warrant specific treatments, which may include the use of medications.

Chemical dependency—whether the dependence is on alcohol or drugs—is unfortunately a disorder in which treatment and recovery are often interrupted by relapses. As parents, you may have strong feelings of anger or failure when your teen fails to maintain abstinence. It's important, however, that while remaining firm in demanding abstinence, you also provide support and encouragement after such relapses.

Drug Abuse

Although the abuse of all drugs—everything from laxatives to nasal sprays to prescription sleeping pills—is widespread in our society, as a parent when you think of drug abuse you probably envision a group of teenagers passing around a marijuana joint at a party. That's often an accurate picture—and as far as it goes. Many teens and young adults, however, move beyond marijuana and may well abuse an array of other mood-altering illegal drugs. These may include:

- **Marijuana.**
  This is the most popular drug among teens in the United States; two-thirds of all American teens admit to trying marijuana at least once during high school, and many smoke it on a daily basis. The marijuana business, in fact, is thriving and is thought to be the third largest agricultural crop in annual revenue in the United States.

While the parent who smoked marijuana twenty or thirty years ago may be tempted to downplay the seriousness of a teen's marijuana use, you should know that the marijuana today's teens are getting is much more potent than what you may have tried when you were in high school or college.

A teen who smokes marijuana feels its effects almost immediately. Most will experience a feeling of relaxation and mild euphoria. Depending upon the level of intoxication, marijuana users often have trouble remembering what happened while they were high and may have difficulty with concentration and coordination. High doses can produce behavior similar to alcohol intoxication.

There is continuing debate and ongoing research as to whether marijuana is a "gateway" drug that opens the door to the use of other illegal substances. It is known, however, that some heavy long-term users experience the signs of mild *physical dependence* (a tolerance to drugs and withdrawal after drug use stops). Those who use marijuana regularly may also become psychologically addicted (*addiction* implies a compulsive use of alcohol or drugs in spite of negative consequences). Neurobiological changes occur with addiction, meaning that physiological changes take place in the brain that result in the addict not being able to use alcohol or a drug in moderation.

Marijuana also results in short-term

memory loss, making the user appear dull-witted, and, like alcohol, impairs driving ability. Marijuana can contribute in later life to lowered sperm counts in males and lung cancer in men and women. If used regularly, it can also lead to a loss of motivation (*amotivational syndrome*).

• **Cocaine.**

It used to be that cocaine was a drug that most teens couldn't afford. In recent years, however, this "champagne drug" has been converted to a form that will fit even a beer budget. Teens who use this potent drug may smoke it in its crystalline form (crack cocaine) or snort the pricey cocaine powder through their noses.

Crack cocaine is highly addictive; users become dependent almost immediately. Within seconds after it is smoked, the user feels an intense high, followed within a few minutes by an extreme low. Because of this, the crack user often feels a desperate need to recapture the high. This drug can cause serious heart and lung problems, which are sometimes fatal to healthy young people.

• **Hallucinogens.**

In the 1960s and 1970s, hallucinogenic drugs such as LSD (lysergic acid diethylamide) enjoyed widespread popularity and then went out of fashion. Today, however, many young people have rediscovered LSD. A teen who takes LSD experiences vivid perceptual changes, which may be good or bad. In a good

trip, colors may appear more vivid, an ordinary sound may seem like a symphony. A simple object—a blade of grass, a window pane—suddenly becomes a masterpiece. Time loses all meaning. Those who have a good trip on LSD often come away extolling the virtues of the drug; not so for those who have a bad trip. A person on a bad LSD trip may have overwhelming fear. She may feel she is dying or losing her mind. Some LSD users have died under its influence when they confused reality with drug-induced fantasy and tried to fly or, out of fear, flee from the upper storys of tall buildings.

While LSD does not produce a physical dependency in its users, it can become addictive and may also produce profound changes in mood and thought processes that may result in true visual hallucinations and a state resembling psychosis.

• **PCP.**

Like LSD, PCP, also called angel dust, is a powerful hallucinogenic drug. Once used to sedate large animals, PCP was abandoned by veterinarians when it became clear that the animals were acting bizarrely before they fell asleep.

PCP is a potent drug that in very small doses causes its user to lose inhibitions and produces a state of euphoria. In larger doses, the drug can produce extremely violent behavior. PCP may also result in seizures and serious heart, lung, and blood pressure problems.

- **Heroin.**

Like morphine, heroin is derived from opium, and when given in large doses over a period of time is highly addictive. In recent years, heroin has experienced a resurgence in the United States, and today more teens are being exposed to this devastating drug. As with marijuana, heroin today is available in a purer and stronger form than in the past.

Heroin users either inject the drug into a vein or snort the drug in a powdered form. Because users are generally more concerned about getting their high than about their health, many use contaminated needles if nothing is readily available. This exposes them to infectious diseases such as HIV and hepatitis.

- **Anabolic Steroids.**

In the last twenty years, androgenic (male) hormones have been abused, usually by boys, to improve strength, athletic performance, and physical appearance. Chronic use can result in growth retardation and damage to testicles. In high doses, these drugs can also produce uncontrollable rage and mood changes, ranging from mania to depression.

- **Inhalants.**

Airplane glue, aerosol sprays, gasoline, and nitrous oxide are common inhalants abused by teens. Each substance has a characteristic high, but most cause dizziness and intoxication. Chronic use can damage many internal organs and occasionally lead to death, usually as a result of heart-rate irregularities. Heavy use may also result in permanent brain damage.

- **Sedatives.**

Valium, Xanax, and prescription sleeping pills are drugs that can be abused and may produce a high characterized by a loss of inhibitions. In larger doses, these drugs cause a depressed state of alertness and eventual loss of consciousness. After prolonged use, sudden withdrawal from these drugs in addicted teens can be life-threatening.

■ IDENTIFYING THE SIGNS

Unless you actually catch your teen high or in the process of using drugs, it is often difficult to know for sure whether she has a problem.

Some general behavior changes, however, may provide clues, although they are not definitive.

- **School.**

It is common for drug-abusing teens to have problems in school. She may refuse to go, or she may head off to school every day, only to meet her friends and spend the day in the park or at a home where the parents are gone. If you are suspicious, call her school and make sure that she isn't missing classes.

Another potential clue is a change in grades. The student who goes from A's and B's to C's and D's may be using drugs.

- **Appearance.**

It may seem to you that your teen has no interest in her looks, what with her torn jeans and shapeless shirts. Most teens are, in fact, *very* concerned about their appearance, and the often unusual or antifashion clothes they wear is their attempt at a fashion statement. They think they look great, even if you don't. So if your teen suddenly becomes apathetic about her appearance—doesn't wash her hair, lets her skin go, no longer cares about her clothes—suspect a problem.

- **Health.**

Most parents are in awe of their teenager's energy level. Despite a grueling day filled with school, activities, and homework, most teens—if you let them—are still going strong when you're entering the dream state of your sleep cycle. True, on weekends or vacations she may spend half her day in bed trying to catch up on the sleep she has lost during the week, but for the most part, sleep is not a high priority for most teens. If, however, your teen begins to sleep a lot and/or becomes listless and apathetic, she may be using drugs or have another emotional disorder.

Other physical signs that may indicate drug use include insomnia, moods that abruptly swing from exhilaration to exhaustion, a lack of interest in food, weight loss, eyes that are bloodshot or have a dazed expression, gazing at objects for long periods of time, excessive sweating or flushed skin, an unexplained rash, an irritated nostril or runny nose, and a steady cough. Sudden and radical changes in behavior may also be indicators of drug abuse.

■ CAUSES AND CONSEQUENCES

What causes a teen to use drugs? Often the first exposure is the result of availability and curiosity. Peer pressure may be involved, too. Typically, a teen's first exposure to an illegal drug begins with beer, wine, and cigarettes. Marijuana follows—the teen may be at a party or with a group of friends and everyone is smoking marijuana. She may feel outright pressure from her friends as they goad her into trying it. Or the pressure may be more subtle; she may simply feel that she isn't one of them if she doesn't smoke. Many teens will progress from using marijuana occasionally to problem drinking. Experimentation with other, more powerful drugs may be next, such as LSD, prescription pills, cocaine, and heroin.

In many cases, teens who use drugs regularly are unhappy and don't have many friends. Most have poor self-esteem. The teen most vulnerable to drug abuse is one with a family history of substance abuse; a strong rebellious streak; a tendency to impulsiveness; a limited social life; extreme shyness; and parents who are permissive toward substance abuse, who neglect their teenage children by not paying them enough attention or spending little time with them.

The consequences of drug abuse can be dire. Teens who are caught using drugs or, worse, selling drugs can be prosecuted. Those who regularly use drugs usually experience academic and social problems in school, which can compromise their future. A teen who is high is one with diminished inhibitions and as such is more likely to engage in dangerous behavior, such as unprotected sex or driving under the influence of drugs. The three leading killers of adolescents—accidents, murder, and suicide—are more prevalent among the alcohol- and drug-using population.

Drugs can be devastating to the body. Some drugs such as crack and heroin are highly addictive. Aside from addiction itself, the physical toll of drug abuse is high. A teen who smokes crack, for instance, increases her risk of heart attack and lung problems such as emphysema. An overdose of angel dust can lead to stroke or a psychotic state that resembles schizophrenia. Teens who inject heroin into their veins may expose themselves to numerous serious infectious diseases, including HIV-AIDS and hepatitis B. Even regular marijuana smoking jeopardizes the teen's long-term health. This popular drug when used on a regular basis can decrease lung capacity, cause lung infections, impair the body's immune system, cause irregular menstrual cycles, temporarily impair fertility, and, according to some studies, cause premature birth or birth defects if used during pregnancy. Moreover, marijuana is sometimes contaminated by animal droppings containing salmonella and can make a user sick with diarrhea, abdominal pain, and fever.

■ HOW TO RESPOND

Prevention is the best approach. Try to foster an environment in which your child feels good about herself—low self-esteem is common among young substance abusers. Communication between parent and teen also is essential. Many young drug users and alcoholics admit to professionals that it was impossible to talk with their parents about issues of concern.

Talk to your children about drugs, the effects and potential dangers. Although schools have become more involved in drug education, parents also should have a strong voice in shaping their children's attitudes. Remember, too, that your actions are even more important than your words. Children who routinely see their parents abusing drugs (or alcohol) are more likely to follow suit.

If your teen is using drugs, the sooner you are aware of it, the sooner you can find the help necessary to prevent the problem from escalating. Upon discovering your teen uses drugs, the treatment options will depend upon the severity of the problem. A good starting point is usually your child's physician, who can answer questions you may have and recommend a child and adolescent psychiatrist or another treatment approach. The recommendation will likely depend on the seriousness of the problem. (See *The Four Stages of Substance Abuse*, page 285.)

If the drug abuse appears to be a one-night-only event—a graduation party, perhaps, or a post-game celebration where your teenager joined her peers in their "partying"—then an open discussion, an appropriate consequence (a Saturday night at home or an earlier curfew), and ongoing conversations and monitoring may be appropriate. If, however, the problem is a more serious one, other strategies may be in order.

The treatment will depend upon the severity of her substance-abuse problem.

Substance Abuse Treatment. Getting both the teen and the family to commit to treatment is the first goal. As parents, you must be willing to invest the time and energy to participate in your teenager's treatment. Other family members may need to be included in the process as well.

The degree to which the adolescent is willing or able to control the impulse to use drugs is a major factor in determining the appropriate treatment approach. Outpatient care can be successful if the youngster acknowledges the problem, indicates a desire for help, and is willing to abstain from all substance abuse. This means, as well, a willingness to cooperate with random urine tests and to attend regular therapy sessions.

Inpatient care may be appropriate for teens who have other psychiatric problems; who continue friendships with peers who are substance abusers; who are not motivated to change their behaviors; or who have failed in previous attempts in outpatient settings.

Twelve-step programs such as the Alcoholics Anonymous approach are often the model for drug as well as alcohol treatments, especially at stage three or four of use (see *The Four Stages of Substance Abuse,* page 285), as they promote abstinence, cost nothing, and may provide supportive adults or peers. Other strategies may also prove valuable, too; among them may be social skills training, in which youngsters are helped to master social behaviors and adjust their own behavior accordingly; behavioral therapy that targets impulsiveness and attempts to help the teen learn to manage the addictive behavior (see *Cognitive-Behavioral Therapy,* page 323); and family therapy, in which problems in the home that may contribute to the teen's impulse to seek escape in drug use (for example, severe marital conflict or other family members who are depressed or themselves alcohol or drug abusers) can be identified and addressed (see also *Family Therapy,* page 326).

Many teens have other problems, such as attention-deficit/hyperactive disorder (see *Attention-Deficit/Hyperactive Disorder,* page 225) or depression (see *Depressive Disorders,* page 209), that warrant specific treatments, which may include the use of medications.

Chemical dependency—whether the dependence is on alcohol or drugs—is unfortunately a disorder in which treatment and recovery are often interrupted by relapses. As parents, you may have strong feelings of anger or failure when your teen fails to maintain abstinence. It's important, however, that while remaining firm in demanding abstinence, you also provide support and encouragement after such relapses.

15

Sleep Disorders

■　■　■

As an adult, perhaps you've learned not to take a good night's sleep for granted. While occasional sleep problems are something that most of us come to expect as we age, we tend to think that our teenagers are so exhausted after a busy day of school and extracurricular activities that the minute their heads hit the pillow, they sink into slumber.

In actuality, adolescents, like adults, don't always sleep well. Though falling into a sound sleep at the end of a busy day should be the most natural thing in the world, many adolescents often encounter roadblocks that come between them and their ability to get the rest they need. The result may be daytime sleepiness, which is a more common adolescent compliant than actual insomnia.

Why do adolescents develop sleep problems? Although genetics play a role in some sleep disorders, many teens have difficulty sleeping simply because they are too busy to go to bed at night. Others simply enjoy staying up late, unrestricted by the regulated bedtimes of their childhood. They begin staying up later and later and when the alarm clock rings in the morning, the last thing they want to do is get up and get ready for school. But they drag themselves off, repeat the cycle the next night, and before too long are sleep-deprived.

Other adolescents may have disturbed sleep as a result of substance abuse. The use of certain drugs and alcohol can produce insomnia, either as a direct effect or as daytime sleepiness after a night of partying.

In this chapter we will explore some of the most common sleep problems that occur in adolescence. We are indeed fortunate to live in an era when sleep problems are taken seriously, and there are health-care professionals who specialize in the research and treatment of sleep disorders. Unlike the sleep problems that sometimes affect young children, adolescent sleep problems tend to be more persistent and often require the expertise of specialists.

Narcolepsy

Narcolepsy, characterized by the abnormal tendency to fall asleep during the day, is a persistent sleep disorder that typically surfaces during adolescence and adulthood, although the problem sometimes occurs in children during the late elementary school years.

Adolescents with narcolepsy typically have difficulty staying awake in class. If left undisturbed, the teen will nod off into rapid eye movement (REM) sleep for anywhere between twenty and forty minutes. Unlike sleep apnea—another disorder characterized by excessive daytime sleeping—the adolescent with narcolepsy awakens from his rest completely refreshed and wide awake. However, in another two or three hours, the pattern is repeated.

■ **IDENTIFYING THE SIGNS**

A teen with narcolepsy will experience uncontrollable episodes of daytime sleepiness no matter how well he has slept the night before. Often, though not always, the sleepiness occurs after a meal. The desire to sleep supersedes all else. Your teen can be in the middle of a test, trying out for the football team, or engaged in a conversation when all of a sudden he slips into slumber.

Many people with narcolepsy also have *cataplexy*, in which the teen experiences a sudden loss of muscle tone, causing the youngster to collapse. As he is drifting into sleep, the adolescent may feel his jaw drop or lose control over his limbs. Many people with narcolepsy experience cataplexy even during wakeful periods. Injuries from falls are common during these episodes. Cataleptic attacks typically last only a few moments. Sometimes strong emotional states such as laughter or anger may bring on attacks. They may occur as often as several times a day or as infrequently as a couple of times a year. Upon awakening, the teen may be unable to move for a few minutes, a condition called sleep paralysis that can be very frightening.

Hallucinations just prior to falling asleep also are common among teens with narcolepsy.

■ **CAUSES AND CONSEQUENCES**

Narcolepsy is thought to be a defect in the way the central nervous system regulates the state of alertness and the phase of dreaming sleep. Genetics plays a role in this disorder. Environmental factors—shift work, lack of sleep, stress—do not cause narcolepsy but may aggravate it. The symptoms of narcolepsy are sometimes confused with the inattention and restlessness characteristic of attention-deficit/hyperactivity disorder. (See page 225.)

This disorder is a lifelong, chronic condition, though symptoms such as cataplexy, sleep paralysis, and hallucinations may wane in time. Narcolepsy is a serious disorder that can complicate many aspects of a teen's academic and social life. Moreover, it can be dangerous if he falls asleep at the wheel of his car.

■ HOW TO RESPOND

If your teen has the symptoms of narcolepsy, he should be evaluated by a specialist in sleep disorders or a physician, frequently a neurologist, familiar with the problem

Although this is a chronic disorder, the prognosis is good as long as the attacks can be controlled. The medication your doctor will prescribe will depend upon the nature and severity of your teen's symptoms. Psychostimulants and antidepressants, alone or in combination, are two types of medications frequently prescribed.

As a parent, you also will be asked to encourage your teenager to set consistent bed and waking times. Regularly scheduled naps during the day may also help reduce the number of sleep attacks. Working closely with your teen's school staff will be helpful, since modifications to the school day may be required. Your teenager will need your support as he learns to adapt his social life to the disorder.

Psychotherapy may also be recommended for adolescents with narcolepsy because low self-esteem and depression are common secondary problems among teens with narcolepsy.

Circadian Rhythm Sleep Disorders

If your teen is having increasing difficulty falling asleep at night and getting up in the morning, he may be suffering from circadian rhythm sleep disorder, also known as delayed sleep phase syndrome.

This sleep disorder is thought to affect as many as 7 percent of all teens. It is due to prolonged periods of sleep deprivation or frequent sleep irregularities.

Ironically, adolescence is a time when the body has an increased need for sleep. Yet many adolescents, usually because of social and academic commitments, begin staying up later and later during the week, the result of which may be only six hours of sleep at night. In the morning, you may practically have to drag him out of bed to get ready for school. The weekends are another story. In an attempt to make up for his sleep deficit, he collapses, often sleeping away the entire morning and well into the afternoon.

Unfortunately, extra sleep is not like money. You can't save it up for the days when there isn't time to get the rest your body needs. After awhile the biological clock is disrupted or reset. When this happens, it doesn't matter how early the adolescent goes to bed or how exhausted he feels: He is apt to lie there for hours until he finally drifts into sleep. He may go to bed at ten or eleven o'clock in the evening, but his biological clock doesn't allow him to go to sleep until one or two o'clock in the morning

∎ IDENTIFYING THE SIGNS

Is your teen increasingly burning the midnight oil and then sleeping past his morning alarm? If this is happening only occasionally, you probably needn't worry. But if it is a frequent occurrence, he may be well on his way to developing circadian rhythm sleep disorder.

Even when you insist on lights out at 10 P.M., the adolescent with circadian rhythm sleep disorder will toss and turn in an attempt to get to sleep. Sleep logs kept by adolescents with this disorder show that even those who stay up well past midnight typically have insomnia for anywhere between one and three hours after they go to bed. It isn't difficult to see how a teen who falls asleep after 2 A.M. is going to have to struggle to catch the 7:30 A.M. school bus. Understandably, adolescents with this disorder are frequently grouchy and report that they even fall asleep in class during the day.

Even during vacations or other times when the teen is able to sleep as long as he wants, his sleep rhythm remains disrupted, although it may be not so apparent because the youngster isn't required to get up before noon.

∎ CAUSES AND CONSEQUENCES

The growing teen needs more sleep, yet consistently gets less, only to fall into bed utterly exhausted on the weekends. This repeated cycle of short sleep periods fol-

lowed by a marathon sleeping session disrupts natural sleep patterns, the result of which is this disorder. This sleep disorder may last from months to decades. It is a major concern because of its potential to interfere with academics and other aspects of the adolescent's life.

∎ HOW TO RESPOND

Sleep problems, especially when the sleep phase is delayed three hours or more, are generally best treated by experts who specialize in sleep disorders. Your teen may try to follow your instructions and go to bed earlier but, because his biological clock has been reset, he may still be unable to sleep.

If your teen has the symptoms of circadian rhythm sleep disorder, the first step in treatment typically involves a thorough evaluation of all of his activities. The physician may ask him to keep a daily log of his activities and of his sleeping and waking patterns. In some cases, setting a consistent bedtime may eventually improve the problem, but often the teen's biological clock needs to be reset before treatment is successful. This is best done during summer vacation. In an attempt to shift the sleep onset time to one that is more appropriate, the clinician develops a regimen that both delays bedtime and rising times by 2 to 3 hours each day, resulting in 26 or 27 hour days. This pattern is continued until the teen is going to bed at 10 or 11 p.m, having reset his biological clock.

Tranquilizers or sleeping pills do not improve this disorder and are not recommended.

Nightmares

When he was younger, he would summon you in the middle of the night to protect him from the monster that had laid claim to an otherwise pleasant dream. Now that he's a teenager, he may not run to you every time he has a nightmare, but that doesn't mean they don't bother him.

A teen's night, like an adult's, is punctuated by dreams during rapid eye movement (REM) sleep, a sleep stage that occurs four or five times over the course of an average night. Most dreams are relatively benign and easily forgotten. Some are wonderful while others classify as nightmares.

■ Identifying the Signs

Nightmares usually occur late in the night as the periods of REM sleep grow longer. The adolescent awakens from the nightmare, fully aware of what's going on. Depending upon his nature and on how frightened he is, he may come into your bedroom to tell you about the nightmare. More typical of a teen, however, is that he will awaken from the nightmare afraid, calm himself, and then go back to sleep. In the morning, he will usually be able to recall the dream.

■ Causes and Consequences

Nightmares are often a response to stress or anxiety and will increase in frequency and intensity when a person is under pressure. Fears can bring on nightmares as can traumatic events in your teen's life. Certain medications or the withdrawal of certain drugs also can induce bad dreams.

■ How to Respond

Occasional nightmares are not cause for alarm. Bad dreams are most common during times of transition or when your adolescent is under more stress than usual.

Persistent nightmares may eventually take a toll on a teen's daytime behavior. If this is happening in your house, you may wish to talk to your physician about consulting a child and adolescent psychiatrist or other mental health professional, especially if there has been a traumatic event in the adolescent's life recently. (See also *Childhood Trauma and Its Effects,* page 205.) Strategies may be developed to deal more effectively with his fears and to develop coping skills for dealing with stresses in the youngster's life. In some instances, too, chemical agents can cause nightmare symptoms to occur, and the physician may wish to review any medications your adolescent is taking.

Sleepwalking

Sleepwalking is a sleep arousal disorder that is thought to occur when the brain has difficulty making the transition from non-REM sleep to REM sleep, the sleep stage in which we dream.

Sleepwalking is actually a term that encompasses more than simply the action of walking. Sleepwalkers have been known to dress, pick flowers in the backyard, rearrange furniture, and, in extreme cases, sleepwalkers have even been caught driving their automobiles.

Sleepwalking is relatively rare in adolescence, although as many as 40 percent of children under the age of 12 have one sleepwalking incident; 1 to 6 percent have anywhere from one to four attacks weekly.

■ IDENTIFYING THE SIGNS

Sleepwalking typically occurs during the first one to three hours of sleep. Some people who sleepwalk will not actually walk but will simply sit up in bed, appearing to be awake when they actually are asleep. Some sleepwalkers will actually get out of bed and walk around the house. A young sleepwalker's body movements are poorly coordinated and he doesn't seem to have a particular destination in mind as he aimlessly wanders throughout the house. Although his eyes are open during the episode, he will appear to be in a daze. If you wake him, he will be confused and disoriented. In the morning, the sleepwalker will have no recollection of the incident. Most episodes last anywhere from a few seconds up to thirty minutes.

■ CAUSES AND CONSEQUENCES

Sleepwalking tends to run in families. Other factors thought to induce an episode of sleepwalking include fatigue and prior sleep loss. During childhood, the highest incidence of sleepwalking is found in children between the ages of six and twelve. Most sleepwalkers outgrow the problem by early adolescence.

Sleepwalking in young people is not a sign of an emotional illness. The biggest problem posed by adolescent sleepwalking is the risk of injury. Sleepwalkers have been known to fall down stairs, hurt themselves bumping into furniture, or endanger themselves by leaving the safe confines of the home.

■ HOW TO RESPOND

Since arousal disorders such as sleepwalking are difficult to predict, it is important that the parent and the adolescent sleepwalker create a safe environment to minimize the risk of injury when these incidents occur.

Sealed windows, locked doors, and perhaps a gate at the top of the staircase will help protect your sleepwalker. To make the house safer, you also may want to avoid leaving objects, electrical cords, or small furniture in the middle of the bedroom where it can be tripped over.

Sometimes sleepwalking incidents can be reduced by encouraging a brief late-afternoon nap and by reducing stress.

Medication. In severe cases, the antianxiety medication diazepam (Valium) has been successful in reducing the frequency of sleepwalking episodes, although a tolerance may develop and when the drug is discontinued, the sleepwalking may resume. If your child continues to sleepwalk into adolescence, a neurological examination to rule out sleep-related seizures may be warranted.

Part 4

SEEKING HELP

■　■　■

In these two chapters you will find practical advice and useful information to guide you when you think professional mental-health intervention may be called for. This section presents the who, where, when, and why of getting help and the kinds of mental health treatment available—individual psychotherapy, medication, behavioral and cognitive techniques, family and group therapy, and psychiatric evaluation and diagnosis.

16

When and Where to Seek Help

■ ■■ ■

As parents, we want our adolescents to do well, to thrive and mature into healthy, happy, well-adapted individuals. Despite our expectations and efforts, however, few youngsters pass through adolescence without some challenges. Many must deal with illness, neurological problems, learning disabilities, a move, a divorce, or a death in the family, or parental remarriage. A teenager's development can be impeded by trauma, abuse, or parenting that is not well matched with an adolescent's temperament or special needs or is routinely neglectful or inconsistent.

For most teenagers, such events pose only a temporary challenge. They are resolved over time and the youngsters are able to continue on their developmental course. Sometimes, however, adolescents and their families need outside help in coping with these challenges or in dealing with their repercussions. Such teens and their families may require professional help or treatment to address their difficulties so that the youngster can resume healthy development. Seeking to help your teen cope with such problems is an indication of the parents' commitment; in most cases, the adolescent's problems are no one's fault.

Determining when adolescents need help

in addition to what their families can provide is not always easy for parents or other adults. Nor is it always clear what kinds of help are best suited to a given teen's family and problems. In this chapter, we will discuss the actual process and procedures involved in seeking help; the signposts indicating that professional intervention is warranted; what mental health treatment means; and what it can accomplish.

When and Where to Seek Help

Parents are often in the best position to recognize when their teenager is having a problem. Even when parents do recognize that their adolescent is having trouble, however, it is not always apparent whether professional help is necessary.

The first step in assessing the cause of the difficulty is to ask the youngster. Sometimes, gently asking your adolescent questions— *Why are you constantly sad? What happened that led to that fight after school? You seem upset; is something bothering you? Why are you so mad?*—will open discussions about the issues with which she's struggling. Giving her adequate time to respond is necessary; talking honestly with your teen about her feelings may also be helpful.

Consulting your child's physician, teachers, or your minister, priest, or rabbi may help to identify problems—both in the youngster and within the family—that could be causing the upset. Frequently, a teacher will notice your adolescent's trouble and call you in. Working together, you can often get the teen back on track before schoolwork, self-esteem, or social interaction is affected.

As a rule, it is the combination of parents' growing concerns and the observation of outsiders such as teachers, physicians, and family members that lead parents to consult a clinician for their adolescent. There are a few signs that indicate that your teenager has problems that could benefit from treatment. These signs include:

- Marked decrease in school performance
- Poor grades in school despite the fact that the adolescent is trying hard
- Excessive fears, worry, anxiety, or crying
- Hyperactivity or fidgeting beyond that observed in other adolescents
- Persistent risk-taking
- Constant disobedience, aggression, or provocative opposition to authority
- Inability to make or keep friends
- Inability to cope with problems and daily activities
- Striking weight loss or weight fluctuation not related to a known medical condition
- Significant change in sleeping and/or eating habits
- Obsessive fears of becoming obese with no relation to actual body weight
- Excessive complaints of physical ailments
- Aggressive or nonaggressive violation of other people's rights, opposition to authority, truancy, thefts, fire-setting, or vandalism
- Threats to run away

- Self-mutilation, self-destructive or other dangerous behavior
- Sustained, prolonged sadness and withdrawn mood and attitude, often accompanied by poor appetite, difficulty sleeping, or thoughts of death
- Frequent outbursts of anger
- Frequent thoughts or worries about death
- Alcohol or drug abuse

Not all of these signs mean you must seek immediate treatment, but each of them, especially when present over an extended period of time or observed in combination with one or more others, strongly argues for getting your adolescent professional help.

Once you decide that help is necessary, making your way through the mental health system can be perplexing. Researching and selecting the right kind of professional help is like other decisions you make for your adolescent. It is a matter of timing, gathering and considering options, and making a commitment to your choice.

Unlike selecting a school or camp, however, parents often bring their own conflicted and troubled feelings to the process of seeking help. A teenager's emotional distress and internal pains cause considerable disruption to the youngster's and the parents' worlds, as parents, too, get caught up in this turmoil and anguish.

In the midst of so much internal and external distress, parents may have difficulty being objective. Parents frequently blame themselves or fear that others—teachers, family members, or friends—will blame them.

Keep in mind that an adolescent in crisis reflects a family in crisis. Parents who are involved in intense marital conflict, divorce, grief, physical illness, substance abuse, or their own emotional, psychiatric disturbance are not always able to make the best determinations about how to seek help and obtain the best treatment for their youngster.

If you are concerned about your adolescent's emotional health but don't know where to start, ask friends, family members, your spiritual counselor, your teenager's school counselor, or anyone else you know who has had experience with psychiatric treatment. Once you start asking questions, you may be surprised at how many people you know have sought help for their family's or adolescent's emotional and behavioral problems.

Your youngster's pediatrician or family physician can often help you decide on the best options. You can also contact your teen's school counselor. If there is an Employee Assistance Program at work, speak to the representative. Many insurers and managed-care plans have 800 telephone numbers that will connect you to services that can assist you in finding behavioral health services covered by your health insurance. Consult your local medical society, local mental-health association, or county mental-health administrator. National organizations such as the American Academy of Child and Adolescent Psychiatry (3615 Wisconsin Avenue, NW, Washington, DC, 20016; http://www.aacap.org) and the American Psychiatric Association (1400 K Street, Washington, DC 20005–2492) can be contacted for referrals at their national headquarters or at local branches found in many cities and regions. Some of these organizations have information on their Web page through the Internet. Often, local hospitals, medical centers, or the department of psychiatry at a nearby medical school will offer mental-health services. You can also find names in the yellow pages under "Mental Health Services," "Physicians (Psychiatry, Child)," "Psychologists," or "Psychotherapists." Parents should be cautious, however, about using the yellow pages or the Internet as their sole source of information and referral: Get as much information about this important decision as possible from friends, school personnel, professionals, and other sources.

What Professional Help Really Means

In consulting with a child and adolescent psychiatrist or other professional many parents worry about being judged. They are anxious and have many questions: *Is my adolescent normal? Am I normal? Am I to blame? Am I silly to worry?* Teenagers will have similar concerns or may be upset with the suggestion that they need to see a mental-health clinician (*I'm not crazy!*).

As you start the process, remember that the professional is there to support and help the family find a solution to the problem, not to place blame. The clinician will listen to your concerns, help you and your adolescent define the problem, and identify some short- and long-term treatment goals.

Parents and their teens frequently have other questions about treatment. *Can you help us? Can you help our adolescent? Does my teenager really need treatment? Do I? What is the diagnosis? How can the family help? What's next? How long will it take?*

Remember: No brief treatment, however effective, is capable of "fixing" you or your adolescent. Treatment will not transform a headstrong and highly active teenager into an obedient, malleable individual. Nor will therapy transform a youngster who is shy and thoughtful into an assertive, boisterous go-getter. Treatment *can* help individuals and families find solutions and ways to cope better together with some very complex problems. Treatment may relieve painful symptoms that, if left untreated, could prevent youngsters from mastering the developmental tasks of their age.

Practitioners vary enormously in style and method. Traditional dynamic psychotherapies focus on identifying emotional conflicts and bringing them into clearer awareness. Some clinicians endorse expression of feelings in the session as a way to lessen the tendency to act out or express feelings through behavior. In therapy directed to families, the professional will work to foster direct and open communication in the family rather than communications that are covert or contradictory. The clinician will work to insure that the communications and feelings of all family members—adults and children—are heard and respected.

Psychotherapy means change but is not about the clinician changing your adolescent. People enter therapy because *they* want change, to alter in some way their thinking, feelings, or behavior. Therapy allows or *facilitates* changes in individuals, couples, and families. In treating adolescents, the treatment focuses on the teen's emotional conflicts or on parenting or family problems that may be interfering with development and normal functioning (i.e. school, learning, and socialization).

While the child and adolescent psychiatrist or clinician guides this process, your adolescent and family must do the actual work to institute change. Change is never easy, yet great anxiety or distress often provides the opportunity for change. Once the initial problem has been resolved (or becomes less disruptive to the teenager and family), the treatment may end. Nonetheless, other problems (for example, marital problems, stress, or depression in family members) may also need attention. When family members are willing, treatment may continue, shifting the focus to other problems for work and resolution or moving on to building new strengths in order to be better prepared for future stresses.

The length of treatment is determined by many different factors, including the severity and the complexity of the problem or problems that need to be addressed; the amount of time, effort, and emotional tension a family can tolerate; the responsiveness of the adolescent and family to particular treatment methods or techniques; and the cost of treatment. In the best of all circumstances, therapy ends when all who are involved agree that a better level of functioning has been reached.

Profiling the Practitioners

The variety of mental-health practitioners can be bewildering. There are psychiatrists, psychologists, counselors, pastoral counselors, psychiatric nurses, psychiatric social workers, and people who call themselves simply therapists. Few states regulate the practice of psychotherapy, so people with much (or little) experience can call themselves "psychotherapists."

On the other hand, most states do recognize and license *psychiatrists, psychologists, nurses,* and *social workers.* While having a degree or other credentials does not ensure that someone is a skilled and effective clinician with children, chances are that practitioners who hold a state license or certificate will have more skills and training than those who have not met such standards. It may be helpful to understand some of the distinctions between these practitioners as you search for a mental-health clinician to treat your adolescent.

Psychiatrist. A psychiatrist is a physician, a medical doctor whose training and education includes a medical-school degree (usually an *M.D.* for "doctor of medicine" or a *D.O.* for doctor of osteopathy) and at least four additional years of study, research, and clinical training in psychiatry. Based on their training, psychiatrists have a thorough understanding of mental *and* medical issues. They also have an in-depth knowledge of medications and are licensed to issue prescriptions. They may be certified as general psychiatrists by the American Board of Psychiatry and Neurology.

Child and Adolescent Psychiatrist. These medical specialists are fully trained psychiatrists with an M.D. or D.O. degree who have had two additional years of advanced training in normal child and adolescent development; the assessment of children, adolescents, and families; and the psychiatric diagnosis and treatment of children and adolescents. Those who have completed their training may take a national examination administered by the American Board of Psychiatry and Neurology. If they pass this examination, they are then board-certified in child and adolescent psychiatry. Child and adolescent psychiatrists are the only clinicians with nationally accredited training and certification in child and adolescent mental health.

Psychologist. Although some psychologists possess only a master's degree in psychology (M.A.), many have earned a doctoral degree in clinical, educational, or research psychology (Ph.D. or Ed.D.). During their four-year course of study, most psychologists are trained in the evaluation and nonmedical treatment of emotional problems and become knowledgeable about research techniques and psychological testing procedures.

Social Worker. Usually a social worker has earned a master's degree (M.S.W.) at a college or university. In most states, social workers can take an examination to be licensed as clinical social workers (L.C.S.W.). Some social workers are employed by general medical hospitals and government agencies to help families cope with a variety of issues, including child abuse, spouse abuse, delinquency, and poverty. Other social workers who are in private practice or are employed by mental health centers or psychiatric hospitals may provide counseling, casework, or psychotherapy for individuals, groups, couples, or families.

Psychotherapist. The term *psychotherapist* does not denote a particular degree or training. It refers only to the fact that one is engaged in the practice of psychotherapy. (See *Individual Psychotherapy,* page 320.) Many who practice psychotherapy, however, have earned professional degrees and completed postgraduate training (for example, psychiatrists, child and adolescent psychiatrists, psychiatric nurses, psychologists, and social workers).

Psychiatric Nurse. Nurses can have a variety of educational backgrounds but are all Registered Nurses (R.N.). Some have obtained additional education at the masters or doctoral level and are certified as Specialists in Psychiatric Nursing by the American Nurses Credentialling Center. This certification is either in adult psychiatric nursing or child and adolescent psychiatric nursing. In most states these specialists are authorized to provide therapy and prescribe medications. They generally do this in collaboration with psychiatrists.

Often, various clinicians perform specific functions in the treatment process. In this book we often use the general terms *clinician* or *professional* to describe individuals who are treating mental disorders and illnesses. Yet, as we've just discussed, not all such professionals are equally well trained to provide for the needs of your adolescent. For example, certain kinds of psychological testing are typically the province of psychologists with Ph.D.'s, while social workers usually have training in family therapy. On the other hand, the training of a child and adolescent psychiatrist prepares that clinician to integrate medical understanding when performing a psychiatric evaluation and treatment. (See *The Psychiatric Evaluation,* page 309.) In the same way, when medications are required, the only clinicians licensed to issue prescriptions are physicians and psychiatrists or, in some states, a nurse practitioner under the supervision of a physician.

It is advisable for parents to attempt to find a clinician who has advanced training in child, adolescent, adult, and/or family therapy. Yet it is also important to find a comfortable and productive match between your adolescent, your family, and the clinician.

FINDING THE RIGHT CLINICIAN

Although clear thinking can be difficult during times of stress, consider carefully what you and your adolescent want and need.

Try to think through these questions:

- What are the problems or concerns for which you want help?
- What style of interaction will you find most helpful? Will you and your teenager work better with someone who offers advice and direction in a structured way? Who listens and solicits your thoughts and solutions? Or a combination?
- Are you looking for individual or family therapy with a medical or nonmedical person?
- Would you and your teenager be more comfortable with a male or female clinician?

Be honest and voice your concerns and questions directly to the mental health clinician from the beginning. During the first interview, observe how your youngster and other family members respond after meeting with the child and adolescent psychiatrist or clinician. Did each of you feel as if you had been listened to? That you, your adolescent, and your feelings were respected? Was there a sense of safety or support or understanding? Listen to your instincts—although it may require more than one session to be sure, find a second candidate if the first clinician doesn't seem to connect solidly with you and your teenager.

Before you make the decision to have your adolescent enter treatment, you should clarify some basic issues. Ask these questions:

- What clinical areas does the clinician identify as crucial for you and your adolescent?

- How often will you meet and for how long? What is your role as a parent in therapy?

- How will the proposed intervention address the problems? How will progress be evaluated?

- How is confidentiality handled?

- How much does the clinician charge? Is there a sliding scale? Does your insurance or health plan cover some or all of the charges?

- Is there a charge for missed appointments? How much notice is required to cancel without being charged?

- Does the clinician work collaboratively with other professionals in case other needs arise, such as testing or medication?

- How do you reach the clinician between appointments or during a crisis?

Once treatment has begun, a child and adolescent psychiatrist or other skilled clinician will help you find ways of coping or solving problems and will build on existing individual and family strengths. Families that have reached an impasse or are in crisis still have some healthy ways of behaving, reacting, and coping.

Even when you find the right fit for you and your teen, however, you must remember that the clinician is only part of the solution. It is essential for you and your family to establish a partnership with that professional.

The Psychiatric Evaluation

Professional help for your adolescent frequently starts with a comprehensive psychiatric evaluation. Whether the family goes to a child and adolescent psychiatrist or other clinician in private practice, a mental health clinic, guidance center, or hospital emergency room, the problem should be carefully defined and understood before the work begins. Typically performed by a child and adolescent psychiatrist or a team of mental health clinicians, the psychiatric evaluation will establish the plan and goals for treatment.

Usually the evaluation consists of a series of interviews, requiring several hours during one or more sessions. During these interviews, the adolescent, family, and clinician work together to understand the nature of the problem or problems. They will also examine possible causes, exacerbating circumstances, and other related problems.

A psychiatric evaluation will involve all areas of the teen's and the family's lives. With the family's help, the clinician will identify the youngster's strengths and assets. At times, the inquiry may strike you as irrelevant or embarrassing. The more information a clinician has, however, the more accurate will be the understanding of the problems and issues.

The clinician will want to know when the problem started, whether anything in particular seems to make it worse, what has been done to address it, and what worked and what didn't. Questions will be asked about the adolescent's overall health (including immunizations) and developmental progress.

When did your child learn to read? Have there been difficulties in school? Does she have many friends? The questions may extend back to early childhood. *When did your child begin to sleep through the night? To talk, walk, feed himself, and complete toilet training?* Questions will also be asked about the pregnancy and delivery, siblings and their individual histories, relationships, school, social functioning, work, drug and alcohol use, and sexual activity. This information assists the clinician in determining what constitutional factors and what experiential factors have contributed to your teen's difficulties.

Parents' health is also relevant, in particular if there is a history of mental or physical illnesses, health problems, or substance abuse. In addition, questions will be asked about problems in the extended family or in previous generations. *Has treatment been sought before? What helped and what didn't?*

To answer questions about the adolescent's physical health and emotional or cognitive functioning, the clinician may arrange for specific tests (for example, blood tests or X rays) and special psychological, educational, and speech and language consultations. With permission from you or your teen, your family physician, school personnel, relatives, and other mental health clinicians involved with the family may be contacted for information as part of the comprehensive evaluation.

By combining biological, psychological, and social information with developmental history and the strengths of the family and the adolescent, the clinician lays the foundation for formulating a diagnosis and developing a treatment plan.

The Interviewing Process. Questions early in the evaluation tend to be open-ended to allow for you and your teen to convey your experience of the problem, its meaning to you, your coping mechanisms, and your immediate concerns. As a diagnostic picture takes shape, the clinician may focus questions to test hypotheses. As a clearer understanding emerges, the clinician will share these observations with the parents and adolescent.

The evaluation process is more than simply gathering information and developing hypotheses. A partnership will be developing between the adolescent, the family, and the child and adolescent psychiatrist or other professional. Within this partnership, the actual work of treatment takes place.

INTERVIEWING THE ADOLESCENT. Adolescents may meet the clinician initially in the company of their parents. But during the evaluation, clinicians will want an opportunity to interview the teenager alone. Many adolescents will require several contacts before they trust the clinician enough to speak honestly about feelings or behaviors. In general, teens are the best reporters of their feelings, while parents can provide information across time and are often better able to describe observable behavior.

During the evaluation, the clinician will note the adolescent's attention span, mood, and thought patterns and look for signs of persistent or intense anxiety or depression. A reluctant teenager will generally not be pressed for answers. Parents should talk with the clinician about how confidentiality will be handled.

INTERVIEWING THE FAMILY. The clinician will want to talk about how you and your family operate. The family is, after all, the context within which children develop emotionally, physically, socially, and cognitively. The behavior of one family member inevitably influences the others and is, in turn, influenced by them. A child and adolescent psychiatrist cannot assess an adolescent's problem without assessing the family, too.

The clinician will also want to understand life in your household. She may ask about the time you spend together, whether the teen meets family expectations, and if you feel you are responsive to your adolescent's needs. The clinician may ask about your worries. *What made you seek help now? Has the problem become worse or less tolerable? What do you think caused the problem? What have you done about it?*

Some personal questions may seem unrelated to your teen's problem, such as how happy your marriage is and how well you and your spouse negotiate disagreements. Parental conflict is often an important circumstance, so the clinician will try to get a sense of any serious problems in the home or in the family. Depression, unresolved grief, illness, financial difficulties, or a family move can each have a profound effect on your adolescent. Sometimes the influence is different from one child to another in the same family.

The clinician will ask about the intensity and quality of your adolescent's peer and sibling relationships. *How many other teens does your youngster routinely socialize with? Is she involved with sports or other extracurricular activities? What are your youngster's favorite hobbies or pastimes?*

In both family and adolescent interviews, a child and adolescent psychiatrist will want to learn about your teenager's behavior and achievement at school. With your permission, the clinician may add to the information that you provide by inquiring directly of middle-school or high-school personnel about the adolescent's relationship with teachers and other students, her ability to attain academic potential and achievement, and the existence of any disciplinary concerns. All earlier records can help the professional reach a fuller understanding.

UNDERSTANDING THE CLINICIAN. The evaluation process is interactive. It provides an opportunity for the clinician to get to know your youngster and your family *and* for you to get to know this professional. During the evaluation sessions, you and each member of your family should feel supported, valued, and listened to.

Watch how the clinician interacts with your adolescent and your family. Tone, posture, and choice of words are indicators of how well the clinician understands the family's worries, fears, and hopes. Over time, you will need to discuss information such as test results and treatment planning; you may need explanations of complex medical or psychiatric information in a way that each of you can understand. Your teenager—and you— needs to feel comfortable with the clinician.

As much as families want to be told everything will be all right, not even the best child and adolescent psychiatrist can predict how things will turn out in the long run. Experienced clinicians know that many teens and their families can be helped through treatment. When that vision is communicated, it eases suffering and builds relationships. Many families feel apprehension and anxiety when they seek help. When a child and adolescent psychiatrist or other clinician communicates professional competence and concern, the adolescent and parent are reassured.

Preparing Your Adolescent for Therapy: What Parents Can Do

Since children are strongly influenced by their parents and families, the appearance of an emotional or behavioral problem in an adolescent is often linked to the family. Many times, parental troubles—marital conflicts, preoccupation, neglect, depression, stress, or general chaos—are expressed through an adolescent. Sometimes family problems can inadvertently reinforce an adolescent's natural vulnerabilities or problems.

The solution to a teen's emotional or behavioral difficulty often lies *within* the family. When parents seek therapy out of concern for their teenager's health or behavior, that search alone sends a message to the adolescent that the parents recognize a problem and are prepared to try to help. You should be involved in your teen's treatment from beginning to end. Your important parental role includes being a historian during the evaluation and a consultant during the treatment. You yourself may also seek treatment, whether it's individual therapy, family therapy, or a family support group.

If your adolescent is in individual therapy, parallel work with parents and siblings can lead to important shifts in the equilibrium within the family. Such work within the family can improve the long-term outcome for the adolescent's future development.

Preparing your teenager for treatment involves being receptive to and curious about the therapy process yourself. Allow yourself to ask questions, since you are a partner in the process. You need to be willing to look at things honestly and directly, to change and grow along with your youngster.

Many teens will be apprehensive or nervous about meeting with a clinician. From the very beginning of the evaluation, be straightforward with your adolescent. Explain in clear language why you are taking her to a professional. For example, tell her that you and her teachers are concerned about how she is feeling and behaving. Explain that it often helps to talk to someone who understands teenagers and that together you will try to understand exactly what is bothering her. Explain why you think she needs treatment. Acknowledge that you may need help to be a more effective parent.

At each step in the process, describe to your adolescent the professional with whom you will be meeting, the setting, the people who will be there, the length of the session, and the other arrangements. Your teenager should know the clinician's name. Having this information can help her feel more in control. Encourage your youngster to be open and honest when answering questions. Tell her she will have time to ask her own questions. Sometimes it is helpful to reassure your teenager that it may take some time to feel relaxed enough to talk freely. Explain that therapy is a special and private time set aside to allow her to talk and think about anything she wants. Tell her that she and the clinician will work together to understand why she feels troubled and behaves the way she does.

To engage in a therapeutic relationship, your adolescent needs your support and encouragement. This is not always easy. Sometimes your teenager will leave a session with an idealized image of the clinician. You may feel competitive, sensing that someone else is helping your teen in a way you could not. At such times, you may have doubts about the therapy. At other moments, your adolescent may storm out of a therapy session very angry and complaining about the clinician or about having to continue in therapy. You may worry that your child will talk critically or reveal embarrassing secrets about you.

Deal honestly with the clinician about your feelings and concerns. You, too, need to have trust in the clinician and believe in the process to effect change for your teenager and family.

DEALING WITH MANAGED-CARE SYSTEMS

Managed care is a review and approval process that monitors the need, type, and use of medical services in an effort to provide necessary and appropriate care while containing (or managing) costs. In recent years, this approach has been used more and more by insurance companies. Managed care can control costs, but it also influences treatments, emphasizing short-term treatment and focusing on dealing with a current crisis or on rapidly changing specific, concrete behaviors.

In these systems or plans, care is authorized by a *utilization review*. This review is usually done by social workers, nurses, or others (often referred to as *case managers*) either by phone or by reviewing a written report prepared by your clinician. If there is a disagreement about the treatment the clinician recommends, a good managed-care company will, upon request, assign a reviewer who has a level of training comparable to the clinician's. Many managed-care companies direct their enrollees to obtain treatment from clinicians in a specific network.

Frequently the clinician evaluating or treating your adolescent will be required to present the evaluation or treatment to a case manager *before* your insurer authorizes payment for additional treatment. If this is not done, you could be responsible for paying all the charges yourself. To avoid delays in evaluations or disruptions in treatment, contact the insurer when you are considering seeking treatment. The appropriate phone number (one open twenty-four hours a day, perhaps an 800 number) is usually on the health-care card provided by your plan.

Case managers use guidelines developed by the managed-care company hired by your health-care plan. Written case summaries and treatment plans prepared by the child and adolescent psychiatrist or mental-health clinician may be required. Sometimes an entire medical record may be requested for review. This practice should be questioned, because it can be a significant intrusion on the confidentiality of your medical record. A good managed-care company will prefer a summary and treatment plan, except perhaps during the final levels of an appeals process. In the case of psychiatric disorders, managed-care reviewers typically authorize payment for a limited number of outpatient sessions or days of inpatient care. To obtain approval for additional treatment, the clinician must discuss the adolescent's progress and needs with a case manager in the managed-care organization.

The utilization review by the managed-care company may give rise to problems about confidentiality when there are issues or "family secrets" that you appropriately regard as private communications with your clinician and are reluctant to have revealed and discussed by your clinician with the case manager. Formerly, these were kept between you and your doctor. These may be important matters that affect the clinician's request to the managed-care company to pay for treatment, but their revelation will infringe on your private relation with the clinician.

You and your teenager should discuss such concerns with your clinician. Often, she will respect your desire for privacy, but be aware, too, that some of the information that you regard as private may also be helpful in getting your adolescent's treatment approved by managed care. In other words, this information may help justify to the insurer the need for continued treatment.

If treatment is denied but you and the clinician think that additional treatment is necessary and covered by your health plan description of benefits, follow the appeals process outlined in your health plan. Your children and family may also benefit from treatment that does not qualify as "medically necessary," as the term is defined in your plan, or is simply not covered by your health plan. If that is the case or if you wish not to use your health plan in order to avoid the infringement on the confidentiality of your communications with your clinician, you may wish to consider contracting with your clinician to pay for treatment the way you purchase other valuable services.

Some managed-care plans limit your choice of child and adolescent psychiatrist or other mental health clinician to their *preferred providers*, a group of doctors, social workers, or psychologists enlisted by your insurer at contracted rates. Typically, these preferred providers have agreed to accept a reduced fee. If you choose to consult with someone else, your insurer may not pay for these services. In the same way, care given at *out-of-network* hospitals may not be covered by your insurance. Some states require health plans to offer a *point of service option*. If your plan has a point of service option, you may consult a practitioner who is not a preferred provider in your plan but your co-pay fee may be significantly higher.

Traditionally, insurers paid only for inpatient and outpatient care. Today, depending upon your plan, a fuller array of services such as day hospital, day treatment, home-based care, respite care, and family-support services may be covered at least in part. These lower-cost and less restrictive services may offer a number of advantages over inpatient hospitalization. (See also *What Are the Treatment Options?*, page 318.)

Some mental-health plans set maximums on annual or lifetime costs for mental health-care. Prudent parents and employers study these limits closely before signing up for any health insurance. Once this amount is used up, coverage ends and an adolescent's subsequent mental-health bills will be the responsibility of the parent. If this happens and your teen needs continued care you cannot afford, you may need to seek help from your state-supported public mental-health system. Unfortunately, this may mean changing clinicians and disrupting your youngster's care.

As you purchase health-care insurance for your family, carefully evaluate the mental-health coverage. Consider the following questions in evaluating the plans:

■ Is the mental-health coverage managed by an outside company? How do we access this company for approvals of needed services?

■ Is there a list of preferred providers? Are adolescent specialists included? Are there child and adolescent psychiatrists? What happens if we want to see someone not on the list?

■ Are you responsible for a *deductible*? (Many insurance programs do not cover treatment from the first dollar but require you to pay for an initial annual increment or deductible of $100 to $500 or more.)

■ What are the co-pays, if any? (*Co-pays* are the out-of-pocket portion of the cost of each service for which you are responsible.)

■ What are the limits on the number of visits covered? Who sets the limits?

■ What hospitals are covered under the plan? Does the plan cover other services such as day treatment or respite care? Is there any recourse (such as appeals or grievance procedures) if you are not satisfied with the provider or the recommendations of the utilization review?

■ What, if any, diagnoses or pre-existing conditions and treatments are excluded?

■ Does the plan cover all types of practitioners?

There may be times when you will have to act as your adolescent's advocate to get services that are not covered by your plan. Mental health and family advocacy groups and professional associations such as the American Academy of Child and Adolescent Psychiatry may provide you with assistance and important information about local services. The support of other parents may also be helpful when you are trying to obtain needed services for your teenager.

Emergencies

Teenagers in crisis may turn to friends, their parents, or other adults for help. Parents may be anxious, angry, or distracted. School counselors or teachers may be overwhelmed or unaware. As a result, these adults are at a loss as to how to help the adolescent. Some adults realize the seriousness of the situation and seek immediate outside help for the teen.

Some adolescents keep the crises to themselves or seek help independently, feeling there is an insurmountable barrier in communicating with their parents. Some crises with teens can be an indication of homes that are chaotic, negligent, or abusive (physical and/or sexual). Psychiatric emergencies are often linked to troubled family relationships and stress in the home. Family crises that threaten family stability include divorce, abandonment, illness, or death.

Clear-cut psychiatric emergencies include suicidal or homicidal threats or behavior. Other possible emergency situations include severe anxiety or panic attacks, psychosis, drug overdoses, drug use by young adolescents, and violent, assaultive, or destructive threats or behavior.

In all emergencies, the first order of business is to ensure the safety of the teenager. Call your health plan's emergency number or consult your family physician. If there is any delay, go to a hospital emergency room. Psychiatric hospitalization is often useful in helping a suicidal, impulsive, or psychotic adolescent regain control, or for a teenager who is very depressed and has not responded to intensive outpatient therapy. Inpatient stays are usually brief. In some communities, less restrictive but safe environments such as a crisis residence or group home may be available.

Many young adolescents are brought for emergency treatment by their parents or relatives. Others are sent for emergency treatment on the recommendation of school, juvenile court, police, health and mental-health organizations, and other community agencies, the family physician or pediatrician, and neighbors.

During the evaluation of a psychiatric emergency, the clinician will assess your adolescent's physical, emotional, intellectual, educational, and social functioning. Recent events will be carefully reviewed, in particular any that indicate trauma, drug use, and other emotional stressors. During the evaluation, the clinician will also review family structure and relationships and will explore whether relatives or friends can give support.

Emergency assessment seeks to clarify what precipitated the crisis. Was it a severe stress or loss? Other underlying conditions may also emerge, such as a severe depression (see *Depressive Disorders,* page 209), conduct disorder (see *Conduct Disorders,* page 236), a psychotic disorder (see *Psychotic Disorders,* page 270), an anxiety disorder (see *Anxiety and Avoidant Disorders,* page 196), or a medical problem with psychiatric symptoms.

Once the adolescent and family can feel safer and less stressed—when the panic, anxiety, and chaos of the emergency has subsided—the clinician can begin to investigate underlying issues and consider how to prevent future crises. It is important that everyone understands that the emergency problem is often not just a temporary crisis but rather a reflection of complex personal and family difficulties that need a longer-term and more painstaking solution.

17

What Are the Treatment Options?

■   ■   ■

Once you and your adolescent have seen a child and adolescent psychiatrist or other qualified professional and the evaluation process has been completed, you should have some idea of the complexity of the problem and a proposed plan of treatment. The treatment might include one or more psychotherapies (individual, couple, family, or group). In addition, medication may be prescribed for your adolescent.

Treatment is based on the adolescent's diagnosis and the course of his problems over time. There are other important conditions, including the family's emotional strengths, their comfort with different types of therapy, the availability of services, and insurance or financial resources.

Clinicians develop treatment plans according to their training. Whether the clinician is a child and adolescent psychiatrist, psychologist, clinical social worker, pastoral counselor, or psychiatric nurse will influence the shape of the plan. If your teen is being treated in a hospital or mental-health clinic, the recommended course of treatment will be affected by institutional policies, attitudes, and styles. Your managed-care company may also favor certain treatment approaches.

This chapter will explain and discuss some of the language, concepts, and therapeutic services that are part of psychiatric treatment for adolescents and their families.

The Continuum of Mental Health Care

Different communities have different treatments available for teenagers with emotional and behavioral difficulties. The range of programs and services is called the *continuum of care*. Not every community has all services, but some of the more common services are described briefly in what follows.

- **Private or outpatient clinic.**

  In such settings, clinicians will meet with teens (individually, with their families, or in groups) for scheduled sessions (typically, thirty to fifty minutes). The frequency of visits depends on the therapeutic plan for the adolescent and family and often upon the policies of the managed-care program.

- **Intensive case management.**

  Case managers coordinate the psychiatric, financial, legal, educational, and medical services to ensure that the teenager can function successfully at home, in school, and in the community.

- **Home-based treatment.**

  This service consists of a team of individuals who visit at home and provide a treatment program to help the adolescent and family by working with the youngster and other family members.

- **Family support services.**

  Some community agencies offer a range of services, which may include parenting training, parent support groups, nutritional counseling, and play groups to help families care for their children.

- **Day treatment.**

  These intensive programs provide psychiatric treatment and school or special-education services. Youngsters usually attend five days a week.

- **Partial hospitalization or day hospitals.**

  Here adolescents receive the intensive treatment services of a psychiatric hospital during the day and return home at night. This enables them to maintain regular family activities.

- **Emergency/crisis services.**

  These are twenty-four-hour-per-day psychiatric emergency services provided in hospital emergency rooms or by mobile crisis teams.

- **Respite care services.**

  While receiving respite care, a patient stays with trained individuals outside of the home for brief periods of time to provide parents with a time free from the intense demands of caring for their youngster. In some communities, in-home respite care services are also available.

- **Therapeutic group home or community residential care.**
  These special residences will accommodate small numbers of teens whose home life does not provide sufficient support, structure, and nurturance or whose needs are severe enough to warrant twenty-four-hour-a-day care. Youngsters in these settings often also attend a day treatment or special educational program if they are not enrolled in school.

- **Crisis residences.**
  These settings offer short-term (usually fewer than fifteen days) crisis intervention and treatment for small numbers of teens. Patients are supervised twenty-four hours per day and often attend their own schools.

- **Residential treatment facility.**
  Seriously troubled teens receive intensive and comprehensive biopsychosocial treatment in a campuslike setting over a long period of time, typically twelve to eighteen months. Some facilities have treatment programs dedicated to specific problems or age groups.

- **Hospital treatment.**
  Adolescents receive comprehensive psychiatric treatment in a hospital. The length of treatment varies. Some communities have specialized psychiatric hospitals. Others have special units for psychiatric services within a general, pediatric, or community hospital.

Individual Psychotherapy

Psychotherapy is based on the development of a therapeutic relationship between the adolescent and the psychotherapist. One important feature of this relationship is the development of sufficient trust on the part of the adolescent to allow the youngster to share with the therapist his thoughts, feelings, and inner experiences. The clinician, by using his or her knowledge of psychological processes, human development, and psychiatric disorders, is able to work to relieve the teen's discomfort and suffering and to promote the development of new skills and ways of coping.

The goals of psychotherapy are to relieve suffering; to restore emotional stability; to increase tolerance of a full range of emotions, including anger and frustration; to promote age-appropriate independence in thought and action; to maximize the adolescent's use of his innate abilities; and to resume healthy development. Psychotherapy is a method of treating psychiatric disorders, emotional and behavioral problems, and developmental crises and delays. To the extent these goals are accomplished, a teenager will find more pleasure and meaning in his life and will build greater resilience and be able to respond more flexibly to the challenge of his age.

The practice of psychotherapy includes different approaches, styles, techniques, and interventions. Most psychotherapies encourage self-exploration while offering some support and direction. Most clinicians, regardless of their training, draw from various schools of psychotherapy theory and modify their approach according to each adolescent's needs and capacities. The frequency and length of psychotherapy sessions vary in accordance with the nature of the problem.

In the privacy of the clinician's office and within the safety of a therapeutic relationship, the teenager will begin to talk (thus, the term *talk therapy*). The clinician observes the adolescent and listens very carefully, noting patterns and themes. During psychotherapy sessions, which are often scheduled once or twice a week and last from thirty to fifty minutes, the youngster is encouraged to explore thoughts, experiences, and feelings. Without moral judgment or criticism, the clinician listens to the teenager and encourages self-exploration during these times. The clinician may ask for clarification, offer tentative interpretations of internal emotional conflicts, make connections between current problems and past experiences, and help the youngster develop different ways of coping.

Psychotherapy works as a result of the development of an alliance between the clinician and the adolescent and because the clinician utilizes a range of specific psychotherapy techniques. Within the safety of that relationship, the youngster is encouraged to become curious about and to discuss feelings, behavior, and inner struggles. By exhibiting a caring, understanding attitude toward the teenager, the clinician allows greater expression and minimizes embarrassment. Clinicians who work with adolescents understand that teenagers often express both positive and negative feelings about their therapy and therapists. Even with very nervous or apprehensive youngsters, good therapeutic relationships can absorb much of the anxiety and promote open discussion. The therapist also helps the teen become more optimistic that he can be helped to get better.

Parents usually play several essential roles when their adolescent is in psychotherapy. In spite of the teenager's emerging independence, the teen is still quite dependent on parents and the parents' judgment about the recommendation for psychiatric care and treatment. This requires that the parent understand the teen's problem and feel confident in the clinician. The teenager may also rely on the parent to see that he goes regularly and to provide payment for treatment.

Another key component of individual psychotherapy with youngsters is the *parent work*. Sometimes the parents will meet with the adolescent's therapist or with another clinician for the purpose of understanding the teen's difficulties and how these difficulties influence the teen's life, development, and the rest of the family. Parents are offered guidance in developing new approaches to parenting and family management. One goal in therapeutic work with parents is to help them tailor their parenting to the particular needs of their adolescent.

In therapy, the adolescent has the opportunity to review his experiences and feelings and to put them in perspective. When having difficulty dealing with painful life circumstances, the teen in therapy has a chance to understand his feelings and move on to adapt to reality.

The length of any course of psychotherapy varies. When symptoms improve, teenagers or their parents may understandably wish to end treatment. The time of ending, however, is best determined in conjunction with the clinician, who is able to assess whether the underlying problems are sufficiently resolved so that the gains can be maintained. At some point the course of treatment may appear to worsen, and the adolescent or parents may protest the treatment. It is essential that parents meet with the clinician periodically to understand what is occurring, so they can make an informed decision to continue and to support the psychotherapy or to end the treatment.

Different forms of individual psychotherapy include psychodynamic (see *Psychodynamic Psychotherapy,* below), cognitive-behavioral (see *Cognitive-Behavioral Therapy*, page 323), and supportive therapies (see *Family Therapy* and *Group Therapy,* pages 326 and 328). For each, the length and frequency of sessions and the duration of the treatment vary, but the practitioner of the therapy should be able to articulate the goals and methods of treatment in a manner that can be clearly understood and seems relevant to the specific problem of the individual teenager.

Psychotherapy is not a quick or easy fix. Rather it is a complex, intense, and rich process that can provide self-understanding and foster new coping mechanisms. Psychotherapy can assist the adolescent to more fully utilize his abilities.

PSYCHODYNAMIC PSYCHOTHERAPY

Psychodynamic psychotherapy is also called *psychoanalytically oriented psychotherapy* and includes concepts used in psychoanalysis. Its purpose is to understand the psychological forces that motivate a person's actions and that color a youngster's thoughts and feelings.

Psychodynamic psychotherapy helps identify characteristic patterns of response to inner struggles. Such patterns are called *defenses.* This therapy assumes that once the underlying issues and patterns are brought to light, the adolescent can better master his emotions and choose more wisely what he wants to say and do. Psychodynamic psychotherapy is part of the foundation for many other forms of psychotherapy.

Psychodynamic psychotherapy is often the preferred treatment for complicated conditions, particularly because so often there is more than one problem that affects the youngster. Such adolescents have more than one diagnosis and may have experienced medical or social trauma. Often these problems have been resistant to treatments. Psychodynamic treatment is especially useful when the adolescent's problems have led to delays in social and emotional development. It is an important treatment option in many psychiatric conditions, including depression, anxiety disorders, eating disorders, and gender identity disorders. For teenagers who are experiencing significant life stresses (for example, from divorce, illness, or death of a family member), psychodynamic psychotherapies are also frequently the treatment to consider.

Psychoanalytically oriented psychotherapy consists of thirty- to fifty-minute sessions where privacy and protection from interruption are assured. The frequency of the sessions and the duration of treatment vary in accordance with how much inner change is to be accomplished and how strongly entrenched the adolescent's defenses are. In stressful life situations where the goal is to help the teenager understand and adapt to new circumstances, the treatment may be less frequent and of brief duration. With more complex and long-standing problems, the treatment may be more frequent (for example, twice a week) and of longer duration. The lengthiest and most intense form of psychodynamic psychotherapy is psychoanalysis in which the adolescent may be seen three to four times per week for several years. Psychoanalysis is an effective treatment for adolescents with severe and complicated personality problems.

In psychodynamic psychotherapy, the clinician assists the teenager in gaining an understanding of his inner world in order that he may develop his own effective response to his environment. Rather than giving advice, the clinician assists the teenager in implementing his own coping strategies. The youngster improves because he has gained insight into and mastery of his feelings and inner struggles within the context of a compassionate, respectful, and reliable therapeutic relationship in which he has felt deeply understood. The adolescent gains the freedom to relate to his environment in a more adaptable manner.

Cognitive-Behavioral Therapy

In the past few years, cognitive-behavioral approaches have proved especially useful in the treatment of young people with certain emotional and behavioral problems, among them depression, anxiety disorders, and a wide range of others. As the name implies, *behavioral therapies* focus on external behavioral symptoms rather than internal feelings and motivations. Behavioral therapy addresses the symptomatic behavior directly. By improving behavior, a change in emotion often follows.

A cognitive approach improves an adolescent's moods and behavior by addressing faulty patterns of thinking. How a person understands events shapes how he feels and acts. Cognitive therapy guides a teenager toward more realistic and positive thinking. The focus is on how the teen's distorted thinking leads to emotional and behavioral problems.

In cognitive therapy, adolescents learn to identify, test, and correct specific distortions in their thinking. They learn to recognize negative thoughts and to see the relationship between thinking, feelings, and behavior. Common errors in thought include exaggerating events and fears; anticipating disastrous outcomes; overgeneralizing from negative experiences; and ignoring times when things go well. Once an adolescent understands and recognizes that he has been automatically reacting negatively, he can examine how realistic those reactions are, consider alternative explanations, and imagine other outcomes.

Cognitive-behavioral therapy offers youngsters tools for thinking about their world. These therapies work especially well with children and teens because the techniques are active and specific to a given problem. The therapy sessions may be shorter in duration than in psychodynamic therapy (perhaps one or two twenty-minute sessions per week), which suits many teenagers.

As with psychodynamic psychotherapy, the initial goal is to develop a rapport between the adolescent and clinician and to gather information. Through a collaborative relationship, the clinician attempts to engender interest in the adolescent, and together they examine, experiment with, and assess the youngster's belief system and perceptions.

Teenagers with excessive anxiety or phobias may be encouraged to chart automatic thoughts and disturbed feelings, to explore worse-case scenarios, and to use self-soothing mental images and fantasies.

Highly anxious or phobic adolescents might be encouraged to use relaxation techniques or to talk themselves into a more soothing or reasonable emotional position. Through *systematic desensitization* (gentle, repeated exposure to a situation or object that frightens or upsets the adolescent), the youngster may learn to conquer the phobia or avoid an anxiety state. A teenager with obsessive-compulsive disorder, for example, may be asked to outline his rituals and obsessional thoughts. Strategies to alter these are developed, which may include facing the feared behavior gradually (*exposure*) and stopping the behavior (*response prevention*) or unwanted thoughts (*thought-stopping*). (See *Obsessive-Compulsive Disorder,* page 201.)

Cognitive theory holds that depression stems from irrational beliefs and distorted thoughts. Usually a depressed teenager personalizes failure, magnifies negative events, and minimizes positive occurrences and attributes. These negative thought patterns may be the result, for example, of the loss of a parent at an early age, whether through death, divorce, or adopting the thought patterns of a depressed parent. Often these negative thoughts are not based on a realistic perception by the adolescent of his abilities and circumstances. In cognitive therapy, the clinician and teenager identify unpleasant thoughts, explore their origins, and devise more realistic and more positive ways of dealing with day-to-day problems.

Behavioral therapy targets specific symptoms, such as social withdrawal, low activity level, self-deprecating behavior, and aggressive behavior. An adolescent then learns through cognitive techniques to monitor negative thoughts he has about himself, to evaluate their validity, and to reinforce positive alternatives. The youngster is taught to set more realistic goals and standards of performance, to refrain from punitive self-statements, and to think of himself in kinder, more encouraging terms.

The cognitive-behavioral clinician working with a teenager with conduct disorder or antisocial behavior will start by determining to what degree the youngster can anticipate and control his aggressive acts and whether the adolescent feels remorse or concern after such episodes. Clinicians frequently use *problem-solving training* to help aggressive teens deal with difficult social and interpersonal situations. The clinician helps the adolescent learn to identify and express his feelings of upset more appropriately prior to the unacceptable action and to devise alternative behaviors. The teen learns the consequences of his behavior and how to make his behavior correspond to what he says he wants to do. The focus is on the adolescent being accountable for his choices, decisions, and behavior. The youngster then begins to see the advantages in changing his behavior.

Gradually he may be able to interact more successfully in social situations. After a few successes, he starts to consolidate what he has learned, his behavior improves, his thinking becomes more positive, and he feels better. Family and friends respond positively to the more considerate teenager, reinforcing the new behavior.

Cognitive-behavioral therapy, when coupled with medication, is also quite effective in treating an adolescent with attention-deficit/hyperactivity disorder. The teenager may be able to improve academic performance, as cognitive-behavioral techniques can assist in reducing impulsiveness and help him control his motor activity. These techniques, however, must be implemented in the home and in the classroom, as well as in the clinician's office. The clinician often works with the school and family to implement or reinforce positive behaviors.

Parent Management Training helps parents learn principles and strategies for managing their adolescent's behavior. In the home, parents are taught to use positive reinforcement—in which the youngster is praised and rewarded for exercising self-discipline or accomplishing other agreed-upon goals—to help the teen operate independently and improve social interactions. Parents learn to use appropriate consequences and limit-setting, such as the loss of privileges. Self-control techniques are taught, such as self-monitoring (*What am I doing? How am I feeling?*), self-evaluation (*What happened here? Could I do this differently next time? Should I?*), and goal-setting (*What are my expectations?*).

Cognitive-behavioral therapy isn't the answer to all problems in adolescence. In some instances, cognitive therapy may reduce some symptoms but fail to alter the overall problem, or the therapy may fail to produce lasting therapeutic change. In others, cognitive therapies can produce significant, positive results, especially when the symptoms are mild, the adolescent is motivated, and the parents actively involved.

Family Therapy

Research has shown that family therapy, whether used as the primary treatment or in conjunction with other treatments such as individual, group, or medication therapies, has proved remarkably helpful in treating a wide range of emotional, behavioral, and psychiatric disorders in teenagers, including psychotic disorders, depression and bipolar disorder, anxiety disorders, substance abuse, eating disorders, and conduct disorders.

In many cases, family therapy provides support and education as the family tries to manage an adolescent and his problems. In some cases, parents enter into therapy to help their teenager get better but come to understand that other, family-related problems are finding expression through their youngster's troubles. At first, the issues that come to light in therapy may seem tangential and unrelated, but when marital problems, unresolved grief, or a family secret are unmasked and discussed, therapy may move in an unanticipated but highly productive direction. With the focus shifted to family tensions, the adolescent may well be released to proceed in a more productive and developmentally appropriate manner. Family therapy can dramatically alter family relationships in very positive and healthy ways.

A clinician may ask that each family member participate, including siblings and even grandparents. At its best, therapy addresses all family members, their private feelings and thoughts, personal and family developmental history, and biological and health-related concerns, as well as their interactions with other members of the family. An effective family clinician must engage each family member during the session and be able to view each individual within the larger context of the family. The clinician will learn from each member's point of view something of the nature, cause, and effects of—and possible solutions to—the problems of the individual and family. In family therapy, the transactions and roles of family members with respect to one another are often the focus for treatment.

Therapy can help the family deal with the stress generated by living with and caring for a troubled adolescent. A sibling can feel neglected, overly burdened, or even embarrassed by another sibling's behavior. During treatment, a parent may be found to have a psychiatric disorder (such as depression) causing the parent and other family members distress. Such a therapeutic finding will be incorporated into the treatment, either by making an appropriate referral for the individual to receive treatment or by addressing the issues in family therapy.

Family therapy offers parents and children

less defensive ways of communicating with one another. It fosters mutual support, positive reinforcement, direct communication, clarification of age-appropriate roles of the members, and more effective problem-solving within the family. It may offer instruction on conflict resolution and can decrease a parent's likelihood of engaging in physically and emotionally abusive behavior. Working to reduce parent-adolescent power struggles, therapy may bring about more satisfying and appropriate parent-teenager interactions. It can support parents as they negotiate the precarious balance between furthering appropriate independence in their adolescent and maintaining sufficient supervision and accountability.

Family therapy addresses problems that unwittingly perpetuate or promote symptoms in teens, among them a lack of generational boundaries, severe marital conflict, rigid or chaotic rules, projection of parental feelings onto a child, or neglectful or overly involved relationships.

There are numerous schools of thought and theory that influence family therapy practice. Accordingly, the way in which clinicians frame or understand problems will determine their intervention. If, for example, a clinician observes a problem in the way parents discipline and guide their adolescent, he or she may use techniques to help parents use positive and negative reinforcement more effectively. (See *Cognitive-Behavioral Therapy*, page 323.) If a teen's symptom serves some function within the family (such as distracting parents from dealing with their conflicts with each other), a clinician may then reframe the

symptom in terms of its function and offer the family different, less damaging ways of obtaining comparable benefits.

Some family therapists look at the process by which the family maintains the need to protect and preserve itself and the need to adapt in the face of inevitable developmental and environmental change. Still others examine how communication patterns and unspoken rules maintain or cause problems for the family members.

In some cases the clinician may move the focus away from the immediate family to the extended family and social support networks and examine the way in which the parents have brought expectations and experiences from their own childhoods into their present family life.

A popular tool and technique in family therapy is the *genogram,* a pictorial representation or "map" of the family. By working with the family to sketch out a genogram, the clinician can more closely investigate the most complex family relationships, family history, and multigenerational issues. As they look at their own diagram, individuals, as well as families, can understand their histories in a new context.

Family therapy is diverse, both in theory and in practice. An eclectic approach to family therapy, however, tends to be more useful than a strict adherence to a particular school of thought. Most family clinicians draw upon different theories for the unique situations different families present. In short, family therapists aim at understanding an adolescent's problems within the family context; what is working to cause or maintain the problems; and what assets, strengths, and resources within the family can help resolve the problem.

Group Therapy

Group therapy uses the power of group dynamics and peer interaction to further understanding and hope in participants. Group therapy is used for a wide range of emotional, behavioral, and life problems. Groups in therapy may consist of several families or only adults or only adolescent peers. Many teenagers respond well to group therapy with peers because of their developmental need to be separate from parents and accepted by peers.

Participating in a group with their peers can assist the teenager in developing social skills for a greater sense of mastery and self-esteem. Some teenagers find it easier to express feelings in a supportive group of their peers. Similarly, parents often feel supported, understood, and able to gain helpful insight and parenting skills in a support group with other parents facing similar challenges. For both the adolescent and the parent, hearing other people talk about familiar problems and ways to resolve them can have powerful, supportive effects.

At any one time in a community, a number of groups, in a number of settings, will be able to address different needs. Groups in schools, community centers, churches and synagogues, health or mental-health clinics, residential treatment centers, or hospitals may address such problems as poor peer relations, low academic achievement, and delinquency or the impact of chronic illness on development. Groups can help teenagers deal with divorce and abuse, somatic and terminal illness. There may be groups for children of battered women or alcoholics, crisis and trauma groups, educational and prevention groups, parent and family groups. Substance abuse treatment is typically conducted with group therapy as a cornerstone of the intervention. Such groups may meet once or twice a week or even every day in a hospital, intensive outpatient program, or long-term treatment center. With adolescents, groups may form not only according to disorder and severity of the difficulties but also according to age. Not all of these groups, however, are organized and led by mental health clinicians.

Consideration for group therapy usually begins with an interview between the clinician and the parents and adolescent. Once in the group, each member will be asked by the group leader what he wants from group therapy. In turn, the leader will explain what is expected of the members. For progress to be made in groups, participants need to be interested in their own thoughts and feelings; to speak within the group as honestly as possible about those thoughts and feelings; to cultivate an awareness of their own behaviors in relation to the others; and to offer suggestions and feedback about topics under discussion.

Initially, members tend to look to the leader for guidance. As the group progresses, members connect with one another. Eventually, each member of the group assumes greater responsibility for his or her individual growth, improvement, and progress.

When working with adolescents, a group leader offers support, spontaneity, and flexibility while fostering a sense of safety and trust. The leader must establish adequate limits and rules for the group. Young people seem to respond best (as, in all likelihood, do adults) when the group leader assumes an attitude of controlled curiosity and sophisticated ignorance, rather than an overly intellectual or authoritarian approach, which is likely to produce silence, fear, withdrawal, and withholding.

Group therapy can move a teenager toward greater communication with others while the clinician observes behaviors, clarifies diagnoses, and gradually interprets the meaning of the discussion and group interactions. Some groups use discussion of a videotape, physical exercise, games, role playing, or genograms, in which the teenagers and clinician create "maps" of each adolescent's family. By mapping the emotional and social landscape of the family, a genogram can help a teenager focus on questions of his parents' marriage(s) or separation, new family alliances, or catastrophic family events.

The degree of permissiveness, structure, and limit-setting in a group format depends upon the activity level, age, and expressiveness of the group. The group therapist imparts meaning, insight, and interpretations when appropriate. As the adolescent feels accepted into the group and connected to his peers and the therapist, he will begin to express his feelings and gain confidence in himself and his role in the group.

Medications

The use of medications to treat psychiatric disorders is called *psychopharmacological treatment*. Certain psychiatric disorders, syndromes, and symptoms respond well to medications. A medication may be chosen to treat a particular target symptom or set of symptoms. The usefulness of the medication can then be monitored by observing changes in the target symptoms. Some medications are prescribed to facilitate attention and learning; others may be used for anxiety and mood disorders. Antipsychotic medications can benefit adolescents with thought disorders, delusions, or hallucinations.

When a medication is being considered, both the teen and his parents need to be included in the discussions. Parents need complete information about any medication prescribed for their youngster. They need to understand when and how the medication is to be taken; the goals for medication use; and the possible side effects. The more parents are involved in the decision to use medications, the more supportive they can be. Sometimes, when parents, teachers, or other mental-health clinicians become frustrated and desperate in their efforts to manage especially difficult behavior, they request medication for the adolescent. Such a request is carefully evaluated by the child and adolescent psychiatrist, who determines whether the use of the specific medication is indicated or what alternative form of treatment would be helpful in resolving the crisis.

A teenager should be given age-appropriate information to help him understand the medication's effects and the reasons for taking it. Adolescents may have many questions about taking a medication. Developmental issues such as independence and concerns about their bodies frequently contribute to teenagers' reluctance to take medications. They often are concerned about how peers or family members will react to their use of *psychotropic* medications (drugs that affect psychic function, behavior, or experience). The better the teen understands the reasons for taking the medication and the benefits it can offer, the more cooperative he will be with the use of the medication.

Prescribing the Medication. Prescribing medications for adolescents begins with a consultation between the psychiatrist, the teen, and parents. The child and adolescent psychiatrist needs a clear understanding of the youngster's medical history and current state of health, allergies, and previous experience with psychiatric medications.

The child and adolescent psychiatrist will target symptoms and discuss the goals and anticipated effects of the medication. This discussion will also include information as to possible side effects and any precautions the teenager and parents should take during treatment. The psychiatrist will discuss the anticipated length of treatment; when and what follow-up will be given; and at what point or under what conditions medication will be adjusted or discontinued. A plan will be formulated, on the basis of a baseline mental status examination, for measuring the adolescent's progress. Medication will be prescribed only after parents, and with many

child and adolescent psychiatrists, after the youngster, have given consent. (See also *Your Adolescent's Medication: Questions to Ask the Doctor,* page 340.)

After the teenager has begun his course of medication, the child and adolescent psychiatrist will review the youngster's response to and progress on the medication on a regular basis. Dosage adjustments or even changes in medication are made when needed. Parents should discuss with the physician any doubts or concerns they may have about the medication. The question of whether teenagers should be personally responsible for managing their medications depends upon the specific diagnoses, developmental level of the youngster, and other specific factors that may influence the adolescent's compliance with medication instructions.

Many medications are prescribed to treat psychiatric disorders in adolescents. The categories of psychotropic medications include stimulants, antidepressants, mood stabilizers, anxiolytics, hypnotics, and antipsychotic drugs. *Appendix A: Psychiatric Medicines* contains detailed information about each of these families of medications, including common side effects, generic and brand names, and other important pharmaceutical information.

Community Resources and Prevention Services

Most communities offer resources providing support to adolescents, especially those whose biological vulnerabilities, family lives, and socioeconomic circumstances put them at risk. By reducing the risk factors and lessening stress on the youngsters, their parents, and their families, some community programs attempt to prevent or limit the later development of behavioral and emotional disorders. Although the nature and number of programs vary in each community, some examples that may be available in your community are given below:

COMMUNITY INTERVENTION PROGRAMS address specific stresses in an adolescent's life. Some hospitals offer programs that aim to alleviate some of the anxiety youngsters experience when they must spend time in a hospital. Some hospitals or agencies also offer programs for teens with chronic physical illnesses.

Adolescents whose parents suffer from serious psychiatric illnesses or substance-abuse disorders are at higher risk for developing emotional and behavioral difficulties. Programs offered through mental-health agencies and hospitals can improve family stability and parenting skills, decrease marital discord, and increase the availability of family supports in these difficult situations.

When a teenager's parents divorce, the adolescent is recognized as being at an increased risk for emotional and behavioral problems. There are immediate and long-term effects of parent separation and divorce, as well as the burden of adapting to new family configurations. Some intervention programs offer youngsters and parents who are involved with divorce a chance to participate in preventive interventions that aim to reduce much of the stress of the events. Children of Divorce Intervention Programs, for example, are mandated in some states before a divorce can be finalized. These programs seem to promote healthier adaptation for children of divorce. Some schools offer teen support groups to deal with divorce.

BIG BROTHER/BIG SISTER PROGRAMS offer youngsters from single-parent families the opportunity to develop a relationship with an adult, usually of the same gender as the adolescent. The adult offers the adolescent regular mentoring, assistance, understanding, and acceptance as they share activities and time together.

FOSTER HOMES offer a homelike environment for youngsters who experience significant turmoil in their lives and must be removed from their own homes in order to assure their safety or adequate care. Foster homes provide the teenager temporary care and nurturance as well as shelter. (See also *Foster Families,* page 110.)

In order to become foster parents, adults must be licensed, but they rarely have any specific training, other than their own life experience. In recent years, there has been an increase in therapeutic foster homes and "special" foster homes, such as those designed for HIV-infected youngsters. Usually, an adolescent ends up in foster care only after protective services has become involved with a family in which abuse or neglect has occurred. Some parents, when overwhelmed and fragmented, will request temporary placement for their children in a foster-care home.

Intensive Outpatient, Partial Hospitalization, and Day Treatment

Intensive outpatient, partial hospitalization, and day treatment represent important options for providing psychiatric care to adolescents in settings that are less restrictive and less expensive than a hospital. Day hospitals and day treatment offer more intensive care for teens for whom one or two office visits per week is insufficient. These programs can be located in hospitals, schools, or other mental-health settings, or be freestanding. In these programs, the adolescent lives and sleeps at home.

With the advent of managed care and other recent health-care reforms, the demand for partial hospital and outpatient or day treatment programs has increased, since they provide an alternative to more costly inpatient hospital stays. In many cases, access to these programs makes hospitalization unnecessary. These programs provide short-term crisis intervention, which can be either an alternative to hospitalization or a transitional setting to shorten hospital stays.

Providing intense, highly structured outpatient treatment, day hospitals and day treatment programs utilize a variety of therapeutic modalities: individual, group, and family therapy (see *Individual Psychotherapy,* page 320, *Group Therapy,* page 328, and *Family Therapy,* page 326); educational and/or vocational therapy; recreation and activity therapy; medical and nursing services; and, in some cases, medications. Such an array of services requires the involvement of an interdisciplinary staff typically drawn from psychiatry, psychology, social work, educational or vocational therapy, occupational or recreational therapy, and nursing.

Day treatment is useful for moderately to severely disturbed teenagers who can be safely managed in less restrictive settings than a hospital or residential care. Some communities have specialized day treatment programs for adolescents with eating disorders, alcohol- and drug-abusing adolescents, and teens with nonpsychiatric conditions such as epilepsy, head trauma, asthma, and sickle-cell disease. Victims of physical and sexual abuse and youngsters with severe emotional and/or behavioral disturbances often do well in these treatment settings.

The goal of these nonresidential programs is to provide treatment for teenagers requiring intensive therapeutic intervention with the least amount of disruption in their normal daily functioning. The evaluation process, however, determines whether the adolescent can be treated safely in a community setting or needs a more restrictive setting such as a hospital or residential treatment center. Youngsters who do well in such open treatment systems usually show a greater ability to control their impulses and comply with program rules.

These open systems rely on family supports and strengths as well as community agencies and programs. Because the adolescent remains in the home, nonresidential treatment encourages the teen and family to maintain higher levels of interaction and more normal functioning than settings that remove the adolescent from the home. Parents, however, must be able to provide adequate control and support at home during evenings and weekends. Techniques that are used in treatment must be used at home. Parents must be receptive to and involved in most treatment strategies and techniques. Parents might also engage in their own therapy and usually must be able to provide transportation for the teenager to the day treatment program.

Treatment is based on a plan developed by a treatment team. An adolescent's progress in treatment is continuously monitored, with changes made to the plan as needed. The length of treatment varies according to diagnosis, severity, and the needs of the youngster and family and on insurance coverage and the managed-care company reviewing the treatment, but discharge planning is an integral part of each adolescent's treatment plan. Before the teenager leaves the treatment milieu for another less intensive treatment setting, there must be a comprehensive plan for aftercare, including plans for continuation of his therapy, schooling, and follow-up.

Hospitalization

Occasionally, because of severe symptoms or a concern for the safety of the adolescent or others, the youngster will require psychiatric treatment in a hospital. Depending on what's available in the community, an adolescent may be admitted to a special unit in a general hospital or to a psychiatric hospital. The goal of inpatient psychiatric treatment is to provide a safe setting for a comprehensive evaluation involving a number of different disciplines and treatments.

Today, psychiatric hospitals tend to provide evaluation, crisis intervention, and crisis stabilization rather than long-term treatment. They are staffed by specialized multidisciplinary treatment teams with child and adolescent psychiatrists, pediatricians, psychologists, social workers, nurses, and teachers, who may also have access to high technology diagnostic testing, including brain imaging, electroencephalography, and chromosomal analysis. Treatment typically includes an individualized mix of group, family, and individual psychotherapies along with medication.

By its very nature, hospital treatment is the most restrictive, taking place in an out-of-home institutional setting. The level of restrictiveness varies among psychiatric hospitals and depends largely on whether the admission is voluntary or involuntary; on whether the unit is locked or unlocked; on policies regarding parent participation (it may be encouraged or discouraged); and on whether visits to the home community are facilitated or prevented.

The average length of stay varies from setting to setting. In many cases, the stay is dictated by diagnostic considerations, the progress of medication therapies, and funding availability or insurance coverage. In some areas, managed care has reduced the availability and utilization of hospital treatment even though the benefit may be included by insurance coverage. At present, the stays are typically defined as up to three days for emergencies; up to fourteen days for acute conditions; up to thirty days for short-term treatment; between one and three months for intermediate treatment; and more than three months for long-term treatment. Managed care has had a profound impact on the use of inpatient care. Fewer children and adolescents are being admitted to hospitals, the length of stays have been decreased, and fewer patients gain access to longer-term treatment.

Hospitalization may be helpful for adolescents with a broad group of disorders, including adjustment disorders, thought disorders, eating disorders, substance-abuse disorders, and pervasive developmental disorders.

Usually psychiatric hospitals separate patients by age. Optimally, adolescents should be separated into middle-school and high-school age grouping. This may not be available, however. Mixing adolescents with adults in psychiatric hospitals is not recommended.

Inpatient treatment includes many different modalities and many different clinicians. Special education programs are also an important aspect of inpatient treatment. A majority of teenagers hospitalized on psychiatric inpatient units have significant cognitive and/or academic difficulties. Identification of these disabilities and the development of remedial teaching strategies can play an important part in an adolescent's progress.

When appropriately and effectively utilized, hospitalization results in safety, stabilization, and a comprehensive understanding of the adolescent's problems, context, and treatment needs. Often the treatment team can then provide linkages with an array of services in the community, such as the school system, day treatment, in-home services, therapeutic foster care, protective services, medical providers, traditional outpatient services, housing resources, and recreation programs. The goal is to enable the youngster to return to his home and community and continue with healthy development.

Residential Treatment

Some adolescents need stable, long-term treatment, especially when their emotional, behavioral, and therapeutic needs are great, and their family and environmental resources are overwhelmed, inadequate, or uncertain. Residential treatment provides stability and intensive therapeutic and remedial interventions in a setting away from home.

Residential treatment typically takes place in a campuslike setting that is not a hospital. It provides individually planned programs of psychiatric services in conjunction with twenty-four-hour-a-day residential care. The professional staff at a residential treatment center may include teachers, social workers, child and adolescent psychiatrists, pediatricians, nurses, and psychologists.

Residential centers offer a setting in which there is space for therapy programs, school, and evening and weekend activity programs. Youngsters live in small groups. Depending on the individual center, teenagers have private or shared bedrooms and communal living and dining rooms. Recreational facilities, classrooms, medical services, and various community resources are usually located nearby.

Each residential center has its own admission process. Most centers are relatively targeted in terms of the type of disorders and age of youngsters they serve.

Residential treatment is often appropriate for adolescents who are out of control. These youngsters lack age-appropriate internal controls and therefore require external controls. Residential treatment is often appropriate for adolescents who have moderately to severely antisocial (delinquent) and aggressive behaviors or psychotic symptoms. (See *Psychotic Disorders*, page 270.) Many teenagers admitted to residential treatment also have severe learning problems.

Children and adolescents with clinical diagnoses of pervasive or specific developmental disorders, attention-deficit/hyperactivity disorder, conduct disorder, depression, bipolar disorder, or severe anxiety disorders may be referred for residential placement. Problems such as organic brain damage, severely disturbed or chaotic families, and impoverished socioeconomic backgrounds may lead a youngster to longer stays in residential treatment. A background that includes parental deprivation, loss, and sexual or physical abuse may also result in residential center placement.

Most adolescents admitted to residential treatment have been through the community mental-health system with little success. They have often been seen by one or more clinicians and been to a child guidance clinic, juvenile court, or state welfare agency. Typically, previous attempts at outpatient treatment and foster home or other custodial placement have not been able to help these adolescents.

Admitting the Adolescent. Admission usually begins with an intensive evaluation process. Information is gathered from previous clinicians and treatment centers. Family and individual interviews, psychological testing, and neurological examinations are conducted when indicated. The needs of the adolescent, the skills and training of the staff, the balance of the youngster's strengths and problems, and the probabilities that the teenager will be helped are some of the variables weighed during the admissions process. Parents may or may not be directly involved in the youngster's treatment, though participation is essential if the teenager will be eventually returning to the family home.

The adolescent's evaluation is usually a collaborative effort of the staff. A treatment program is tailored to meet the teen's needs, and then progress is monitored.

The largest amount of time in the youngster's life—and therefore, the bulk of the therapeutic work—is spent in group living. Behavioral therapy and psychoeducational principles are applied to address such problematic behaviors as temper tantrums, fighting, withdrawal, bedwetting, poor feeding habits, and inadequate peer relations. Teens are involved in intensive individual and group therapy. Some take medication for specific symptoms or disorders. School problems that are rooted in severe learning disabilities and disruptive behavior are routinely assessed and addressed in the school either on campus or in the community.

The goal is improvement in the ability to relate to others and to function in and out of school. Many of the teens have the opportunity to work through certain types of past trauma during this residential phase of treatment. When teenagers leave residential treatment, they may react with feelings of loss and a temporary regression may occur, with heightened acting out and aggressive behavior.

Follow-up after discharge varies. Many residential treatment centers have their own step-down programs, so a teen moves from residential treatment into a day-treatment program or off-grounds school program. Most youngsters eventually return to their families but continue with community and outpatient treatments in order to further consolidate and enhance progress. A smaller group of those unable to return to their families go into group or foster homes, boarding school, further residential treatment, or custodial care.

APPENDICES

APPENDIX A

Psychiatric Medications

Prescription medications have become an important part of treatment for a number of psychiatric disorders in children and adolescents. Medications, however, are seldom used in isolation but as one element of an overall approach. A psychiatric medication should be prescribed for your youngster only after a thorough psychiatric evaluation has been completed. (See *The Psychiatric Evaluation*, page 309.) These medications cannot cure all problems but can be effective treatments for specific troubling symptoms, problem behaviors, or certain psychiatric disorders.

The medication must be part of a comprehensive treatment plan, which usually includes individual or other psychotherapeutic approaches (See *Individual Psychotherapy,* page 320; *Psychodynamic Psychotherapy,* page 322; *Cognitive-Behavioral Therapy,* page 323; *Family Therapy,* page 326; or *Group Therapy*, page 328.) As with other prescription medications, psychiatric medications can only be prescribed by a licensed

physician. Psychiatrists, however, are physicians who are specifically trained in using psychiatric medications, and more specifically, child and adolescent psychiatrists are trained to use these medications in young people.

When a child and adolescent psychiatrist prescribes a medication, both parent and youngster may have concerns and questions: Full explanations should be given for why the medication is being prescribed, what benefits may result, the potential side effects, and other treatment alternatives, if any. (See also *Your Adolescent's Medication: Questions to Ask the Doctor,* page 340.)

Most medications have some side effects. These can range from minor (for example, dry mouth, constipation, or stomach upset) to serious (such as liver inflammation, kidney dysfunction, or changes in heart rhythm). Fortunately, the most common side effects are minor and the serious ones rare. Your adolescent's psychiatrist should discuss these risks with you.

YOUR ADOLESCENT'S MEDICATION
QUESTIONS TO ASK THE DOCTOR

When a medication is prescribed for your child or adolescent, you have a responsibility as a parent to learn as much as you can about the medication. The prescribing psychiatrist will explain to you the expected role the medication is to play in the comprehensive treatment plan and will monitor and evaluate the effectiveness of the drug. The following issues should also be discussed with you and your adolescent.

■ **The Name of the Medication.**
What is the generic name of the medication? The brand name? Are there other brand names by which it is known?

■ **Indications.**
Why is this medicine recommended? Medications are tested in a variety of trials before being marketed. The Food and Drug Administration (FDA) reviews the data and deems them sufficient before permitting drugs to be sold. FDA approval will specify that a given medication has efficacy in treating a given disorder— that is the disorder for which the drug is *indicated.* It is common, however, that a medication is valuable in treating other disorders for which there are no FDA *indications* and, as a result, the medications may be prescribed in such cases. Be aware that most trials are conducted on adults, most often men. Before your adolescent begins taking a medication, discuss its indications with the prescribing physician.

■ **Action of the Medication.**
How does the medication work? How does it affect your adolescent's brain or body to produce the desired emotional, behavioral, or cognitive changes? What is known about its efficacy in other teenagers with similar conditions?

■ **Instructions.**
How is the medication to be taken—before, after, or with meals? With water? How many times per day? Are certain foods or other medications to be avoided while using the prescribed medication? Are there activities that should be avoided while taking it?

■ **Side Effects.**

What are the potential side effects? Are some of them permanent or life-threatening? What should be done if side effects occur? Is the medication potentially addictive?

■ **Laboratory Tests.**

Are any laboratory tests (for example, electrocardiogram or blood test) required prior to the youngster's taking the medication? Are lab tests necessary to monitor the effects of the medication during use?

■ **Drug Interactions.**

If your youngster is also taking medications prescribed by his pediatrician for a common disorder such as acne or asthma, is there a potential problem? Discuss this, too, with your adolescent's psychiatrist.

■ **Follow-Up.**

How often will the adolescent need to see the doctor to determine how the youngster is responding to the medication and whether the dosage should be changed? How long will this medication be necessary?

■ **Cost.**

How much does it cost? Are there less expensive generic brands of the same medication on the market?

Ask these questions *before* your child or adolescent starts taking the medication. If you are not satisfied with all the answers, seek a second opinion.

The Medication Directory

In the pages that follow are individual entries for medications that are commonly prescribed by child and adolescent psychiatrists. The organization is alphabetical; for ease of reference, both brand and generic names are included. Because new products continually arrive on the market, this list cannot be all-inclusive. Nor is the inclusion of a medication in these pages an endorsement.

When a medication is first developed, it is given a **generic** name, approved by government agencies, which identifies it as being different from all others. In this appendix, generic names are listed in **boldface** type.

When a medication is marketed, the maker gives it a proprietary name, its *brand* name. Brand names are listed in *italic* type. Brand names are the exclusive property of the original manufacturer who, for a fixed period, has the sole right to sell that medication under its own brand name. When the patent expires, other drug companies may produce and sell the medication under its generic name or their own brand names. That's why some drugs are available under a variety of names.

When taking any medication, your youngster needs to follow carefully the psychiatrist's instructions regarding administration, dosage, and proper storage. If any side effects occur, consult your pediatrician, psychiatrist, or pharmacist immediately. Always tell your physician about other prescriptions, over-the-counter drugs, and health supplements that your adolescent may be taking. Beneath the entry for each generic name, you will find the medication family to which the medication belongs; the brand names under which it is sold; the common uses and indications; and some of the potential side effects. If you don't see the reason cited that your child is taking a specific medication, ask your doctor. There are occasionally extenuating circumstances for the use of certain medications beyond the typical ones.

■ ■ ■

ADDERALL
> Brand name of the psychostimulant medication dextroamphetamine/amphetamine

ALPRAZOLAM
> *Medication Family:*
> A benzodiazepine antianxiety medication
> *Brand Name:*
> Xanax
> *Common Uses and Indications:*
> Separation anxiety disorder, panic disorder, generalized anxiety
> *Potential Side Effects:*
> Drowsiness, lethargy, dependence, loss of inhibition

AMITRIPTYLINE
> *Medication Family:*
> Tricyclic antidepressant medication
> *Brand Names:*
> Elavil, Endep
> *Common Uses and Indications:*
> Depressive disorders

> *Potential Side Effects:*
> Dry mouth, constipation, cardiovascular changes, dizziness

ANAFRANIL
> Brand name of the tricyclic antidepressant medication clomipramine

ATENOLOL
> *Medication Family:*
> Beta-blocker antihypertensive medication
> *Brand Name:*
> Tenormin
> *Common Uses and Indications:*
> Anxiety, performance anxiety, impulse-control disorders
> *Potential Side Effects:*
> Lethargy, numbness in fingers, decreased heart rate and blood pressure

ATIVAN
> Brand name for the antianxiety medication lorazepam

BENADRYL
Brand name for the antihistamine medication diphenhydramine hydrochloride

BENZTROPINE
Medication Family:
Anticholingeric
Brand Name:
Cogentin
Common Uses and Indications:
Control of muscular spasms and other side effects of certain antipsychotic medications
Potential Side Effects:
Increased heart rate, constipation, dry mouth, confusion, blurred vision

BUPROPION
Medication Family:
Antidepressant medication
Brand Names:
Wellbutrin, Zyban
Common Uses and Indications:
Major depression, attention-deficit/hyperactivity disorder, smoking cessation
Potential Side Effects:
Appetite reduction, nausea, sleeplessness, dry mouth, constipation; rarely, seizures, dizziness

BUSPAR
Brand name of the antianxiety medication buspirone

BUSPIRONE
Medication Family:
Antianxiety medication
Brand Name:
BuSpar
Common Uses and Indications:
Anxiety, extreme anger

Potential Side Effects:
Nausea, headache

CALAN
Brand name for the calcium-channel-blocker antihypertensive medication verapamil hydrochloride

CARBAMAZEPINE
Medication Family:
Anticonvulsant medication
Brand Name:
Tegretol
Common Uses and Indications:
Major depression, bipolar disorder, impulse-control disorder
Potential Side Effects:
Double vision, nausea, drowsiness, poor coordination, reduced white blood cell count

CATAPRES
Brand name for the antihypertensive medication clonidine

CHLORPROMAZINE
Medication Family:
Antipsychotic medication
Brand Name:
Thorazine
Common Uses and Indications:
Schizophrenia, psychotic symptoms, agitation
Potential Side Effects:
Drowsiness, dry mouth, constipation, weight gain, blurred vision, muscle spasms, restlessness, involuntary movements, tremors, blood pressure changes

CLOMIPRAMINE
Medication Family:
Tricyclic antidepressant medication

Brand Name:
Anafranil
Common Uses and Indications:
Obsessive-compulsive disorder
Potential Side Effects:
Drowsiness, headache, dry mouth, constipation, stomach upset, excess sweating, tremor, cardiovascular and blood pressure effects, weight gain

CLONAZEPAM

Medication Family:
Antianxiety medication, anticonvulsant
Brand Name:
Klonopin
Common Uses and Indications:
Anxiety, panic disorder, separation anxiety, seizures
Potential Side Effects:
Drowsiness, irritability, dependence, lethargy, diminished inhibitions

CLONIDINE

Medication Family:
Antihypertensive medication
Brand Name:
Catapres
Common Uses and Indications:
Attention-deficit/hyperactivity disorder, Tourette's disorder
Potential Side Effects:
Drowsiness, cardiovascular and blood pressure changes, stomach upset, depression

CLOZAPINE

Medication Family:
Antipsychotic medication
Brand Name:
Clozaril
Common Uses and Indications:
Schizophrenia and bipolar disorder
Potential Side Effects:
Drowsiness, exaggerated salivation, constipation, weight gain, nausea, dizziness, decreased white blood cell count, seizures

CLOZARIL

Brand name of the antipsychotic medication clozapine

COGENTIN

Brand name of the anticholingeric medication benztropine

CYLERT

Brand name of the psychostimulant medication pemoline

DALMANE

Brand name of the sedative/hypnotic flurazepam

DDAVP

Brand name of the analogue of antidiuretic hormone desmopressin

DEPAKENE

Brand name of the anticonvulsant medication valproic acid

DEPAKOTE

Brand name of the anticonvulsant medication valproic acid

DEPRENYL

Brand name of the selective monoamine oxidase inhibitor selegiline

DESIPRAMINE

Medication Family:
Tricyclic antidepressant medication
Brand Name:
Norpramin
Common Uses and Indications:
Depression, attention-deficit/hyperactivity disorder

Potential Side Effects:
Drowsiness, dry mouth, blood pressure and cardiovascular effects, weight gain, constipation, blurred vision

DESMOPRESSIN
Medication Family:
Synthetic antidiuretic hormone
Brand Name:
DDAVP
Common Uses and Indications:
Enuresis (bedwetting)
Potential Side Effects:
Nasal dryness, headaches

DESYREL
Brand name of the antidepressant medication trazodone

DEXEDRINE
Brand name of the psychostimulant dextroamphetamine

DEXTROAMPHETAMINE
Medication Family:
Psychostimulant medication
Brand Name:
Dexedrine
Common Uses and Indications:
Attention-deficit/hyperactivity disorder
Potential Side Effects:
Appetite reduction, sleeplessness, irritability, weepiness, increased heart rate, decreased growth rate

DEXTROAMPHETAMINE/AMPHETAMINE
Medication Family:
Psychostimulant medication
Brand Name:
Adderall
Common Uses and Indications:
Attention-deficit/hyperactivity disorder

Potential Side Effects:
Appetite reduction, sleeplessness, irritability, weepiness, increased heart rate, decreased growth rate

DIAZEPAM
Medication Family:
A benzodiazepine antianxiety medication
Brand Name:
Valium
Common Uses and Indications:
Anxiety, night terrors
Potential Side Effects:
Drowsiness, reduced inhibitions, dependence, lethargy

DILANTIN
Brand name of the anticonvulsant medication phenytoin

DIPHENHYDRAMINE HYDROCHLORIDE
Medication Family:
Antihistamine
Brand Name:
Benadryl
Common Uses and Indications:
Sedation, control of side effects of antipsychotic medications
Potential Side Effects:
Drowsiness, rash, decreased blood pressure, unsteadiness, gastrointestinal disturbances

DOXEPIN
Medication Family:
Tricyclic antidepressant medication
Brand Name:
Sinequan
Common Uses and Indications:
Major depression
Potential Side Effects:
Dry mouth, constipation, dizziness, cardiovascular changes

EFFEXOR
>Brand name of the antidepressant medication venlafaxine

ELAVIL
>Brand name of the tricyclic antidepressant medication amitriptyline

ENDEP
>Brand name of the tricyclic antidepressant medication amitriptyline

ESKALITH
>Brand name of the mood stabilizer lithium

FLUOXETINE
>*Medication Family:*
>>A selective serotonin reuptake inhibitor antidepressant medication
>
>*Brand Name:*
>>Prozac
>
>*Common Uses and Indications:*
>>Obsessive-compulsive disorder, major depression, eating disorders
>
>*Potential Side Effects:*
>>Nausea, diarrhea, upset stomach, appetite change, sleeplessness, drowsiness, jitteriness, excess sweating

FLUPHENAZINE
>*Medication Family:*
>>An antipsychotic medication
>
>*Brand Name:*
>>Prolixin
>
>*Common Uses and Indications:*
>>Psychotic symptoms, schizophrenia, Tourette's and similar conditions
>
>*Potential Side Effects:*
>>Drowsiness, restlessness, muscular rigidity, tremor, blurred vision, constipation, dry mouth, involuntary movements, blood pressure changes, weight grain

FLURAZEPAM
>*Medication Family:*
>>Sedative/hypnotic
>
>*Brand Name:*
>>Dalmane
>
>*Common Uses and Indications:*
>>Insomnia
>
>*Potential Side Effects:*
>>Drowsiness, dizziness, dependence

FLUVOXAMINE
>*Medication Family:*
>>A selective serotonin reuptake inhibitor antidepressant medication
>
>*Brand Name:*
>>Luvox
>
>*Common Uses and Indications:*
>>Depression, obsessive-compulsive disorder
>
>*Potential Side Effects:*
>>Nausea, diarrhea, sleeplessness, jitteriness, stomach upset, excess sweating

GUANFACINE
>*Medication Family:*
>>An antihypertensive medication
>
>*Brand Name:*
>>Tenex
>
>*Common Uses and Indications:*
>>Attention-deficit/hyperactivity disorder
>
>*Potential Side Effects:*
>>Drowsiness, headache, dry mouth, constipation, nausea, cardiovascular and blood pressure changes

HALDOL
>Brand name of the antipsychotic drug haloperidol

HALOPERIDOL
>*Medication Family:*
>>Antipsychotic medication

Brand Name:
  Haldol
Common Uses and Indications:
  Schizophrenia, psychotic symptoms, Tourette's disorder
Potential Side Effects:
  Drowsiness, muscle rigidity or tremor, restlessness, dry mouth, blurred vision, constipation, involuntary movements, weight gain

IMIPRAMINE
Medication Family:
  Tricyclic antidepressant medication
Brand Name:
  Tofranil
Common Uses and Indications:
  Attention-deficit/hyperactivity disorder, major depression, panic disorder, separation anxiety disorder, enuresis (bedwetting)
Potential Side Effects:
  Dry mouth, drowsiness, blood pressure and cardiovascular effects, constipation, blurred vision

INDERAL
  Brand name of the beta-blocker propranolol

KLONOPIN
  Brand name of the benzodiazepine medication clonazepam

LITHIUM
Medication Family:
  Mood stabilizer medication
Brand Names:
  Eskalith, Lithobid
Common Uses and Indications:
  Bipolar disorder, extreme anger, major depression

Potential Side Effects:
  Nausea, vomiting, sedation, diarrhea, weight gain, tremor, acne, increased urination, thirst, decreased concentration, kidney dysfunction, hypothyroidism

LITHOBID
  Brand name of the mood stabilizer medication lithium

LORAZEPAM
Medication Family:
  Antianxiety medication
Brand Name:
  Ativan
Common Uses and Indications:
  Anxiety, agitation, insomnia
Potential Side Effects:
  Drowsiness, dizziness, unsteadiness, diminished inhibition, dependence, diminished concentration

LUVOX
  Brand name of the selective serotonin reuptake inhibitor medication fluvoxamine

MELLARIL
  Brand name of the antipsychotic medication thioridazine

METHYLPHENIDATE
Medication Family:
  Psychostimulant medication
Brand Name:
  Ritalin
Common Uses and Indications:
  Attention-deficit/hyperactivity disorder, impulsivity
Potential Side Effects:
  Appetite reduction, nausea, sleeplessness,

headaches, weepiness, increased heart rate, decrease in growth rate

MOBAN

Brand name of the antipsychotic medication molindone

MOLINDONE

Medication Family:
Antipsychotic medication
Brand Name:
Moban
Common Uses and Indications:
Schizophrenia, psychotic symptoms
Potential Side Effects:
Drowsiness, muscle rigidity or tremor, restlessness, dry mouth, blurred vision, constipation, involuntary movements, blood pressure changes, weight gain

NARDIL

Brand name of the monoamine oxidase inhibitor antidepressant medication phenelzine

NAVANE

Brand name of the antipsychotic medication thiothixene

NEFAZODONE HYDROCHLORIDE

Medication Family:
Antidepressant
Brand Name:
Serzone
Common Uses and Indications:
Major depression
Potential Side Effects:
Decreased blood pressure, headache, dry mouth, nausea, drowsiness

NORPRAMIN

Brand name of the tricyclic antidepressant medication desipramine

NORTRIPTYLINE

Medication Family:
Tricyclic antidepressant medication
Brand Names:
Pamelor
Common Uses and Indications:
Attention-deficit/hyperactivity disorder, major depression, panic disorder
Potential Side Effects:
Drowsiness, dry mouth, blood pressure and cardiac effects

OLANZAPINE

Medication Family:
Antipsychotic medication
Brand Name:
Zyprexa
Common Uses and Indications:
Schizophrenia, psychotic symptoms
Potential Side Effects:
Drowsiness, weight gain, cardiovascular and blood pressure changes, dry mouth, blurred vision, constipation, muscle spasms or rigidity, tremor

ORAP

Brand name for the antipsychotic medication pimozide

PAMELOR

Brand name of the tricyclic antidepressant medication nortriptyline

PARNATE

Brand name of the monoamine oxidase inhibitor antidepressant tranylcypromine

PAROXETINE

Medication Family:
A selective serotonin reuptake inhibitor antidepressant medication
Brand Name:
Paxil

Common Uses and Indications:
  Major depression, obsessive-compulsive disorder
Potential Side Effects:
  Nausea, diarrhea, appetite changes, stomach upset, sleeplessness, jitteriness, excess sweating, dry mouth

PAXIL
  Brand name of the selective serotonin reuptake inhibitor paroxetine

PEMOLINE
  Medication Family:
    Psychostimulant medication
  Brand Name:
    Cylert
  Common Uses and Indications:
    Attention-deficit/hyperactivity disorder
  Potential Side Effects:
    Appetite reduction, nausea, sleeplessness, decreased growth rate, irritability, increased heart rate, headaches, liver inflammation

PERPHENAZINE
  Medication Family:
    Antipsychotic medication
  Brand Name:
    Trilafon
  Common Uses and Indications:
    Schizophrenia, psychotic symptoms
  Potential Side Effects:
    Drowsiness, tremor, muscle rigidity, restlessness, dry mouth, blurred vision, constipation, blood pressure changes

PHENELZINE
  Medication Family:
    Monoamine oxidase inhibitor antidepressant medication
  Brand Name:
    Nardil

Common Uses and Indications:
  Depression
Potential Side Effects:
  Lowered blood pressure, weight gain, dizziness, high blood pressure after eating foods containing tyramine

PHENYTOIN
  Medication Family:
    Anticonvulsant
  Brand Name:
    Dilantin
  Common Uses and Indications:
    Seizure disorders
  Potential Side Effects:
    Balance and coordination problem, confusion, slurred speech, nausea, gum and other dental problems

PIMOZIDE
  Medication Family:
    Antipsychotic medication
  Brand Name:
    Orap
  Common Uses and Indications:
    Tourette's disorder
  Potential Side Effects:
    Drowsiness, muscle rigidity, tremor, restlessness, dry mouth, blurred vision, constipation, cardiovascular and blood pressure changes, involuntary movements

PROLIXEN
  Brand name of the antipsychotic fluphenazine

PROPRANOLOL
  Medication Family:
    Beta-blocker antianxiety and antihypertensive medication

Brand Name:
Inderal

Common Uses and Indications:
Anxiety, performance anxiety, impulse-control disorders, migraine

Potential Side Effects:
Lethargy, depression, decreased heart rate, decreased blood pressure, wheezing

PROZAC
Brand name of the selective serotonin reuptake inhibitor fluoxetine

RISPERDAL
Brand name for the antipsychotic risperidone

RISPERIDONE
Medication Family:
Antipsychotic medication

Brand Name:
Risperdal

Common Uses and Indications:
Schizophrenia, psychotic symptoms, impulse-control disorders

Potential Side Effects:
Drowsiness, restlessness, weight gain, muscle rigidity, decreased blood pressure, diminished concentration, dry mouth, constipation, blurred vision, involuntary movements

RITALIN
Brand name for the psychostimulant methylphenidate

SERTRALINE
Medication Family:
A selective serotonin reuptake inhibitor antidepressant medication

Brand Name:
Zoloft

Common Uses and Indications:
Major depression, obsessive-compulsive disorder, panic disorder

Potential Side Effects:
Nausea, diarrhea, stomach upset, sleeplessness, jitteriness, excess sweating, drowsiness

SERZONE
Brand name of the antidepressant medication nefazodone hydrochloride

SINEQUAN
Brand name of the tricyclic antidepressant medication doxepin

STELAZINE
Brand name of the antipsychotic medication trifluoperazine

TEGRETOL
Brand name of the anticonvulsant medication carbamazepine

TENEX
Brand name for the antihypertensive guanfacine

TENORMIN
Brand name for the beta-blocker atenolol

THIORIDAZINE
Medication Family:
Antipsychotic medication

Brand Name:
Mellaril

Common Uses and Indications:
Schizophrenia, psychotic symptoms, impulse-control disorders

Potential Side Effects:
Drowsiness, dry mouth, constipation, weight gain, blurred vision, muscle rigidity, restlessness, blood pressure changes, weight gain, involuntary movements

THIOTHIXENE
Medication Family:
Antipsychotic medication
Brand Name:
Navane
Common Uses and Indications:
Schizophrenia, psychotic symptoms
Potential Side Effects:
Drowsiness, dry mouth, blurred vision, constipation, muscle rigidity, restlessness, blood pressure changes, weight gain, involuntary movements

THORAZINE
Brand name of the antipsychotic chlorpromazine

TOFRANIL
Brand name of the tricyclic antidepressant medication imipramine

TRANYLCYPROMINE
Medication Family:
Monoamine oxidase inhibitor antidepressant medication
Brand Name:
Parnate
Common Uses and Indications:
Major depression
Potential Side Effects:
Decreased blood pressure, dizziness, elevated blood pressure after eating foods containing tyramine, restlessness, jitteriness

TRAZODONE
Medication Family:
Antidepressant medication
Brand Name:
Desyrel
Common Uses and Indications:
Depression, insomnia

Potential Side Effects:
Drowsiness, persistent penile erections, blood pressure changes

TRIFLUOPERAZINE
Medication Family:
Antipsychotic medication
Brand Name:
Stelazine
Common Uses and Indications:
Schizophrenia, psychotic symptoms
Potential Side Effects:
Drowsiness, dry mouth, blurred vision, constipation, muscle rigidity, restlessness, blood pressure change, weight gain, involuntary movements

TRILAFON
Brand name of the antipsychotic perphenazine

VALIUM
Brand name of the benzodiazepine diazepam

VALPROIC ACID
Medication Family:
Anticonvulsant medication
Brand Names:
Depakene, Depakote
Common Uses and Indications:
Bipolar disorder, major depression
Potential Side Effects:
Stomach upset, vomiting, nausea, weight gain, drowsiness, tremor, liver toxicity

VENLAFAXINE
Medication Family:
Antidepressant medication
Brand Name:
Effexor

Common Uses and Indications:
Major depression, obsessive-compulsive disorder

Potential Side Effects:
Drowsiness, dry mouth, nausea, excess sweating, constipation, blurred vision, elevated blood pressure, decreased appetite, tremor

VERAPAMIL HYDROCHLORIDE

Medication Family:
Calcium-channel-blocker antihypertensive

Brand Name:
Calan

Common Uses and Indications:
Bipolar disorder, hypertension

Potential Side Effects:
Constipation, low blood pressure, headache, dizziness, fatigue

WELLBUTRIN
Brand name of the antidepressant medication bupropion

XANAX
Brand name of the benzodiazepine alprazolam

ZOLOFT
Brand name of the selective serotonin reuptake inhibitor sertraline

ZYPREXA
Brand name of the antipsychotic medication olanzapine

APPENDIX B

Medical, Psychological, Educational, and Developmental Tests

In arriving at a diagnosis, your adolescent's physician, child and adolescent psychiatrist, or other clinician may require specialized information about your youngster. In addition to talking to you, examining your teenager, and obtaining a range of information about your youngster's symptoms, behavior, and development, the clinician may order one or more diagnostic tests.

The nature of testing will vary according to specific symptoms. If a physician suspects lead poisoning, a blood test may be conducted to determine the serum level of lead. Specialized tests such as the Continuous Performance Test may be done to evaluate a youngster's ability to concentrate on specific tasks, which can be useful in diagnosing attention-deficit/hyperactivity disorder. Intelligence and developmental tests may be conducted to evaluate an adolescent's intellectual, speech, motor, and other areas of development.

In the pages that follow, the diagnostic tests most commonly used in evaluating cognitive, behavioral, and developmental problems in children and adolescents are discussed.

Medical Tests

A wide range of medical tests is routinely used by medical professionals to help diagnose—and often to rule out—many disorders, both psychiatric and physiological. This appendix does not attempt, however, to cover the full catalog of medical tests but only those that are most commonly used by the child and adolescent psychiatrist seeking to diagnose psychiatric disorders.

Blood Tests Blood tests are conducted to identify the presence of certain conditions. A blood sample can be examined in multiple ways. Some tests measure the levels of the different types of blood cells; others seek to identify enzymes, toxins, or certain chemicals in the blood. The volume of blood required for some blood tests is as small as a few drops, in which case a small prick of a fingertip will produce the required amount. For other studies, a larger amount of blood is required, in which case a thin needle inserted into an arm vein will allow the blood to be withdrawn into a syringe. While this is a bit painful, a skilled technician can help the patient relax and make the procedure as easy as possible.

THE COMPLETE BLOOD COUNT (or CBC) is the most commonly conducted blood test. Most often done as part of a complete checkup, the CBC measures the amount of hemoglobin in the blood, as well as the red blood cells (*hematocrit*), the number and types of white blood cells, and the platelets (which help in clotting the blood) in a given sample. The CBC can be used to monitor the side effects of certain medications.

BLOOD SERUM CHEMISTRY TESTS measure the amounts of sodium, potassium, chloride, and phosphorus (the electrolytes) in the blood; blood sugar (glucose); and a variety of enzymes and chemical by-products produced by the body. Some blood serum chemistry examinations may also be done to monitor the possible side effects of some medications on kidney and liver function.

THYROID FUNCTION may be ascertained by drawing blood to measure serum levels of hormones such as thyroxine and thyroid-stimulating hormone. These tests can be used in evaluating certain mood disorders and the possible side effects of some medications.

CHROMOSOMAL ANALYSIS may be done to evaluate for genetic disorders such as Down's Syndrome and Fragile-X Syndrome.

SCREENING TESTS may be conducted to identify antistreptococcal antibodies, mononucleosis, or Human Immunodeficiency Virus (HIV), each of which can be a factor in certain emotional or behavioral problems. A screening test may also be done to identify elevated levels of lead in the blood, which may be linked to attention-deficit/hyperactivity disorder.

MEDICATION LEVELS can be measured in monitoring correct dosages of medications such as lithium, carbamazepine, depakote, and certain antidepressants.

SERUM TOXICOLOGY studies may be ordered to identify the presence of unknown drugs, alcohol, or other chemicals in the body, which can help explain sudden behavior changes or toxic delirium or confirm substance abuse.

Urine Tests Urine tests are a routine part of a comprehensive health examination. Your adolescent's physician will usually order a urinalysis at your youngster's periodic checkups, typically testing for protein and levels of sugar (glucose) as well as a microscopic examination of the sediment in the urine. All your youngster needs to do is provide a small amount of urine in a cup, which is then sealed in a special container, labeled, and sent to a laboratory for testing.

When treating certain psychiatric disorders, there are two other circumstances when urine tests may be appropriate. Some medications, including certain mood stabilizers and antidepressants, may on rare occasions damage the kidneys, so the child and adolescent psychiatrist or other physician may conduct a *routine urinalysis* to monitor kidney function. If substance abuse is suspected, a *urine drug screen* may be ordered to test for the use of drugs. Some substances, such as marijuana, may appear in the urine for several days or weeks after use, depending on the amount of substance ingested. Finally, female adolescents may require a urine *pregnancy test*. Pregnancy can also be determined by a blood test.

Imaging Tests   For decades, doctors have been employing *X-ray* examination to view the internal structures of the body. The technology has proven its worth countless times in diagnosing injuries and disorders of the skeleton, the teeth, and a variety of internal organs. Recently, new types of procedures such as *computerized tomography* (CT scanning) and *magnetic resonance imaging* (MRI) have added to the range of choices your physician has in seeking to understand the anatomy within the body. For the child and adolescent psychiatrist, too, each of these imaging techniques has a number of uses.

X rays, CT scans, and MRIs each involve immobilizing the patient on a specially designed table, while the X rays or electromagnetic energy are used to create an image. The X ray takes only a few seconds to complete, while the MRI and CT scan may require an hour or more. Other than the discomfort of being still for a period of time, which can sometimes be frustrating for youngsters, none of these examinations results in pain for the adolescent.

The Skull X Ray.   The skull X ray can be an invaluable tool for evaluating certain conditions that may affect your emotions or behavior.

The film image produced can be examined ("read") for evidence of abnormalities or to investigate for skull fractures. The skull X ray can be particularly useful in cases of trauma and physical abuse.

CT Scans and Magnetic Resonance Imaging.   As with the traditional X ray, the CT scan employs an X-ray beam that passes through the body. In the case of computerized tomography, the beam is then processed by a computer to produce an image. The CT scan is many times more detailed than an X ray.

The MRI is also used to generate a picture of the body's internal structure, but unlike the X ray, the MRI employs electromagnetic energy to provide image information. No ionizing radiation is required, as with conventional X rays and CT scans.

The greater sensitivity of both the MRI and the CT scan means they are valuable in providing images of soft tissues, the heart, and the blood vessels, as well as the brain. For the child and adolescent psychiatrist, these scanning technologies can be useful in examining for structural changes in the brain that can produce certain emotional and behavioral changes.

Electrical Tests   The human body has its own complex circuitry, and devices have been developed that record electrical activity in the heart and brain. When these recordings are examined, they may reveal a wide variety of symptoms or abnormalities, some of which may prove to be valuable diagnostic clues.

Electrocardiograph.   The EKG or ECG records electrical currents in the heart. The pattern of electrical impulses that is produced can then be examined in detail. For the child and adolescent psychiatrist, an EKG may be used to monitor the side effects of medications that can affect cardiac function. The EKG procedure involves the attachment of electrodes to the chest, wrist, and ankles that record the electrical activity in the heart. Typically about fifteen minutes are required for an EKG, which is painless.

Electroencephalograph. The EEG measures and records the patterns of electrical activity that are produced by the brain and is used typically to identify possible seizure disorders. Electrodes will be attached to the adolescent's scalp using a special glue. The electrodes will then detect the electrical activity of the brain, which can be recorded as a "brain wave" on a moving sheet of paper. Typically the test requires only about half an hour. Often the adolescent is given a mild sedative to evaluate patterns of brain activity during sleep. If an unusual seizure disorder or a sleep disorder is suspected, the electrodes may be left in place overnight.

To alleviate anxiety about any of these tests, it may be helpful to discuss them with your teenager prior to the scheduled test so that the youngster has an opportunity to ask you any questions. If you do not have all the answers, encourage your teen to pose the questions to the technician or physician on the day of the test.

Psychological, Educational, and Developmental Tests

Many psychological, educational, and developmental tests are in general use. Some are regularly employed in educational settings, so virtually every adolescent will at one time or another take an achievement test in a school setting. Other tests are used either to identify disorders or to explain abnormalities in behavior or development. Thus, when a psychiatric disorder is suspected, one or more developmental tests, adaptive functioning assessments, or personality or neuropsychological tests may be utilized, as well as screening tools to assess problems with paying attention.

Standardized psychological testing constitutes an important complement to more informal clinical interview techniques. Because most psychological tests were developed using large samples of youngsters, and because the same procedures are used for all individuals being tested, these psychological tests allow for quantitative comparisons between the performances of specific adolescents and their peers. Specialized tests are recommended for youngsters for whom English is a second language.

Psychological testing usually proceeds from a comprehensive examination of such major areas as verbal and visual-spatial skills to more specialized testing of specific problem areas (such as with paying attention, memory, or receptive and expressive language). This process ensures that no deficits are missed and that specific problems are examined closely. Each adolescent's unique strengths are identified, and specific recommendations for intervention made.

Intelligence Tests. Intelligence tests are designed to measure a youngster's cognitive capabilities. Generally, these tests evaluate the youngster's capacity to act purposefully, to think rationally, and to deal effectively with the environment. By using such tests, professionals can identify strengths and weaknesses in such areas as comprehension, attention span, math ability, verbal ability, and spatial reasoning. If specific deficits are identified, additional tests of language, memory, spatial perception, or motor functioning may be conducted. In conjunction with achievement tests, intelligence tests are used to identify learning disabilities. When mental retardation is suspected, intelligence tests and measures of adaptive functioning are employed. Only very low or very high scores are interpreted as indicating significant delays or giftedness. While there are a number of widely used intelligence tests, the most commonly used in testing adolescents is the *Wechsler Intelligence Scale for Children—Third Edition* (WISC-III), which is designed for youngsters six to sixteen years of age. For older teenagers and young adults (the recommended age range is seventeen to seventy-four), the test commonly administered is the *Wechsler Adult Intelligence Scale—Revised* (WAIS-RC).

Academic Achievement Tests. These tests are used to assess the student's learning potential and the degree to which an adolescent has acquired knowledge compared to other youngsters in the same grade and of the same age. Academic achievement tests are standardized, so they measure school achievement without the potential subjectivity of the teachers. They can be useful in identifying specific learning disorders and academic problems.

One commonly used achievement test today is the *Woodcock-Johnson Psycho-Educational Battery (Revised)*. This battery evaluates primarily school-age youngsters' progress in reading, writing, and arithmetic. The subjects of science, social studies, and the humanities, however, can be assessed as well. The *Wechler Individual Achievement Test* (WIAS) has a recently developed achievement counterpart to the WISC-III. Less common achievement batteries include the *Wide Range Achievement Test—Third Edition* (WRAT–3) and the *Kaufman Test of Educational Achievement* (K-TEA).

Personality Tests. Personality is the collection of qualities and characteristics that make a person a distinct individual. It represents a pattern of cognitive, affective, and overt behavioral traits that persist over extended periods of time. Personality testing may play an important part in diagnosing such mental illnesses as psychotic, anxiety, or depressive disorders. In addition, they can also be helpful in evaluating an adolescent at risk for suicide, interpersonal conflicts, and adjustment difficulties.

Personality tests seek to discover important psychological themes or issues that may not be readily apparent in clinical interviews or other tests. In most projective tests, the adolescent is presented with an ambiguous picture, a situation, or an incomplete scenario and is asked to respond to it. Though there are certain guidelines for each test, it is important for the adolescent to free associate. The expectation is the teenager will perceive and interpret the ambiguous stimulus and, in doing so, will reveal interpersonal conflicts, defense mechanisms, and underlying anxieties, as well as the capacity to cope realistically with the environment. In other words, the adolescent's conscious or unconscious thoughts reveal his or her way of coping with reality.

Among the many personality tests used with adolescents are the *Roberts Apperception Test for Children* and the *Rorschach Test,* in which youngsters are asked to respond to inkblots. Other tests used to gain information include the *Draw-a-Person* and the *Kinetic Family Drawing.*

Neuropsychological Testing. These sophisticated tests are used to identify the presence of brain damage in adolescents and to determine the extent and even the location of the brain damage. The tests can be used both to diagnose the nature of the brain dysfunction and to direct rehabilitation strategies. The two neuropsychological tests in common use are the *Halstead-Reitan Battery* and the *Luria-Nebraska Neuropsychological Battery (Children's Revision)*.

Other Tests. There are a number of other instruments that are used in evaluating an adolescent. For those who appear to have attention difficulties, such as youngsters with attention-deficit/hyperactivity disorder, the tests include the *Connors' Continuous Performance Test* (CPT) and the *Test of Variables of Attention* (TOVA). When hearing problems are suspected, as may be the case with certain behavioral or learning problems, an *audiological evaluation* or hearing test may be done, either in the pediatrician's office or by an audiologist. Speech and language problems may be evaluated and appropriate therapies designed using such tests as the *Peabody Picture Vocabulary Test* (PPVT), the *Expressive One Word Picture Vocabulary Test* (EOWPVT), and the *Test of Language Competence* (TLC). These tests are usually performed by a speech pathologist.

Rating Forms and Questionnaires. Various surveys may be used to assist with making diagnoses and/or following progress during treatment. These surveys may be completed by the adolescent, the parents, or others involved with the teenager, such as teachers. Many rating scales are available, some of them very specific for what they evaluate (for example, the *Beck Depression Index*). When assistance is needed to evaluate difficulties in paying attention in the adolescent, there are different forms and rating scales used by parents, teachers, and professionals. If there are concerns about anxiety, the *Revised Children's Manifest Anxiety Scale* (RCMAS) is often used. There are other more general scales as well.

One commonly used test is the *Child Behavior Checklist* (CBCL), in which parents or teachers are asked to rate a very wide variety of specific behaviors for a particular teenager. The pattern of responses may then be compared to the standards for the questionnaire to help determine types and seriousness of the problems. Other rating forms document the seriousness of certain disorders, such as depression, ADHD, or obsessive-compulsive disorder.

Glossary

Medicine in general and psychiatry in particular make use of technical terms that enable the clinician to identify the symptoms, progress, and other aspects of a patient's health or disorder.

In this book, we have attempted to keep such terms to a minimum, introducing psychiatric and medical terminology only for reasons of specificity or because you, as a parent, will encounter them in discussing your youngster's status with his child and adolescent psychiatrist or other professional clinician. The definitions in the following pages are brief and intended to be immediately useful rather than all-inclusive. Particularly when your concern is specific disorders, refer to the main text of the book for comprehensive discussions.

■ ■ ■

Acute. Of short duration or rapid onset.

ADHD. See *Attention-Deficit/Hyperactivity Disorder.*

Affect. Feelings; observable aspects of an emotional state, such as sadness, anger, or euphoria.

Aggression. Forceful action against another person, which may be physical, verbal, or symbolic, and is meant to cause pain. Such behavior may be hostile or destructive or it may be for self-protection.

Allergen. Agents, such as pollen particles, dust mites, certain foods, inhalants, and drugs, which may cause an allergic reaction.

Anorexia nervosa. Potentially life-threatening eating disorder involving the loss of weight at least 20 percent below minimal normal levels.

Antidepressant. Medication used to treat depression.

Anxiety. Feeling of nervousness, apprehensiveness, fear, or dread.

Anxiolytic. Medication used to treat anxiety.

Articulation disorder. Inability or delay in producing speech appropriate to age and dialect, such as when sounds are omitted, distorted, or substituted, as in saying *w* for *r* and *f* for *th.*

Asperger's disorder. Pervasive disorder of development characterized by seriously impaired social interactions and repetitive behaviors, interests, and activities. Asperger's disorder resembles autism, but language development is less affected in children with Asperger's disorder.

Asthma. Disease of the respiratory system characterized by increased responsiveness to stimuli, including pollens, air pollutants, and *allergens,* in which the smaller bronchial airways constrict, causing wheezing and shortness of breath.

Attention-Deficit/Hyperactivity Disorder (ADHD). Disorder characterized by impulsivity, distractibility, inattention, and sometimes excessive activity.

Autism. Pervasive disorder of development that affects socialization, speech, and thinking.

Autonomy. Independent control over one's actions. This term is used to describe the emerging behaviors of children around age two, who have just learned to walk and talk.

Avoidant disorders. Social anxiety, characterized by an adolescent's avoidance of or failure to seek contact with others.

Behavioral. Relating to how a person acts.

Behavioral therapy. See *Cognitive-Behavioral therapy.*

Behavior modification. Method of treatment used to help children and adolescents change behaviors by rewarding desired behaviors and establishing consequences for undesirable ones.

Bipolar mood disorder. Mood disorder characterized by cycles of depression and mania (excitement).

Birth order. Sequence in which siblings are born within a family.

Body image. Perception an individual has of his or her own body, which may include size, shape, and attractiveness.

Bonding. Sense of connection (attachment) between parents and babies that forms the foundation of the parent-child relationship.

Brief reactive psychosis. Short episode of severely disturbed thinking, with loss of contact with reality, in response to a stressful event.

Bulimia nervosa. Eating disorder involving repeated episodes of binge eating and purging.

Catatonia. Condition in which a person is unresponsive, immobile, sometimes with rigid muscles, and unable to talk. Catatonia may be seen in schizophrenia or mood disorders.

Cerebral palsy. Disorder resulting from damage to the central nervous system before, during, or shortly after birth. *Spastic* cerebral palsy is characterized by constant muscle contraction and rigidity. *Nonspastic* cerebral palsy involves various types of involuntary muscle movements.

Child abuse. Pattern of behavior in which an adult beats, batters, sexually molests, exploits, or neglects a child or adolescent.

Child and adolescent psychiatrist. Physician whose education after medical school includes at least three years of specialty training in psychiatry plus two additional years of advanced training with children, adolescents, and families.

Childhood trauma. Horrible, often life-threatening events experienced during childhood or adolescence, frequently causing stress reactions.

Chronic disease. Disease of long duration, often of slow progression, which may wax or wane over time.

Closed head injury. Injury in which brain tissue remains within the skull but that may lead to brain bruising, swelling, and irreversible damage.

Cognition. Process of thinking characterized by awareness with perception, reasoning, judgment, intuition, and memory.

Cognitive-Behavioral therapy. Method of psychotherapy used to decrease symptoms of depression and anxiety by examining negative thoughts and ideas associated with these feelings and resulting behavioral changes.

Conduct disorders. Disorder in which behavior exceeds normal range and is socially destructive, such as fighting, stealing, lying, arson, truancy, running away from home, or exploitative actions.

Conflict. Psychic tension that occurs as a result of opposing forces, desires, or needs.

Corporal punishment. Physical punishment such as spanking.

Date rape. Sexual relations between partners known to each other but to which one party has not consented.

Delinquency. Antisocial, immoral, and illegal actions committed by minors.

Delusion. False and perhaps bizarre belief that cannot be changed by logical arguments or evidence.

Depression. Emotional state or mood characterized by sadness, despair, and loss of interest in usual activities.

Diabetes mellitus. Disorder of carbohydrate metabolism due to a decrease in insulin production that results in increased sugar in the blood and urine.

Diagnosis. The name of a disease or syndrome.

Disorder of written expression. Specific learning disability involving written language and fine motor coordination, problems with visual memory, slowness in finding the correct word, spatial disorganization, and inability to arrange thoughts.

Dissociation. Involuntary mental and emotional distance or separation from events, resembling a self-hypnotic state.

Down's syndrome. Congenital disorder usually caused by an extra chromosome in the twenty-first pair, and characterized by mental retardation and a distinct physical appearance.

Dysfunction. Inadequate, impaired, or abnormal function.

Dyslexia. Specific learning disability involving reading, which may include reversing letters and words and word-blindness.

Dysthymic disorder. Disorder characterized by mild to moderate chronic depression.

Ego. Theoretical concept describing the internal mental function that enables a person to perceive needs and to adapt to the demands of reality.

Empathy. Understanding how others feel.

Expressive language. Phase of communication involving the process of putting ideas and thoughts into words and then into speech.

Fetal alcohol syndrome. Congenital syndrome caused by exposure to alcohol in utero, characterized by mental retardation and specific physical characteristics.

Fragile-X syndrome. Congenital syndrome caused by an abnormality of the X-chromosome, characterized by mental retardation, specific maladaptive behaviors, and abnormal physical features.

Gender identity. Perception of one's self as male or female, developing in toddlerhood or early childhood and reinforced by social experience and the changes of puberty.

Genetic. Relating to heredity.

Genogram. Diagram or "map" of a family including notation of medical or psychiatric conditions in family members. A genogram may be useful in investigating complex relationships, family history, and multigenerational issues.

Glucose monitoring. Testing to monitor sugars in the urine or blood usually in a person with diabetes.

Hallucination. Visual, auditory (sound), olfactory (smell), or kinetic (touch) perceptions without external stimulation, such as hearing voices when no one is present.

Handedness. Preference for using the dominant hand, often indicated by learning to write with the right or left hand.

Heredity. Characteristics passed from parent to child through genes.

Human Immunodeficiency Virus (HIV). Virus that causes acquired immune deficiency syndrome (AIDS).

Hyperkinesis. Outdated term for Attention-Deficit/Hyperactivity Disorder referring to excessive motor activity.

Hypnotic. Medication used to induce sleep.

Hypoxia. Inadequate oxygen supply to the tissues of the body.

Identification. Unconscious patterning of one's behavior after that of another person. Important in the development of personality and in the concept of the superego.

Inhibition of choice. Understanding and ability to act, based on knowing that it is often better to pass on a short-term reward for an ultimately better result.

Insulin. Hormone secreted by the pancreas, essential to the metabolism of glucose.

Language and speech disorders. Abnormal or delayed development of language and speech in children and adolescents. Typically these include problems with development of expressive language, receptive language, and/or speech and articulation.

Latchkey children. Children or young adolescents who arrive home from school to an empty household because parents work outside the home.

Learning disorders. Disorders characterized by difficulty in processing, learning, or expressing concepts and information, resulting in academic achievement below expected performance for age, schooling, and intellectual abilities.

Major depression. Disorder characterized by persistently depressed mood for at least two weeks accompanied by other related symptoms, including suicidal thinking in severe cases.

Managed care. Medical or mental health care organized under an administrative system that monitors the need, type, and use of medical services in order to improve quality of care and/or control costs.

Mania. Mood characterized by extreme excitation, euphoria, grandiosity, irritability, hypersexuality, decreased need for sleep, and rapid speech. Psychotic symptoms may also be associated with mania.

Manic-depressive disorder. See *Bipolar disorders.*

Mathematics disorder. Specific learning disorder involving mathematics skills.

Mental retardation. Developmental difficulty characterized by subnormal intelligence and delayed self-help skills.

Migraine headache. Headache, often on one side of the head, usually associated with visual symptoms, intolerance of light, nausea or vomiting, and lasting four to six hours.

Mutism. Lack of speech.

Nebulizer. Machine for making a fine spray or mist, to which medication may be added usually for treatment of asthma when inhalers do not suffice.

Negativism. Refusal to follow requests or commands with oppositional disagreement.

Neurobiological. Regarding the biology of the nervous system.

Neurology. Medical specialty concerned with

the function and malfunction of the nervous system.

Nightmare. A "bad dream," the contents of which arouse fear or anxiety.

Nonverbal. Without words.

Obsessive-compulsive disorder (OCD). Disorder characterized by intrusive thoughts (obsessions) and repeated, ritualized actions (compulsions).

OCD. See *Obsessive-compulsive disorder.*

ODD. See *Oppositional defiant disorder.*

Open head injury. A severe skull fracture and open wound to the head that may lead to brain damage.

Oppositional behavior. Behavior that is defined as negative or hostile.

Oppositional defiant disorder (ODD). Disorder characterized by a pattern of uncooperative, defiant, and hostile behavior toward authority figures that seriously interferes with a youngster's day-to-day functioning.

Paranoid ideation. Thoughts involving suspiciousness or exaggerated feelings of unfair treatment or harassment.

Parasomnias. Disturbances that occur during sleep or in the transition between wake and sleep, including night terrors, sleepwalking, and sleep talking.

Parent Management Training (PMT). Therapy in which parents are taught principles and strategies for managing their adolescent's behavior, including positive reinforcement (praise and tokens) and consequences and mild punishments (time-outs and the loss of privileges).

Personality. Mental traits, characteristics, and styles of behavior that are stable over time.

Pervasive developmental disorders (PDD). Disorders, including autism, characterized by qualitative impairments in the development of social interaction and communication skills

and in imaginative activity.

Phenylketonuria (PKU). Hereditary disease in which the amino acid phenylalanine is not metabolized. Without strict dietary control, mental retardation develops.

Phobia. Persistent and irrational fear of particular objects, people, animals, or situations.

Posttraumatic stress disorder (PTSD). Anxiety disorder following exposure to trauma, characterized by recall of the event and avoidance of stimuli associated with the trauma. See also *Childhood trauma.*

Precocious puberty. Signs of sexual maturation prior to age eight in girls and age ten in boys.

Preferred provider. Physicians, social workers, nurses, or psychologists enrolled by a particular insurer or managed-care plan.

Prognosis. Prediction of course, duration, and outcome.

Psychiatric social worker. Person with a Master's of Social Work (M.S.W.) or state certification as a Licensed Clinical Social Worker (L.C.S.W.).

Psychiatrist. Physician whose education after medical school includes at least four years of specialty training in psychiatry.

Psychoanalyst. Person, usually a physician, trained in the theory of psychoanalysis, a technique employing free association, careful analysis of the relationship between the psychoanalyst and the patient, and interpretation of unconscious thoughts and feelings.

Psychoanalytically-oriented psychotherapy. See *Psychodynamic therapy.*

Psychodrama. Therapeutic technique of dramatically enacting, as in a play, personal or emotional problems.

Psychodynamic therapy. Therapy based on the assumption that a person can develop better control over his or her own behavior, choices, and actions by understanding unconscious thoughts and feelings and interpersonal relationships. Such therapy often combines discussion, explanation, relaxation, and psychological exploration and support.

Psychologist. Person who has a Master's, Ed.D., Psy.D., or Ph.D. degree in clinical, school, counseling, experimental, or educational psychology.

Psychopharmacology. Medical specialty concerned with the use of psychoactive medications to alleviate symptoms of emotional, behavioral, or mental disorders.

Psychosis. Severely disturbed mental state characterized by loss of contact with reality, which may include disorganized speech or behavior, delusions, and/or hallucinations.

Psychotherapist. Person who uses various psychological principles to help a patient improve behavior, feelings, thinking, or social interactions.

Psychotherapy. Treatment for various emotional, behavioral, or mental problems that uses communication between a trained person and the adolescent to bring about change and to relieve distress.

PTSD. See *Posttraumatic stress disorder.*

Puberty. Stage of physical development when changes of sexual maturation occur and sexual reproduction first becomes possible.

Rapid eye movement (REM). Description of activity of closed eyes during a particular stage of sleep during which dreams occur. This stage of sleep is also called REM sleep.

Reading disorder. Specific learning disorder characterized by difficulties in visually tracking words, in visually discriminating between similar letters (mistaking *d*'s for *b*'s, for example), or in associating sounds with their symbols and interpreting the meaning of words.

Receptive language. Decoding spoken words and sentences requiring discrimination among sounds (auditory discrimination), interpretation of what is heard, and assignment of meaning to words and sentences.

Reflex. Involuntary neurological response to stimulus.

Regression. Return to an earlier pattern of thinking or acting.

REM. See *Rapid eye movement.*

Role modeling. Method of teaching behavior based on patterning by example.

Schizophrenia. Severe psychiatric disorder characterized by psychosis (inability to think logically and rationally), including catatonia, delusions, hallucinations, paranoia, and disorganized language and behavior.

Seizure. Neurological disorder characterized by convulsions or other episodic behavior caused by abnormal electrical discharges in the brain. Epilepsy is one form of seizure disorder.

Serotonin. Neurotransmitter (chemical messenger) involved in regulation of sleep, mood, appetite, and sexual function.

Sexual abuse. Behavior in which an adult commits a sexual act with a child or adolescent for gratification of the adult's sexual and aggressive needs and desires.

Sexually transmitted diseases (STDs). Infections transmitted by sexual activity, including gonorrhea, chlamydia, genital herpes, human papilloma virus (genital warts), HIV, and syphilis.

Sibling. Brother or sister.

Sibling rivalry. Competition between siblings for the affection and attention of parents.

Social-emotional learning disorder. Diagnosis given to children or young adolescents who are unable to make friends and behave in a socially acceptable way. They fail to interpret appropriately the emotional responses of others and make incorrect inferences about others' intentions and behaviors.

Somatoform disorder. A psychiatric disorder characterized by the development of physical symptoms that suggest a medical condition but are not fully explained by any medical condition.

Spelling disorder. Specific learning disability characterized by difficulty spelling words.

STDs. See *Sexually transmitted diseases.*

Stuttering. Involuntary breaks in the rhythm or fluency of speech, such as repetition of syllables, prolongation of sounds, and pauses in which the person seems to be struggling to make any sound at all.

Superego. Theoretical concept describing a person's internal mental functions that are expressed in moral attitudes, conscience, and sense of guilt.

Systematic desensitization. Behavioral therapy technique in which the patient is presented with a graduated hierarchy of anxiety-provoking stimuli; a treatment for phobias.

Talk therapy. See *Psychotherapy.*

Tantrum. Fit of uncontrolled anger, rage, and distress.

Temperament. Predisposing characteristics of a person, including the manner of displaying moods and emotions first noted in infancy.

Thought disorders. Disorders characterized by an impairment of thinking, including disorganized, incoherent, or vague speech, delusions, hallucinations, or paranoia.

Tics. Involuntary, repetitive muscle contractions, involving any muscle group but most commonly the face, eyes, or neck.

Time-out. Technique used to isolate briefly a disruptive child in order to interrupt and avoid reinforcement of negative behavior.

Tourette's disorder. Disorder characterized by multiple motor tics along with vocal tics, such as grunting, humming, and tongue clicking.

Toxic delirium. Disorder in which psychotic symptoms are caused by an ingested chemical or accumulation of the body's toxic by-products.

Tranquilizer. Medication that reduces anxiety, agitation, or emotional tension.

Trauma. Injury, physical or psychic, caused by shock, violence, or abuse.

Utilization review. Monitoring of care and services in a medical or mental-health setting, for the purposes of improving quality of care and/or containing cost of care.

Verbal. Related to words.

Withdrawing. Retreating or avoiding contact with people and experiences.

Withholding. Keeping information or feelings inside or away from interactions with people.

INDEX